SEASONAL DIMENSIONS
TO RURAL POVERTY

WARNING: It is ~~illegal~~ ... a day 365 days a year.
~~...~~ to mutilate Library material or to keep it overdue.

PLACE IN RETURN BOX to remove this checkout from your record.
TO AVOID FINES return on or before date due.

DATE DUE	DATE DUE	Date DUE
MAR 0 2 1991		
Apr 01 '91	OCT 2 7 2008	
Apr 29 '91		
May 29 '91		
Jul 1 '91		
173		
SEP ... 1992		
5/10 1987258		
JUL 2 6 1993		
208		
SEP 25		
JUN 1 1 1996		

MSU Is An Affirmative Action/Equal Opportunity Institution

MICHIGAN STATE UNIVERSITY LIBRARY
MAY 02 2025
WITHDRAWN

SEASONAL DIMENSIONS TO RURAL POVERTY

EDITED BY
ROBERT CHAMBERS, RICHARD LONGHURST
ARNOLD PACEY

Frances Pinter (Publishers) Ltd
Allanheld, Osmun Publishers

Published in Great Britain in 1981 by
Frances Pinter (Publishers) Limited
5 Dryden Street, London WC2E 9NW

ISBN 0 86187 200 2 (UK)

Published in the United States of America in 1981
by Allanheld, Osmun & Co. Publishers, Inc.
(A Division of Littlefield, Adams & Company)
81 Adams Drive, Totowa, New Jersey 07512

Copyright © 1981 by Institute of Development Studies

All rights reserved. No part of this publication may
be reproduced, stored in a retrieval system, or
transmitted in any form or by any means, electronic,
mechanical, photocopying, recording, or otherwise,
without the prior permission of the publisher.

Library of Congress Cataloging in Publication Data
Main entry under title:

Seasonal dimensions to rural poverty.

   1. Rural poor—Tropics—Addresses, essays, lectures.
2. Seasonal variations (Economics)—Addresses, essays,
lectures. 3. Seasonal variations (Diseases)—Addresses,
essays, lectures. I. Chambers, Robert, 1932-
HC79.P6S38   306'.3   81-2838
ISBN 0-86598-057-8 (US)   AACR2

81 82 83 84 / 10 9 8 7 6 5 4 3 2 1

Printed in the United States of America

To every thing there is a season, and a time to every purpose under the heaven; a time to be born, and a time to die; a time to plant, and a time to pluck up that which is planted

Eccles. 3 : 1-2

CONTENTS

List of Tables x
List of Figures xii
Preface xv

INTRODUCTION, *Robert Chambers* 1

1. CLIMATIC SEASONALITY IN THE TROPICS 9
1.1 Introduction 9
1.2 The Nature of Climatic Seasonality, *R.P.D. Walsh* 11
1.3 Case-Studies 21
1.4 References 29

2. SEASONAL ENERGY RELATIONSHIPS AND FOOD 30
2.1 Seasonality and Labour in the Rural Energy Balance,
    Tim Bayliss-Smith 30
2.2 Food Consumption in Relation to Labour Output,
    Margaret Haswell 38
2.3 Nutrition and Disease in Machakos District, Kenya
    Simeon R. Onchere and R. Slooff 41
2.4 Seasonal Aspects of Nutrition, *Richard Longhurst and
    Philip Payne* 45
2.5 Agriculture and Nutrition in Matlab Thana, Bangladesh,
    *A.K.M. Alauddin Chowdhury, Sandra L. Huffman and Lincoln
    C. Chen* 52
2.6 Energy Needs and Technology, *Arnold Pacey* 61
2.7 References 63

3. ECONOMIC RELATIONSHIPS AND THE
   SEASONAL USE OF LABOUR 67
3.1 Seasonality in the Rural Economy (of Tropical Africa),
    Philip Raikes 67
3.2 A Case-Study in Food Production, Sale and Distribution,
    Emmy B. Simmons 73
3.3 Labour and Subsistence in a Pastoral Economy, *Jeremy
    Swift* 80
3.4 The Seasonality of Prices and Wages in Bangladesh, *Rafiqul
    Huda Chaudhury* 87
3.5 Seasonal Patterns of Agricultural Employment in Bangladesh,
    Edward J. Clay 92

Contents

3.6	References	100
4.	THE SEASONAL ECOLOGY OF DISEASE	102
4.1	Introduction	102
4.2	Diarrhoeal Diseases, *B. S. Drasar, A. M. Tomkins and R. G. Feachem*	102
4.3	Diarrhoeal Diseases: Rotavirus Infection in Children, *W.A.M. Cutting*	111
4.4	Respiratory Diseases, *R.N.P. Sutton*	112
4.5	Infectious Skin Diseases, *Michael J. Porter*	114
4.6	Insect-Borne Diseases: Malaria, *R. S. Bray*	116
4.7	Insect-Borne Diseases: Filarial Infections and Kala-Azar, *B. A. Southgate*	121
4.8	Guinea-Worm Infection, *R. Muller*	125
4.9	Seasonal Variables in Infective Disease: A Summary, *David Bradley*	127
4.1	References	131
5.	SEASONAL PATTERNS IN BIRTHS AND DEATHS	135
5.1	Causes of Seasonal Fluctuation in Vital Events, *Tim Dyson and Nigel Crook*	135
5.2	Data on Seasonality of Births and Deaths, *Nigel Crook and Tim Dyson*	141
5.3	Seasonal Patterns of Vital Events in Matlab Thana, Bangladesh, *Stan Becker and M. A. Sardar*	149
5.4	Seasonality of Births in the Solomon Islands, *Sheila Macrae*	154
5.5	Births, Work and Nutrition in Tamil Nadu, India, *S. Rajagopalan, P. K. Kymal and Pu-ai Pei*	156
5.6	References	161
6.	FAMILY HEALTH AND SEASONAL WELFARE	163
6.1	Introduction	163
6.2	Seasonality and the Growth of Infants in a Gambian Village, *M.G.M. Rowland, Alison Paul, A. M. Prentice, Elisabeth Müller, Melanie Hutton, R.A.E. Barrell, and R. G. Whitehead*	164
6.3	Poverty, Housing and Disease, *B. B. Waddy*	175
6.4	Seasonal Health Problems in the Zaria Region, *Andrew Tomkins*	177
6.5	A Study of Childhood Disease in Tanzania, *James P. Goetz*	182
6.6	Pastoralists and Cultivators in Bagamoyo District, *D. K. Ndagala*	186
6.7	References	191

Contents

7.	THE SOCIAL DISTRIBUTION OF SEASONAL BURDENS	193
7.1	Social and Familial Inequalities	193
7.2	Seasonal Dimensions of Women's Roles, *Ingrid Palmer*	195
7.3	The Sociology of Seasonal Food Shortage in Hausaland, *Michael Watts*	201
7.4	Seasonality and Dependence in South Asia, *John and Barbara Harriss*	206
7.5	Seasonal Out-Migration and Rural Poverty, *Henry Rempel*	210
7.6	References	214
8.	CONCLUSIONS AND PRACTICAL IMPLICATIONS	218
8.1	Seasonality in Rural Experience, *Robert Chambers, Richard Longhurst, David Bradley and Richard Feachem*	218
8.2	Government Perceptions and Responses, *Ian Carruthers*	224
8.3	Practical Implications, *Robert Chambers and Simon Maxwell*	226
8.4	References	238

Appendix to Chapter 5 241
Appendix: Ode to the Seasons Conference 248
List of Contributors 250
Index 254

LIST OF TABLES

1.1 Indices of the relative seasonality of rainfall 13

1.2 Provisional classification scheme of tropical climates on the basis of rainfall seasonality 19

1.3 Summary of climatic classifications and rainfall data for the six case-study areas 22

2.1 Predicted crop production in different climates, based on 3 per cent conversion of light received during wet months 32

2.2 Shifting cultivation of rice: comparative data on person-hours of labour per rice crop per hectare 35

2.3 Effect of rainfall seasonality on the amount of work required each month in order to produce rice through shifting cultivation 36

2.4 Breast milk yield per stage of lactation according to season, Machakos, Kenya 43

2.5 Energy intake (kcal) by season and region, Ghana Nutrition Survey 51

2.6 Wholesale price of medium rice (1976-77), agricultural labourer wage rate (1977-78), and average household cereal stocks (1976-77), in Matlab thana, Bangladesh 55

2.7 Body weight of mothers by month and landownership in Matlab, Bangladesh 59

3.1 Land ownership and use, seven cattle-owners, ten non-cattle-owners, Hanwa, 1966/67 and 1970/71 75

3.2 Seasonal work patterns: on-farm and off-farm (income-earning) labour for seventeen farmers, Hanwa, 1966-7 76

3.3 Sales, prices, and seasonality: eighteen Hanwa farmers, 1970-1 79

3.4 Social and religious obligations of eighteen households, Hanwa, 1970-1 79

3.5 Major crops in Bangladesh 88

3.6 The annual crop labour requirements of selected 'traditional' and 'new' crop rotations in Bangladesh 94

List of Tables

4.1 Deaths from diarrhoeal disease at various ages in England and Wales, 1911 and 1971, and in Mexico and Egypt, 1971 104

4.2 Seasonal transmission of guinea-worm infection in various geographical regions 126

5.1 Correlations between the average monthly distribution of births and the mean minimum temperature nine months previously, 1962-4 147

5.2 Percentage distribution of leading causes of death for infants under one month old and adults over forty-five years in Matlab DSS, 1972-73 153

6.1 Simplified annual events calendar for the Gambian village of Keneba 166

6.2 Diseases of particular prevalence in the Zaria region of northern Nigeria 178

6.3 Diseases of particular prevalence among different population groups within one village area in Zaria region of northern Nigeria............................. 180

6.4 Diseases of particular prevalence in Bagamoyo District, Tanzania 183

7.1 Seasonality in selected South Asian regions 207

8.1 The variation of various factors by month in Gambia 221

8.2 The variation of various factors by month, in Matlab, Bangladesh 222

8.3 Checklist on the policy implications of seasonality 237

Appendix Table 5.1 Seasonal measures of births (and marriages) by month of birth, for countries with available data, grouped into regions 241

Appendix Table 5.2 Seasonal measures of deaths, by month of death, for countries with available data, grouped into regions 244

Appendix Table 5.3 Comparison of state urban and rural birth indices of seasonality for ten states, by month, India 1962-64 247

LIST OF FIGURES

1	Schematic 'map' of some of the factors discussed in this book	7
1.1	Spatial distribution of rainfall regime types in the tropics	12
1.2	Seasonality index maps for Brazil, the Indian Subcontinent and Sub-Saharan Africa	14
1.3	Sub-Saharan Africa: dry months per annum	16
1.4	Sub-Saharan Africa: tropical climatic types based on rainfall seasonality	19
1.5	The Indian Subcontinent and Brazil: tropical climatic types based on rainfall seasonality	20
1.6	Bangladesh, showing District boundaries and the location of Matlab in Comilla District, which is in the Matlab thana case-study area	23
1.7	South India, showing boundary of Tamil Nadu and the location of North Arcot and Thanjavur Districts	25
1.8	Map of the main area of bimodal climate in East Africa, locating the Machakos and Bagamoyo Districts, both of which have E3*-type climates	26
1.9	The three case-study areas in West Africa in relation to the main climatic zones	27
2.1	Predicted maximum yield of agricultural crops in tropical climates differing in rainfall seasonality	33
2.2	Seasonal pattern of food availability for Matungulu and Mbiuni locations of Machakos District	42
2.3	Graph of food storage at farm level over time, Machakos District, Kenya	43
2.4	Mean body weight of 216 mother children pairs by month of observation, Matlab thana, Bangladesh	53
2.5	Median of suckling time during 8 hours of daytime observation and month of observation of 216 mother child pairs, Matlab thana, Bangladesh	56
2.6	Number of patients admitted to ICDDR,B hospital during calendar 1976 and 1977 by etiology and month of admission	58

List of Figures

2.7	Household food stocks on the day of interview by month of interview of eight landowner households and seventeen landless households, Matlab thana, Bangladesh	60
3.1	Median dates of planting and harvesting in Hanwa village, northern Nigeria, 1966/7	73
3.2	Food consumption in relation to work done for cattle-owners and non-cattle-owners in Hanwa village, northern Nigeria, 1970/71	77
3.3	Labour requirements and milk production in a flock of fifty goats, north Mali	82
3.4	Labour requirements and milk production in a herd of twenty-five camels, north Mali	83
3.5	Labour requirements and milk production in a herd of twenty-five cattle, north Mali	84
3.6	The wholesale price of coarse rice in Bangladesh: an adjusted seasonal index for 1953-68 and 1968-76	89
3.7	An index of real daily wage rates for agricultural labour in Bangladesh	90
3.8	The impact on labour requirements of changes in cropping patterns	96
3.9	The impact on labour requirements of changes in cropping patterns	97
3.10	Histograms showing the seasonal distribution of crop labour requirements in four administrative districts of Bangladesh	99
4.1	Hourly readings of faecal coliform and streptococci concentrations with associated rainfall and river temperature data	109
4.2	Rainfall and the incidence of respiratory illness in Trinidad; data recorded in 1961-62	113
4.3	Malaria prevalence and density among mothers and infants 0-6 months old in Gambia, 1976	118
4.4	Malarial antibody levels in the blood of mothers and infants in Gambia, 1976, and in cord blood samples	120
4.5	Seasonal variations in rainfall and in the man-biting rate of two species of mosquito, *Anopheles funestus* and *Anopheles gambiae* sensu latu, at Tingrela, Upper Volta	122
4.6	Rainfall, kala-azar diagnoses, abundance of sandfly vector, and presumed infection potential, Kitui District of Kenya, 1961-2	124

List of Figures

5.1	A simplified diagram of some of the main interrelationships likely to bring about a seasonal fluctuation in births	136
5.2	A simplified diagram of some of the main interrelationships likely to bring about a seasonal fluctuation in deaths	140
5.3	Average monthly percentage variation in births and deaths by region	143
5.4	The monthly percentage distribution of 'conceptions' and the mean minimum air temperature for the urban population of the Punjab, over a three-year period (1962-64)	147
5.5	Deaths and rainfall in two Indian states	148
5.6(i)	Live births in the Matlab Surveillance System (both areas) 1972-1974 by month and fitted regression curve	151
5.6(ii)	Total deaths in the Matlab Surveillance System (both areas) 1972-1974 by month and fitted regression curve	151
5.6(iii)	Neonatal mortality rates in the Matlab Surveillance System (both areas) 1972-1974 by month and fitted regression curve	151
5.7	Climatic seasonality and agriculture in Tamil Nadu	157
5.8	The seasonality of births and conceptions in rural Tamil Nadu, and the seasonality of women's agricultural work in the North Arcot District of Tamil Nadu	158
6.1	Contrasting growth in Gambian children born in different seasons	168
6.2	Seasonal variations in breast milk intake for babies at Keneba, Gambia	169
6.3	Seasonal variations in energy intake of women in Keneba, Gambia	171
6.4	Gambia: weight loss and gain among women in Keneba, showing that even pregnant women lose weight during the rains	172
6.5	Gambia: seasonal changes in disease prevalence, Keneba village	173
6.6	The time of year at which babies are completely weaned off the breast in the Malumfashi area, northern Nigeria	179
6.7	Monthly occurrence of cases of lower respiratory tract disease and of measles in children under 15 years admitted to Bagamoyo District Hospital, Tanzania, 1976	184
6.8	Monthly occurrence of cases of severe protein-energy malnutrition (PEM), diarrhoea, and malaria/fever in children under 15 admitted to Bagamoyo District Hospital, Tanzania, 1976	185

PREFACE

The process which has led to this book was sparked off by the discovery in a seminar at the Institute of Development Studies at the University of Sussex that in both northern Nigeria and a part of Bangladesh there was a peak in births in the late wet season. This led organisers and participants to examine the ramifications of tropical seasonality, paying particular attention to inter-relationships among various disciplines — geography, economics, sociology, medicine, nutrition and demography, to mention but some. The Conference on Seasonal Dimensions to Rural Poverty which followed was organised jointly by Robert Chambers and Richard Longhurst of IDS and by David Bradley and Richard Feachem of the Ross Institute of Tropical Hygiene, London School of Hygiene and Tropical Medicine. The conference was financed by IDS, and held from 4-7 July 1978.

This book is based on the conference papers and discussions, but it is not a conventional conference volume. Arnold Pacey worked out a logical framework, reflected in his schematic diagram (page 7). With the generous consent of contributors, he did the major work of shortening, editing, and organising the papers into coherent chapters, with the other two editors undertaking the later stages. The final chapter includes practical implications contributed by the editors and by many others who have corresponded from different parts of the world. Elsewhere in the book, sections for which no author is cited are the joint responsibility of the editors.

In summary, the findings of the conference and its follow-up suggest that most of the very poor people in the world live in tropical areas with marked wet and dry seasons. Especially for the poorer people, women and children, the wet season before the harvest is usually the most critical time of year. At that time adverse factors often overlap and interact: food is short and food prices high; physical energy is needed for agricultural work; sickness is prevalent, especially malaria, diarrhoea and skin infections; child care, family hygiene, and cooking are neglected by women overburdened with work; and late pregnancy is common, with births peaking near harvest. This is a time of year marked by loss of body weight, low birth weights, high neonatal mortality, malnutrition, and indebtedness. It is the hungry season and the sick season. It is the time of year when poor people are at their poorest and most vulnerable to becoming poorer.

Some of these points, and others in this book, are almost embarrassingly obvious; and some are surprising. Rural people have always known about the seasons, but planners and policy-makers have difficulty grasping their full significance. Urban-based professionals travel less during the rains and so underperceive adverse seasonality. In addition, specialisation makes it difficult for professionals to see the seasonal linkages between food, energy, morbidity, malnutrition, indebtedness, dependence, exploitation, and poverty.

Preface

It is difficult to find any aspect of rural life in the tropical third world which is not touched by seasonality. In consequence, any attempt to come to terms with it involves many disciplines. Lip-service to multidisciplinarity is easy, but to bring many professions together invites the mutual incomprehension of a Tower of Babel. One good thing about tropical seasonality is the common framework it provides for different disciplines and professions, making communication simpler and new insights more likely. We hope that readers will not limit themselves to what they find more familiar but will launch out into domains other than their own and share the excitement of finding cross-disciplinary linkages, many of which have taken us by surprise, and many of which no doubt remain to be uncovered.

We hope, too, that this is only a beginning. Many research questions and practical implications are suggested by seasonal analysis. Perhaps all rural research and all rural planning should have a seasonal dimension; perhaps *counter-seasonality* — offsetting biases against seeing the hungry and sick seasons, and then offsetting adverse seasonality itself — should be in the minds of all who are concerned with rural poverty and rural development.

Many people have contributed to the development of this book. The earlier work of Susan Schofield on seasonal nutrition has been a recurrent point of reference and source of ideas. Those who presented the case studies — from Gambia, Mali, northern Nigeria, Kenya, Tanzania, Tamil Nadu and Bangladesh — are named in the text. Others have contributed special studies. The research on the seasonality of births and deaths was carried out by the Centre of Population Studies at the London School of Hygiene and Tropical Medicine. The families and friends of contributors and editors have suffered in silence or otherwise. Many at IDS have helped, not least with tolerance. Philippa Baxter, Teresa Dearlove, Lyn Gorman and Ann Segrave have given administrative and technical advice and support. Anita Hall organised the original conference and made it a pleasure. Pauline Cherry drew the diagrams, and Christopher Heaps most of the maps. Above all, we want to thank Susan Saunders. She played a major part in preparing the conference, managed the follow-up to it, and typed, checked and organised the final manuscript, and all this with a calm, good humour and accuracy which we can only envy and admire.

Robert Chambers   Richard Longhurst

Figure 1.1 has been redrawn from a map in K. Nieuwolt *Tropical Climatology* and is reproduced by permission of the publishers, John Wiley.

INTRODUCTION
Robert Chambers

> I settled down in the village on August 28 last year but by mid September I had already learned of the hard days of the 'enzala', i.e. hunger or famine which annually occurs between February and May. The food grains harvested in December have run out and the next harvest begins in May. It is certainly a tragedy that officialdom (e.g. agricultural reports, etc.) say nothing about this annual plight. But this is a fact which everyone in the village knows . . . . I cannot forget how on two different occasions on exchanging greetings as I arrived to carry out interviews the women informed me that they had not eaten anything for three days.
>
> (Joseph Ssennyonga, describing research in western Kenya: Ssennyonga, 1976, p. 11n)

Explaining rural poverty

The extent of rural poverty needs no elaboration. What has perhaps been new over the past few years has been the increasing concern with the poorer rural people. It is notorious that the poorer majority of rural people in third world countries have not shared proportionately in the fruits of economic growth — that they have usually benefited rather little, or not at all, or become worse off. The explanations are many. Rural poverty is variously and to varying degrees attributed to a continuing condition of undevelopment; to an active process of underdevelopment and the extraction and transfer of surplus through colonialism, neo-colonialism and the forces of capitalism and unequal exchange; to ill-health and poor nutrition; to war; to natural disasters; to famines; to population growth and its pressure on resources; to degradation of the environment; to the impact of inappropriate capital-intensive technology; and to the failure of government services to provide for basic needs. Other factors mentioned are the 'talents effect' (Pearse, 1977) — the tendency for those who are relatively better off and more powerful in rural areas to capture the benefits of programmes and to accumulate wealth; and the exploitation of rural areas and people by urban areas and people (Lipton, 1977). There are many persuasive explanations, and many variants of them. One may reasonably conclude that there are many forces which act and interact to sustain, deepen and extend rural poverty.

Compared with these explanations, rather little attention has been paid to tropical wet-dry seasonality. Climate has been out of fashion as an explanation of poverty; but the location of richer countries in temperate latitudes and poorer countries in the tropics is so marked that climatic factors cannot lightly be dismissed, whether they are fashionable or not. One possibility is that climatic influences have been underestimated because of a failure to see that seasonally adverse factors interact and reinforce each other at certain times of the year. Tropical seasonality tends to be overlooked anyway; and where it is noticed, it is usually along a single disciplinary dimension. It is only rarely (as for example in Haswell, 1975, Schofield, 1974) that the interactions of multiple seasonal adversities (medical, nutritional, agricultural, family, economic, social, and so on) have been analysed.

Against this background, we can ask:
(1) are there reasons why tropical seasonality should tend to be overlooked?
(2) what linkages are there between concurrent seasonal stresses and adversities?
(3) what seasonal factors matter — when, where, how much, and to whom?
(4) does seasonality make some people poor and keep them poor?
(5) what practical measures does seasonal analysis suggest?

This book seeks to open up discussion of topics such as these, to present some of the relevant research that has been done in Africa and South Asia, and to assess the implications.

Two caveats are in order. First, a seasonal perspective does not necessarily imply an explanation of rural poverty with some sort of causal primacy. This is simply one mode of analysis among many, but one which has been neglected. Second, there is no intention to draw attention away from other explanations. Self-critical introspection is often uncomfortable but salutary. To the extent that observers have vested interests in rural poverty, they may prefer explanations or modes of analysis which do not threaten those interests. Some from rich countries may prefer to find explanations in, say, population pressure on resources rather than in low commodity prices; and some from urban sectors in third world countries may prefer to find explanations in unequal exchange between countries rather than unequal exchange between the urban and rural sectors within countries. In adopting a seasonal mode of analysis we must be careful that we are not subconsciously attracted by an activity which conveniently diverts attention from more painful issues such as these. At the same time we may note that there is nothing in a seasonal mode of analysis which excludes other explanations listed; to the contrary, it should illuminate the manner in which they operate.

The case for exploring a seasonal mode of analysis rests on two further arguments: first, that there are systematic biases against this mode, tending to its neglect; and second, that the hypothesis that adverse seasonalities operate to keep poor people poor or make them poorer is sufficiently plausible to deserve examination. These will be considered in turn.

Seasonality unobserved

Rural poverty itself, seasonal or not, tends to be underperceived (Chambers, 1980). Reasons for this are that officials, researchers and other travellers in rural areas tend to meet the wealthier and more influential people; they tend to meet men rather than women; and they often visit or study model villages or projects which have received special attention. This underperception of poverty is reinforced by four distinct biases which make it more difficult to find out what happens to the poor under the adverse conditions of rainy seasons:

Introduction

(1) *tarmac bias*. The areas visited during the rains tend to be those accessible by all-weather roads, especially tarmac. These tend to be the more prosperous and more densely settled areas closer to urban centres, and less exclusively agricultural and less subject to seasonality than those which are more remote and harder to reach. Often, too, the better-off people have bought up plots beside tarmac roads to become a roadside elite (Ssennyonga, 1976, pp. 9-10) and built good houses on them, while the poorer people who are more vulnerable to seasonal problems have shifted back out of sight.

(2) *activity bias*. During the rains there is often much activity in the fields. This can attract attention away from what goes on in the villages, in the houses and huts, where those who are weaker, sicker and shorter of food, including women and children, may be found.

(3) *irrigation bias*. John Harriss (1977, pp. 30ff) has shown for India for the late 1960s and early 1970s, that social science research was concentrated in the richer areas with assured irrigation, to the neglect of vast areas relying only on rainfall. Indeed, irrigation generally exercises an attraction which draws to it disproportionate attention and research. Irrigated agriculture has, of course, its own seasons. But compared with rainfed agriculture, in the seasonal wet-dry tropics, it is more reliable, provides a steadier supply of crops to cultivators and work to labourers, and may spread the peaks of adverse factors more around the year, weakening their interaction.

(4) *dry season bias*. Perhaps the most significant bias results from the tendency for rural visits and research to be undertaken in the dry seasons. (See Appendix for a little verse which touches on this subject.) There may be exceptions with epidemiologists and agriculturalists who have to work during the rains. But generally, officials, experts, researchers and professionals of all sorts are restricted in their travel at those times. Some areas are officially closed to movement and others are inaccessible unless on foot or by horse, hovercraft, helicopter or aircraft. In parts of the South Sudan, for example, there are months every year when the roads have become impassable but the rivers are not yet high enough for travel by boat. During rains, the risks of getting stuck or damaging a vehicle are high. And rains and mud are physically unpleasant. So research institutes concentrate their fieldwork in the dry season. In a revealing sentence, a manual on assessing rural needs warns about the unexpected in rural surveys and says 'once, the jeeps needed for transporting the interviewers were recalled for a month *during the few precious months of the dry season*' (Ashe, 1979, p. 26, our italics). The resulting dry season bias gives exaggerated impressions of well-being, as with nutrition surveys conducted after harvest when food is abundant. The privations of the wet hungry season, the period, in Ssennyonga's words, of 'slow and quiet famine' (1976, p. 8), go unseen.

In addition to these specific biases, there is a more general anti-seasonal bias in data collection and processing. Much seasonal analysis requires detailed year-round data; but these are costly to obtain. They require sustained and expensive organisation, especially difficult for academic researchers with teaching obligations. But even when year-round data are obtained, they may not be processed because both researchers and funds tend to be exhausted once fieldwork is over, and because seasonal data are bulky and burdensome if they have been well collected. Short surveys are less risky and more digestible and lead to earlier and easier consummation. Thus 'one-point' nutrition surveys are more common than seasonal all-the-year-round surveys (Schofield, 1974, p. 22). With economic data, too, a seasonal breakdown may be all too rare, and C. T. Kurien's lament for Tamil Nadu may apply elsewhere:

> To estimate the percentage of agricultural labourers living below the poverty line we need information about man-days worked in a year and wage rates. It is impossible to get accurate data relating to these which will reflect the wide variety of patterns . . . during different periods of the year. (1976, p. 35)

It is not surprising that a subject should be neglected for which data are scarce because they are difficult and laborious to collect and analyse.

Finally, disciplinary specialisation hinders the understanding of seasonal linkages between different factors. There is no discipline, except perhaps geography, which could claim competence to explore the links between climatic seasons and poverty. But the geographical school which sought explanations of development and undevelopment in terms of climate long since ceased to be respectable; and as climate itself has been subjected to sophisticated mathematical analysis, geographers and climatologists may have been forced to narrow their vision more and more to the physical aspects of climate and their measurement and analysis. As for other disciplines, if they focus on seasonality, the sustained organisation for data collection and processing may make such heavy demands that they have no time or energy for considering concerns other than their own. They may then identify some seasonal changes which deepen poverty but not explore how these are linked with others. An economist may note seasonal fluctuations in wage levels, but not in the incidence of malaria. A doctor may observe seasonal patterns of morbidity but not of indebtedness. In any case, even without the special difficulties of seasonal studies, professional brainwashing trains observers in tunnel vision. They see those parts of the whole on which they have learnt to direct a light but they see them at the cost of a balanced view. Rural people, unimpeded by professional blinkers, often see more of the whole. For outside professionals to see that whole may require many disciplinary searchlights; and these are expensive and difficult to bring together, especially between the social sciences and the natural sciences.

To the extent that these biases operate, it is not surprising that seasonal dimensions to rural poverty should be neglected.

An initial scenario

The suggestion that tropical seasonality may reinforce rural poverty can most concisely be presented as a composite scenario, in which each statement is a hypothesis open to testing.

Introduction

The scenario starts with a tropical environment where a wet season follows a dry season, and where cultivation is practised. Towards the end of the dry season, food becomes scarcer, less varied and more expensive. The poor people, who may be landless or have small plots of land, experience food shortage more acutely than their less poor neighbours. Some migrate in search of work and food. Others undertake non-agricultural activities near their homes in which the returns to labour are low. More work is involved in fetching water.

When the rains come, land must be prepared, and crops sown, transplanted and weeded. If animals are used for ploughing, they are weak after the dry season. Delays in cultivation reduce yields. For those with land, food supplies depend on the ability to work or to hire labour at this time. For those without land, work in the rains and at harvest often provides the highest wages of the year. This is the time of year when food is most needed for work, but it is also the hungry season when food is shortest and most expensive. It is, too, a sick season when exposure to tropical diseases is at its greatest, when immunity is low, and when women are most likely to be in late pregnancy. So the rains bring crisis. Vulnerable to hunger, sickness and incapacity, poor people are undernourished and lose weight. Seasonal stress drives them into debt and dependence. The knowledge that there will be future seasonal crises constrains them to keep on good terms with their patrons. They are thus screwed down seasonally into subordinate and dependent relationships in which they are open to exploitation. The poor are subordinated to the less poor and the weak to the strong. Stress is passed down to the weakest — women, children, old people and the indigent. Sometimes the screw becomes a ratchet, an irreversible downward movement into deeper poverty as assets are mortgaged or sold without hope of recovery. This is, then, a time when poor people are kept poor and a time when they become poorer.

With the harvest things improve. Grain prices are lower, a benefit to those who must buy food but a disadvantage to those small farmers who must sell their crops to repay debts or raise money for ceremonies. After the harvest, ceremonies, celebrations and marriages take place. Body weights recover. The dry season sets in. And then the cycle begins all over again.

There are dangers in presenting this composite scenario. First, it is written descriptively but each statement is in fact a separate hypothesis which may be mistaken for a widely established truth. An ideal type may be created in the mind of the reader, with which experience will not fit. Many exceptions may be found, and each environment must be analysed separately.

A second danger lies in extrapolation from situations of exceptional seasonality to rural areas more generally. Seasonality may be most studied and written about where it is most marked. This book, for example, deals with savannah areas in Africa and monsoon climates in Asia rather than with equatorial areas where seasonal contrasts are less. Within those regions, the book takes some half-dozen areas for closer examination. These case-study areas have been chosen, not only for their seasonal characteristics but also because of the availability of data. This may seem to have biased the choice unduly, but when the distribution of rural population in the third world generally is examined, this appears less distorting than at first sight. While exact figures cannot be given, well over half the rural population of the third world outside China probably lives in areas characterised by high climatic seasonality (ranging from D3 to F5 in the classification presented in Chapter 1). Such areas include most of the Indian Subcontinent and much of Africa south of the Sahara, besides parts of Central and South America and of Southeast Asia. After excluding areas of lower seasonality, the affected rural population in the Indian Subcontinent alone was over 600 millions in 1980 and in Sub-Saharan Africa over 200 millions.[1]

A third danger in making generalisations about seasonality is that agricultural seasonality does not always reflect the seasonality of climate because of irrigation. By using stored or non-seasonal water (whether from dams, rivers, or the ground) cultivation may be artificially spread more around the calendar, bringing new and different flows of food and income, labour demands and threats to health. As irrigation spreads, especially in the Indian Subcontinent, annual patterns of variation along many dimensions can be expected to change.

An approach for all disciplines

Seasonal variations occur in most of the human activities and natural processes which directly concern rural life. The schematic 'map' of some of the factors discussed in this book (see Figure 1) illustrates the considerable range of elements concerned in this, and some of their linkages. It is evident that many disciplines are required for a comprehensive understanding of seasonality as it affects rural people. With this in mind, the chapters which follow are organised to concentrate in turn on climate (Chapter 1), nutrition (Chapter 2), agricultural economics (Chapter 3), epidemiology (Chapter 4), and demography (Chapter 5). These specialised chapters reveal shared insights which later chapters draw together. Thus Chapters 6 and 7 are concerned with the welfare of poor rural people and its seasonal variations, Chapter 6 dealing with family health and Chapter 7 with social issues. Finally, in Chapter 8, an attempt is made to derive the more important practical implications for rural development policy and practice.

The experience of the conference which gave rise to this book and of subsequent work and correspondence has shown that seasonal analysis has a capacity both to excite intellectually, and to draw together the different professions. It provides a frame of questions which specialists can share, and which makes it easier to accept and relate to the concerns and findings of other disciplines. The divisive effects of professional training and of departmentalism are well known, and often give rise to complaints of lack of coordination and lack of integration in rural development. Seasonality provides one integrating concept which, as this book seeks to show, makes it easier to understand processes in rural environments and in rural life, and easier to see interactions between sectors and between programmes.

The hope is, then, that this book will do three things: first, raise *awareness* of seasonality and of seasonal linkages; second, provide practitioners and researchers of different departments and disciplines with a *common frame of questions*, which will draw them together; and third, and above all, help to identify *feasible measures* which will make things less hard for those rural people who, so often unseen, suffer seasonal hardship and impoverishment.

Introduction

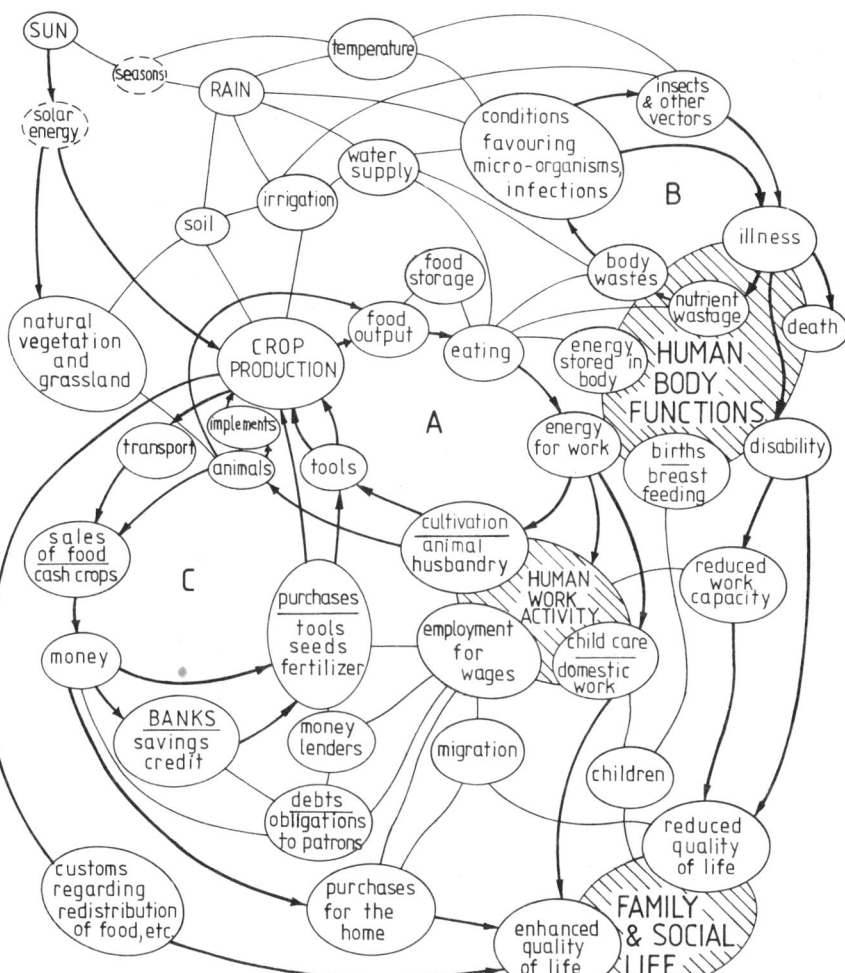

Figure 1   Schematic 'map' of some of the factors discussed in this book. Chapter 2 is concerned mainly with the cycle of food and energy relationships marked 'A', Chapter 3 with the cycle marked 'C', and Chapter 4 with 'B'. The overall argument of the book proceeds from top left to bottom right in its general subject matter.

Seasonal Dimensions to Rural Poverty

Note

1. These very approximate estimates have been derived from three sources: (1) the maps presented by Walsh in Chapter 1 below; (2) estimates of world rural population by country in 1975, supplied by FAO, and updated; (3) maps in Davies (1973).

References

Ashe, Jeffrey (1979), *Assessing Rural Needs: a Manual for Practitioners*, VITA (Volunteers in Technical Assistance), 3706 Rhode Island Avenue, Mt. Rainier, Maryland 20822, USA.

Chambers, Robert (1980), 'Rural Poverty Unperceived: Problems and Remedies', *World Bank Working Paper* No. 400, Washington D.C.

Davies, H.R.J. (1973), *Tropical Africa: an Atlas for Rural Development*, Cardiff, University of Wales Press.

Harriss, John (1977), 'Bias in Perception of Agrarian Change in India', in *Green Revolution? Technology and Change in Rice-Growing Areas of Tamil Nadu and Sri Lanka*, ed. B. H. Farmer, London and Basingstoke, Macmillan.

Haswell, Margaret (1975), *The Nature of Poverty: a Case-history of the First Quarter-century after World War II*, London and Basingstoke, Macmillan.

Kurien, C. T. (1976), *Rural Poverty in Tamil Nadu, India*, Rural Employment Research Programme, Working Paper, Geneva, International Labour Office.

Lipton, Michael (1977), *Why Poor People Stay Poor: Urban Bias in World Development*, London, Temple Smith.

Pearse, Andrew (1977), 'Technology and Peasant Production: Reflections on a Global Study', *Development and Change, 8* (2).

Schofield, Sue (1974), 'Seasonal Factors Affecting Nutrition in Different Age Groups and Especially Pre-school Children', *Journal of Development Studies, 11* (1), pp. 22-40.

Ssennyonga, Joseph (1976), 'The Cultural Dimensions of Demographic Trends', *Populi, 3* (2).

Chapter 1
CLIMATIC SEASONALITY IN THE TROPICS

1.1 Introduction

An ecological scenario

What is seen all the time is often not fully perceived. In the seasonal tropics, the alternation of wet and dry seasons is easily taken for granted. It is in comparison with an equatorial climate, where seasonal change is much less marked, that the full significance of the wet and dry seasons of higher latitudes becomes evident.

What tropical wet and dry seasons mean to people in rural areas can hardly be overstated. Such people, dependent on animal husbandry and agriculture for their livelihood, live in close contact with communities of plants, animals, insects, and micro-organisms. Indeed, the people themselves are an integral part of such natural communities. With the yearly ebb and flow of the seasons, domestic animals have their times for breeding and giving milk; crops germinate, grow and mature; and insects complete whole life cycles, some of them meanwhile pollinating crops or spreading disease.

In regions where seasonal contrasts are particularly sharp, and where there is a long dry season, that season is often, to begin with, a time free from severe pressures. Agricultural work-loads are small and there is often less disease. In contrast, the end of the dry season and the beginning of the rains is often a time of intensifying pressure, with more work to be done, more illness to contend with, and a shortage of food.

This picture of what happens in a highly seasonal climate can be elaborated as a scenario, stressing climatic, ecological, and human factors. We do not suggest that in any one place all the factors will vary together as described here. We do suggest, however, that many of them do commonly vary together, and that there is a widespread tendency for adverse factors to operate concurrently during wet seasons, and for these adverse factors to hit the poorer people harder.

The three climatic variables which most strongly influence the balance between adverse and positive factors are rainfall, evaporation, and solar radiation. The solar radiation which reaches the earth's surface is the ultimate energy source for all growing vegetation; its seasonal and geographic variations influence the potential productivity of food crops.

The other two variables, rainfall and evaporation, affect the availability of water in the local biological environment. Rainfall brings water into the environment, and it is then lost by direct evaporation, by transpiration through

---

This section draws on contributions by Deryke Belshaw and David Bradley, and on a paper by Chambers *et al.* (1979).

plants, by deep percolation and by stream flow. Evaporation and transpiration are greatest when temperatures are high, when humidity is low, and in windy weather. A standard measure here is the 'potential evapotranspiration' (PE). This represents the loss of moisture that would theoretically be experienced by a green crop covering the whole ground surface, and measures the amount of water needed by that crop if it is to flourish.

Where there is a long dry season, by the time it ends most plant life is dormant. So when the rains start, there are no green leaves from which moisture can be lost, and hence transpiration is negligible. However, some of the rain will penetrate the soil to be held there as soil moisture. In the early part of the rainy season, there is usually a gradual build-up of soil moisture which then forms a reservoir on which plants can draw as they resume growth. When the soil is saturated, further rainfall will percolate to the water table, perhaps causing springs to start flowing. Some rain reaches the river system more rapidly by running off the ground surface without penetrating the soil, and some more slowly by flowing laterally downslope at a shallow depth in the soil; ponds fill and river flow starts.

As moisture accumulates at these different locations in the environment, it is quickly exploited by various forms of life. Soil bacteria start to multiply and to break down the dead plant matter left by the dry season; seeds germinate and grow, using nitrogen released by this bacterial activity; perennial plants put out new leaves; insects begin breeding; and as grazing and water supplies improve, cattle and other herbivores give birth to young and produce milk.

In many tropical regions, rainfall is not sufficient to sustain transpiration losses from plants for more than a short period, and the reservoir of soil moisture is quickly depleted. One problem for the farmer, if he does not have irrigation, is to make maximum use of this soil moisture during the short period when it is available. But while that is a major concern for agriculturists, in this book we need to look at seasonal changes in environmental moisture from a wider perspective. Where rainfall is low compared with evaporation, sources of drinking water used by rural communities may tend to dry up very quickly. Contamination of drinking water may occur when the rains begin. The rainfall/evaporation relationship may affect the size of ponds in such a way as to determine the time of year when different organisms will breed or be most prevalent, including the mosquitoes which spread malaria, the waterfleas (cyclops) that carry guinea-worm infection, and the water-snails which spread schistosomiasis.

It is not always easy, however, to predict how some of these organisms will be affected. In very dry climates, the brief rainy season may be the only time when mosquitoes can find water in which to breed. In wetter climates, the mosquitoes may prefer the small ponds which persist in the dry season to the large expanses of water which are found while the rains are in progress. Temperatures may also play a part in limiting the activity of some animals during the season when water is available.

Implications for the human population

It would be possible to analyse the ecology of any specific area by means of a detailed study of climatic variables (rainfall, temperature, PE), their effect on different habitats (soil, ponds, vegetation), and their consequences for all forms of life. That kind of analysis lies in the background of this book, but an awareness of it must to a large extent be taken for granted. What is of greater importance here is the end-result of climatic and ecological relationships for the human population, and the way in which human welfare is affected.

For example, the start of the rains often brings a crisis for the community because much work is required in the fields to plant the new crops, but at the same time food is short and disease increasingly prevalent. This time of year is often known as the 'hungry season' or 'lean period'. Success with the new crop may depend on making prompt use of the often brief period when the soil is in the right state for ploughing or hoeing. Crops planted early in the rains frequently do better than those planted later (Gray, 1970). This is because of seasonal cycles in the activity of soil bacteria; the start of the rains stimulates bacterial activity in the soil which releases a 'flush' of nitrogen (Kowal and Kassam, 1978). If crops can take advantage of this, they are likely to yield well. But in many areas, a short delay in planting causes this benefit to be missed and weeds can be the main beneficiaries of the nitrogen flush if they are not removed in a timely manner.

All too often, though, it is the poorer farmers who are slow in preparing the land, because of inadequate tools, or because they lack draught animals; so it is they who are late putting in their seeds. Nor can they afford the fertilizer that might help the crop catch up. Thus their harvest is smaller than that achieved by richer neighbours, and the following year, they are more likely to be short of food during the planting season, and may then be forced to buy grain at inflated prices. In these circumstances, the poorer people are often driven to distress sales or borrowing.

In analysing the factors which create human situations of this kind, we need to study food production, nutrition and disease. We also need to consider man-made conditions in the social and economic order which may be causally more fundamental than climate. But the way social and economic processes work themselves out in rural tropical environments can only be fully understood by including their climatic, and especially seasonal, contexts.

1.2 The Nature of Climatic Seasonality
R.P.D. Walsh

What is seasonality?

In temperate regions, seasonal variations are usually identified on the basis of temperature contrasts during the year, but in the tropics, rainfall is the important criterion since mean temperatures vary so little from month to month. Thus in most tropical areas, the year is described in terms of wet and dry seasons. In monsoon regions, though, the year is customarily divided into three on the basis of both rainfall and temperature, and there are cool dry, hot dry, and hot rainy seasons.

The rainfall regimes of the tropics occur as a series of zones running roughly parallel with the equator; they are a response to a low-pressure system or trough which migrates between positions to the north of the equator in July, and generally to the south of the equator in January. Jackson (1977) has characterised the rainfall regimes caused by this equatorial trough as follows:

Seasonal Dimensions to Rural Poverty

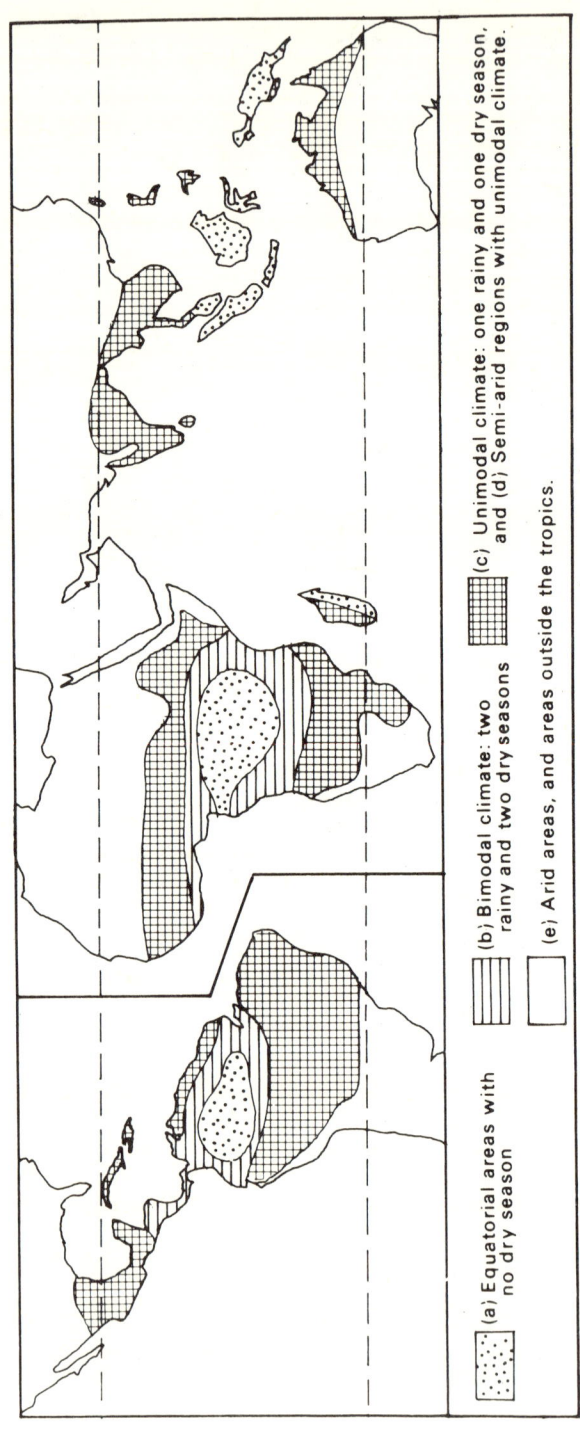

Figure 1.1 Spatial distribution of rainfall regime types in the tropics

Redrawn and reprinted, with permission, from K. Nieuwolt (1977) *Tropical Climatology*. London, John Wiley & Sons

Climatic Seasonality in the Tropics

TABLE 1.1. Indices of the relative seasonality of rainfall

Index	Formula	Range of values
Seasonality Ratio (SR)	$\dfrac{\bar{x}_{max} - \bar{x}_{min}}{\bar{R}}$	0.00 – 1.00
Seasonality Index (SI)	$\dfrac{\sum_{n=12}^{n=1} \left\| \bar{x}_n - \dfrac{\bar{R}}{12} \right\|}{\bar{R}}$	0.00 – 1.83

where: $\bar{x}_{max}$ = mean rainfall of wettest month
$\bar{x}_{min}$ = mean rainfall of driest month
$\bar{R}$ = mean annual rainfall
$\bar{x}_n$ = mean rainfall of month n
n = month, where 1 = January, 2 = February, etc.

Note: A high value of either index indicates a climate with sharp contrasts between wet and dry seasons.

(a) on the equator: no real dry season;
(b) close to the equator: double rainfall maxima, with pronounced winter dry season and short midsummer dry season — a bimodal climate;
(c) further from the equator: a single rainy season and a single dry season — a unimodal climate;
(d) on the poleward fringes of the zone in (c): a semi-arid region with a short wet season and a long dry season — a dry unimodal climate;
(e) in the subtropical margins, there is generally an arid region with no wet season capable of supporting crops.

The distribution of these different rainfall regimes is mapped in Figure 1.1. This shows the areas with double and single rainfall maxima, that is, areas with bimodal and unimodal climates. However, an approach based solely on this distinction is not only imprecise, but also precludes objective comparison of different areas of the tropics. In fact, at least four additional characteristics of rainfall regime are important, namely, (1) 'relative seasonality', (2) 'absolute seasonality', (3) timing of rainfall maxima and minima, and (4) year-to-year reliability of rainfall.

Relative seasonality

The 'relative seasonality' of rainfall refers to the degree of contrast in relative terms between the amounts of rain at different times of year. No attempt is made to define 'dry' and 'wet' months in an absolute sense, and indices measuring relative seasonality are thus only concerned with seasonal contrasts.

Table 1.1 defines two ratios which can be used as indices of relative seasonality. The first is a ratio of the *range* of the mean monthly rainfall ($\bar{x}_{max} - \bar{x}_{min}$) and the mean annual rainfall. This will be referred to as the 'seasonality ratio' and takes account only of the wettest and driest months and not of others. A second index, which takes into consideration all months of the

Seasonal Dimensions to Rural Poverty

year, is the 'seasonality index' (Walsh, 1980). This is simply the sum of the absolute deviations of mean *monthly* rainfall from the overall mean, divided by mean *annual* rainfall. In theory this index can vary between 0.00 (if all months have equal amounts of rain), and 1.83 (if all rain is concentrated into a single month). Maps of seasonality index for Brazil (based on data for forty stations), the Indian Subcontinent (sixty-eight stations) and Sub-Saharan Africa (224 stations) are presented in Figure 1.2.

The index reflects differences in rainfall regime well. The only disadvantage is that it takes no account of the temporal distribution of monthly rainfalls and does not directly distinguish between regimes with one or two maxima. However, most tropical regimes conform to relatively simple patterns, and

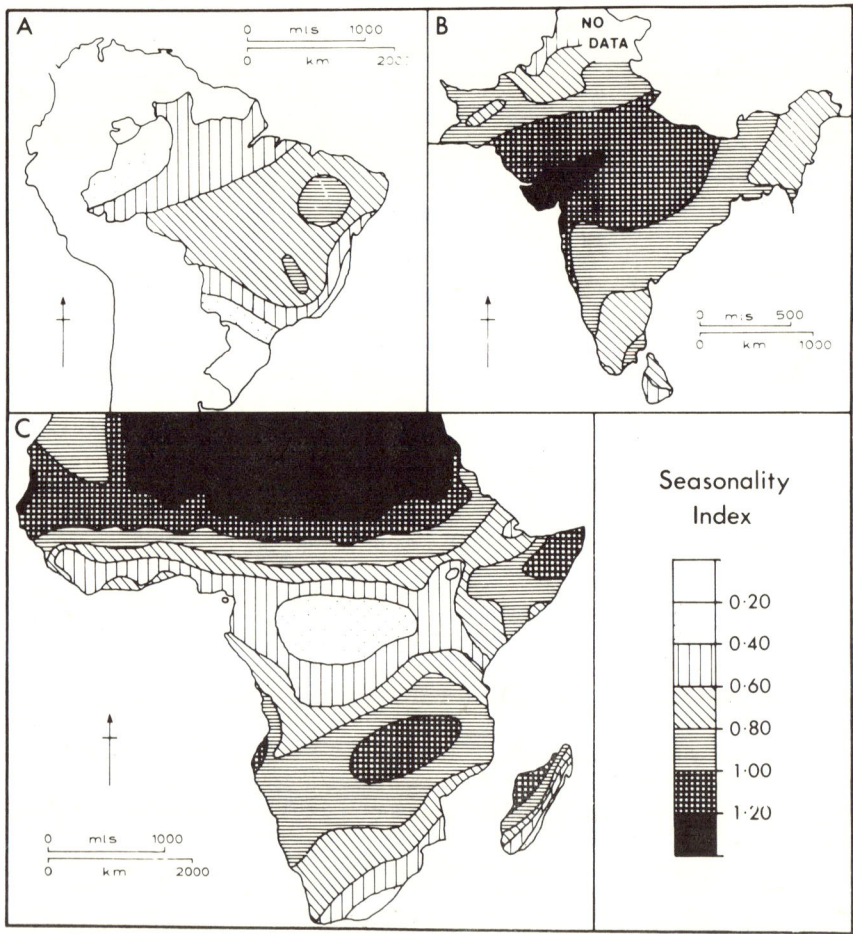

Figure 1·2 Seasonality index maps for Brazil, the Indian Subcontinent and Sub-Saharan Africa.

Climatic Seasonality in the Tropics

areas with double maxima (bimodal climates) tend to have lower seasonality index values than those with only one maximum (unimodal climates).

In the Indian Subcontinent (Figure 1.2), the pattern is interesting, and reflects the differences in rainfall regimes and origins of rainfall very clearly. Indices are relatively low in South India and Sri Lanka because these regions are near the equator and have a longer rainy season, often with a double peak in rainfall. In the Bay of Bengal area, the index is again low, this time because the summer rainy season is extended into autumn because of tropical cyclones and lesser disturbances. The very high indices of the centre and west of India are the result of almost all the rain falling in a very short summer period of three to four months. In northern India and northern Pakistan, the combined effect of the decreased intensity of the summer monsoon and the appreciable winter rainfall due to temperate depressions results in more equable rainfall distribution and hence lower seasonality index values than further south. The seasonality index values of the Indian Subcontinent are, in general, very high in comparison with the rest of the world, reflecting the monsoonal nature of the climate. In Africa, the pattern is relatively simple, with increasing seasonality as one moves farther from the equator. The Sahel region ranks with monsoonal India in its very high seasonality index, often in excess of 1.20.

The indices described above have all been calculated from mean monthly figures. The indices can, however, be calculated for individual years, when they are denoted by SI_i. It should be noted that the mean value of SI_i (denoted $\overline{SI}_i$) will be significantly higher than the seasonality index calculated from mean monthly figures alone.

Absolute seasonality

Although relative seasonality is important, most emphasis has traditionally been placed on definitions of 'dry' and 'wet' seasons in *absolute* terms. It is generally agreed that a dry period is one where insufficient water is available to meet the potential needs of plants as measured by potential evapotranspiration (PE). The problem is that PE is very difficult to measure directly, and complicated formulae have been introduced for estimating it from other meteorological data. Thornthwaite (1948) pioneered calculations of this kind, but his method is complex and is based on assumptions which are to some extent arbitrary. Penman's (1963) method of estimating PE is more accurate, but requires detailed data that are often not available.

Thus for most purposes it appears that relatively simple indices are as useful and perhaps just as realistic as complicated formulae. Indeed, it can be argued that a 'dry' month can be defined in terms of a single figure. Thus Koeppen and Geiger (1936) stressed a rainfall figure of 60 mm (2.4") in their classification, Miller (1953) and the New Oxford Atlas (Lewis, 1975) have mapped the frequency of months with less than 50 mm rainfall. However, water deficits arise in the tropics at monthly rainfalls well in excess of 50-60 mm, and Mohr, Van Baren and Van Schuylenborgh (1972) found that a 100 mm (4") limit was more realistic.

Some workers have used 4" (102 mm) to indicate 'dry' months (e.g. Stoddart and Walsh, 1979), and in Figure 1.3 the annual frequency of dry months so

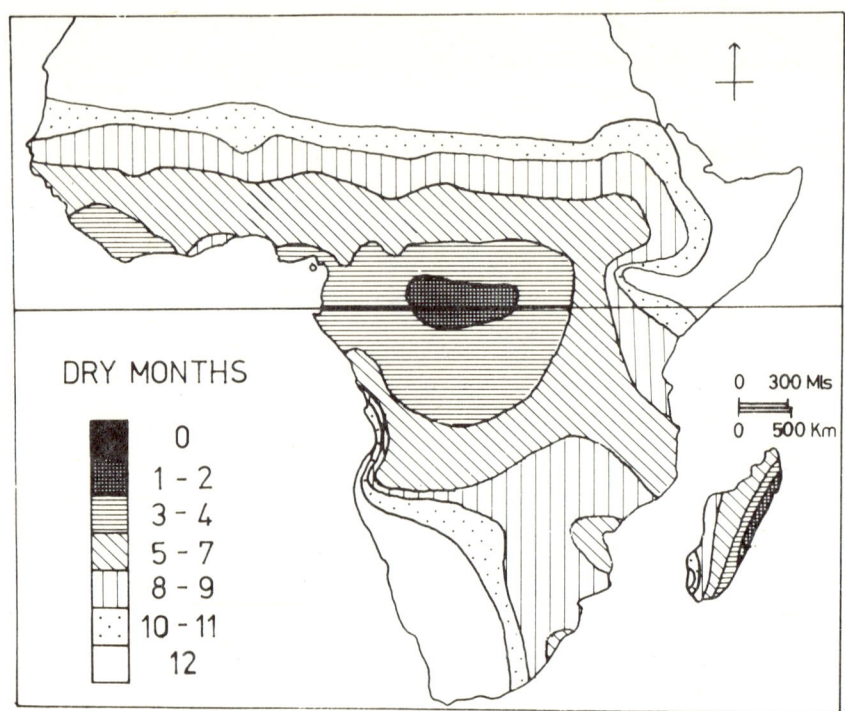

A dry month has a mean rainfall of less than 4 inches (102mm)
Figure 1.3 Sub-Saharan Africa: dry months per annum.

defined is mapped for Sub-Saharan Africa. The data are again derived from long-term averages; if the figures were re-calculated by averaging the frequency of dry months for individual years, the mean would be somewhat larger.

Timing of rainfall maxima and minima

The timing of rainfall maxima and minima can only be qualitatively expressed. Important here are the season of maximum rainfall and the number and timing of rainfall peaks. In equatorial or near-equatorial areas, double peaks of rainfall tend to occur near the equinoxes; away from the equator, they tend to occur in early and late summer. In almost all other tropical areas, a single summer maximum occurs.

Reliability and seasonality

The reliability of the onset of rainy seasons and of rainfall within them strongly influences farmers' decisions about the timing of agricultural activities. Reliability is reflected in the variation of rainfall for the same month as between years. Reliability tends to be lower, the lower the mean annual rainfall. Reliability also tends to be lower the higher the relative and absolute

Climatic Seasonality in the Tropics

seasonality. In other words, the more marked the seasonality of the rainfall, the less reliable the rainfall is during the rainy season.

Seasonality of other climatic elements

In the subtropical margins, temperature shows significant changes with season, particularly in continental areas. Annual temperature range is often only 2°C at the equator, but rises to around 10°C at latitudes 20°N and S; however, even at latitudes 30°N or S, annual ranges are still only around 5°C in maritime areas (Paffen, 1967).

Associated with temperature changes are seasonal changes in potential evapotranspiration (PE), which increase quite sharply with latitude, reflecting increasing contrasts in day length and temperature. Nearer the equator the PE is more nearly constant from month to month.

Seasonal changes in *relative humidity* tend to follow seasonal changes in rainfall, with higher relative humidities in the wet seasons. However, the degree of variation can differ markedly. At Brazzaville, in the equatorial zone, relative humidity shows very little seasonal change. At Fort Lamy, in Chad, however, relative humidity varies immensely from 81 per cent in August, during the short summer wet season, to as low as 23 per cent in March. The very low relative humidities in winter are the direct result of the 'Harmattan' which blows from the north-east from the dry Sahara over almost all of West Africa during the winter months.

In many tropical locations, wind *directions* also change systematically with season. The Harmattan of West Africa is a classic example, another being the monsoon of the Indian Subcontinent. In some tropical areas, also, the cyclone or hurricane is an important climatic element. Cyclones generally show distinct seasonality in occurrence; they tend to occur in late summer and autumn. Because of the extreme damage associated with hurricanes, a knowledge of their seasonality is of considerable importance.

Seasonality and the classification of tropical climates

Seasonality of rainfall and amounts of rainfall have formed the basis of almost all systems for classifying tropical climates. For example. Koeppen's world classification is based on the rainfall and temperature limits of different types of plants (Koeppen and Geiger, 1936). Tropical areas are then considered to lie within a boundary formed by the 18°C (64.4°F) isotherm drawn for the coldest month of the year, this isotherm being critical for certain tropical plants. Boundaries are then drawn between tropical rainy and dry climates, and within the dry climates between semi-arid and desert types. These divisions are based upon simple empirical expressions involving mean annual temperature and mean annual rainfall.

The Koeppen system has the advantage of simplicity, but rainfall seasonality is only incorporated in the classification in a rudimentary way, and many places with quite different rainfall regimes are classified as the same.

Thornthwaite's climatic classification (Thornthwaite, 1948) gives primary place to the water balance, and in particular, to a moisture index which he defined to express the state of the *annual* water balance in an area. In areas with a long dry season, where potential evapotranspiration (PE) measured over a full year is likely to exceed the annual rainfall, this moisture index is negative. But in areas with high rainfall and a short dry season, the moisture index is positive.

Thornthwaite classified arid and semi-arid climates as those for which the moisture index was between -100 and -33; he defined sub-humid climates as those with an index between -33 and $+20$; and he defined humid climates as those where the index was between $+20$ and $+100$.

These figures indicate little about seasonality, and for that purpose Thornthwaite introduced various subdivisions which describe whether the wet season comes in summer or winter. The result is a more precise classification than Koeppen's, but it is highly debatable whether it is accurate in its PE estimates, particularly in the tropical context.

Jackson's (1977) classification of tropical climates has no pretensions to precision, and concentrates on the broad characteristics of rainfall: annual rainfall total, number of rainy and dry seasons, and the length and intensity of the dry season(s). He makes a basic threefold division into 'humid', 'wet and dry', and 'dry' tropics. The main problem is the imprecision of some of Jackson's class limits, with no clear indication as to what exactly constitutes 'a few' months, and so on. However, the interesting aspect of this classification is that it is linked directly to different types of agriculture and crops (see Jackson, 1977, pp. 189-93).

It should be stressed that the three classifications of climate discussed here have had rather different aims. Koeppen's system sought only to describe the climatic limits of natural vegetation types; Thornthwaite's system is based on the water balance; Jackson's system seeks to relate rainfall regimes to agricultural crops and practices.

A new climate classification based on rainfall seasonality

Tentatively presented here is a simple scheme of describing and classifying tropical climates in terms of absolute and relative seasonality of rainfall. Two main criteria are employed:

(a) the length of the dry period, as given by the number of months with less than 4" (102 mm) rainfall on average; this number is denoted as $\overline{DM}$;

(b) the seasonality index, $\overline{SI}$, defined above.

A simple categorisation of these two criteria is given in Table 1.2. The length of dry period factor is divided into seven primary classes ranging from 'perennially wet' (A), with no dry months, to 'arid' (G), with twelve dry months. If there are two wet and two dry seasons, as in bimodal climates, then the symbol * may be added. However, most areas with a double maximum of rainfall tend to have only one dry season in the absolute sense, with less than 102 mm rain per month, so this symbol is rarely used.

When the seasonality index is also divided into seven categories, the two factors may be combined to yield forty-nine possible climate types. But in practice, there is a degree of correlation between aridity and seasonality, and so a number of types do not occur, such as A3-A6, B4-B6, C4-C6, F0-F1, and G0-G1. Maps of the climatic types based on rainfall seasonality are presented in Figures 1.4 and 1.5. In Africa, there is almost a full range of possible types,

TABLE 1.2. Provisional classification scheme of tropical climates on the basis of rainfall seasonality

Absolute Seasonality			Relative Seasonality		
Length of dry season (DM)			Seasonality Index ($\overline{SI}$)		
Symbol	Type	$\overline{DM}$ (Months <4" or 102mm)	Symbol	Type	$\overline{SI}$
A	Perennially wet	0	0	Very equable	<0.20
B	Wet with short dry season	1–2	1	Equable but definite drier season	0.20–0.39
C	Wet seasonally dry	3–4	2	Rather seasonal	0.40–0.59
D	Wet and dry	5–7	3	Seasonal	0.60–0.79
E	Dry seasonally wet	8–9	4	Markedly seasonal; long drier season	0.80–0.99
F	Dry with short wet	10–11	5	Most rain in ≤3 months	1.00–1.19
G	Arid	12	6	Extreme; almost all	>1.20

Note: Symbol * is added (e.g. C*, D*) where there are two dry seasons.

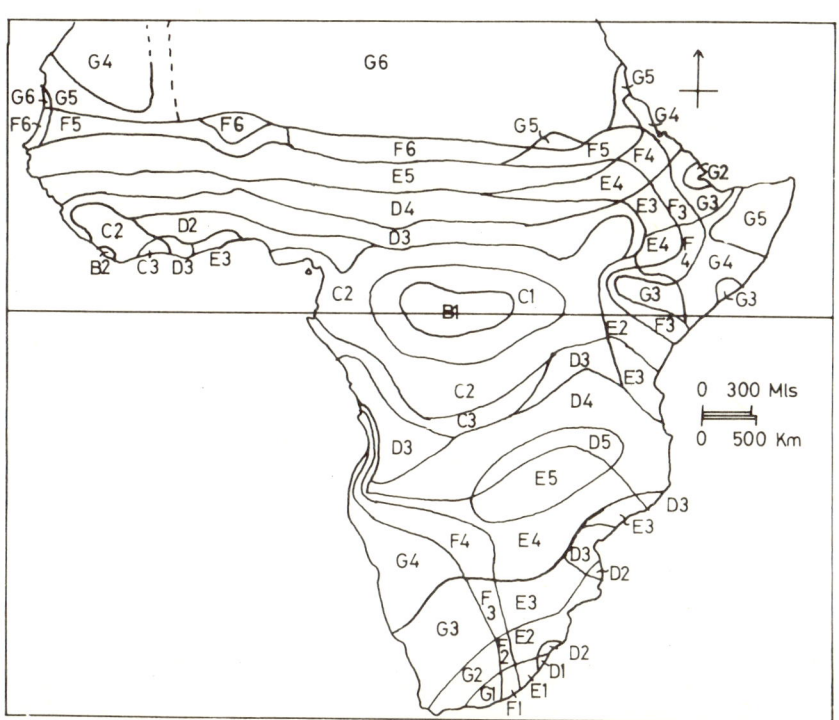

Figure 1·4 Sub-Saharan Africa tropical climatic types based on rainfall seasonality.

19

Seasonal Dimensions to Rural Poverty

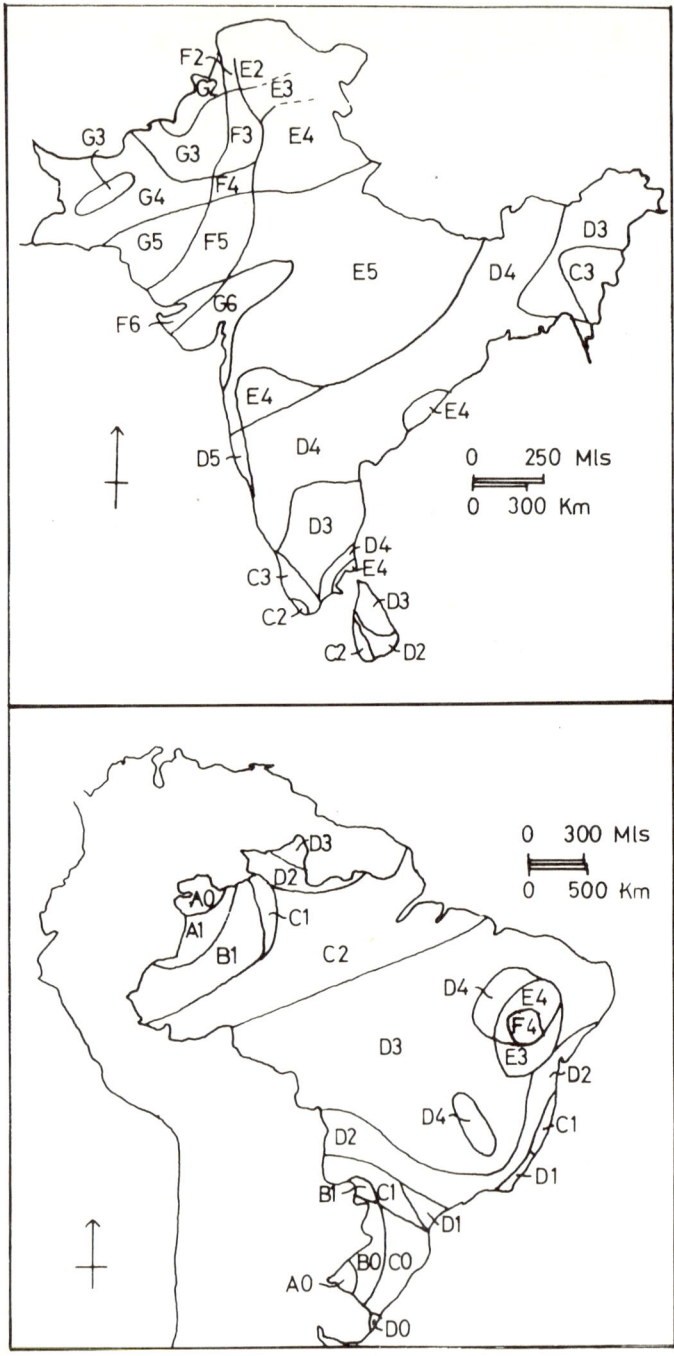

Figure 1·5 The Indian Subcontinent and Brazil: tropical climatic types based on rainfall seasonality.

broadly arranged in latitudinal zones north and south of the equator, but there is a marked absence of perennially wet (A) climates, even in equatorial areas; for examples of those one must look to Brazil (Figure 1.5). The Indian Sub-continent is very seasonal, with long dry seasons and very peaked rainfall regimes, and hence very high seasonality indices. There are no A or B climates; South India and Bangladesh stand out as the areas with lowest seasonal contrasts.

This classification scheme can be regarded as slightly arbitrary in its definition of dry months. Clearly also, the scheme is not sufficient for all purposes; no climatic classification can ever be. This one is specifically geared to *rainfall seasonality*, which is the aspect of seasonality of greatest interest for this book.

Seasonality in climatic change

There is now a very large body of evidence to show that large areas of the tropics have been subject to quite substantial climatic changes, even over the past hundred years. Over wide areas of the tropics, strikingly similar trends in annual rainfall have been noted: a very wet phase in the late nineteenth century; a drier phase in the first twenty to thirty years of this century; a return to wetter conditions in the 1930s, 1940s, and 1950s; and a markedly drier phase from 1960 onwards (Goudie, 1977, Winstanley, 1973).

Many of these changes have been accompanied by changes in the nature of seasonality (Stoddart and Walsh, in press). For example, at Roseau, Dominica, in the Eastern Caribbean, there was a double maximum in rainfall, with the peaks occurring in July/August and November. However, in the drier phases of climatic change, the November secondary maximum disappeared. In the rest of the tropics, marked changes in seasonality have also been reported by Winstanley (1973), who showed that the summer wet season rainfall of stations in the Sahel zone of Africa and in north-western India and Pakistan was only 50 per cent of 1955-9 levels during the dry years 1968-72. A tendency for rainfall changes to be most marked at the beginning and end of the wet season during drier epochs was found by Kraus (1954) in Australia, and a similar pattern occurred in the Caribbean (Walsh, 1980).

Clearly, then, aspects of seasonality of climate in the tropics are not static in nature, but have often been subject to marked changes, even during the past century. Studies of the influence of climatic seasonality on cultural, economic, and physical systems in the tropical world should take this fact into account.

1.3 Case-Studies

An attempt to describe the effects of seasonality on human populations in all the climatic zones defined in the previous section would either entail a formidably detailed treatment, or an undesirable degree of generalisation. So although this book does attempt to reach some general conclusions, there is constant reference to the local ecology or economy of specific areas; in particular, there are six case-study areas which receive detailed attention (see Table 1.3).

None of these case-studies is located in A and B climates, or in climates such as C2 or D2, because these all represent places (mostly close to the equator),

Seasonal Dimensions to Rural Poverty

TABLE 1.3. Summary of climatic classifications and rainfall data (mm) for the six case-study areas (* denotes a bimodal rainfall regime)

Case-study area	Climate class	Annual rainfall	Rainy season(s)	Reference
1) Monsoon Climate, *Bangladesh*				
Matlab, Comilla District	C3	2000-2500	May-Nov	Chapters 2, 5
Comilla District	C3	2000-3200	May-Nov)	
Dacca District	C3	1700-2500	May-Nov)	Chapter 3
Faridpur District	C3/D3	1650-2200	May-Nov)	
Kushtia District	D3	1420-1630	May-Nov)	
2) Monsoon Climate, *Tamil Nadu*				
North Arcot District	D3/E3	850-1000	Aug-Nov)	Chapters 5, 7
Thanjavur District			)	
(Old and New Deltas)	E4	1200-1400	Oct-Nov)	
3) Bimodal Climate, *East Africa*				
Machakos District Kenya	E3*	600- 950	Mar-May) Oct-Nov)	Chapter 2
Bagamoyo District, Tanzania	E3*	750-1100	Mar-Jun) Oct-Nov)	Chapter 6
4) Unimodal Dry Climate, *Northern Nigeria*				
Zaria area (Hanwa village)	D4	900-1250	May-Oct	Chapter 3
Malumfashi	D4/E5	800-1100	May-Oct	Chapter 6
Katsina	E5	550- 850	Jun-Oct	Chapter 7
5) Unimodal Dry Climate, *Gambia, West Africa*				
Keneba, Gambia	E5	600-1100	Jun-Oct	Chapter 6
Genieri, Gambia	E5	500-1000	Jun-Oct	Chapter 2
6) Arid Climate, *Mali, West Africa*				
Northern Mali	G5/G6	70- 200	Jun-Sep	Chapter 3

where rain occurs in nearly all months of the year, and where the seasonal contrasts relevant to this book are likely to be less marked. However, two equatorial regions which are discussed, though not at case-study length, are Java (Chapter 7) and the Solomon Islands (Chapter 5). These are places where, despite low *climatic* seasonality, some seasonality still occurs in other events; they thus serve as a warning that climate is not a unique determinant of all cyclic changes. For example, although the Solomon Islands have a climate classed as A0 and A1, with remarkably equable weather throughout

Climatic Seasonality in the Tropics

the year, the human birth rate shows seasonal changes.

Among the principal case-studies, the region with the least climatic seasonality, and the lowest number of dry months, is Bangladesh. The country is divided between areas of only two classifications: C3 and D3 (Table 1.3). About 75 per cent of the rainfall comes in a short wet season between May and October. However, the average annual amount of rainfall is very high — 1880 mm in Dacca, about 2000 mm in the Matlab case-study area, and up to 3000 mm in some other places. Thus even the small proportion of rain that falls outside the wet season can give a considerable total in some months, and few

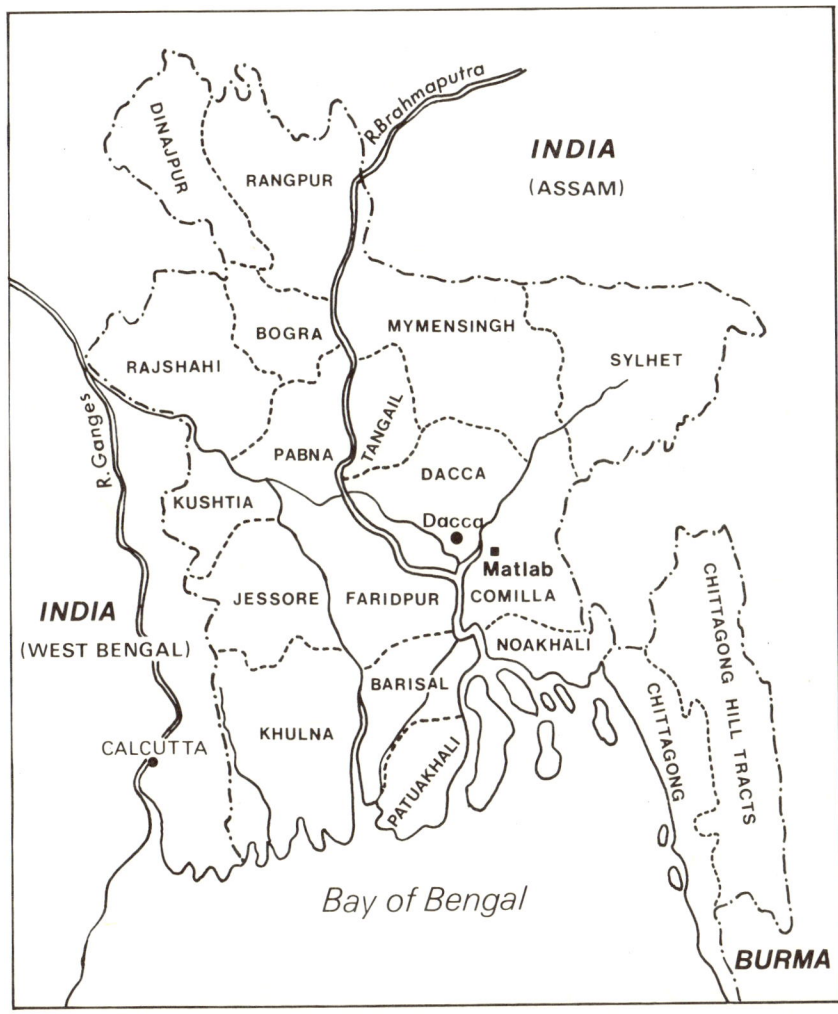

Figure 1.6 Bangladesh, showing District boundaries (dashed line) and the location of Matlab in Comilla District, which is in the Matlab thana case-study area

places have more than four 'dry' months as defined by Walsh in the preceding section. The result is that the classification of climate shows Bangladesh as an area with relatively little rainfall seasonality.

The material from Bangladesh presented in Chapters 2, 3, and 5 includes two reviews which concentrate on one locality (Matlab thana), and two which discuss wider areas. The latter focus on some of the more important geographical contrasts by taking a transect across the country from Kushtia District in the west (with a D3 climate) to Comilla District in the east (C3). These areas can be located on the map in Figure 1.6.

One unusual feature of Bangladesh is that many areas are low-lying delta land where fields are regularly flooded at the end of the monsoon season. The main crop in these areas is a variety of rice which can withstand deep floods by means of its long stems. The population of such areas tends to experience food shortages during September and October, when these monsoon floods are in progress, and the harvest from the deep-water rice crop is awaited.

Among other case-study areas, the one with greatest climatic similarity to Bangladesh is the State of Tamil Nadu in southern India. Although total rainfall is much less than in Bangladesh, the seasonal distribution of the rain is similar. The largest amount of rain comes in the four months August-November (Figure 5.7), but in the two or three months preceding the wet season, there is significant precipitation in some places. The climatic classification varies according to the district from D3 to E3 and E4.

Tamil Nadu is outstanding among the six case-studies for the extensive development of irrigation. Two areas are of particular interest. In Thanjavur District (see Figure 1.7) large-scale irrigation works involving river dams and canals have enabled large parts of the Old and New Delta areas to be intensively irrigated. By contrast, in North Arcot District irrigation is principally of a localised kind based on tanks or wells. However, this also can be very intensive, and it is estimated that, on average, there is one irrigation well for every 2.4 ha of cultivated land.

In areas such as these, it is important to draw a distinction between climatic seasonality and agricultural seasonality. In the C3 and D3 climates of Bangladesh, one knows that there are only four to five dry months in the year, and therefore it comes as no surprise that two rice crops can be grown each year. In the E3 and E4 climates of Tamil Nadu, however, one expects eight to nine dry months and therefore only one cropping period in the year. However, irrigation makes two and sometimes three cropping periods possible for many farmers. Thus although the seasonality of rainfall is classed as E3 or E4, the seasonality of irrigated agriculture is more closely comparable to what one would find in a C3 or even a B2 climate.

Bangladesh and Tamil Nadu have *unimodal* climates, but East Africa appears on the maps (Figure 1.4) as a region of relatively low seasonal contrast because its *bimodal* climate gives it a low seasonality index. East African case-studies come from two areas: Machakos District in Kenya (Chapter 2), and Bagamoyo District in Tanzania (Chapter 6). Although these areas are a considerable distance apart, they both have an E3*-type climate. Figure 1.8 indicates their locations, and at the same time illustrates the extent of the area in East Africa where bimodal rainfall regimes are experienced. On this map an

Climatic Seasonality in the Tropics

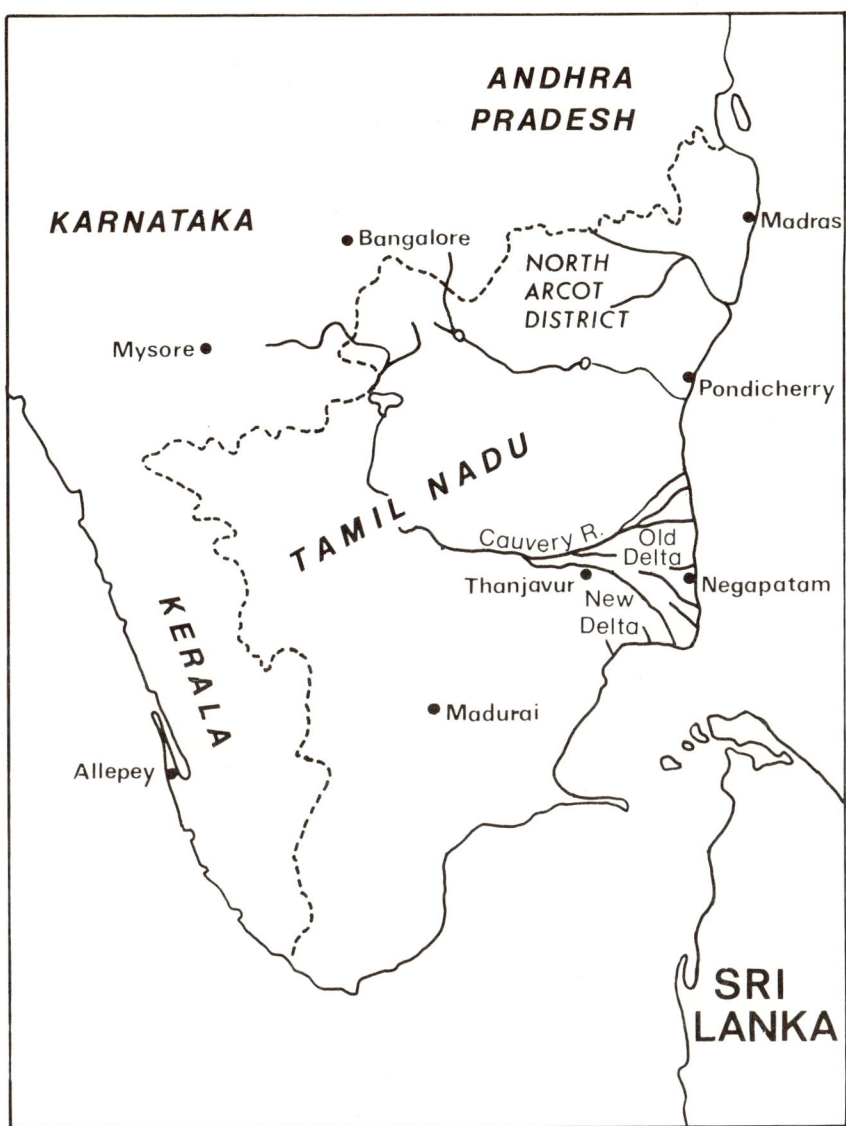

Figure 1·7 South India, showing boundary of Tamil Nadu and the location of North Arcot and Thanjavur Districts.

Seasonal Dimensions to Rural Poverty

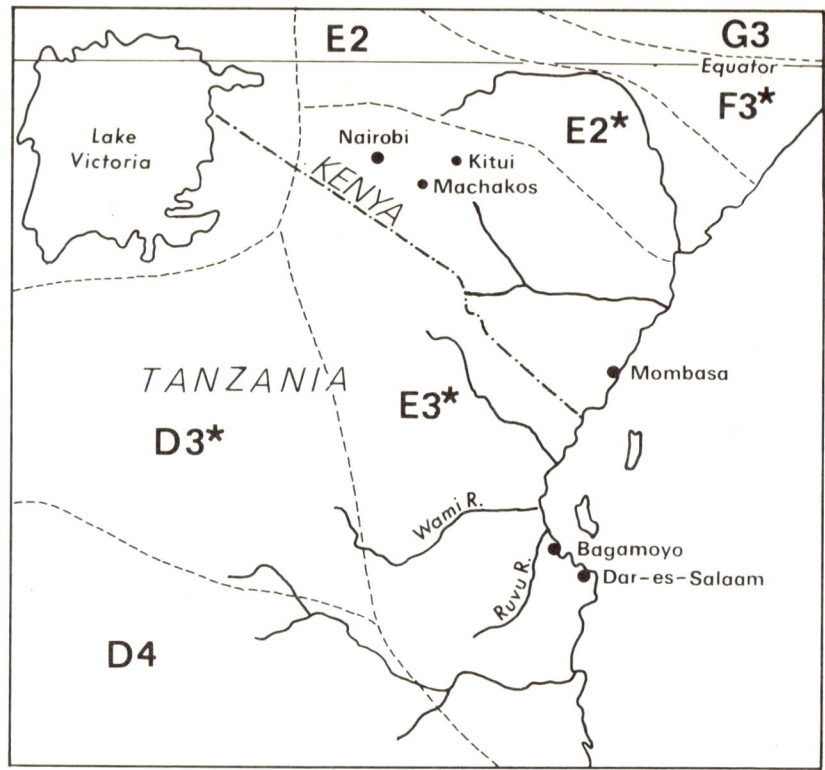

Figure 1.8 Map of the main area of bimodal climate in East Africa, locating the Machakos and Bagamoyo Districts, both of which have E3*-type climates. The map shows that D, E, F, and even G types of climates all occur in the region with bimodal rainfall regimes. (Dashed lines are very approximate boundaries of climatic types; compare Figure 1.6)

asterisk is used to denote bimodal rainfall even when one of the two rainy seasons is not strictly wet enough to merit this. The asterisk is normally used only when *both* rainfall peaks produce a month with more than 102 mm of precipitation.

It is difficult to compare the data from East Africa with the very precise and detailed information available from Bangladesh. But it does appear that a bimodal climate offers some advantage to a rural population, provided that enough rain falls in the two wet seasons for crops to be grown in both. In the East African case-study areas, there is a *long* rainy season from mid-March until at least May, and a *short* rainy season centred on October. Crops are grown in both seasons. In Machakos District, food produced during the short rains lasts until the long-rains harvest. Short-rains maize is harvested green when food stocks are low, but the main short-rains crop, pigeon peas, matures slowly after the rains are over, and is harvested later.

West Africa provides three case-studies for this book, all of them with

26

Climatic Seasonality in the Tropics

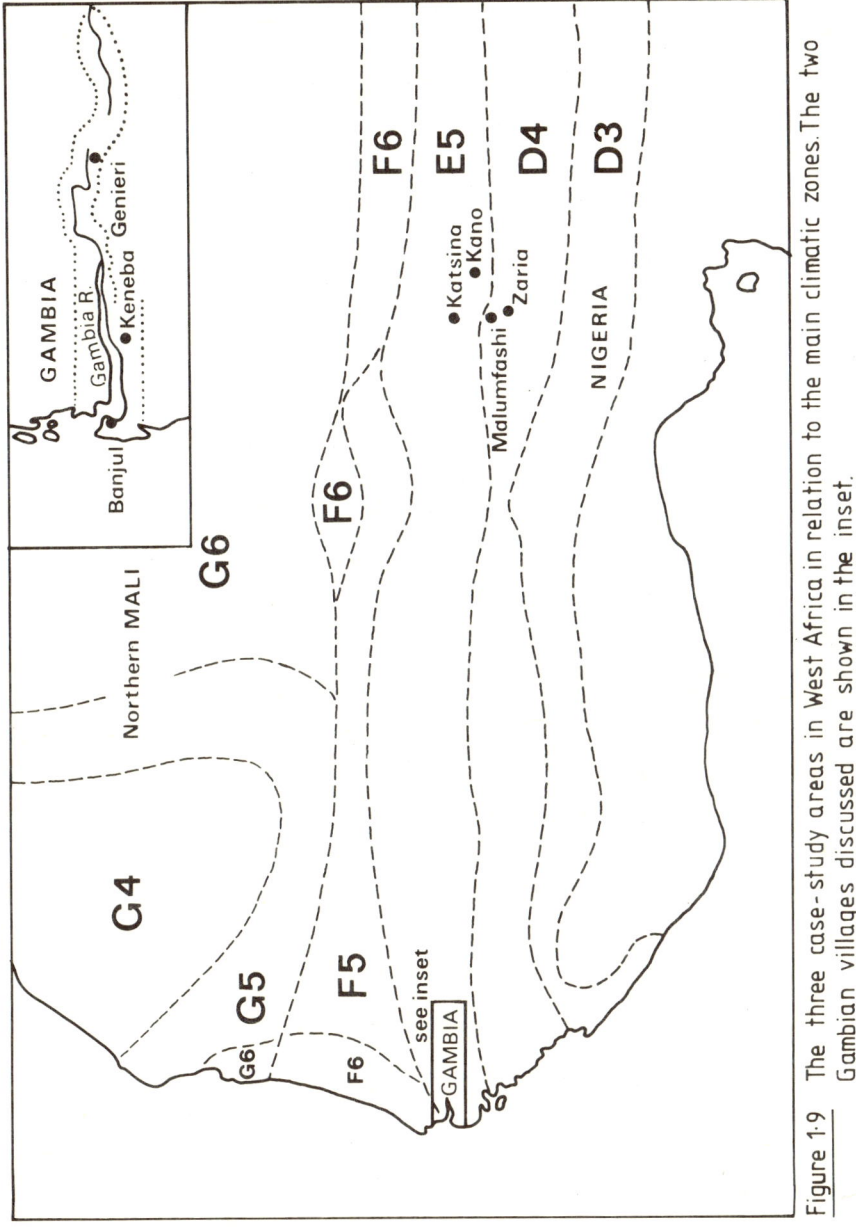

Figure 1.9 The three case-study areas in West Africa in relation to the main climatic zones. The two Gambian villages discussed are shown in the inset.

sharper contrasts between wet and dry seasons than those so far discussed. These range from a part of northern Nigeria with a D4 climate, through Gambia with an E5 climate, to the arid climate of northern Mali. The latter overlaps classes G5 and G6, which indicates some of the most extreme rainfall seasonality to be found in the tropics. All these West African areas have unimodal climates; locations of the places concerned are shown in Figure 1.9, and the dates of rainy seasons and amounts of rainfall are summarised in Table 1.3.

Information from Gambia* is derived mainly from two villages, Genieri (discussed in Chapter 2), and Keneba (Chapter 6). Although there are differences in cropping pattern and in other respects, the two villages share many common features. The short unimodal rainy season in Gambia is marked by shortages of food and money, a low energy intake for women, exacting agricultural work, high incidence of infections, including diarrhoea and malaria, increased contamination of well water and food, lower body weights of mothers, and high child mortality. Poorer families suffer a severe labour crisis during the rains.

In the northern Nigeria case-study area, annual rainfall becomes less as one travels further north. Katsina, the most northerly Nigerian settlement discussed, has a very similar climate to that in Gambia according to Table 1.3. Further south, however, are the Malumfashi and Zaria areas where the rains are more ample and seasonality is less — the climatic classification is D4 instead of E5 (Figure 1.9). In the two latter areas, the period of pre-harvest food shortage certainly presents fewer problems than in Gambia, though this may be due to good management more than differences in climate (Chapter 3). Seasonal peaks in the need for agricultural labour are met by higher food intakes for the family as a unit, although the nature of allocations within households is not known.

Conclusion

The purpose of this book is to examine the effect of all these seasonal contrasts, especially on the poorest sectors of society. However, care is needed when generalising from the case-studies. For example, although Gambia and Zaria both come within a band of unimodal rainfall south of the Sahara, they show the effects of seasonality in different ways. And even where rainfall is bimodal, or where cropping follows more complex patterns under irrigation, concurrent seasonal peaks of several factors are still found. In the East African cases, for example, although bimodality may have smoothing effects, there remain peaks, for example in labour demand for agricultural activities. Moreover, Bangladesh has complex patterns of irrigated cropping and labour demand, but still shows considerable seasonality in demography and disease.

One should also be aware that failure of the rains — an irregular occurrence — may be more significant than the regular rhythm of the seasons, and may play a bigger part in accentuating and sustaining rural poverty. We shall return to this and other issues in later chapters, as evidence from the case-studies, and from more general surveys accumulates.

*This abbreviated name is used throughout to refer to the small West African republic of The Gambia.

1.4 References

Blüthgen, J. (1966). *Allgemeine Klimageographie,* 2nd edn., Berlin, Walter de Gruyter.

Chambers, R., Longhurst, R., Bradley, D., and Feachem, R. (1979), 'Seasonal Dimensions to Rural Poverty: Analysis and Practical Implications', Discussion Paper 142, Institute of Development Studies, University of Sussex.

Goudie, A. S. (1977), *Environmental Change,* Oxford, Clarendon Press.

Gray, R. W. (1970), 'The Effect on Yield of the Time of Planting of Maize', *East African Agric. Forestry J., 35,* pp. 291-8.

Jackson, I. J. (1977), *Climate, Water and Agriculture in the Tropics,* London, Longmans.

Koeppen, W., and Geiger, R. (1936), *Handbuch der Klimatologie,* Berlin, Gebruder Borntraeger.

Kowal, J. M., and Kassam, A. H. (1978), *Agricultural Ecology of Savannah,* Oxford, Oxford University Press.

Kraus, E. B. (1954), 'Secular Changes in the Rainfall Regimes of South-east Australia', *Quart. J. R. Met. Soc., 80,* p. 591.

Lewis, C. (ed.), (1975), *The New Oxford Atlas,* London, Oxford University Press.

Miller, A. A. (1953), *Climatology,* 8th ed., London, Methuen.

Mohr, E.C.J., van Baren, F. A., and van Schuylenborgh, J. (1972), *Tropical Soils,* 3rd ed, The Hague, Mouton-Ichtiar Baru-van Hoeve.

Nieuwolt, K. (1977), *Tropical Climatology,* London, John Wiley & Sons.

Paffen, K. (1967), 'Das Verhältnis der Tages−zur Jahreszeitlichen Temperaturschwankung', *Erdkunde, 21,* pp. 94-111.

Penman, H. L. (1963), *Vegetation and Hydrology,* Technical Communication 53, Harpenden, Commonwealth Bureau of Soils.

Stoddart, D. R., and Walsh, R.P.D. (1979), 'Long-term Climatic Change in the Western Indian Ocean', *Phil. Trans. R. Soc. Lond., 273B,* pp. 11-23.

Stoddart, D. R., and Walsh, R.P.D. (in press), 'Environmental Variability and Environmental Extremes in the Island Ecosystem', *Proc. 13th Pac. Science Congr.,* Vancouver, Canada, August 1975.

Thornthwaite, C. W. (1948), 'An Approach toward a Rational Classification of Climate', *Geogr. Rev., 38,* pp. 55-94.

Walsh, R.P.D. (1980), *Drainage Density and Hydrological Processes in a Humid Tropical Environment: the Windward Islands,* Ph.D. thesis, University of Cambridge.

Winstanley, D. (1973), 'Recent Rainfall Trends in Africa, the Middle East, and India', *Nature, Lond., 243,* pp. 464-5.

Chapter 2
SEASONAL ENERGY RELATIONSHIPS AND FOOD

2.1 Seasonality and Labour In the Rural Energy Balance
Tim Bayliss-Smith

Introduction

The energy balance of a rural community is the difference between its *available energy resources* and the *energy input required* from the people at a given point in time if they are to maintain their existing and future livelihood. Available energy resources consist mainly of food (and sometimes fuel also), and so depend largely on how much of the fruits of agriculture remain from the preceding harvest. If food is short at seasons when people must provide a large energy input to manual work in the fields, they may reach a state of *negative energy balance*, or energy deficit. Adults will then lose weight as energy stored in the body is utilised, and the pressure on food available to children may be such as to present serious risks to their health. They may also begin to show signs of protein-energy malnutrition (PEM). These latter aspects of the problem will be considered by other authors later in this chapter, and also in Chapter 6.

Crop production and the sun's energy

The ultimate source of the energy available to a rural community from its food and fuel is, of course, the sun. And one paradox of tropical regions — especially those with humid climates — is that they receive lower levels of energy as solar radiation than do temperate zones during the summer season. A rough calculation by Best (1962) showed that during the growing season of most cereal crops the average radiation in temperate regions is approximately 1.5 times that of the tropics. Chang (1968a) extended this approach to show that tropical regions have lower potential crop production over four and eight month growing periods than temperate regions, and only offer an agricultural potential comparable to that of warm temperate climates when the full twelve months are taken into account.

The advantage of the tropics for agriculture lies in the potential for year-round crop production. The absence of any restriction on plant growth through low temperatures means that tree crops (e.g. oil palm, cocoa) or crops with long vegetative period (sugar cane, bananas) are particularly suitable, as they intercept the maximum amount of light.

This advantage of year-round growth is what seasonality threatens. In the absence of irrigation, soil moisture reserves are quickly reduced at the onset of a dry season. At a certain point, photosynthesis and plant growth cease, and they do not recommence until soil moisture begins to accumulate at the outset of the next rainy season.

The effect of seasonality on plant growth is not merely to reduce the duration of the growing season. Near the equator, vegetation is also likely to receive less solar radiation per month in the wet season than in the dry, because of the effects of cloud cover. Towards sub-tropical latitudes, the varying day length may reduce or enhance this cloudiness effect, according to whether or not the wet season occurs in the winter months.

Usually the dry season, being the sunniest period of the year, is a time when crops could, in theory, be most productive. However, this is precisely the period when very little agricultural activity is possible without irrigation, so most crop production is restricted to the season of the year which is least favourable for maximum rates of photosynthesis and growth.

Seasonality in agricultural production

The basis of the Walsh classification of rainfall seasonality, presented in Chapter 1, is the assumption that a monthly rainfall of 102 mm represents an average threshold above which conditions are sufficiently wet for continuous plant growth, and below which relative drought prevails. The research reviewed by Chang (1968b) and Jackson (1977) suggests that such an assumption is reasonable. Crops may not, of course, achieve a complete ground cover in the first 'wet' month of a wet season, but on the other hand, growth is likely to continue for a few weeks into the first 'dry' month of the following dry season. As an approximation, therefore, the number of 'wet' months (rainfall 102 mm or more) can be taken as representing the duration of the growing season for annual crops.

This consideration can provide the basis for a theoretical model of crop production, if we assume that farmers do not practise irrigation. If the crop can be said to maintain a complete ground cover during the wet months, it intercepts all the available solar radiation during those months. However, slightly less than half this radiation is light suitable for photosynthesis (Caldwell, 1975), and of that half, only about 3 per cent is converted into plant growth in a crop such as rice. In other words, less than 1.5 per cent of the total solar energy received by crops is converted by them into the chemical energy of plant tissues.

The chemical energy contained in a growing plant is represented by its increasing weight, referred to as its net primary production (NPP): 1 g of dry matter from a plant represents energy amounting to 17.8 kJ or 4.25 kcal (Cooper, 1975). From this fact, and from data on solar radiation during the growing season, it is possible to calculate what yield of dry matter per hectare might theoretically be expected from the crop.

When these calculations are made for sites representative of all the important Walsh seasonality types (see Table 2.1), then we have a set of figures which describe the relative importance of seasonal drought for tropical agriculture (see Figure 2.1). To convert the figures for dry matter production per hectare into food yields, one would need some partition factor: for cereals, perhaps 50 per cent of the dry crop would represent harvested yield, the remainder consisting of inedible roots, stems, chaff, etc. But actual harvest prediction is not the object of this exercise, since very few farmers (especially non-capitalised ones) can hope to achieve the efficiency of crop growth assumed. In practice, soil nutrients and moisture will often be less than op-

TABLE 2.1 Predicted crop production in different climates, based on 3 per cent conversion of light received during wet months (rainfall > 102 mm)

Walsh seasonality type	Station	Wet months		Net primary production of crop per year	
		Number of Months	Total solar radiation received (kJ/cm^2/month)	kJ/cm^2	t/ha dry matter
A0	Puyo, Ecuador	12	33.14	5.6	31.5
A1	Singapore	12	54.20	9.2	51.5
B0	Eala, Zaire	11	50.78	7.9	44.3
B1	Yangambi, Zaire	10	51.93	7.3	41.1
B2	Colombo, Sri Lanka	10	50.15	7.1	39.7
C1	San Juan, Puerto Rico	9	55.15	7.0	39.3
C1	Santa Elena, Venezuela	9	58.45	7.4	41.7
C2	Khao Chong, Thailand	8	59.89	6.8	38.0
C3	Cochin, India	8	49.32	5.6	31.3
C3	Kinshasa, Zaire	8	51.95	5.9	32.9
D2	Havana, Cuba	6	53.03	4.5	25.2
D2	Benin, Nigeria	7	44.91	4.4	24.9
D3	Beira, Mozambique	6	68.46	5.8	32.5
D3	Manila, Philippines	6	42.73	4.2	23.7
D4	El Salv., San Salvador	6	36.91	3.1	17.5
D5	Bissau, Port. Guinea	5	60.30	4.3	23.9
D5	Samaru, Nigeria	5	59.82	4.2	23.7
D5	Lubumbashi, Zaire	5	56.89	4.0	22.5
E2	Palmira, Colombia	4	38.18	2.2	12.1
E2	Lourenco Marques, Moz.	3	68.91	2.9	16.4
E3	Kitui, Kenya	3	70.37	2.1	16.7
E4	Malakal, Sudan	4	59.53	3.4	18.9
E4	Townsville, Australia	4	64.59	3.6	20.5
E4	Bulawayo, Zimbabwe	3	67.20	2.8	16.0
E5	Iscia Baidoa, Somalia	3	75.03	3.2	17.8
E5	Katherine, Australia	4	62.69	3.5	19.9
E5	Tete, Mozambique	3	65.65	2.8	15.6
F3	Honolulu, Hawaii	1	44.10	0.6	3.4
F4	Maun, Botswana	2	65.62	1.9	10.4
F4	Barcelona, Venezuela	2	65.44	1.9	10.4
F5	Dakar, Senegal	2	56.79	1.6	9.0
F5	Porto Viejo, Ecuador	1	42.80	0.6	3.4

Sources: Solar radiation data from Black (1956), Qasim *et al.* (1968), Griffiths (1972), Kira (1975), Schwerdtfeger (1976); climatic typology based on rainfall data in the same sources or in Wernstedt (1972).

Seasonal Energy Relationships and Food

PREDICTED MAXIMUM CROP YIELD t d.m./ha/yr

	0	1	2	3	4	5	6
G							
F				3	10	6	
E			14	17	19	18	
D			25	28	18	23	
C		41	38	32			
B	44	41	40				
A	32	52					

Figure 2.1 Predicted maximum yield of agricultural crops in tropical climates differing in rainfall seasonality.
Climates A - G differ in the number of 'dry' months, while 0-6 is an index of the relative seasonality of the rainfall received (see Walsh, Chapter 1.2). The predicted yields are in tonnes of dry matter per hectare, and they were calculated by assuming the crops utilise 3% of light received during 'wet' months.

timum, and crop cover will be incomplete. So although a crop conversion efficiency of 3 per cent is low by comparison with the results of some agricultural trials (Cooper, 1975), in relation to the reality of tropical farming practices, this and the other assumptions made here are wildly optimistic.

The figures for dry matter production (in tonnes per hectare) presented in Figure 2.1 suggest that without irrigation the maximum potential of agriculture will fall steadily as one moves from A and B climates to E and F climates — in other words, as the number of dry months in the year increases. Nevertheless, the greater solar radiation per month that is usually received in the more seasonal climates can compensate to some extent for the shorter growing season. Production at the E4 sites, for example, is 50 per cent that at the A0 and A1 sites, even though their growing season is only four months rather than twelve.

Seasonal labour requirements in agriculture

Although the sun provides the energy for crops to grow, farmers must expend additional energy to create suitable soil conditions, to remove weeds, and finally to harvest the crops. The influence of seasonality on annual yield is therefore related not only to seasonal changes in available solar energy, but also to the energy resources available to the farmer, chiefly in the form of labour. In highly seasonal climates, yields are inevitably lower than elsewhere (Figure 2.1). Adaptation to this lower level of total output would, however, be much easier were it not for the substantial peaks that occur at certain times in the year in both output and the necessary inputs.

Peaking in labour needs cannot be approached in a generalised way, since different crops vary so greatly in the amount and timing of the work required to produce them. Here we consider the labour requirements for one crop, rice, when grown in two different ways — first, as a rain-fed crop under shifting cultivation, and second, as paddy rice. In the latter instance, the control of water reduces the uncertainty of seasonal rainfall, but does not by any means reduce the problem of labour seasonality.

Six stages in the cultivation of the dry rice crop can be distinguished, corresponding to six different months in the agricultural calendar. These are clearing scrub and burning (in the dry season); then tillage and planting the crop (by broadcasting the seed); two phases of weeding are necessary, and efforts may be needed to protect the crop from pests. The final stage is harvest, which occurs four months after planting.

Detailed studies in Sarawak, the Philippines and Tanzania suggest that the total labour input per hectare for one rice crop ranges between 700 and 1080 hours (mean 915 hours; see Table 2.2). Peak labour input is required at harvest, which absorbs 32 per cent of the total labour time. The average number of days needed for each stage is as follows:

Month	Stage	Person-days per hectare per rice crop	
1.	Clearing	18	(14%)
2.	Burning	6	(4%)
3.	Tillage, sowing and fencing	26	(20%)
4.	First weeding	20	(15%)
5.	Second weeding	20	(15%)
6.	Harvest	43	(32%)
	Total	133	

Although specific to hill rice, these figures are also likely to be fairly representative of the distribution of labour in any cereal crop (e.g. maize) grown under conditions of shifting cultivation. The data have been converted from hours to days by adopting as a unit a seven-hour working day.

A number of records of dry rice crops suggests that yields are variable, but average 1446 kg/ha of paddy (Hanks, 1972). With an average processing loss

TABLE 2.2. Shifting cultivation of rice: comparative data on person-hours of labour per rice crop per hectare

Stage	Task	Iban, Sarawak Primary forest	Iban, Sarawak Secondary forest	Hanunoo, Philippines Primary forest	Hanunoo, Philippines Secondary forest	Kilombero, Tanzania Grassland
		Person-hours of work per rice crop per hectare				
1.	Clearing	83	190	104	111	168
2.	Burning	23	46	47	59	
3.	Tillage, sowing, fencing	118	118	189	208	260
4.	Weeding, replanting, protecting	91	102	220	184	108
5.	Weeding, protecting	91	102	221	185	108
6.	Harvest	294	294	300	300	328
Total		700	852	1081	1047	972
Rice yield, t/ha		1.5-2.0	1.5	2.3	2.3	1.7

Notes and sources:

Iban— Freeman, 1955. In both cases total labour inputs into all activities other than harvesting have been reduced by 20 per cent, since about this proportion of the swidden is occupied by non-rice crops. In the case of primary forest swiddens, the initial inputs into clearing and burning have been halved, since the swidden lasts for two consecutive crops.

Hanunoo— Conklin, 1957, cited by Clark and Haswell, 1964. Initial inputs have been divided by 4 (primary forest) and 2 (secondary), since these are the respective numbers of years that each new swidden is cultivated. Weeding, replanting and fencing work inputs have been halved, since the totals refer to work with the succeeding maize crop as well as to the rice crop that concerns us.

Kilomdero— Ruthenberg 1971. Man-days are converted to hours using the conversions in his Table 3.4.

of 30 per cent (Grist, 1959), this implies a net edible yield of 1012 kg, which approximately represents the quantity of food that would fulfil the total energy needs of a household of five persons. (We must assume the household's age structure is the same as that of the population, where on average 800,000 kcal/3360 MJ is required per person per year.) To this total subsistence requirement (1108 kg per household), we must add next year's seed, estimated by Hanks (1972) and by Harriss (1977) as 60-62 kg, to make a total requirement of 1170 kg of rice.

We can calculate from the data above that the total subsistence energy needs of a household will be met if it has 1.156 ha of land under cultivation, which in turn will require 154 person-days of work in a year. We can now begin to calculate the effect of seasonality on the monthly distribution of this workload. Four different degrees of seasonality are considered in Table 2.3, of which three warrant further comment, as follows:

A or B climates (0-2 dry months). The dry season in such climates is

Seasonal Dimensions to Rural Poverty

TABLE 2.3. Effect of rainfall seasonality on the amount of work required each month in order to produce rice through shifting cultivation

(Data represent days of work required per month for the average household to achieve subsistence, in four different climates.)

Seasonality type:	A or B climate	C climate	D climate	E climate
Number of dry months:	0-2	4	6	8
	Number of days of work per wet (W) or dry (D) month			
Month 1	W/D - 12	D - 0	D - 0	D - 0
2	W/D - 12	D - 22	D - 11	D - 0
3	W - 13	D - 6	D - 11	D - 7
4	W - 13	W - 11	D - 3	D - 7
5	W - 13	W - 18	D - 3	D - 7
6	W - 13	W - 15	W - 11	D - 2
7	W - 13	W - 24	W - 18	D - 2
8	W - 13	W - 16	W - 15	D - 2
9	W - 13	W - 10	W - 34	W - 31
10	W - 13	W - 8	W - 24	W - 23
11	W - 13	W - 8	W - 8	W - 23
12	W - 13	D - 16	D - 16	W - 49
Annual work input per household (days)	154	154	154	154

Note: One average household is assumed to comprise five persons, cultivating 1.16 ha in order to satisfy all subsistence energy needs from rice. In the table, the monthly inputs of work to this land (clearing, burning, planting, weeding, harvesting) are staggered in order to achieve the most equable distribution of labour through the year that is feasible in each climate. The predicted peaks in labour requirement are thus the minima that are achievable.

neither sufficiently long nor sufficiently acute for the growth of crops to be seriously affected. On the other hand, the burning of cleared vegetation is not always possible, and much of it may be left to rot in situ. Agricultural activities can continue throughout the year, and by staggering planting dates, seasonal peaks in either work load or production can be avoided.

C climate (4 dry months). If cleared vegetation can be burned, it makes available plant nutrients and discourages weeds, but this advantage cannot be achieved in the C climate without some peaking in dry season labour. In the long wet season, though, planting times can be staggered into three distinct cropping periods, two of which overlap somewhat.

E climate (8 dry months). The very short wet season means that all the land must be in simultaneous cultivation. Severe peaks will therefore occur in the month of sowing and, especially, at the time of harvest.

The peak labour needs illustrated by this analysis may seem well within the capacity of an average household of five persons (see Table 2.3). However, the analysis is based only on the agricultural work needed for bare subsistence. If, say, a 50 per cent surplus must be aimed at, for exchange purposes, or to in-

Seasonal Energy Relationships and Food

sure against a bad harvest, then the monthly labour inputs in Table 2.3 must also be increased by 50 per cent. This may well put enormous strain on a household's resources during peak months.

It is useful to compare these patterns of seasonality in shifting cultivation with the effect of the seasons on perennial, wet rice cultivation. Here, water control has the advantage of reducing the influence of rainfall variability, but the effects of seasonality on employment are not thereby diminished. Unless there is large-scale water storage or pumping, there is little that can be done in the dry season, except perhaps the cultivation of minor crops (Ruthenberg, 1971).

Detailed information concerning the more intensive transplanting method of paddy cultivation is available for North Arcot in the Tamil Nadu State of India (Chinnappa and Silva, 1977; Chinnappa, 1977). With traditional varieties grown in the wet season, yields in the early 1970s averaged 2292 kg of paddy (1604 kg of rice) per hectare, from a labour input of 239 person-days. This implies that the same average household considered above (five persons, total needs 1170 kg rice) would require 0.729 ha in cultivation with a single annual crop. This in turn would require 174 days of work per annual crop, distributed between months as follows:

Month	Stage	Person-days per crop	
1.	Nurseries, irrigation works, first ploughing	47	(27%)
2.	Ploughing, manuring, transplanting	38	(22%)
3.	Weeding, fertilizer application	21	(12%)
4.	Weeding, pesticide application	19	(11%)
5.	Harvest, transporting	26	(15%)
6.	Threshing and winnowing	23	(13%)
	Total	174	(for 0.729 ha)

We can assess the effects of seasonality on the distribution of this work-load by using the same method of analysis as with rice grown under shifting cultivation. The results again suggest that, particularly in D and E climates, there will be enormous and unavoidable peaks in labour input, separated by periods of enforced inactivity in the dry season.

The rural energy balance

Recent reviews of the energetics of agricultural systems suggest that when inputs and outputs are all reduced to energy units, and when annual data are used, then pre-industrial technology is found to be the most efficient at producing food per unit of total energy used. This kind of farming shows ratios of food output to labour input which, in energy terms, almost always exceed 10, and which rise to 50 in some cases (e.g. Harris, 1971; Leach, 1976; Bayliss-Smith, 1977). By contrast, industrialised methods of food production, especially of animal products, have output/input ratios of just over, and even below, unity. In such systems, mechanisation enormously increases the energy output per hour of human work, but the overall energy efficiency is very low.

The two kinds of rice cultivation considered here do not happen to differ greatly in energy efficiency when inputs and outputs are assessed on an annual basis. We can convert person-days of work into an energy input by adopting 175 kcal (735 kJ) per hour as the likely average rate of energy expenditure by an adult worker. This implies an average energy ratio of food output to work input (human work only) of 21 for shifting cultivation and 19 for paddy cultivation. The addition of those labour inputs needed to look after the draft animals would no doubt reduce slightly the efficiency ratio for wet rice.

In the more seasonal climates, however, the ratios of energy output to energy input in rice cultivation fluctuate enormously from month to month. Even if, optimistically, we divide the rice harvest into twelve monthly portions and regard each twelfth as the monthly output, the output/input ratios of the average household will still vary greatly:

	Shifting cultivation				Paddy cultivation			
Climate:	A,B	C	D	E	A,B	C	D	E
Output/input ratio:								
annual average:	21	21	21	21	19	19	19	19
peak labour month:	21	11	8	6	11	8	6	6

When we consider that food output is *not* equally available in all months, and that the labour inputs assumed in the model are only those needed to achieve subsistence, then it becomes clear that in seasonal climates many people may be in energy deficit at certain times of year. Thus a finer-grained analysis of agricultural systems that appear to be efficient users of energy on an annual basis might lead to a very different conclusion, as will become evident later in this chapter. The supposed 'primitive affluence' of subsistence farmers, and the 'ecological efficiency' of pre-industrial agriculture may often be achieved only at the cost of considerable seasonal stress. Papers presented later in this chapter will more fully document the nature of this seasonal stress, and the energy deficits which cause it, and will show that it has consequences for the whole community, including young children.

2.2 Food Consumption In Relation to Labour Output
Margaret Haswell

Early studies relating food and work

One of the earliest nutrition surveys to include data on work done by people as well as their food intake was carried out in Nyasaland (Malawi) in 1938-9 (Platt, 1943). At the end of the 1939-45 war, a unit of the British Medical Research Council commenced plans for a similar survey to be conducted in Gambia.[1] This survey was begun in 1947 by a medical officer, a nutritionist, and the author as agronomist.

The study centred on the village of Genieri, 190 km upstream from the mouth of the River Gambia, on the south bank. This area of hinterland was then relatively isolated, and was virtually inaccessible during the rains. The programme allowed for a three-year period of research when detailed records were obtained, including data on population structures and the health status of the community, farm layouts, crop yields, livestock, human labour re-

Seasonal Energy Relationships and Food

quirements, cash crops, and labour efficiency.

The seasonal nature of agricultural work was (and still is) an important characteristic of the area. In Genieri, not all harvests were good for all families, nor were stores protected against heavy loss by insect pests. This was exemplified by studies of energy intake per person in the 1947-50 period, which showed highest values in the post-harvest season and wide variations between compounds, with consumption falling off as food stocks dwindled. Where stocks from the previous year's harvest permitted, the balance between food consumption and energy expenditure was maintained to meet heavy work-load peaks at the beginning of the new agricultural season (May-June). Lowest food intakes were found in the July-August pre-harvest 'hungry season' during the period of intensive agricultural work. Energy expenditure during this season on actual farm work was dependent upon the extent to which villagers were prevented by shortage of food from adjusting intake to requirements. In October and November there was some recovery in the body weights of men and women following harvests of the early upland rainfed rice and early millet before the main harvest was taken in December and January.

Seasonal energy use

Among data collected by the author which demonstrate the relationship between food availability and energy requirements were those obtained during 1949-50 (Haswell, 1953). The total energy input was subsequently estimated from this data by applying energy rates for each task, allowance also being made for walking and resting time (Haswell, 1973, p. 61).

In Genieri, upland and swamp rice is grown by women, while the men take responsibility for crops such as millet, sorghum and groundnuts. A detailed study of women working in the rice swamp made it possible to compare their energy expenditure in the wet season and at other times of the year. Average energy expenditures in agricultural work in each quarter of the year were as follows:

June-August (wet season)	1219 kcal/woman/day
September-November (wet season)	1088 kcal/woman/day
December-February (dry season)	799 kcal/woman/day
March-May (dry season)	301 kcal/woman/day

During the wet season, a woman would spend less time and energy on other tasks, such as preparing meals (360 kcal/day), and fetching firewood and water (54 kcal/day). Even so, peak energy expenditures during this period left many women in a state of energy deficit and drawing upon fat stored 'on the back' as a source of supplementary energy.

Converting annual aggregates to a daily basis, the mean energy cost of agricultural work was 852 kcal per woman per day and the quantity of milled rice produced 2.08 kg per woman per day. The energy value of this amount of rice is 7363 kcal. So the ratio of energy gained to energy expended by these women rice cultivators was 7363 ÷ 852, which is equal to 8.6 (Haswell, 1979).

This output/input ratio is not as high as the figure of 21 given by Bayliss-Smith (see Section 2.1) after an analysis of rice grown in shifting cultivation. It is, however, a ratio which might be expected to give some margin of energy for non-agricultural tasks and for feeding the family. However, the rise in energy expenditures shown to have occurred during the wet season confirms Bayliss-Smith's point that average figures taken over the whole year often disguise considerable seasonal stress.

One might have thought that the situation for the people of Genieri would have improved since these figures were obtained in 1949-50. However, the author made further studies in the same village during 1962 and 1973-4, and found evidence of deterioration. For example, we can consider the food stocks of each of the family compounds in the pre-harvest 'hunger season'. Stocks were measured at 1 July 1974, and converted into kcal/head to estimate the number of days' supply, first, on the basis of the 1949 average post-harvest consumption of 2149 kcal/person/day, and second, as if the family were permanently constrained by the pre-harvest 'hunger' 1949 average of 1696 kcal/person/day. Only 2 per cent of the households had sufficient food to last until the next main harvest was gathered. A further 10 per cent had sufficient to last until the next early harvest based on the higher level of consumption, or 18 per cent at the lower pre-harvest 'hunger' level. Thus, whichever criterion was used, 80 per cent of the people were short of food grains.

Between 1950 and 1974, there was a swing away from food crops into cash crop production, and many families could make up their food grain shortage by purchases, using the cash received from the sale of groundnuts. There was, however, a problem of great disparity in income. The few 'rich' households can be identified with the 2 per cent with a surplus of grain. These had a comparative advantage both in human resources and favoured lands, and acquired much of their wealth from lending money to less fortunate members of the community out of the fruits of production, investment, and saving. As an example, the surpluses generated by these families have allowed them to construct modern granaries, and thereby to make greater profits from the off-season sale of food grains. In contrast, 'poor' households remained trapped at a low level of production by shortages of labour, often caused by the out-migration of able-bodied men or by chronic ill-health. Such families have become almost permanently indebted to the rich for the purchase of food at inflated prices, and for loans at high interest rates (Haswell, 1975, 1977).

By 1974, the principal change in technology was the introduction of oxen for ploughing, mainly in the savannah areas used for cash crops. Ownership of oxen was mainly limited to the few 'rich' families. Poorer households faced with a labour shortage or sickness endeavoured to hire oxen, usually incurring further debt and pledging land and crops.

Some technological changes have provided a more even benefit, however. Where no roads existed in 1947, Banjul, the capital, can now be reached by an all-weather road. Where head-loading was the only means of transport in 1947, ox-carts and motor trucks are now available for those who can pay for the service. However, the system of agricultural production still does not guarantee to each person their daily food needs, and still relies upon the female labour force for arduous tasks in the production of food. One can only conclude that the small gains achieved from new technology and from the intensification of agriculture have favoured only a small élite, and have not proved adequate to reverse a process of social and economic decline.

One reason why strategies for tackling these problems have rarely been formulated is that, with few exceptions, economists have been narrowly preoccupied with production and productivity studies at the macro-level. Such studies cannot fully reveal micro-level situations or seasonal constraints on production. It is the energy gain over the energy expended by the human population it supports which should dictate the food production strategy. To formulate meaningful alternatives in strategies for rural development, measurements of energy balance are a necessary prerequisite. In some months of the year, there may be a surplus of labour, but it is questionable whether there are reserves of human energy either for more intensive physical activity, or to summon the will to organise, plan, adapt, and innovate.

2.3 Nutrition and Disease In Machakos District, Kenya
Simeon R. Onchere and R. Slooff

Introduction

Since 1974, a study of food availability and health has been carried out in the Northern Division of Machakos District, Kenya.[2] This study, which constitutes a major element of the Joint Project Machakos, is undertaken by the Royal Tropical Institute of Amsterdam. The basic fieldwork consists of fortnightly visits to every household by locally recruited workers who collect data on child health and food availability.

The study area is about 85 km^2 in extent, and has a population of about 26,000. The area is mostly classed as 'medium potential' land, indicating moderate or poor rainfall. In fact, the area gets between 600 and 1000 mm of rain distributed over two seasons. The short rains (SR) occur during October-December, and the long rains (LR) during March-May.

Machakos District is representative of a sizeable proportion of Kenya's smallholder agriculture. It has a high population in relation to the 'carrying capacity' of the land and its unreliable rainfall. The area is known for food shortages, which were particularly severe in 1961, 1965, 1971 and 1975.

The farming system

The average farm size in the area studied is 2.86 ha supporting 6.25 persons. A typical farm will have around nine animals, most of them cattle, but including some goats. About half the land belonging to the farms is cultivated; crops include maize, pigeon peas (*Cajanus cajun*), beans and cowpeas (*Vigna* spp.). Half of the farms also own a team of oxen and an ox-plough that is regularly used. The remaining farms either borrow or hire from these during peak farm operations. Very few farmers are self-sufficient, and most have an income from non-agricultural activities. Significantly, there is a 10 per cent rate of in- and out-migration each year.

There are two crop plantings every year. The short-rain crop is planted in September or October, and the long-rain crop in March or April. Usually, the harvest from the short-rain crop lasts until the long-rain crop is ready. However, the harvests of the long-rain crop do not last until there is food available from the short-rain crop. Thus the period of greatest food shortage

Seasonal Dimensions to Rural Poverty

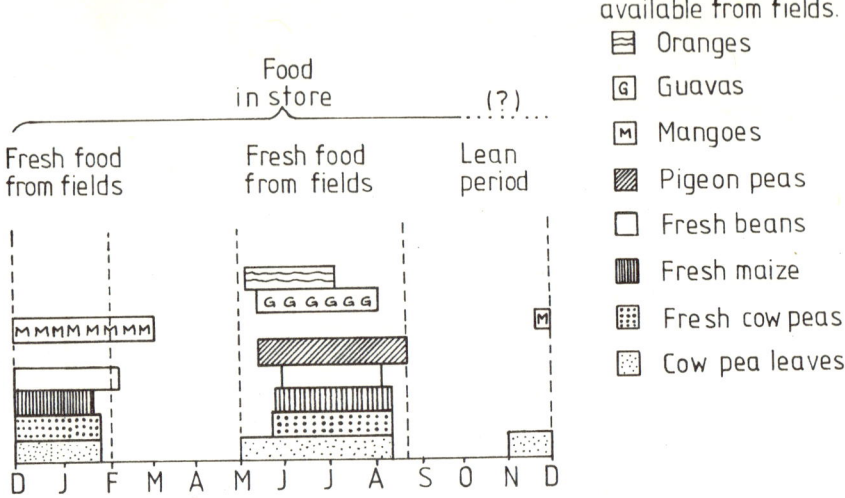

Figure 2.2 Seasonal pattern of food availability for Matungulu and Mbiuni locations of Machakos District

occurs between September and January, when the short-rain crop is in the ground, but before it is ready. But even during this time, there is some green vegetable available from the cow-pea crop (Figure 2.2).

The presence of food in the stores of sample households, monitored throughout the year, provides one way of estimating the extent of food shortages (Figure 2.3). Food stocks are below average from September to February. In January and February, though, young maize is usually eaten straight from the fields, and as this is not suitable for storage, it does not appear in the food stores.

A survey of local shopkeepers showed that people purchased relatively little from shops between January and June, but food purchases were higher between July and December, reaching their maximum level during the last three months of the year. There appears to be a marked variation among the various shops, suggesting that the pattern of food purchasing differs from area to area and from household to household. This can be understood when it is realised that some farmers depend partly or entirely on the cultivation of cash crops like coffee. Observations made by van Steenbergen *et al.* (1978) suggest that no real difference occurs in the availability of food to households between the lean period and the time of harvest, though the type of food differs. However, in the same studies, breast-milk yields of lactating mothers were

Seasonal Energy Relationships and Food

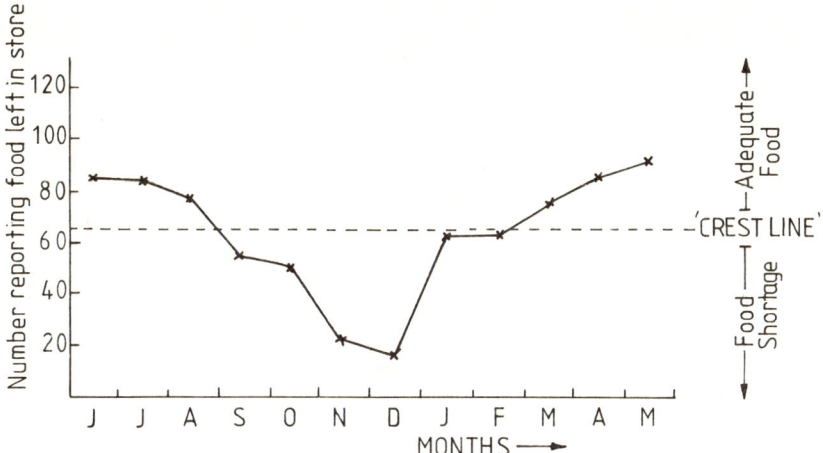

Source: Drawn using data from Onchere (1976) p 44.
The vertical axis represents the number of households (in a total sample of 119) reporting food (maize, beans, pigeon peas) in store for each month represented on the horizontal axis. The 'crest line' is a means of separating probable food shortage months from those that are not serious food shortage months. It is drawn along the year-round arithmetic mean of the number of households reporting food in store. The horizontal axis starts at June which is the month that harvest from long rains crops (beans) starts, followed by maize in July and pigeon pea in August.

Figure 2·3 Graph of food storage at farm level over time, Machakos District, Kenya.

TABLE 2.4. Breast milk yield per stage of lactation according to season, Machakos, Kenya (in ml per 24 hours, S.D. in brackets)

Age (months)	ml/24 hours			
	N	lean season	N	harvest season
0 - 1	0	—	7	778 (190)
2 - 3	7	540 (85)*	6	710 (157)*
4 - 5	4	404 (118)*	5	708 (157)*
6 - 11	8	407 (79)	14	543 (178)
12 - 17	10	405 (122)	12	470 (148)
18 - 23	5	210 (62)	7	366 (156)

Notes: * $P < 0.01$

Intake of mother's milk was assessed by the test weighing technique for three to four days from 07.00–19.00 hours and for one night from 19.00–07.00 hours.

Source: van Steenbergen et al. (1980).

found to vary markedly with the season as Table 2.4 shows (van Steenbergen et al., 1980).

Nutritional status

Although purchases of food in Machakos District seem to compensate effectively for shortages in subsistence food supplies, it should be noted that the period of seasonal subsistence food shortage comes at a time when agricultural work is at its heaviest. From September to October, work must be done in the fields to prepare the ground and plant the short-rain crops. Among the crops planted are pigeon peas, which stay in the fields for roughly one year. Last year's pigeon peas are therefore harvested in August and September, at a time when land preparation for this year's crop may be starting. This overlap produces a very pronounced peak in the labour requirements of agriculture at this time. Families without the means to purchase sufficient food could therefore find themselves in energy deficit during this season. Such problems may contribute to the reduced milk yield of lactating mothers during the lean period, though that could also be a reflection of the reduced time spent feeding infants during a busy season.

In the course of a study of the growth of children up to an age of five years, information was collected on weight, height, and upper arm circumference. At the beginning of the study (June 1974), children below four years of age were included from 500 sample households. During the period from 1974 to January 1977, all these children were followed longitudinally until they reached the age of five years, and children born in the sample households were added to the study (Oomen et al., 1979).

Until the age of about six months, the weight curve of the children usually followed the Harvard standard. After that, the average weight of the Machakos children deviated progressively from this, and approached more and more the 80 per cent weight-for-age line. A similar result was found with height-for-age standards, and for upper arm circumference, though in both these sets of measurements, the deviation from standard was less.

The incidence of protein-energy malnutrition (PEM) varied during the period of the study, but not in a way that was related to the seasons. There was no increase during 'lean periods'. This could be explained by the fact that there are two harvests each year. However, harvests in both seasons are usually poor and most of the crop is consumed straight from the fields with little left to store. The more likely reason why there are no seasonal effects on nutritional status is that many people have income from other sources (cash crops, non-farm income, migrant labour income, sales of handicrafts).

However, one should note that there is a wide variation of farming systems and, consequently, of subsistence harvesting in the area. Also, the dependency on non-farm sources of income varies considerably from household to household. It is therefore plausible that seasonal effects might have been observed if the sample had been drawn from households relatively less self-sufficient in subsistence food crops, and with low incomes from other sources.

Seasonality of diarrhoeas: morbidity and mortality

Diarrhoea among under-fives was studied from June 1974 until June 1977 by Leeuwenburg et al. (1978). There did not appear to be an effect of seasonality on the incidence of diarrhoeal disease but out of forty-six *deaths* associated with diarrhoea and vomiting, thirty-seven (80 per cent) occurred in the months of March-July. The mortality in under-fives due to all causes combined, however, was distributed fairly evenly over the months. It is striking that most of the children who died of diarrhoea were less than one year old (thirty-three out of forty-six).

Other authors, like McGregor *et al.* (1970) in Gambia, Moore (1965) in Costa Rica, and Gordon *et al.* (1964) in Guatemala and India suggested a relationship between diarrhoea incidence and the seasons. However, it remains difficult to explain why diarrhoea deaths in our study area should occur in a clustered way over a period of a few months. The months of March, April and May are wet months, but June and July are relatively dry. The other rainy season has its peak in November, but diarrhoea mortality does not show any increase then. It is unlikely that extended common source infection could take place in March-July. One might also expect other peaks in diarrhoea incidence, for example, during the lean period when weaning foods are of poorer quality and lower quantity than usual. However, this idea is not supported by the pattern of diarrhoea morbidity or mortality, since October and November show neither higher incidence, nor higher mortality, than other months.

2.4 Seasonal Aspects of Nutrition*
Richard Longhurst and Philip Payne

Observations on the incidence of malnutrition

The two previous papers (Sections 2.2 and 2.3) discussed the possible effect of seasonal food shortages and energy deficits on the nutrition of adults in Gambia and of children in Kenya. In such studies, evidence for seasonal occurrence of nutrition problems consists either of direct observations of the numbers of malnourished individuals throughout the year, or has in other cases been inferred from data on variations in the amounts of food consumed in relation to needs. Although many studies of seasonal changes in food supply have been made, we believe that their interpretation is doubtful because of the difficulty of measuring food consumption with sufficient accuracy. We will return to these problems in more detail later, but will first review the direct evidence.

The diagnosis of malnutrition in an individual can be on the basis of clinical signs, on biochemical measurements made on blood or urine, or from measurements of retarded growth in children or weight loss in adults. These 'anthropometric' indicators, weight, height, upper arm circumference, etc., are generally regarded as the simplest and most reliable ways of measuring nutritional status, and it is to such studies that we shall mainly refer. It needs to be remembered, however, that growth is affected by many things other than just food supply, in particular it is affected by infectious diseases not only

---

*The full length paper originally presented at the conference has been published as 'Seasonal Aspects of Nutrition: Review of Evidence and Policy Implications', *Discussion Paper* 145, Institute of Development Studies, University of Sussex, November 1979.

because these disturb the metabolism of the host, but also because infection frequently causes loss of appetite, and hence malnutrition as a secondary effect.

When we describe a child who is underweight as 'malnourished' we are really using weight for age as a proxy indicator which stands for the effects of a number of possible causes or combinations of causes.

Changes in the rate of growth probably give us the most sensitive measure of the impact of seasons. Studies which measure this are relatively few in number, and among the best known are those by McGregor et al. (1968) carried out in Gambia. It was found that increases of mean weight with age did not follow a smooth pattern, but were large during the dry months, and small, or even negative, during the wet months between May and November.

The seasonal effect was slight during the early months of life but became obvious at late ages. Children born in the early part of the year (15 February to 14 May) gained very well until nearly the end of their first rainy season, when there was a short set-back. Those born during the earlier part of the dry season received a sharp check to growth soon after entering the wet months. Thus, season of birth as well as age dictated the average pattern of gain in weight during the first year of life. Thereafter, average weights were unusually good during the dry months and poor during the wet months. By two years of age the differentials had evened out, so that children on this and subsequent birthdays had about the same average weight, irrespective of season of birth. (McGregor et al., 1968, p. 343).

Other studies in Gambia have shown similar results of faltering weight gain (Marsden and Marsden, 1965) and higher incidence of malnutrition in the wet season (Spalding et al., 1977), as have other studies from unimodal situations in Sekhukumiland in South Africa (Waldemann, 1973), and in Ghana (Davey, n.d.). In Uganda where there are two rainy seasons from March to May and October to November most cases of malnutrition presented at a clinic occurred at the end of the second wet season when harvesting was taking place (Poskitt, 1972). Since infections such as malaria and measles correspond to these rainy periods, it was believed that the precipitation of overt kwashiorkor was the result of infection at this time.

Some studies have not shown this pattern of weight loss in the wet season. In Thailand, elementary school children gained more weight during the rainy season than at other times (Hauck et al., 1960) and in a rural community in Jamaica no seasonal changes in growth rates were observed (Standard et al., 1969).

Very few studies have been carried out of changes in *adult* weight by season. The best known is Fox's work in Gambia (Fox, 1953). He showed that changes in body weight were related to the seasonal pattern of farming activity and food availability. Weight was gained from November to mid-March (dry season) and lost from July until the beginning of November (mid-end rainy season).

In a nutrition survey in Ghana, it was found that body weights of people in all parts of the country showed a distinct cycle of seasonal change:

In the northern savannah some body weights of adults fall steadily for

Seasonal Energy Relationships and Food

the first eight months of the year, then rise sharply after the next harvest. Total loss in the middle of the year may be as high as nine or ten pounds. In the forest zone the pattern varies somewhat . . . . On the coast and coastal plain weight was lost at the beginning of the year and gained in the middle. (Davey, n.d., p. 7).

Nutrient requirements

Where studies are made of people's food intake, and an effort is made to assess inadequacies in diet independently of symptoms of malnutrition, there is a considerable problem in deciding what constitutes an adequate diet. Two kinds of statement are commonly made about people's nutrient requirements. First, figures may be given for amounts of nutrients which could safely be recommended as adequate for practically all individuals even though they may be living under a wide variety of situations. In contrast to these 'recommended intakes', and of more relevance to this book, are 'safe levels'. These are figures for minimum physiological requirements, and are levels of food intake below which there is an increasing probability that some specified symptoms of deficiency will appear.

In practice, most experimental measurements of requirements have sought to determine intakes which will prevent the appearance of symptoms when fed for *an indefinite period of time*. Most of the research of the past fifty years has aimed at insulating the subjects under study from any environmental change. Thus we know quite a lot about the steady-state behaviour of individuals and animals, but relatively little about their response to fluctuations in intake or to factors which might alter requirements.

A person who is able to eat fruit in season in large quantities can build up a store of vitamin C in his body as much as 2000 mg. To assess his 'requirement' for vitamin C during the rest of the year, we would need to know how large these stores must be in order to insure that when the intake drops to a low level, the risk of some critical disfunction does not become unacceptable.

In fact, because the experimental approach to requirements has concentrated on the steady-state, we cannot answer these questions for any nutrient in much more than a qualitative fashion. What is clear, however, is that for all those nutrients, the lack of which most commonly gives rise to problems and of which the supply is affected by seasonality, the body has evolved very effective storage mechanisms which are able to smooth out seasonal peaks and troughs of supply. These stores have 'half-lives' of the order of magnitude of the period between seasonal peaks. Thus vitamin C, vitamin A, thiamine, niacin, folic acid, iron, calcium and energy can all be stored for long periods, so that many months of deficient diets are needed to produce symptoms of malnutrition in previously well-nourished subjects.

Another dynamic aspect of requirements in relation to seasonality is adaptability. By this is meant that the requirement in some way changes in response to a change in intake without necessarily incurring an important loss of function. Such a response may be more or less immediate, or it may only develop over long periods of exposure to low intakes, or may even develop in a community or racial group over generations. Thus there is evidence of population adaptation to low intakes of thiamine and calcium, and recently,

Nicol and Phillips (1976) have demonstrated that African adults are able to metabolise protein more efficiently and therefore to maintain themselves on lower intakes than can Caucasians.

Perhaps the most important example of adaptability is that which takes place as a response to reduction in energy intake. This is through a number of mechanisms. A reduction in physical activity may be accompanied by metabolic changes which reduce the amount of energy needed for maintenance. At the same time, the body energy stores are drawn upon so that there is a progressive decline in total body weight, which is itself a contributory factor in the reduction of maintenance energy needs.

The effects of the seasonal work load and of variations of energy supply in terms of changes in body tissues has been examined by computer simulation (Dugdale and Payne, 1977). Loss of body fat is probably of little or no functional consequence. However, some lean tissue is also lost during the deficit part of the cycle, and to the extent that this is muscle, must result in loss of work capacity. Individuals vary one from another in their propensity to store and release energy as fat rather than lean tissue, and the study shows a comparison between a genetically 'fat' individual (preferentially fat storing) and a genetically 'lean' person (preferentially lean storing).

Requirements for protein are not affected by changes in physical activity. However, when energy is in deficit, dietary protein will be used as an energy source. Also, during periods of growth or repletion of body weight, an adequate supply of dietary energy is a necessary precondition for the laying down of protein in body tissues. The current view about the relative importance of protein and energy as factors causing malnutrition is that protein deficiency is most often secondary to a deficiency of energy, and is rarely a primary cause in its own right.

Our main conclusion therefore is that firm inferences about malnutrition on the basis of seasonal fluctuations of food intakes should be made with some caution, simply because we cannot at present interpret them in relation to needs. Nevertheless, in many of the studies we quote below, food supply data have been expressed as a percentage of energy requirements. We have adhered to this since it does at least facilitate comparisons across communities: a seasonal cycle in percentage adequacy should not in our view be regarded as more than suggestive evidence that malnutrition will be seasonal.

Seasonal change in food supply

Schofield (1974) analysed a number of village studies (twenty-five in Africa), and found that for the entire sample, 92 per cent of energy requirements were met in dry seasons, but that energy intake dropped to 85 per cent in wet seasons. She also found that villages with a bimodal distribution of rainfall have less seasonal variation in their diet: 'In the 15 villages with a unimodal rainy season, the . . . fulfilment of calorie requirements was 100% in the dry season and 88% in the wet season'. For the ten villages with bimodal seasons, 'the percentage fulfilment of calorie requirements in the wet and dry seasons were not significantly different' (Schofield, 1974, p. 24).

Since these studies did not involve logging people's work activities, they could not have been based on seasonally adjusted estimates of requirements.

The analysis therefore demonstrates only that seasonal fluctuations in food intakes occur most often where seasonality is unimodal than where it is bimodal.

Many of the studies on seasonal differences in intake have been carried out in West Africa and have been reviewed by Annegers (1973). His careful interpretation points to highest energy intakes in November and December post-harvest periods with minimum intakes in July and August, although one study in Senegal (Boutillier et al., 1962) found per capita intakes almost identical in wet and dry seasons. Another departure from this stereotype West African situation has been found in the Zaria region of northern Nigeria, where per capita energy intakes were found to be lowest in the period following the grain harvest (Simmons, 1976a). Per capita intake was 2264 kcal on an average daily basis for the whole year. However, underlying this is a variation from a low of 1949 kcal in the November-December period to a high of 2458 kcal in April-May, which are the first two months of the planting season, and which might be expected to be the traditional 'hungry season'. Simmons speculates that these departures from conventional wisdom are due to changes in body needs rather than available supply. The greater energy needs are in the April-May period and the November-December period also presents the farmers with demands of gifts and cash. Families may well plan and ration their intake accordingly.

Variations in nutrient intake may differ not only seasonally but also between regions, income classes and family members. A comment on the last group is provided at the end of this section and the data on regional differences are presented now. No quantitative evidence on the differential impact of seasons on nutrient intake by income class has been found.

The results of four country-wide nutrition surveys have been analysed to assess regional differences and seasonality. These are from the two bimodal locations of Kenya (Bohdal, Gibbs and Simmons, n.d.) and Bangladesh (Ministry of Health, Pakistan, 1966; Institute of Nutrition and Food Science, Dacca University, 1977) and the bimodal locations of Swaziland (Jones, 1963) and Ghana (Davey, n.d.).

The Kenya survey supports the view of small variations in intake in places with bimodal seasonality, confirming the impression gained from the Kenya case-study (Section 2.3) in this chapter. On a regional basis the data were somewhat inconclusive. In Bangladesh, clearer trends were derived from the two surveys carried out in 1962-4 and 1975-6. Strong seasonal trends emerged when food intake data obtained from different rural locations were averaged for each month of the survey. Particular crops were consumed predominately in their seasons: rice after the *aus* (July-September) and *aman* harvests (November-January); wheat (October) and white and sweet potatoes (March-May). Overall energy and protein intakes are sensitive to the availability of rice. There is a lower intake in the two lean periods of early monsoon (June-July) and early winter (November-December). Vitamin A intake increased sharply in the fruit season (May), thiamine was always satisfactory (because of rice parboiling), riboflavin intake was low and vitamin C intake, although never deficient, also fluctuated with the supply of fruit. Urban areas showed similar seasonal variations. However, in the agricultural cooperative villages in Chittagong, compared to villages in Rangpur and Dacca Districts, seasonality in cereal supply has been eliminated by growing three crops of rice the year round, leading to a less varied diet. This has been achieved by modernisation of agriculture with use of fertilizer and powered irrigation.

Another study from Bangladesh, presented later in this chapter (Section 2.5), confirms the seasonal variations in food availability and intake, but argues that these fluctuations are only a small part of the overall problem.

With the unimodal rainfall distribution in Swaziland, there is the additional factor that rainfall varies greatly in amount from one region to another. The Highveld region has ample rain, the Middleveld somewhat less and the Lowveld has virtually a semi-arid climate suited only to drought-resistant crops such as sorghum, though maize is also grown. A comprehensive nutrition survey conducted in the 1960s (Jones, 1963) shows sharp contrasts between these regions. The contrasts are, however, exaggerated by the seasons during which the data were collected. Thus figures for the most productive agricultural area, the Highveld, refer to the time of year when the food is most plentiful. But the data for the semi-arid Lowveld were collected in the 'hungry season' which may begin in July or August and extend to late January. Food supplies normally improve steadily from January until the main maize harvest in March-May. There is no information about maximum food intakes in the Lowveld immediately after harvest, but subjective assessments support the idea that there are marked seasonal alternations between plenty and hunger.

In Ghana, despite being unimodal, two crops of maize harvested in July and October are possible in the long growing season in the southern parts of the country. In the north the agricultural season is more compressed (May-December) and sorghum and millet are the main staples. Although there were problems with data collection, Table 2.5 shows that in all regions there were consistent patterns of low intakes before harvest.

Most of the studies we have quoted show per capita average intakes for energy and protein which are close to estimates of average requirements. However, these average figures may conceal maldistribution in the community, both between households and between individuals in the households. In the Bangladesh survey (of 1962), 45 per cent of households did not meet the average level for energy intake, and 60 per cent of households were below the protein average. Measurement of nutrient intake by individual family members is most difficult, but available evidence, summarised by Schofield (1974) shows that intakes in relation to requirements may be unequal and biased in favour of the adult male.

However, as pointed out, the storage of nutrients in the body makes it difficult to know precisely what the needs of different sectors of the population really are. Schofield's analysis suggests that there is great inequality in fulfilment of requirements among pre-school children and women. We do not doubt that problems exist for these groups, but suggest that direct indicators of nutritional status and health show the problems more unambiguously than evidence of poor nutrient intake.

Energy storage mechanisms

It is clear that variations in periods of plenty and scarcity are most marked in areas where there is dependence on one harvest only. In such situations, the

Seasonal Energy Relationships and Food

TABLE 2.5. Energy intake (kcal) by season and region, Ghana Nutrition Survey

	Coastal zone		Forest zone			Northern zone	
	Fishing village	Farming village	Town + village	Town + village	Large town	Farming village	Scattered village
January–February	2785	2817	2268	2415			
March–April	2598	2518	2310	2200	4109		1415
May–June	1440	1987	2202	2926		2199	
July–August	2127	2210	2024	2135	2117		2625
September–October	3094	2776	2194	1735	1883	1666	
November–December	2370		1917	2627	1847	2112	
Village name	Mouree	Mafi-Kumasi	Juaben & Jacobu combined	Kokuma & Acherensua combined	Damongo	Binduri	Yorog

Source: Davey (n.d.)

rural poor replenish their body stores after harvest in anticipation of losing weight towards the next harvest. They are no doubt aware of what is coming, and ration their food stocks accordingly, as far as they are able. When the next season's cultivations start, their energy requirements increase, and at this time adults start to lose weight. It is interesting to consider whether using their bodies for storing energy might be a better strategy than leaving food in their granaries. However, calculations show that the efficiency of storage of energy in the body is around 25 per cent for 'lean' type individuals and 60 per cent for 'fat' type individuals, implying 'losses' therefore of 75 per cent and 40 per cent respectively. These calculations are drawn from the results of the computer simulation carried out by Dugdale and Payne (1977) where for the 'fat' individual the maximum changes in body stores are 5.9 kg of fat, 0.8 kg of slow lean and 0.7 kg of fast lean and for the 'lean' individual these are 1.7 kg, 3.0 kg and 2.2 kg respectively. However, several studies of actual measurements (notably Boxall *et al.*, 1977) show grain losses from farmers' granaries to be lower, probably less than 10 per cent. On the face of it therefore, the use of the body as a store appears to be a less efficient option.

2.5 Agriculture and Nutrition In Matlab Thana, Bangladesh
A.K.M. Alauddin Chowdhury, Sandra L. Huffman, and Lincoln C. Chen

Introduction

Previous papers in this chapter have discussed energy deficits which arise when seasonal peaks in labour demand coincide with periods of food shortage. In discussing the nutritional status of a group of mothers and children in Bangladesh, this paper points out that energy deficits may also occur because of 'nutrient wastage' associated with illness or with lack of time for proper feeding of infants at times of peak labour demand.

All the data presented come from Matlab thana, Comilla District, Bangladesh,[3] where the International Centre for Diarrhoeal Disease Research, Bangladesh (ICDDR,B) has a field station providing diarrhoeal health services and undertaking field research since 1963. Like much of monsoon Asia, Matlab thana has three seasons: monsoon (June-October), cool winter (November-February), and a hot-dry season (March-May). The major crop, known as *aman,* is deep-water floating rice, grown during the monsoon. During the winter, a smaller amount of land is devoted to *boro* rice, to high-yielding rice, and to wheat, millet and vegetables. The people are predominantly Muslim. About 50 per cent of families are either absolutely landless, or own less than the subsistence holding of 0.6 ha. Education and literacy standards are low, as are the role and status of women.

The micro-level individual and household data employed in this paper were collected between March 1976 and February 1977 as part of a longitudinal study on the relationship between nutrition and fertility among 205 mothers and children living in eighty-six Matlab villages (Huffman *et al.*, 1978).

Seasonality of nutritional status

Nutritional status, particularly among vulnerable mothers and children, fluctuates markedly by season. Evidence for this is presented in Figure 2.4,

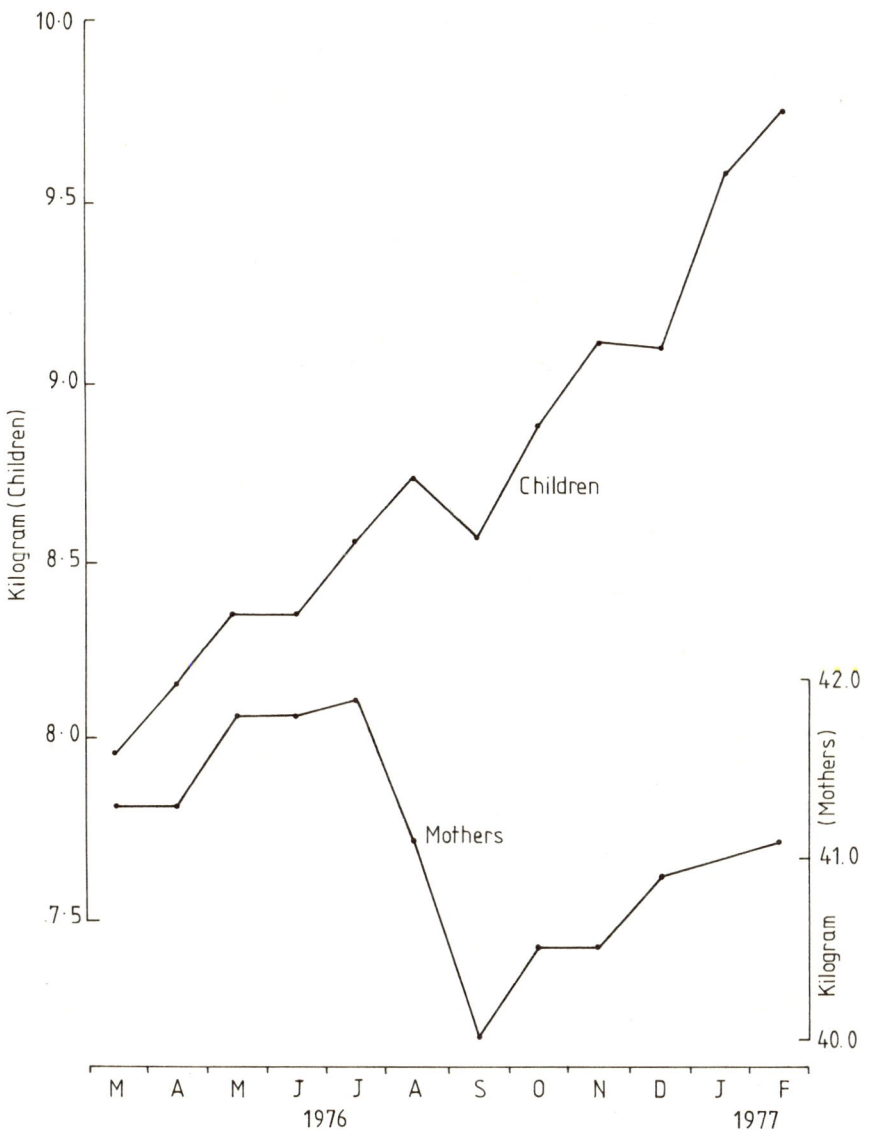

Figure 2.4 Mean body weight of 216 mother children pairs by month of observation, Matlab thana, Bangladesh.

which shows monthly fluctuations of body weight among 216 mother children pairs. Among the cohort of children, weight gain appeared to be adequate in the first and last months of the study year. However, retarded growth—or even weight loss—characterised the critical months of August-September.

During the development of a pre-school child, 'nutrient wastage' may occur due to infections and parasitic diseases. In these conditions, nutrient loss may occur in several ways (Briscoe, 1977). An ill child may experience interruption of breast feeding or reduced food intake due to anorexia. Food that is consumed may be malabsorbed due to functional problems and rapid transit time in the gastro-intestinal tract. The child may also suffer from catabolic losses induced by infection. Through fever and other mechanisms, infection may cause body tissue to be broken down, sequestered, and excreted.

A child's nutrient intake is determined by the diet of mother and child. During pregnancy, the maternal diet and maternal nutritional reserves are important factors affecting foetal nutrition (DHEW, 1970). In most rural areas of poor countries, breast-feeding is universal and intensive in the first and second years of life (Jelliffe, 1968).

Nutrient wastage during illness can take place in several different ways which should be seen as interdependent. Infection, for example, may not only result in biological wastage of nutrients through malabsorption and catabolism, but may also influence dietary practices during and after illness. Another factor may be reduced availability of food in the family if wage income is reduced by illness of adult earning members.

The importance of looking at these different factors together is that they illustrate the interdependence of agricultural and public health measures. Significantly, in those less developed countries that have made major strides towards eliminating protein-energy malnutrition (e.g. China), policies have simultaneously acted on all three major determinants of nutritional well-being: food availability, food behaviour, and nutrient wastage.

Family food availability

In a predominantly agrarian economy, the seasonal nature of family food availability will obviously be dependent upon agricultural cropping patterns. Even a superficial examination of cropping patterns in Matlab thana reveals marked seasonal variation. Of singular importance is the monsoon *aman* rice crop which accounts for over half of cereal production. Land preparation, ploughing, and broadcast planting work for this major crop occur during February-April, while harvesting work is concentrated in November-December. Significantly, most of the agricultural work related to the other crops takes place between December and July. Virtually no field work is undertaken during the second half of the monsoon, and in the immediate post-monsoon periods.

Monthly data on rice prices, agricultural wage rates, and household food grain stocks shown in Table 2.6 accurately reflect this agricultural cycle (Huffman *et al.*, 1978, CAMO, 1978). The wholesale price of medium quality rice in Matlab rose steadily from April to October 1976, falling precipitously with

TABLE 2.6. Wholesale price of medium rice (1976-77), agricultural labourer wage rate (1977-78), and average household cereal stocks (1976-77), in Matlab thana, Bangladesh

Month	Wholesale price of medium rice[a] (taka/mound)	Agricultural labour wage rate[b] (taka/day)	Average household cereal stock[c] (mounds)
March	116	10.0	2.1
April	111	8.0	2.9
May	122	7.5	5.1
June	118	7.5	3.1
July	123	6.0	2.8
August	123	*	2.1
September	123	*	1.0
October	125	6.0	0.7
November	105	7.5	3.2
December	111	7.5	5.3
January	113	7.0	2.8
February	118		1.1

Note: *Extremely limited agricultural work opportunities exist between August and October, except jute stripping.

Sources: a. Chandpur Subdivisional Marketing Office, Ministry of Agriculture, Government of Bangladesh, June 1978.
b. Three anonymous farmers in Matlab. Data were obtained in Bengali months, which usually begin and end in the middle of Western calendar months.
c. Huffman et al. (1978).

the harvest of the *aman* crop in November. Monthly surveys of cereal food stocks in 205 households displayed a bimodal pattern, peaking in May and December. Crude wage rate data suggest high labour demands in March-April for *aman* land preparation work together with the harvest of some winter crops and a lower peak during the *aman* harvest. Taken together, these data show that the period of greatest scarcity is August-October, when rice prices are highest, household food stocks lowest, and agricultural labour demand weakest.

The seasonality of the agricultural cycle may affect household food behaviour and diet in several ways. The most obvious are changes in food distribution within the family. A second mechanism would be seasonal changes in work generating varying energy requirements for different individuals in a family. A third factor is that work patterns may also affect the *time* allocated for preparing food and breast-feeding infants.

In July 1978, the total daily energy intake for various individuals in one family in Matlab thana was measured. Total daily food consumption was 6157 kcal, which was distributed as follows: father, 32 per cent; mother, 31 per cent; brother, 22 per cent; and child, 15 per cent. Observation such as this over an entire calendar year is required to examine possible seasonal fluctuations in food availability. Although data are lacking, it is possible that seasonal

Seasonal Dimensions to Rural Poverty

food shortages may be disproportionately absorbed by nutritionally vulnerable family members (mothers and children), so amplifying for them the impact of seasonal food scarcity.

Seasonal variations in a mother's work may not only alter her energy needs, but may reduce the time available for child-rearing. During much of the year, 40-50 per cent of women spend their day predominantly on crop-related work (particularly crop processing). Peak work-loads occur in May, July and November, and one possible effect is shown in Figure 2.5, which presents data on the suckling time of one group of mothers during daytime observation.

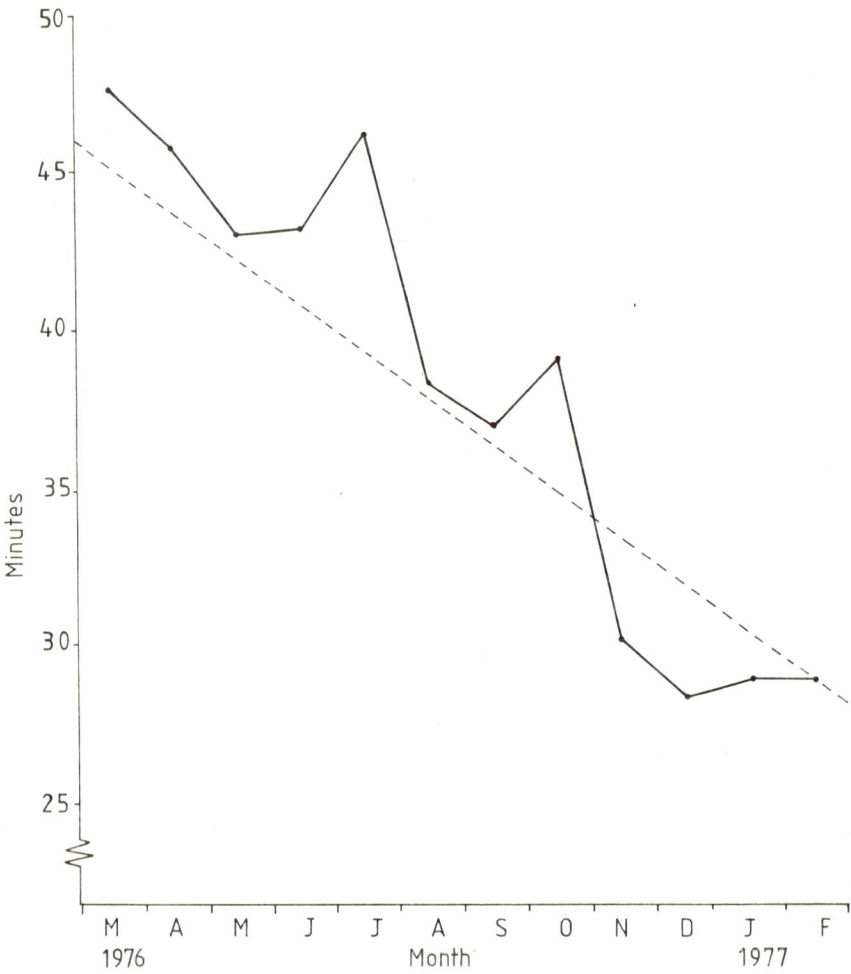

Figure 2.5 Median of suckling time during 8 hours of daytime observation and month of observation of 216 mother and child pairs, Matlab thana, Bangladesh.

Because of gradual weaning, the average suckling time declined from forty-eight to twenty-nine minutes over the twelve months of observation. To highlight possible seasonal fluctuations, a regression line was plotted which helps to show up a slightly steeper reduction in suckling during November-December. These are the months when energy and time devoted to post-harvest work on the *aman* rice crop would be most intense.

Infection and diarrhoeal disease

Fluctuations of nutritional status may be conditioned both by seasonal changes in food consumption, and by the seasonal incidence of infectious diseases, which are important causes of nutrient wastage. Although many infections have an adverse nutritional impact, the diarrhoeal diseases have received particular attention because of their prevalence among the most vulnerable age group (pre-school children). They directly affect the gastro-intestinal tract, causing greater anorexia, food witholding behaviour, and nutrient malabsorption than most other infections (Rowland *et al.*, 1977; Rohde, 1978). Figure 2.6 shows the number of diarrhoeal admissions to the ICDDR,B Matlab hospital for 1976 and 1977 combined. Two peaks, in March and September, are noted. Although the agent responsible for most of these admissions is not known, bacteriological diagnosis was possible in the cases of cholera, non-agglutinating vibrios (NAG), shigella, and salmonella. Relatively few cases of the last were seen. However, cholera shows a striking seasonal pattern, with about 700 admissions in September. Recent studies show that a substantial portion of the previously undiagnosed diarrhoeas in children are due to rotavirus and toxigenic *E. coli* (Merson and Black, 1978). These, too, have seasonal patterns. The former attacks children of six months to two years old, peaking during the winter months, and the latter, also common among children, has a probable spring peak.

Available evidence is too limited to document the role of these seasonal infections on nutritional status (Chen, 1978). Much more detailed analysis would be needed, with clinical studies to document the various nutrient wastage pathways (intake, malabsorption, and catabolism), and the quantitative significance of each. Finally, seasonal patterns of other nutritionally important infections, such as measles and pertussis, would need to be documented.

With cholera, there are large seasonal fluctuations, and there are also marked year-to-year variations in incidence. No one single year is truly representative. Twelve years of cholera monitoring at the ICDDR,B hospital in Matlab show that the most common peak for cholera is November-December, but the peak may occur at any time between September and January in any given year.

Two final points regarding the role of infection should be noted. First, data on individuals are the only means of documenting the nutritional effects of infection; aggregate figures mask seasonal changes and effects on particular age groups. Second, infections may affect nutritional status in other ways apart from nutrient wastage, and particularly by compromising the work capacity of the labour force. Infections in particular seasons may even create effective labour shortages in the midst of underemployment.

Seasonal Dimensions to Rural Poverty

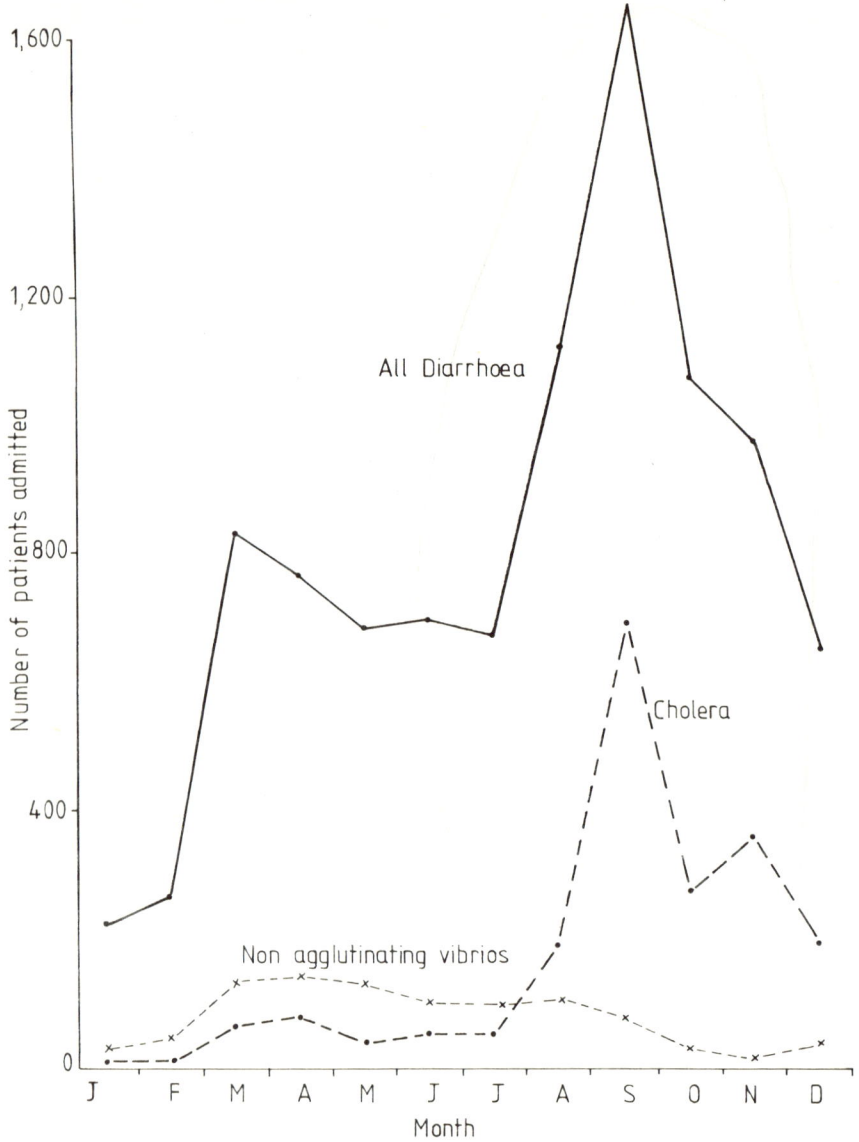

Figure 2.6 Number of patients admitted to ICDDR,B hospital during calendar 1976 and 1977 by etiology and month of admission.

Impact on the rural poor

An *a priori* hypothesis of this book is that seasonal fluctuations bear more heavily on the poor than on other social groups. An attempt was therefore made to examine the impact of seasonal factors on the nutritional status of the rural poor.

Table 2.7 presents data on the body weight of 205 mothers by month. The same data are provided on eight and seventeen mothers who come from land-owning and landless households respectively. In all three groups, monthly fluctuations of maternal body weight were observed. Although fluctuations among the landless are not extreme, the degree of variation was greater among them than among the landowning mothers (this was not statistically significant, however). In addition, the mean body weight averaged over all months was lower for the landless mothers.

Interestingly, though, landless mothers spent more time breast-feeding their infants. Landowning mothers, who breast-feed less, may experience either greater availability of supplemental weaning foods, or reduced time available for child care because of heavier post-harvest work loads.

Equally pronounced differential fluctuations are shown in Figure 2.7, where monthly cereal food stocks for these landowning and landless households are presented. Both groups displayed bimodal peaks, but the differences in quantity of food were striking. Among landless families, stocks were entirely depleted during the critical lean month of October. However, landowning families theoretically had sufficient stocks to maintain adequate family consumption throughout the year without resort to market purchases.

There are other seasonal factors that may operate against the nutritional welfare of the rural poor. Physical work in the fields requiring heavy expenditures of energy is more likely to be concentrated among the landless. And during the critical lean months, interest rates may be high and survival pressures may be so intense that assets, such as land, livestock, utensils and

TABLE 2.7. Body weight of mothers by month and landownership in Matlab, Bangladesh

Month	All (n = 205)		Landowners (n = 8)		Landless (n = 17)	
	Weight	% Mean	Weight	% Mean	Weight	% Mean
March	41.3	100	42.9	103	41.9	104
April	41.3	100	42.6	102	40.0	100
May	41.8	102	41.8	100	40.7	101
June	41.8	102	41.3	99	40.9	102
July	41.9	102	41.7	100	40.8	101
August	41.1	100	41.3	99	39.9	99
September	40.0	97	40.7	97	38.3	95
October	40.5	98	41.5	99	39.1	97
November	40.5	98	41.7	100	39.2	98
December	40.9	100	41.7	100	40.2	100
January	41.0	100	41.8	100	40.4	100
February	41.1	100	42.6	102	40.6	101
Mean	41.1	100	41.8	100	40.2	100

Seasonal Dimensions to Rural Poverty

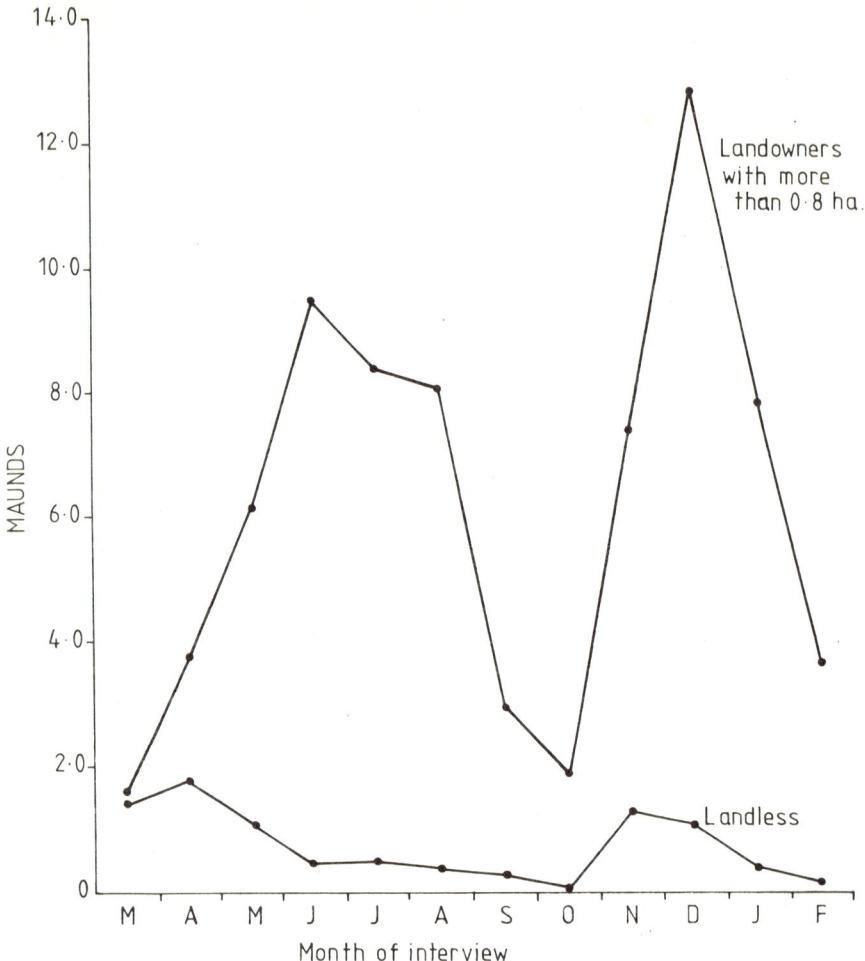

Figure 2·7 Household food stocks on the day of interview by month of interview of eight landowner households and seventeen landless households, Matlab thana, Bangladesh.

tools, may be transferred from the disadvantaged to the wealthy at rates of exchange below the annual average.

Practical implications

Programmes that can ensure basic minimal needs to poor families during these critical periods — even relief to a certain extent — could mitigate the tendency toward the concentration of assets by a small minority.

Wage income opportunities are obviously highly seasonal in character. Large-scale infrastructure projects, such as public works or food-for-work are

Seasonal Energy Relationships and Food

confined to the dry winter season in Bangladesh. At this time, labour demand is not at its weakest annual point. Technological and programme innovations, such as multiple cropping and home-based agro-industries, to generate work during the lean fall months are needed.

Interventions aimed at optimising the utilisation of food resources by families through improved dietary practices need to take seasonal factors into account. Promotion of breast-feeding may be facilitated by a smoother distribution of maternal time and energy use in work throughout the seasons. Supplemental feeding programmes, where indicated, may be more effective if targetted to disadvantaged families and individuals during periods of scarcity.

Infection control, particularly diarrhoeal disease prevention and treatment, also has seasonal dimensions. The transmission of various diarrhoeal diseases is known to be markedly seasonal, so much so that the unravelling of the causes of seasonality would probably result in the delineation of the entire transmission cycle of these diseases. Seasonal diarrhoea in Matlab has prompted the ICDDR,B hospital to shift staff between periods of strong and weak service demand. Preventive work and non-seasonal curative services, such as family planning, may be undertaken during non-epidemic periods. It should be stressed, however, that this increase of staff efficiency may be achieved only at the cost of increased programme complexity. Shifting of staff requires more training, supervision, and other programme support services.

However striking the seasonal pattern of nutritionally related factors in rural Bangladesh, though, it should not be allowed to overshadow the fundamental situation with regard to nutritional welfare. Normative nutrition indicators among rural mothers and children approximate only 70 per cent of Western standards (Jelliffe, 1966). This deplorable condition is several-fold greater than seasonal fluctuations in nutritional status, which deviate about 5 per cent from annual average. Deliberations about policy and programme interventions should therefore begin at the root causes of energy-protein malnutrition.

2.6 Energy Needs and Technology

Seasonal cycles in energy use

The standard of living of any subsistence farming community depends on a favourable energy balance in its farming operations. In the absence of tractors, electricity supplies and fossil fuels, all the energy used by such a community is derived from the process by which plants convert sunlight into chemical energy. This process of photosynthesis is the source of food for people, fodder for animals and firewood for cooking. Some of the energy which the human population gains in this way has to be re-invested in food production, through the labour involved in tilling fields, harvesting crops, and so on.

Many factors which enter into this energy-use cycle are shown schematically in Figure 1 in the Introduction, particularly by the circuit of relationships marked 'A'. The links between these energy relationships and the community's 'quality of life' should be noted, because quality of life can only be improved if the community can produce an energy surplus. Only then do people have the resources to support themselves during years of poor harvest, and only then do they have the energy to innovate, to improve their homes, or to indulge in recreation or social activities.

In Section 2.2 in this chapter, Haswell discussed the energy used by women in rice cultivation, and showed that the ratio of energy produced to energy used in labour was 8.6. It appeared that this ratio was sufficient for survival, but did not represent a big enough energy surplus for the quality of life to be improved. It also seemed that the women were in a state of energy deficit during seasons of peak labour demand. The analysis of another rice-growing system given by Bayliss-Smith (Section 2.1) showed that food production could yield twenty-one times as much energy as the requirement for labour. This is a much more favourable ratio, implying a larger surplus and the possibility of improvement in quality of life. Even so, Bayliss-Smith showed that periods of seasonal energy deficit might occur.

Other papers in this chapter have been rather less concerned to evaluate the re-investment of energy in agriculture, and instead have focused on the energy surplus which should be available to feed children and maintain family life. In these papers, it has been repeatedly shown that during certain seasons, the energy status of mothers can adversely affect children being breast-fed (Sections 2.3, 2.4 and 2.5), and seasonal food shortages may hold back the growth of older children. It has also been pointed out that illness can cause 'nutrient wastage', involving a loss of energy (Chowdhury *et al*, Section 2.5).

Economic relationships and technology

The model of energy use in subsistence communities so far discussed is, of course, only partially valid, because none of the communities considered is solely involved in subsistence agriculture. In every case, some cash crops are grown, some food is bought in, and some people sell their labour for wages, often migrating on a seasonal basis to do so. To complete the picture of energy relationships, therefore, we need a complementary picture of economic relationships, and this is presented in Chapter 3, and is also represented summarily by the cycle 'C' in Figure 1.

If these economic relationships work well, they will drive the energy production cycle harder, enabling it to produce a larger surplus. For example, if people are able to earn some spare cash, this can be used to hire animal-drawn ploughs, to buy seed and fertilizer for high-yielding crops, or to buy tools and equipment which will ease the burden of manual labour. All these are changes in technology which allow unused sources of energy (e.g. oxen) to be mobilised, or which allow energy already available to be used more efficiently.

One of the key functions of the economy, indeed, can be to mobilise new technologies in either of two categories. On the one hand, there are technologies such as irrigation or the breeding of new crop varieties that can help overcome seasonal constraints on crop production. On the other hand, though, there are technologies which may contribute directly to alleviating the seasonal energy deficits on which this chapter has focused.

For example, energy deficits can be reduced by the introduction of extra energy through farm mechanisation. But after much unhappy experience with tractor programmes, and after 'energy crises' which have played havoc with fuel and fertilizer prices, this approach is less often appropriate. Instead, the possibility of using *existing* energy sources more economically is receiving increased attention.

As an example, consider the energy used in growing cereals in the tropics using hand-hoes for tillage. This may amount to 100,000 kcal/ha (420 MJ/ha). There are several ways in which changes in technology can affect economies in this prodigal use of human labour, and so reduce seasonal energy deficits. Three examples are as follows:

(1) the partial replacement of traditional hand-hoes by more efficient hand-tools, especially for weeding, can save over 10,000 kcal/ha (42 MJ/ha);
(2) the use of ox-drawn ploughs and cultivators can transfer a large proportion of the work-load to the animals, allowing the human labour force to cultivate up to three times as much land with the same effort;
(3) the use of 'minimum tillage' with herbicides for weed control can reduce the energy requirements of agriculture to as little as 8000 kcal/ha (35 MJ/ha), for example, in experiments at Ibadan, Nigeria (IITA).

There is no space to discuss details of these technologies. They are relevant here in that they achieve considerable economies in energy, and demand a much reduced effort from the labour force during seasons of peak agricultural work. They also require tools or materials from outside the community, and thus depend on the effective functioning of the cycle of economic relationships.

We can see from Figure 1, then, that a large part of what goes on in rural communities can be modelled in terms of three interacting cycles. The cycle of energy production and use is driven *forward* by an economic cycle capable of mobilising new technology, and is *retarded* by a cycle of infection and disease. We can think of this model almost as three gear wheels meshing together. The problem is that these gears do not turn at uniform speed. In regions where there is a long dry season, that is a time for free-wheeling. But when the rains come, there is an intensification of drive in the food/energy cycle, while at the same time, the brakes are applied via the cycle of infection and illness. The need is to get the economic and energy-use cycles running well together while disengaging the cycle which brings disease.

Notes

1. Subsequently, Gambia has been the focus for much other detailed work on nutrition and energy use in rural communities, and is one of the case-study areas discussed in this book; see the comments in Section 2.4 in this chapter, and also Chapter 6.
2. The parts of East Africa which have a bimodal climate comprise one of the case-study areas in this book. This paper on Kenya should be compared with papers from similar areas of Tanzania which are presented in Chapter 6. The first part of the paper was written by S. R. Onchere, and the second and third parts by R. Slooff.
3. Bangladesh is another of the case-study areas in this book and is also represented in Chapters 3 and 5.

2.7 References

Annegers, J. F. (1973), 'Seasonal Food Shortages in West Africa', *Ecol. Food Nutr.*, 2, pp. 251-7.
Bayliss-Smith, T. P. (1977), 'Energy and Economic Development', in *Subsistence and Sur-*

vival: Rural Ecology in the Pacific, ed. T. P. Bayliss-Smith, and R.G.A. Feachem, London, Academic Press.

Best, R. (1962), 'Production Factors in the Tropics', *Neths. J. Agric. Sci.,* 10, pp. 347-53.

Black, J. N. (1956), 'The Distribution of Solar Radiation over the Earth's Surface', *Arch. Met. Geophys. Bioklim., B 7,* pp. 165-89.

Bohdal, M., Gibbs, N. E., and Simmons, W. K. (n.d.), *Nutrition Survey and Campaign against Malnutrition 1964-1968,* Report to the Ministry of Health (Kenya) on the WHO/FAO/UNICEF assisted project.

Boutillier, J. L., Cantrelle, P. A., Causs, J., and Levant, C. (1962), *La Moyene Vallée du Senegal,* Paris, Ministère de la Coopération.

Boxall, R. A., Greeley, M., Tyagi, D. S., Lipton, M., Neelakanta, J. (1977), 'The Prevention of Farm-Level Food Grain Storage Losses in India: A Social Cost-Benefit Analysis', *IDS Research Report,* Institute of Development Studies, University of Sussex.

Briscoe, J. (1977), 'The Quantitative Effect of Infection on the Use of Food by Young Children in Poor Countries', *American Journal Clin. Nutri.,* 32, pp. 648-76.

Caldwell, M. (1975), 'Primary Production of Grazing Lands', in *Photosynthesis and Productivity in Different Environments,* ed. J. P. Cooper, Cambridge, Cambridge University Press.

CAMO (1978), Chandgur Agricultural Marketing Office, Ministry of Agriculture, Government of Bangladesh, Report dated June 1978.

Chang, J-H. (1968a), 'The Agricultural Potential of the Humid Tropics', *Geog. Rev.,* 58, pp. 333-61.

Chang. J-H. (1968b), *Climate and Agriculture,* Chicago, Aldine.

Chen, L. C. (1978), 'Control and Diarrhoeal Disease Morbidity and Mortality, Some Strategic Issues', *Amer. J. Clin. Nutr.,* 31(12) pp. 2284-90.

Chinnappa, B. N. (1977), 'Adoption of the New Technology in North Arcot District', in *Green Revolution?,* ed. B. H. Farmer, London, Macmillan.

Chinnappa, B. N., and Silva, W.P.T. (1977), 'Impact of the Cultivation of HYV Paddy,' in *Green Revolution?,* ed. B. H. Farmer, London, Macmillan.

Clark, C., and Haswell, M. R. (1964), *The Economics of Subsistence Agriculture,* London, Macmillan.

Conklin, H. C. (1957), *Hanunoo Agriculture. A Report on an Integral System of Shifting Cultivation in the Philippines,* Rome, F.A.O.

Cooper, J. P. (1975), 'Control of Photosynthetic Production in Terrestrial Systems', in *Photosynthesis and Productivity in Different Environments,* ed. J. P. Cooper, Cambridge, Cambridge University Press.

Davey, P.L.H. (n.d.), Ghana Nutrition Survey, 1961-62, Unpublished report to the Government of Ghana (mimeo).

DHEW (1970), *Maternal Nutrition,* U.S. Department of Health, Education and Welfare and National Academy of Sciences, Washington, D.C., Government Printer.

Dugdale, A. E., and Payne, P. R. (1977), 'Pattern of Lean and Fat Deposition in Adults', *Nature,* 266, pp. 349-51.

Fox, R. H. (1953), 'A Study of Energy Expenditure of Africans Engaged in Various Rural Activities', Ph.D. thesis, University of London.

Freeman, J. D. (1955), *Iban Agriculture,* London, HMSO.

Gordon, J. E. et al. (1964), 'Acute Diarrhoeal Disease in Less Developed Countries', *Bull. Wld. Hlth Org.,* 31, pp. 9-20.

Gordon, J. E. et al. (1970), 'Weanling Diarrhoea', *Amer. J. Med. Sci.,* 245, pp. 345-77.

Griffiths, J. F. (1972), (ed.), *Climates of Africa,* Amsterdam, Elsevier.

Grist, D. H. (1959), *Rice,* 3rd ed., London, Longmans.

Hanks, L. M. (1972), *Rice and Man,* Chicago, Aldine.

Harris, M. (1971), *Culture, Man and Nature,* New York, Crowell.

Harriss, B. (1977), 'Paddy and Rice Statistics in Sri Lanka', in *Green Revolution?,* ed. B. H. Farmer, London, Macmillan.

Haswell, M. R. (1953), *Economics of Agriculture in a Savannah Village,* Colonial Research Study No. 8, London, HMSO.

Haswell, M. R. (1973), *Tropical Farming Economics,* London, Longmans.

Haswell, M. R. (1975), *The Nature of Poverty: a Case History of the First Quarter-Century after World War II*, London, Macmillan.

Haswell, M. R. (1977), 'Longitudinal Analysis of Agricultural Change: a Study of Social and Economic Decline', *Civilisation*, 27, No. 3/4.

Haswell, M. R. (1979), 'Economic Choice of Appropriate Technology by Peasant Farmers', *Report of the West Africa Rural Technology Meeting*, London, Commonwealth Secretariat.

Hauck, H. M., Thorangkul, D., and Rajatasilpin, A. (1960), 'Growth in Height and Weight of Elementary School Children', *J. Trop. Pediatrics*, 6 (3), pp. 84-91.

Huffman, S. L., Alauddin Chowdhury, A.K.M., Chakraborty, J., and Mosley, W. H. (1978), 'Nutrition and Post-Partum Amenorrhoea in Rural Bangladesh', *Population Studies*, 32, pp. 251-60.

Institute of Nutrition and Food Science, Dacca University (1977), *Nutrition Survey of Rural Bangladesh 1975-76*, Dacca.

Jackson, I. J. (1977), *Climate, Water and Agriculture in the Tropics*, London, Longmans.

Jelliffe, D. B. (1966), *The Assessment of the Nutritional Status of the Community*, WHO Monograph Series No. 53, Geneva, WHO.

Jelliffe, D. B. (1968), *Infant Nutrition in the Subtropics and Tropics*, WHO Monograph Series No. 29, Geneva, WHO.

Jones, S. M. (1963), *A Study of Swazi Nutrition: Report of the Swaziland Nutrition Survey 1961-62*, Durban, Institute of Social Research, University of Natal.

Kira, T. (1975), 'Primary Production in Forests', in *Photosynthesis and Productivity in Different Environments*, ed. J. P. Cooper, Cambridge, Cambridge University Press.

Leach, G. (1976), *Energy and Food Production*, Guildford, IPC Press.

Leeuwenburg, J., Gemert, W., Muller, A. S., and Patel, S. C. (1978), 'Machakos Project Studies VII: The Incidence of Diarrhoeal Disease in the Under-five Population', *Trop. Geogr. Med.*, 30, pp. 383-91.

McGregor, I. A., Rahman, A. K., Thompson, B., Billewicz, W. Z., and Thomson, A. M. (1968), 'The Growth of Young Children in a Gambian Village', *Trans. Roy. Soc. Trop. Med. Hyg.*, 62, pp. 341-52.

McGregor, I. A., Rahman, A. K., Thompson, B., Billewicz, W. Z., and Thomson, A. M. (1970), 'The Growth of Young Children in a West African (Gambian) Village', *Trans. Roy. Soc. Trop. Med. Hyg.*, 64, pp. 48-77.

Marsden, P. D., and Marsden, S. A. (1965), 'A Pattern of Weight Gain in Gambian Babies during the First 18 Months of Life', *J. Trop. Pediatrics*, 10 (4), pp. 89-99.

Merson, M., and Black, R. (1978), Unpublished communication, Cholera Research Laboratory, Dacca.

Ministry of Health, Pakistan (1966), *Nutrition Survey of East Pakistan, March 1962-January 1964*, A report in collaboration with the University of Dacca and the Nutrition Section, Office of International Research, U.S. Department of Health, Education and Welfare.

Moore, H. A. *et al.* (1965), 'Diarrhoeal Disease Studies in Costa Rica', *Amer. J. Epid.*, 82, pp. 143-61.

Nicol, B. M., and Phillips, P. G. (1976), 'The Utilisation of Dietary Protein by Nigerian Men', *Brit. J. Nutr*, 36, p. 337.

Onchere, S. R. (1976), M.Sc. thesis, University of Nairobi.

Oomen, H.A.P.C, Jansen, A.A.J., and 't Manntje W. (1979), 'Machakos Project Studies XIV: Growth Pattern of Rural Akamba Pre-school Children', *Trop. Georg. Med.*, 31, pp. 421-39.

Platt, B. S. (1943), 'Planning for Better Nutrition in the Colonies', *The Imperial Review*, 12, 3.

Poskitt, E.M.E. (1972), 'Seasonal Variation in Infection and Malnutrition at a Rural Paediatric Clinic in Uganda', *Trans. Roy. Soc. Trop. Med. Hyg.*, 66, pp. 931-6.

Qasim, S. Z., Bhattathiri, P.M.A., and Abidi, S.A.H. (1968), 'Solar Radiation and its Penetration in a Tropical Estuary', *J. Expl. Mar. Biol. Ecol.*, 2, pp. 87-103.

Rohde, J. E. (1978), 'Preparing for the Next Round: Convalescent Care after Acute Infection', Paper presented at the Workshop on Effective Interventions to Reduce Infection in Malnourished Populations, National Academy of Sciences, Haiti, and published in *Am. J. Clin. Nutr.*, 31(12) pp. 2258-68.

Rowland, M.G.M., Cole, T. J., and Whitehead, R. G. (1977), 'A Quantitative Study into the Role of Infection in Determining Nutritional Status in Gambian Children', *Brit. J. Nutr.*, 37, p. 441

Ruthenberg, H. (1971), *Farming Systems in the Tropics,* Oxford, Clarendon Press.
Schofield, S. (1974), 'Seasonal Factors Affecting Nutrition in Different Age Groups and Especially Pre-school Children', *J. Development Studies, 11* (1), pp. 22-40.
Schwerdtfeger, W. (1976), (ed.), *Climates of Central and South America,* Amsterdam, Elsevier.
Simmons, E. B. (1976a), *Calorie and Protein Intakes in Three Villages in Zaria Province, May 1970-July 1971,* Samaru Miscellaneous Paper 55, Institute for Agricultural Research, Ahmadu Bello University.
Spalding, E., McCrea, J., Rutishauser, I.H.E., and Parkin, J. M. (1977), 'A Study of Severely Malnourished Children in Gambia', *J. Trop. Pediat. Envir. Child Health, 23,* pp. 215-19.
Standard, K. L., Desai, P., and Miall, W. E. (1969), 'A Longitudinal Study of Child Growth in a Rural Community in Jamaica', *J. Biosoc. Sci., 1,* 2, pp. 153-76.
Steenbergen, W. M. van, Kusin, J. A., Voorhoeve, A. M., and Jansen A.A.J. (1978), 'Machakos Project Studies IX: Food Intake, Feeding Habits and Nutritional State of the Akamba Infant and Toddler', *Trop. Geogr. Med.,* 30, pp. 505-22.
Steenbergen, W. M. van, Kusin, J. A., and Rens, M. M. van. (1980), 'Lactation Performance of Akamba Mothers, Kenya. Breast Feeding Behavior, Breast Milk Yield and Composition', *Journal of Tropical Pediatrics and Environmental Child Health.*
Waldemann, E. (1973), 'Seasonal Variations in Malnutrition in Africa', *Trans. Roy. Soc. Trop. Med. Hyg., 67,* p. 431.
Wernstedt, F. L. (1972), *World Climatic Data,* Lemont, Pennsylvania, Climatic Data Press.

Chapter 3
ECONOMIC RELATIONSHIPS AND THE SEASONAL USE OF LABOUR

3.1 Seasonality In the Rural Economy (of Tropical Africa)
Philip Raikes

Seasonality and seasonal variability

Huge numbers of rural people throughout the world suffer acute seasonal hardship made worse by *variations* in seasonal patterns. But some suffer more than others, while a minority actually benefit from the hardship of others. The degree of hardship undergone is thus not simply a matter of the severity and unpredictability of climatic seasonality. It also depends on the level of technology and system of socio-economic organisation with which given climatic conditions are confronted. For the individual or family it also depends on the position held within the society and its class structure.

Climate is only one of a large number of seasonal or periodic factors bearing on human social production and life, ranging from daily, weekly and monthly rhythms (the working day, wage-periods, menstruation) to economic cycles occurring over many years. Any 'season' in agriculture, or other human activity, is composed of the interaction of a number of cycles of different periodicity.

This is to be distinguished conceptually from seasonal variability, which refers to fluctuations around a hypothetical mean seasonal pattern. The common distinction between inter- and intra-seasonal variation does not adequately represent this difference, which refers to predictability rather than length of period. In practice, the effects of seasonality in agriculture are invariably compounded by variability.

Seasonality and agriculture

Any agricultural production process is seasonal in that it depends on a climatic sequence which activates the biological-chemical processes of plant (or livestock) growth and generates particular patterns of labour requirement. Generally speaking, the shorter the rainy season, the more likely it is that periods of heavy labour will be condensed and interspersed with periods largely composed of waiting for biological-chemical processes to work themselves out. Apart from this, the seasonal occurrence of harvests implies a seasonal pattern of food shortage, hunger and associated diseases and debilities.

Seasonal cycles in rainfall and temperature generate seasonal patterns of growth in crops and livestock and, through them, cycles in labour requirement, input requirements, and availability of food and income. The way in which the first are reflected in the second depends upon the pattern of production, the techniques in use and the social organisation of production and labour.

Thus seasonal labour peaks can be partially offset by adopting a pattern of crops which are complementary in terms of their labour requirements. Where technical innovations like irrigation are available, this levelling process can be enhanced by dry-season cropping. Other technical innovations can ease seasonal stress on labour requirements by increasing productivity at crucial times (e.g. by ox-cultivation, mechanisation) and by extending or shifting the growing season (e.g. by crop-breeding, dry-planting).

At once problems related to social structure intrude, for where income and control of resources are unequal, the wealthy will have preferential access to most of these means of responding to seasonality. But of equal importance is the way in which a society allocates its available labour in this respect. Very roughly, we can distinguish two opposed responses. In one, social resources, especially labour, are mobilised so as to assist those undergoing the most serious seasonal stress at least to survive, sometimes through the cooperative use of labour. Alternatively, where social divisions are primarily defined in terms of property ownership, those with the control of resources or social position to command the labour of others may 'flatten out' their own seasonal labour peaks by transferring them to others. This may occur where the poor are forced by seasonal hunger to sell their labour during periods when they would otherwise be cultivating their own farms. Where the poor are already in debt, creditors and patrons may stipulate the provision of labour during the peak season as a condition of the loan. In either case, the opportunity cost, in terms of lost production on the poor peasant's own farm, will often exceed the value of the wage earned, leaving him or her worse off than before (and subject to continuing debt).

When one turns to strategies to deal with seasonal variability, one finds a similar range of options and disparity of opportunities between income groups. Technical innovations like irrigation cost money and are thus more easily available to the wealthy and those with access to credit. While risk affects all, it bears more heavily upon those without reserves and for whom crop loss can spell starvation, loss of land or debt bondage. They will thus be less willing to incur risk even if the probability is that a risky strategy will give higher average returns. For example, it is not uncommon for poor peasants to grow a selection of drought-resistant but low-yielding crops for security, foregoing the higher-yielding but more risky crops which might improve their economic situation but which could also ruin them.

The relation between system of production and response to seasonality

The above has indicated that there are substantial differences in the response to seasonality, depending upon the way in which production and society are organised, though it may be thought (with some justification) that the contrast has been rather crudely drawn. If one is to draw conclusions for policies to combat the ill-effects of seasonal stress, it is necessary to pursue this analysis somewhat further and consider the conditions under which these different responses arise.

To begin with, it is worth reiterating the two main components of seasonal stress and their interaction. First, food shortages tend to occur at particular periods of the year since harvests occur at specific seasons and poor rural families are often unable to make the produce of one harvest last until the next. This may arise from failure to produce sufficient food for the period, inadequacies in the system of storage, or because for one reason or another the produce of the harvest has to be sold or repaid soon after the harvest when prices are low. But whatever the reason, the effect, in terms of hunger, will tend to be felt during characteristic 'hungry gaps' specific to each particular pattern of production. This leads to debilitation of both humans and draught animals, reducing their productive potential (often exacerbated by nutritionally-related patterns of disease). The effects will be more serious if, as is often the case, the period of hunger is also a period of peak labour requirements (the second aspect of seasonal stress). Seasonal peaks in field labour may be exacerbated by other calls upon available labour as, for example, the need to travel long distances to collect water.

Short of outright starvation and death, the most serious effects of seasonal stress are processes in which the stress incurred during one season (and especially one of drought or other disaster) leads to a reduction in the control by the peasant family over its means of production, thus adversely affecting its ability to withstand the stress incurred in subsequent seasons. It is in this respect that the most significant differences between systems of social and economic organisation occur. On the other hand, it is not hard to see how seasonal stress and the effects of drought or other climatic hazard provide the occasions (not the reason) for such changes in the control over resources.

Reference was made above to systems in which the effects of seasonal and other stress are combatted through the redistribution of either labour or its products towards those in most dire need. While there is a good deal of romantic nonsense written about such systems, the existence of mechanisms of this type is (or in most cases was) of some significance. It occurs for the most part in relatively small-scale societies in which markets for produce and labour are but little developed and in which control over the labour of others by dominant social groups is primarily political, military or religious and effected through some form of tribute.

We can usefully consider the different social processes occurring in relation to seasonality in the context of various systems of agriculture and societies resting upon the base of production by household units; most of them small in scale of production and performing all or most agricultural labour directly themselves. This would cover a large proportion of the third world and a larger proportion of the population most at risk during periods of seasonal stress. Other systems are in transition from household-based production towards (or based upon) larger-scale production units of various types, worked either by landless labourers or by migrants from peasant households, supplementing a household production which is no longer able to maintain the family. In such cases, these workers are the populations most at risk, though the pattern of seasonal stress which they suffer may have a somewhat different periodicity than that of household-based production as such.

We can start with the two related aspects of seasonal stress: shortage of food, often occurring during periods when more labour than usual is needed, and shortage of labour, concentrated on such peak periods. Other things being equal (i.e. the amount and quality of land which the household has at its disposal, access to means of production) it is clear that those households most likely to be hungry at certain periods of the year are those which have the least satisfactory balance between labour available and consumptive needs. Obviously, in specific cases other factors (and chance) will also play a role. Less diligent, provident and skilled household heads will presumably be more severely affected, as will those afflicted by various misfortunes like disease of humans or stock and insect or hail attack.

A schematic view of history

It seems broadly true to speak of one general historical trend towards the increasing penetration and scope of commodity relations within agricultural societies based on household production and of another trend towards the emergence of larger-scale production units worked for their proprietors by others. Clearly as an account of an actual historical process this would be a laughable oversimplification. But it does have at least sufficient correspondence with reality to serve as the basis for a simple schematic account by choosing systems at three (partly arbitrary) points along this series of processes.

In the first place, we can consider a society, like a number of those in pre-colonial Africa and elsewhere, in which a rather high proportion of total labour is devoted to production for household self-provisioning, specialised production of items of consumption and means of production being, as a corollary, very limited. With limited specialisation, exchange of produce within the basic production system is limited and sporadic, transfers being often made on bases other than any form of economic calculus. In almost all cases, that is, they serve in some political role, their terms being specifically affected by political status and power. Exchanges take place in the context of cementing relations between households, some relatively equal, others tending to patronage and clientage. Gifts, loans and assistance take place within a similar context, while any exactions by dominant groups tend to be based on tribute paid in respect of the political, ideological or military authority of the dominant rather than by reference to any notion of the exchange of goods and services between them and the producers of the tribute. Naturally enough, except in the limiting case where tribute is exacted by pure force, the legitimacy of a ruler or dominant group will depend upon their being seen to maintain social cohesion, ensuring the conditions for the continued existence of the society as a whole and its component households. Yet this certainly could not be described as an exchange of goods and services of equal value and equally certainly would not have been seen that way by those involved.

Another important feature of many such societies is the absence of private property in land, depending in large part upon its relative abundance. Access to sufficient land for household self-provisioning would thus be a concomitant of membership in the society. The strength and viability of the society would then depend in large part upon the number of people which it could include and thus the labour at its disposal; factors which would also affect the status and power of its leaders. One can thus see very good practical reasons for such

Economic Relationships and Seasonal Labour Use

a society and its leaders to organise the redistribution of labour and produce in order to maintain as viable production units those households most vulnerable to misfortune, including seasonal stress. In the first place this is a condition for the reproduction of the social unit. Second, it is a means whereby rulers and dominant groups can legitimate the extraction of tribute. Finally, in the absence of techniques or means of organisation for increased productivity, there are no alternative means by which the strength and viability of the social unit can be enhanced and/or the wealth and power of its ruling groups increased. In short, in such a situation, there is little to be gained by the sorts of ruler or ruling group likely to be found, from using periods of seasonal vulnerability as an occasion for special exaction, and there are very good reasons for them not to do so.

The second case is a simplified version of one possible development in specialisation and social complexity. Here one has a certain degree of specialisation in the production of consumer items and means of production, with the corollary that households must produce a certain amount of produce to be sold in exchange for such goods. In the case under consideration, rural households still produce the vast bulk of their direct food requirements. The existence or development of larger-scale units of production will be ignored for the present.

Regular market exchange of produce, based on specialisation, leads to the emergence of prices based on the commensuration of values and varying in accordance with market 'laws'. One strict corollary of this is that crop prices will be lower just after harvest, when many peasants are trying to sell, and higher during periods of seasonal shortage. One thus sees the emergence of an economically-based class trading in agricultural produce and specifically buying at harvest time and storing for the rise in price which would surely come. By a further extension, the money gained from such trade may then be lent to peasants and in particular to those peasant families finding themselves short of food or of cash for some vital purpose. One can think of a large number of special reasons why families should be forced to incur debts, but one of the more general would be the liability of families lacking in labour and land (which in this case is assumed to be scarce, to have a price and to be unequally distributed) to make their food supplies last to the end of the season before the following harvest. In such cases it is not only heavy debt burdens in cash or produce which worsen the position of the debtors in subsequent years, but a variety of other conditions which may be imposed upon them, including obligations to work on the fields of the creditor. Obviously it will be of most use for the latter to have access to such labour at times of peak labour need and by the same token times when loss of labour is likely to have the most serious negative effect upon the production of the debtor.

It is not hard to see here the seeds of a third situation — though it will seldom be found in historical reality to have developed in such a 'tidy' way — that is, the development of techniques and methods for the organisation of labour, giving a decided advantage, in terms of productivity, to units of production large enough to require more labour than that of the proprietory household. This, in turn, generates the development of a class of capitalist farmers, using the proceeds from such production as capital to be ploughed into further production in process of accumulation. At this point one finds a further change in the situation of the poor and vulnerable as debts which were previously used to bind them to the creditor are used to loosen them from their land.

Considered as 'history', the above would be the most appalling oversimplification and quite untenable. It omits most of the specific features of real historical developments and all of the subtleties and differences between particular cases. The point is simply to indicate how different forms of productive organisation affect what happens to poor peasants in periods of stress.

Seasonality and social form

It might also be questioned what this has to do with seasonality as such. The answer seems to be that in studying seasonality, one is concerned to discover its impact and to combat or ameliorate the ill-effects, especially those which bear with particular force upon the rural poor. Seasonality as such is inherent in the process of agricultural production and nothing is likely to change that. Even the sharply differentiated seasonal patterns which are commonly considered as most stressful are in fact necessary for the growth of some crops. Nor is one concerned simply with the general effect of policies related to seasonality, but with their effect within given social conditions. Mechanisation to release seasonal labour bottlenecks may increase total production in a given area. But if it provides the occasion for marginalising large numbers of seasonal labourers without alternative employment possibilities, or for increasing the size of large farms by foreclosing peasant mortgages, it can hardly be said to improve the lot of those most in need.

It is certainly useful to study the various seasonal cycles which affect different agricultural production processes as a component of any programme to develop them. But knowledge about seasonality alone does not and cannot provide solutions. Since the effects of seasonality are intimately bound up with specific features of the organisation and control of agricultural production and the social forms within which it occurs, 'seasonality' does not form a very useful object of study on its own. One of the reasons I have found it so difficult to provide useful examples of general application for this section (and why the generalisations attempted appear so stark and unsatisfactory) is an abundance of different combinations of periodicities and their interactions with other aspects of production and social organisation which defies tidy classification.

It is reasonable to generalise that food shortage at a point of the year near to harvest and the peaking to labour requirements are among the most important effects of climatic seasonality in agriculture and when they coincide this obviously exacerbates the overall effect. But, as made clear in other contributions to this book, disease patterns, even if nutritionally-related, do not always coincide with periods of greatest hunger, while labour bottlenecks may occur at different points in the production cycle depending upon techniques, soils, patterns of weed growth and insect attack.

What one can say with some assurance is that the specific periods of seasonal stress in a particular agricultural system will constitute the period of maximum vulnerability for the poorer and more defenceless families, in terms not only of hardship but also of loss of control over means of production and subsequent decreased ability to cope with seasonal stress. Where a process of

Economic Relationships and Seasonal Labour Use

expropriation of small peasants is in progress, it is a fair bet not only that such periods of vulnerability will provide the occasion for such changes in status but that technical improvements aimed at ameliorating the situation will accrue primarily to those who already control the more significant resources and access to credit.

3.2 A Case-Study In Food Production, Sale and Distribution
Emmy B. Simmons

Seasonality in the Zaria area

In the Zaria area of northern Nigeria, the rains generally begin in late April or May. Upland fields are then cleared, ploughed, weeded, and ridged — all with hand tools and manual labour. Later, crops are harvested as they ripen, beginning in August with millet, the major grain crop of guineacorn (sorghum) being harvested, dried, and stored by early January (see Figure 3.1). Only if a farmer controls *fadama*, or low-lying lands with year-round groundwater, is it possible to continue farming through part of the dry season.

While the rains are the major element of importance, other seasonal factors play a part in rural lives. The harmattan dust and winds sporadically turn everything cold and grey in October-February. The religious calendar schedules Ramadan, or *Azumi*, the period of daylight fasting. This exerts a significant effect on consumption, altering the time of the major meal from evening to morning in some households. Most people re-arrange their daily routines for work as well; as eating and drinking are done only before dawn, people may work less because of low energy levels.

To look in some detail at the seasonal dimensions of rural household behaviour, information is brought together here from three surveys of eighteen farming households in Hanwa, a village near Zaria (Norman, 1972; Simmons, 1976a and b). One survey in 1966-7 focused on farm management, another on marketing and credit was done in 1970-1, the same year as a third on household consumption and expenditure. All surveys covered complete cropping cycles.

The eighteen sample households are divided into two groups: those which

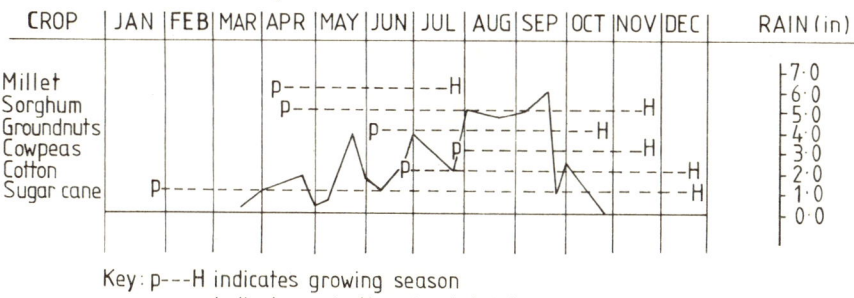

Figure 3.1 Median dates of planting and harvesting in Hanwa village, northern Nigeria, 1966/7. (Source: Norman, 1972)

own milk cattle and those which do not. This division permits comparison of households whose economic existence was closely tied to the land and to the seasons (cattle-owners) with households which appeared to be making a transition to economic lives not wholly dependent on the land (non-cattle-owners).

While the heads of all eighteen households in both 1966 and 1970 identified themselves as 'farmers', secondary occupations indicated their different orientations. *All* of the cattle-owners listed herding activities as their second occupations, while half of the non-cattle-owning household heads reported labour or other wage positions (such as guard or gardener) in Zaria City as their secondary source of employment. It should not be assumed that cattle-owners are more 'subsistence-oriented' or poorer than non-cattle-owners, however. Milk is a 'cash crop' and provides a steady income which supplements production of crops for consumption.

Production and work cycles

Apart from the basic distinction of livestock ownership, cattle-owning households in Hanwa differ from those which do not own cattle in other ways. For example, in 1966-7, they cultivated upland holdings which were considerably larger than those of the non-cattle-owners. This gave them the substantially greater production bases reflected in total output levels (Norman, 1972). The non-cattle-owners, however, had somewhat more *fadama* land, permitting them to grow different crops (e.g. sugar cane) and to spread labour somewhat differently throughout the year.

Between 1966 and 1970, farms of cattle-owners remained about the same size, while the mean size of non-cattle-owner farms decreased by 12 per cent. In relation to the size of households, though, this represents a decrease for both groups. For the cattle-owning households, this decrease was from 0.9 to 0.8 acres (or 0.36 to 0.33 ha) per person, while for non-cattle-owners, the reduction in available land was from 0.6 to 0.5 acres (0.24 to 0.20 ha) per person. Average grain output for millet and guineacorn (sorghum) grown in mixtures was 1229 lb/acre (1380 kg/ha) for cattle-owners and 1087 lb/acre (1220 kg/ha) for those not owning cattle. From this one may estimate that about 0.3 acres or 0.12 hectares can theoretically supply one person's energy needs. With the reductions that took place prior to 1970, two households among those not owning cattle fell below this level. However, none of the cattle-owning households had so little land.

Cattle-owners in Hanwa appeared to prefer cotton as a cash crop, while those without cattle favoured groundnuts (see Table 3.1). Cattle-owners in general grew fewer crops in less complex mixtures; inter-cropping two was most common. Non-cattle-owners put nearly half of their cultivated land to three or more crops (Norman, 1972, p. 73). Both groups of households sold part of their food-crop production, so it is difficult to generalise about cash-crop/food-crop preferences.

Of all the factors of production under the Hanwa farmers' control (as rain is not), allocation of labour is the most sensitive seasonal decision. Seasonal demands for labour vary considerably, and the ability of the household to provide the work effort needed contributes greatly to the success of a production cycle. The farm manager has two options: to draw only upon the household's

TABLE 3.1. Land ownership and use, seven cattle-owners, ten non-cattle-owners, Hanwa, 1966/67 and 1970/71

	Average cattle-owning household	Average household not owning cattle
1970/71: Total crop acreage	11.41	6.00
1966/67: Total crop acreage	11.40	6.84
Upland acreage (%)	98.6	88.0
Fadama acreage (%)	1.4	12.0
Fallow	2.2	2.5
Percentage of acreage allocated to selected crops (1966/67):		
Guineacorn	64.3	58.3
Millet	58.0	49.9
Groundnuts	20.9	31.7
Cowpeas	15.6	52.9
Maize	6.5	16.7
Sugarcane	–	6.0
Cotton	35.3	2.5
Sweet potatoes	9.9	10.3
Cassava	4.1	15.1
Tomatoes	3.7	0.9
Okra	7.9	2.2
Pepper	2.7	1.0

Source: Norman (1972), pp. D2 ff. and Hays (1975), pp. 142.

labour force, or to hire labour. Table 3.2 shows that cattle-owners invested less household labour in crop production than those without cattle, and used more wage labour. They hired 77.5 man-hours per cultivated acre (192 man-hr/ha), as opposed to the 50.6 man-hours per acre (125 man-hr/ha) hired by the non-cattle-owners. This may be because the period of the labour bottleneck in the fields (April-July) coincides with the time when work involving the cattle is also heaviest. Households not owning cattle have a more even work load from month to month. Labourers were hired mainly in July-August by cattle-owners for jobs such as planting cotton and harvesting millet. Non-cattle-owners used hired labour most in April-May for land preparation and planting. The latter group were able to concentrate their greatest amount of off-farm, wage earning activity in December-March, which is the dry season when there is least farm work to do.

Average figures from the farm management survey indicate that the contribution of women in terms of total time spent on farm tasks is miniscule. It is actually less than one per cent, and is concentrated in the harvesting months (September-December). Off-farm employment of women, however, is considerable. All women in cattle-owning households sell milk in Zaria City, keeping only small amounts for household consumption. Some mitigate the seasonal impact of variable milk supplies somewhat by diluting it with *kuka* (cream of tartar) and water. With the proceeds of the milk sales, each buys household food supplies (salt, oil, vegetables, meat). Many of the women in

TABLE 3.2. Seasonal work patterns: on-farm and off-farm (income-earning) labour for seventeen farmers, Hanwa, 1966-7

	Cattle-owners		Non-cattle-owners	
	Farm crops	Off-farm including cattle	Farm	Off-farm
Percentage of annual man-hours by month:				
April	12.5 %	9.0 %	9.0 %	8.5 %
May	12.6	10.1	12.8	7.9
June	11.5	11.5	10.3	7.8
July	13.2	10.8	10.9	9.3
August	9.3	0.9	10.8	9.1
September	7.5	7.7	8.8	5.8
October	8.1	9.4	9.1	5.2
November	10.2	9.1	8.7	6.9
December	6.1	7.8	7.4	10.7
January	4.7	5.8	6.1	10.1
February	3.3	5.3	4.2	10.1
March	1.0	4.6	1.9	8.1
	100	100	100	100
Annual man-hours of household labour	1707.4	665.6	1838.2	494.2
Annual man-hours per cultivated acre	189.8	–	343.0	–
Hired man-hours per cultivated acre	77.5		50.6	
Total man-hours per cultivated acre	267.3		393.6	

Source: Norman (1972).

the case-study households also manufactured millet balls (*fura*) which they then sold with the milk as a midday meal to Zaria workers.

Household food availability

The case-study households all appeared to have adequate grain storage facilities to permit nearly the entire amount to be stored in the compound *rumbu* (granary) in an unthreshed state. The drop in humidity at the time of the guineacorn (sorghum) harvest helps to ensure thorough drying, and minimises storage loss from causes associated with dampness. Those households with carry-over stocks large enough to cause storage problems apparently either sold the excess when they were able to judge the coming yield, or gave away the old stocks as *zakka* (a 10 per cent tithe required by Muslim custom).

According to the food consumption figures collected in 1970-1 and the results of the marketing and storage survey of the same year, the rate of

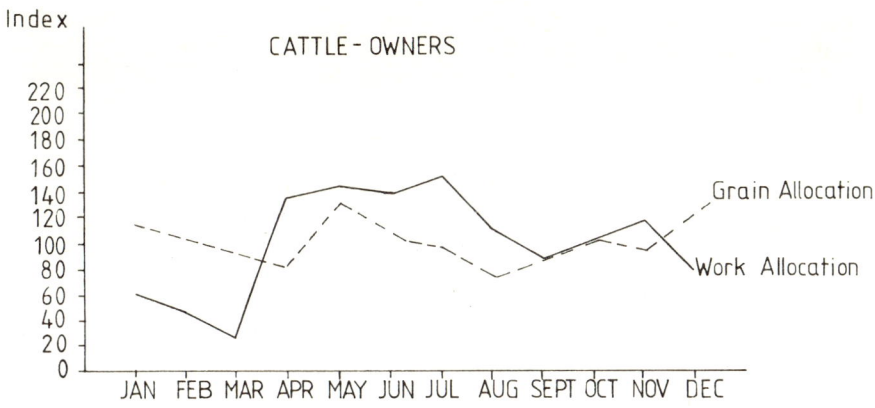

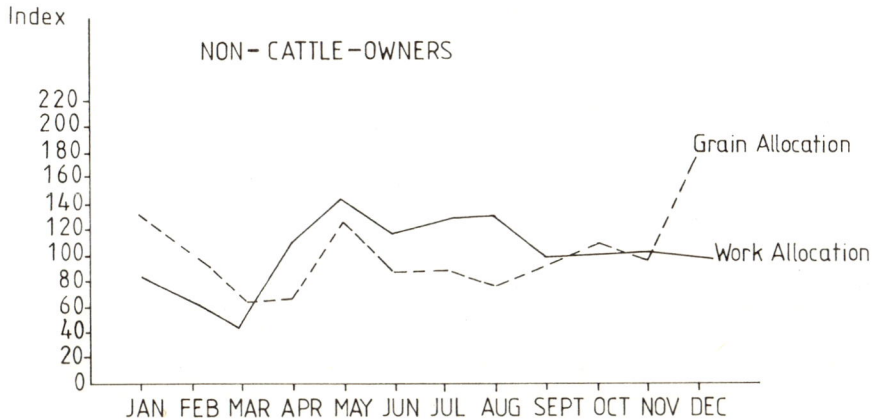

Figure 3.2 Food consumption in relation to work done for cattle-owners and non-cattle-owners in Hanwa village, northern Nigeria, 1970/71. Food consumption is indicated by grain allocations from stored production, purchases, and gifts. Both grain allocation and work allocation are expressed as an index, with monthly means as 100.

removal of grain from storage for consumption seems to be seasonally adjusted. Extra amounts are taken out of storage as labour efforts of household members increase (see Figure 3.2).

This additional intake of food is not expected from the experience of 'hungry seasons' quoted in Chapter 2. There, instances were mentioned where less food was available at the time of year when work demands were highest (see Section 2.4). In the Zaria area, it may be that needs for additional food in the heavy labour season are better planned for than elsewhere. Larger food consumptions at these times may also reflect the fact that women in the area do not work in the fields, so their time for cooking is not cut short when extra agricultural labour is required.

However, even though energy intakes and total food consumptions increase, Figure 3.2 suggests that energy needs to meet seasonal labour demands may still exceed consumption. People may still be 'hungry' at this time. Even so, calculations of the energy required for work suggest that cattle-owning households meet all their 'needs', and households without cattle fall short only in the October-January period.

Of course, all households also have the option to purchase grain to supplement stocks, and some reported receipt of gift grain from others. Of the eight cattle-owning households, only one purchased regularly on a monthly basis, in quantities clearly designed for immediate consumption. The farmer concerned was a newcomer to the village and had only one acre of land, and so was atypical. Three cattle-owners purchased no grain at all, and the four others purchased irregularly in relatively large lots. Non-cattle-owners, by contrast, all reported more or less regular purchases in small quantities. This pattern helps to account for the sustained rise in grain intake in the rainy season.

Sales and gifts of grain

Hanwa farmers who do not own cattle sell less grain than their cattle-owning neighbours simply because their production is lower. Yet sales of millet by farmers without cattle were almost twice as high as those by cattle-owners. As the purchase behaviour of the cattle-owners also indicated the possibility of some minor trade (though none was a trader in a regular way), it is interesting to consider sales behaviour in relation to price (see Table 3.3). Three points are of particular note:

(1) The importance of millet sales in June by non-cattle-owners indicates that cash needs for hired labour and consumption may have been partly met by this means.
(2) Relatively high guineacorn sales in October by cattle-owners correlates with the 'cleaning out of old stock'.
(3) The guineacorn dumping by cattle-owners when prices were relatively high reflects the advantages that Hanwa residents with sufficient stocks have in being able to respond easily to market conditions in Zaria.

Family ceremonies (naming, marriage, death) occur throughout the year. Most require special food preparation, and gifts of food are normally involved. Table 3.4 indicates the extent of both gifts and tithes.

Religious occasions are scheduled on a lunar calendar, and thus do not fall in the same months every year. In the 1970-1 survey year, Ramadan began on 30 October 1970. It was reflected in high expenditures during October-November owing to the emphasis at this time on family gift-giving, particularly of clothing.

The special role of *zakka*, the Muslim tithe, in bringing about immediate post-harvest distribution of food-grain production should also be mentioned. While farmers might be unwilling to admit their inability to meet this obligation, most of the Hanwa farmers reported the approximately 10 per cent *zakka*

Economic Relationships and Seasonal Labour Use

TABLE 3.3. Sales, prices, and seasonality: eighteen Hanwa farmers, 1970-1

	Millet			Guineacorn		
	Relative Zaria price*	Cattle-owners' sales	Non-cattle-owners' sales	Relative Zaria price*	Cattle-owners' sales	Non-cattle-owners' sales
		(percentage of total)			(percentage of total)	
September 1970	—	—	—	49	—	23.0
October	—	—	—	46	45.7	26.6
November	8	—	11.1	-11	4.6	29.0
December 1970	5	31.3	5.2	0	—	—
January 1971	-6	10.5	6.1	-2	—	21.4
February	-2	10.4	11.1	7	—	—
March	2	22.3	6.1	17	4.0	—
April	-6	—	8.4	6	23.1	—
May	-11	5.2	4.4	23	4.6	—
June	5	6.2	34.8	21	13.4	—
July	16	5.2	4.5	18	4.6	—
August	14	9.1	8.5	16	—	—

Note: *The relative Zaria price is the percentage the observed market price was above (or below) the expected price for that month. Thus a high positive relative price would indicate an advantageous time for selling, while a large negative would indicate a price slump.

Source: Hays (1975), pp. 87, 88, and unpublished figures on sales.

TABLE 3.4. Social and religious obligations of eighteen households, Hanwa, 1970-1

	Lbs. of grain given away		Expenditures (all Hanwa)*		
	Cattle-owners	Non-cattle-owners	Meat	Ceremonies, gifts	Clothing
			(shillings/household/week)		
January	190	46			
February	130	40	19.20	35.31	—
March	111	20			
April	55	44	4.98	34.34	
May	78	133			
June	45	34	9.86	8.83	
July	21	7			
August	23	5	4.47	2.42	—
September	452	227			
October	81	31	9.82	9.08	20.20
November	52	53			
December	629	338	9.46	11.81	0.86

Note: *These were tabulated on a bi-monthly basis and are listed here in the first month of the two-month period.

Sources: Hays (1975), unpublished data on monthly sales and Simmons (1976b), pp. 93 ff.

allocation, mainly in September and December.

It is striking that gifts and tithes entail the free disposal of about 22 per cent of crop production for both groups of farmers. This fact, in the face of marginal household supplies for consumption, reinforces the impression one has of the importance of social and religious obligations in the local community.

Taxes are also an annual obligation. They are collected by the village head in December-January. In addition to the tax to be paid by every adult male, cattle-owners are expected to pay *jangali*, or cattle taxes. Their reluctance to reveal the exact sizes of their herds, and their known under-reporting of tax payments make this a seasonal obligation that is very difficult to analyse. Common wisdom has it that farmers are forced to sell their grain at harvest (when prices are low) in order to pay taxes, which are conveniently due just after harvest. In Hanwa, however, cattle-owners harvested cotton for sale, and those without cattle had groundnuts, so it does not appear that tax needs were a major reason for selling grain.

Conclusion

From the above discussion, it should be evident that cattle-owners are self-sufficient in grain, even after sales, gifts, and tithes, but non-cattle-owners are not, and rely on purchases to make ends meet. While seasonal factors do have a major influence on the lives of Hanwa farmers, such factors do not seem to pose major constraints on farmers' capacities to improve their economic situations. Farmers have generally evolved systems which can cope with the normal pattern of seasonal change. In Hanwa, the more important constraints are the amounts of land available and the opportunities for productive employment to supplement farm incomes.

An understanding of the seasonal dimensions of the Hanwa farmers' productive capacity and output patterns does, however, provide some useful information for the programming of development processes. Crop technology innovations which require more intensive labour inputs in the rainy season, for example, are not likely to be adopted by cattle-owners. Those crop changes which can be shown to improve output per acre with no increase in labour demands, especially if they are also responsive to higher levels of fertilization, stand a better chance with the cattle-owning group. Farmers who do not have cattle, on the other hand, are constrained by land and cash availability and, since they are now able to provide a level of living from their farm resources which is only just adequate, can be expected to be slightly more averse to risk than cattle-owners. For the non-cattle-owning households to adopt new crop technologies, improved credit facilities at the beginning of the rainy season will be critical.

3.3 Labour and Subsistence In a Pastoral Economy
Jeremy Swift

Seasonality in milk production

Seasonality is at the very heart of nomadic pastoralism which has its origins in an opportunistic effort to exploit, through the use of domestic animals, the huge potential offered by the rich plant growth caused by the rains each year. A necessary condition is that households should be able to survive the difficult conditions that follow. The pastoral economy is built around this sharp seasonal dichotomy.

The Kel Adrar Twareg of north Mali are nomadic pastoralists. Apart from a declining caravan trade and increasing wage labour migration to north African construction sites and oil fields and west African towns, their livelihood comes solely from herds and flocks. They use Saharan and Sahelian pastures in and around the Adrar mountains, where annual rainfall is between 70 and 200 mm. The Kel Adrar divide their year into three approximately equal seasons: a hot rainy season, starting around June, a cold dry season (when temperatures at night drop, although the days remain hot), and a hot dry season.

Rainfall is not only low, but is seasonally very concentrated. In terms of the classification of climatic seasonality presented in Chapter 1, the area is divided between the G5 and G6 climatic classes, which denote extreme seasonality. The rainfall is also highly variable. Similarly, plant cover is temporally and spatially variable, and shows a marked seasonal peak in growth coinciding with the short period when there is adequate soil moisture. A large proportion of plant cover consists of annual grasses, the seeds of which germinate and grow in a period of weeks after adequate rainfall. Perennial grasses, however, come into leaf after the very first rains, well before the annuals. Shrubs and trees grow more slowly and continue after grass growth has stopped. Thus the perennial grasses extend the availability of good grazing at the beginning of the rains, and shrubs and trees provide food for livestock well after the end of the very short wet season (Breman and Cissé, 1977).

The two main components of Sahelian pastoral diets are milk and millet (and dates in a few places). Milk is an important item in all diets, contributing between 25 and 75 per cent of total food energy. Where pastoralists do not practise agriculture, the contribution of milk does not fall below 40 per cent. Millet (grown or bought) is important in all diets, meat only marginally so (Swift, 1979).

Milk is a highly seasonal food since its production depends on the breeding cycle of the female animals in the household herd. The timing of these cycles is a joint product of biology and management.

Cattle and camels come into breeding condition in the rainy season, responding to the fresh pasture available then. Gestation periods are nine months for cows and twelve months for camels, after which the animals give milk for five to six months (cows) or up to twelve months (camels). Sheep and goats have a five-month gestation and are thus theoretically capable of breeding twice in a year. Ewes lactate for two to four months, goats for five to ten months.

The Kel Adrar and other Sahelian pastoralists modify the effects of climatic seasonality on their animal breeding cycles in a number of ways. Herdsmen commonly manage their camels to give a calving interval of twenty-four months, which ensures good lactation and births in the wet season every second year. Cattle calving intervals tend to be around either twelve or twenty-four months, with a majority of births taking place during the rains. This is clearly advantageous to both pastoralists and calves since it means that cows are well fed during lactation, with correspondingly high milk yields, and also that the calves have plenty of grass to eat at weaning.

Sheep breeding is controlled more directly, both to ensure that lambs are born at the best moment of the year, and to prevent two lambings except in good pasture years. In normal years, rams are prevented from tupping the ewes until December, so that lambs are born early in the rainy season. This timing means that the lambs have grass to eat at weaning, and also that water and fresh grass are available for ewes to ensure a good lactation.

The reproductive cycle of Kel Adrar goats is regulated differently, reflecting the different ecological requirements and economic utility of goats. In a normal year, kids are born from September to January. This is after the rains, but it is the season when tree and shrub growth is still active. There is thus plenty of food for the lactating goats and for the kids at weaning. In good years, the goats are allowed to breed again and two kid crops are produced.

The seasonal arrangement of normal lactation periods for three of the four species of animals can be seen from Figures 3.3, 3.4 and 3.5. Comparison of these diagrams shows the relative success of the Kel Adrar in spreading their

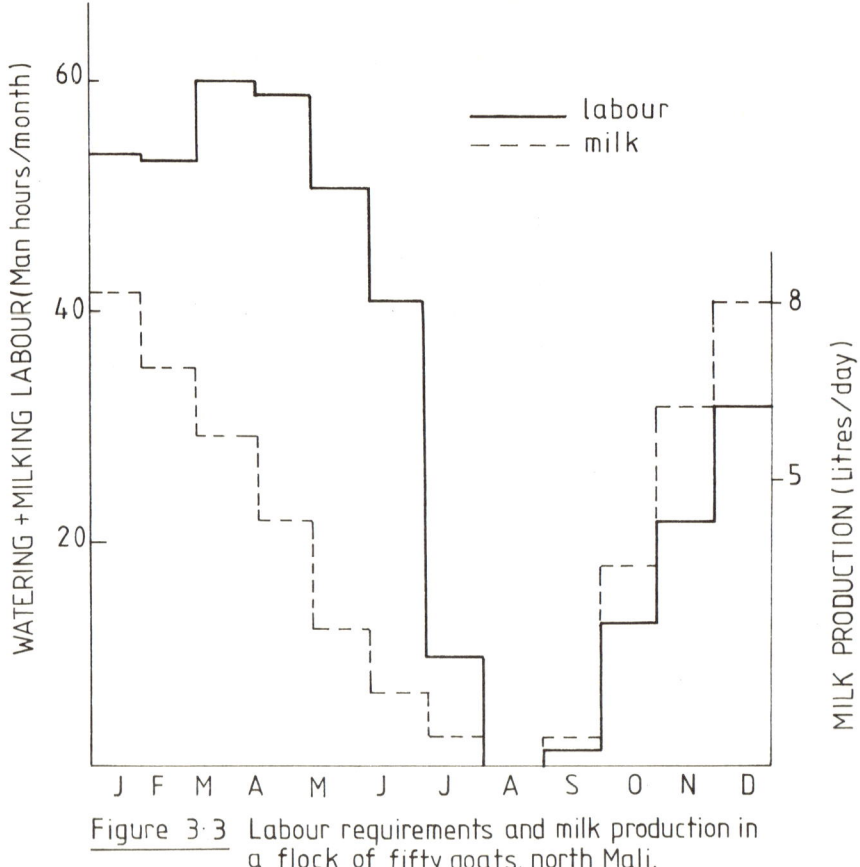

Figure 3.3 Labour requirements and milk production in a flock of fifty goats, north Mali.

Economic Relationships and Seasonal Labour Use

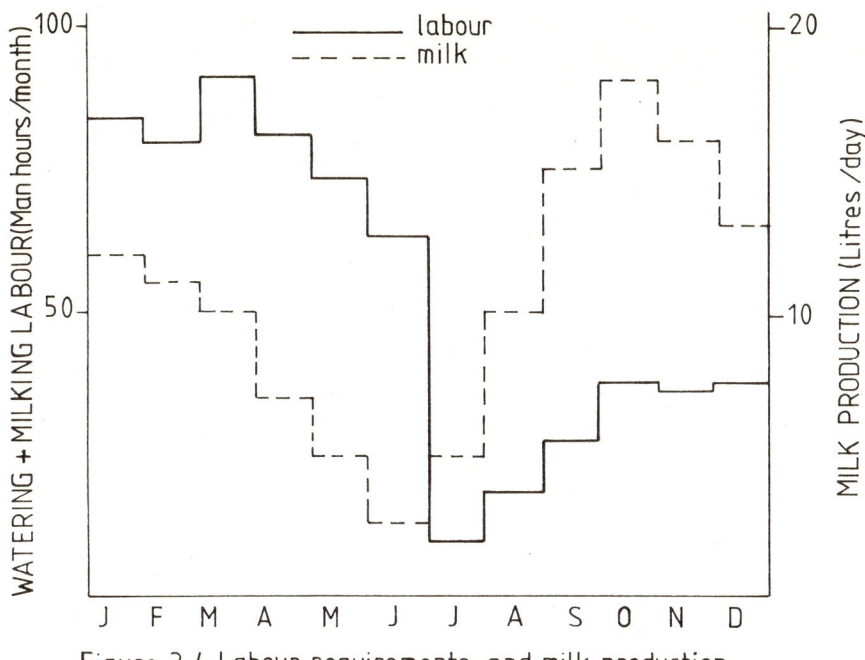

Figure 3·4 Labour requirements and milk production in a herd of twenty-five camels, north Mali.

milk supply throughout the year, as far as the extreme climatic seasonality allows, and also their failure to accomplish this completely. There is a period of variable length in the hot dry season, and especially in April-May, when milk may be scarce or completely lacking.

Of course, not every Kel Adrar household has all four kinds of animal. Poor households rely principally on goats. Rich households not only have more animals, but they have three or four species, thus maximising their chances of some milk supply for much of the year.

The seasonality of milk production is made more serious by the difficulty of storing any milk surplus. Camel milk, of which there may be a large surplus in some months, does not make cheese for biochemical reasons. Cheese and clarified butter are made with milk from other animals, but small daily surpluses are not easy to convert in this way, and neither cheese nor butter are particularly good forms of storage in any case. Traditionally, Twareg (and some other Saharan and Sahelian pastoralists) used to drink very large quantities of milk at times when it was abundant. This was especially true of the women, who got very fat as a result, thereby storing the food energy in their bodies.

Given the difficulty of storing milk, it would be logical for the Kel Adrar to exchange or sell it at the time of greatest milk surplus. This is not possible, because the main milk surplus occurs at the time of year when householders are making use of remote, wet-season pastures unusable at other times, and

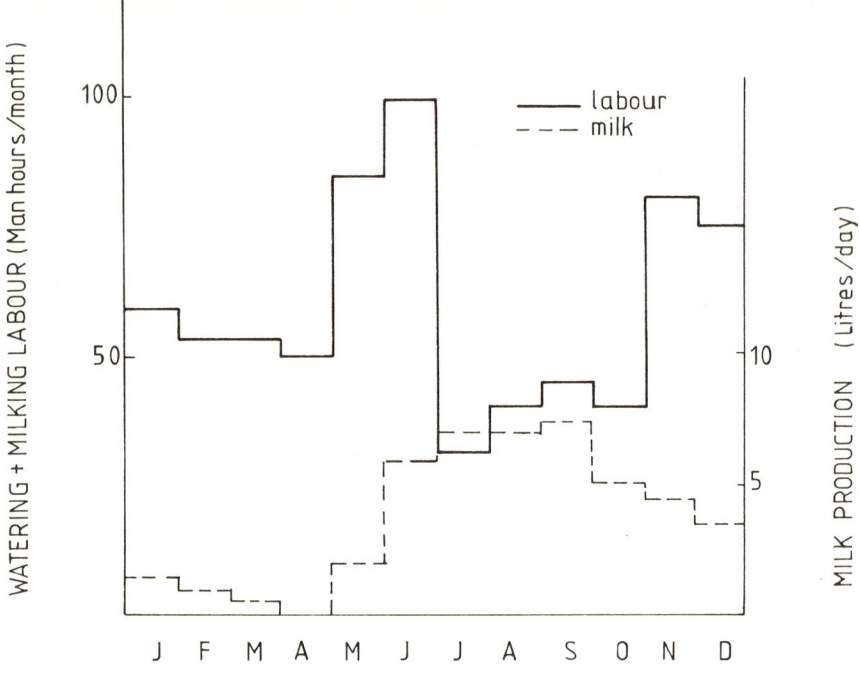

Figure 3·5 Labour requirements and milk production in a herd of twenty-five cattle, north Mali.

are consequently farthest from potential markets. It would also be logical to exchange surplus milk for millet, but there would be difficulty for a nomadic population in storing the large amounts of millet which would be so obtained.

Labour requirements

The labour requirements of Kel Adrar herding vary seasonally. There are three main herding tasks: supervision, watering, and milking. Supervision of animals is largely passive and requires little more than the presence of the herdsman. Milking does not need a large amount of labour either. Camels and cattle are normally milked twice a day by a man, ideally with a boy on hand to keep the calves away. Sheep are milked by men or women, but milking the goats is usually a woman's task, although men do not hesitate to take over when necessary.

Drawing water for the animals is an arduous, energy-consuming task, however. It is also a task for which peak labour requirements occur in the dry season, when milk production is at its lowest. Figures 3.3 to 3.5 illustrate the effect of this. For all species except goats, milk production is lowest in the January-May period, which corresponds to the hot dry season in which maximum watering labour is needed. Goats are an exception, apart from a period from March to June when milk production falls off.

These points principally concern the men, who water the camels and cattle. However, since millet is the main food in the hot dry season, labour for pounding it and for cooking puts a heavy load on the women also. Children may also be fully employed fetching drinking water several miles to the camp. The hot dry season, therefore, is a time when demanding labour requirements affecting the whole community coincide with food shortages.

The Kel Adrar Twareg periodically sell animals from their herds, or salt from the mine at Tawdenni in the Sahara, in order to buy millet. Most sales appear to take place either at the end of the cold season, when a few animals can most easily be taken several hundred kilometres south to the Niger and a good price obtained. During the hot season, animals in bad condition are sold at low prices more locally. Because of the difficulty for nomadic people in storing grain, they have to buy millet as they need it, mainly during the hot dry season when prices are highest.

Adaptations to the seasonal pattern

The Kel Adrar attempt to mitigate the worst effects of the extreme seasonality they experience in a number of ways. Two widely different ones are demographic regulation and occasional slaughter of animals.

In a pastoral economy where food supply varies widely and where output is insensitive to increased labour inputs, there is advantage in keeping human populations small and slowly growing relative to the herds. Although I have no demographic data for the Kel Adrar, there is evidence that African nomadic pastoralists in general have low rates of natural increase compared to neighbouring farming people, and that these are due to low birth and death rates (Swift, 1977). These differences cannot be ascribed to health or nutrition, which are generally better among herding than farming peoples, but seem to be the result of social regulation of the demographic processes. There is little data on this, but in various African pastoral societies, such practices as generation grading coupled with a ban on child bearing in the junior grades, late marriages, and post-natal sexual abstinence are found. There is a suggestion that Somali pastoralists practise sexual abstinence during the dry season and in drought years. This general brake on demographic processes, by keeping population low in relation to resources, should theoretically help households through the difficult season. But this must remain a hypothesis until more data are available.

At quite another level, the Kel Adrar supplement their food supply at the moment of greatest shortage by the slaughter of animals in an informal rain-making ceremony. If the onset of the rains appears to be delayed, animals donated by richer herdsmen are killed and the meat is widely shared, and this is accompanied by prayers for rain. The ceremony is repeated until the rains start. This appears to serve two purposes: first, that of providing meat (which is not a common part of the diet) at a time of nutritional stress, and second, redistributing food from the rich to the poor.

Seasonal Dimensions to Rural Poverty

Seasonality and poverty

In the Kel Adrar and other Sahelian pastoral societies, there is a network of traditional non-market transactions with animals which serves to mitigate seasonal or sudden unexpected food shortages. If a household does not have enough animals to provide a sufficient milk supply, it can go to a richer household and borrow animals according to one of a number of standard agreements, which include the seasonal loan of a lactating animal. In minor seasonal or other crises, these transactions serve as redistributive mechanisms by which the rich help the poor. But in more serious crises, the system works in favour of the rich since, having loaned animals to other people, they have many favours to call in. At such times poor households are unable to borrow animals, and are sometimes forced out of the pastoral economy.

This tends to support the argument put forward in Section 3.1 that many communities have mechanisms for coping with the normal pattern of the seasons, but that they have much greater difficulty in coping with climatic variability. Seasonality, as distinct from variability, is not in the end a critical factor. Certainly it cannot explain the increasingly precarious situation of Sahelian pastoralism. As with many of the situations discussed in Section 3.1, explanations for this deterioration must be sought in the economic, political and ecological changes first set in motion by colonial occupation, which have accelerated in recent years (Swift, 1977). The process by which outsiders buy into the production process (buying rights to water which control access to pasture, buying animals, hiring labour) is well under way, and was hastened by the 1973 drought. The traditional self-help mechanisms of Sahelian pastoralists are breaking down. In these new conditions, seasonality and especially climatic variability may become more important than before. With each drought year, an increasing number of poor people may be forced out of their pastoral lifestyle, being compelled to sell rights to their wells or seek work as hired cow-hands.

The implication of this is that seasonality itself should not be a main target for development policies; these should be directed at more fundamental policy variables such as control of land and water.

However, efforts should be made to understand and combat seasonality in any pastoral development programme in the Sahel. It should be noted, for example, that the effects of seasonality will be accentuated by any effort to promote the permanent settlement of nomadic pastoralists unless irrigated or stored fodder can be provided for much of the year. This is unlikely to be economically viable in most of Africa, so pastoral development policy should seek to preserve and develop the flexibility of pastoral movement.

Among other practical measures, there should be emphasis on maintaining a diversity of livestock species, and on developing simple methods for storing milk or cheese suitable for use in remote places.

Finally, it should be noted that in tropical unimodal climates, maximum milk production from most animals comes during the rainy season, simultaneously with the period of most acute food shortage in any crop-producing economies in the same region. With better means of storing and transporting milk (or cheese), it might be possible to make pastoral and crop production systems complement one another with benefit to both. Communities in southern Africa which combine the raising of cattle and the growing of grain crops already exploit this complementary relationship to some extent: milk production increases before the grain crops are ready and helps to shorten the hungry season (Jones, 1963). In Sahelian west Africa there is also the possibility of increased economic linkages with north African economies belonging to a different climate system. This will be made easier by the trans-Saharan road now nearing completion, and would particularly benefit livestock-rearing people.

3.4 The Seasonality of Prices and Wages In Bangladesh
Rafiqul Huda Chaudhury

Introduction

The seasonal dimensions of rural poverty may be studied by reference to a wide range of criteria. One might consider seasonal variations in employment, in food prices, in wages, or in nutrition and disease. All these criteria of rural poverty are applied to Bangladesh in various parts of this book. For example, in Chapter 2 (Section 2.5), the seasonality of nutrition and disease in the Matlab thana case-study area was discussed. Mention was made there of the way in which seasonal changes in wage rates and food prices affect the amount of food that the poor are able to buy. This theme is taken up here and discussed in relation to the whole of Bangladesh. The complementary theme of seasonal variation in employment is discussed by Clay in the next part of this chapter (Section 3.5).

Crop production, particularly of rice and jute, is the predominant economic activity in Bangladesh, accounting for nearly half of the gross domestic product and over 70 per cent of employment. Thus to understand the seasonality of either food prices or wages in Bangladesh, and their effect on the poor, it is essential to consider the crop calendar in some detail. It is a complex calendar because, in many places, high rainfall and ample groundwater make it possible to raise more than one crop each year. There is added complication because the precise timing of the rice crops depends on whether they are sown broadcast in the fields or grown in a seed-bed and then transplanted. In fact, three main types of rice crop can be distinguished, and are referred to as the *aus, aman,* and *boro* crops. Their distinctive places in the crop calendar are indicated in Table 3.5.

The most important of these crops has traditionally been *aman*. In 1976-7, *aman* accounted for 60 per cent of rice production. The corresponding percentages for *boro* and *aus* were 14 and 26 respectively (Agriculture Ministry, 1977). Thus it appears that the *aman* crop is of over-riding importance among agricultural activities in rural Bangladesh, and this point has to be borne in mind while interpreting the data on seasonal prices and wages.

The cropping calendar creates considerable problems of sharp peaks in the demand for labour. According to one estimate, 40 per cent of the demand for hired labour is concentrated in the months of April and May alone (Ahmed, 1973). Demand for labour in agriculture is spasmodic. This is because

Seasonal Dimensions to Rural Poverty

TABLE 3.5. Major crops in Bangladesh

Type of crop	Abbreviation used in Section 3.5	Growing season	Time of sowing and transplanting	Time of harvest
Rice:				
Aus,[a] broadcast	B. aus)	early monsoon;[b]	March–	June–
Aus, transplanted	T. aus)	*Kharif*	April	August
Aman,[a] broadcast (deep-water variety)	B. aman))	mid to late monsoon;[b]	June–	October–
Aman, transplanted (also called *Shail*)	T. aman)	*Kharif*	August	December
Boro,[a] transplanted	boro	winter,[c] dry season; *Rabi*	January– February	March– June
Jute		early monsoon[b]	April– May	July– August
Wheat and *Barley*		winter,[c] dry season	October– November	February– March
Pulses (lentils, gram)		winter,[c] dry season	December– February	February– March

Notes:
  a) The introduction of modern rice varieties with short growing periods, and the use of mechanised irrigation is obscuring the distinction between these different rice-growing seasons.
  b) These are the main *kharif* crops; other crops grown in the same season include chillies, tropical vegetables, and mung.
  c) Other *rabi* or cool season crops are rape, mustard, and temperate vegetables.

agricultural operations have to be performed within a short and specific time span. For example, harvesting has to be completed very quickly or the paddy is dropped from the stalk, and often the land has to be prepared immediately for a second crop. Sowing must await the onset of the rains, but must then be done very promptly.

Many of the rural poor depend on finding paid employment, and their opportunities are affected by the hectic level of work in some seasons and its slack pace in others. The busiest time is the March-June period, and the slackest is September-October. Some 80 per cent of the monsoon rain comes in the months May-September, and agricultural activity is focused on the earlier part of that season.

Food prices and wage rates

Rice constitutes the basic diet in Bangladesh and other food items (wheat, fish, vegetables and pulses) are usually considered as supplements. According to the 1975-6 nutrition survey, rice on average constituted 61 per cent of the total food intake of the population (Dacca University, 1977).

There is a close relationship between the supply and the price of rice. This can be verified by examining prices during the pre-harvest and post-harvest

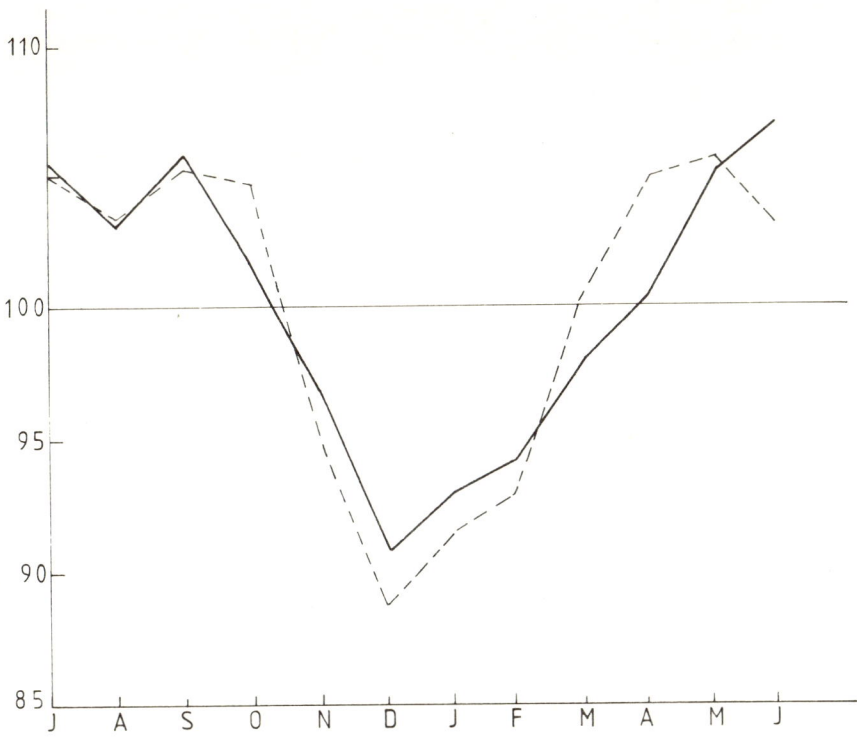

Figure 3.6 The wholesale price of coarse rice in Bangladesh: an adjusted seasonal index for 1953-68 (full line) and 1968-76 (dashed line). Computed from raw data given in Monthly Bulletin in Statistics (various issues), Bangladesh Bureau of Statistics.

periods. As an example, Figure 3.6 illustrates seasonal variations in the price of coarse rice, and shows that prices are high in May and September, before the *aus* and *aman* harvests respectively, and low during the main, *aman*, harvest, especially in December. The price begins to rise in January, and this trend continues up to June. In the June-August period there is often some fall in price as the *aus* harvest comes onto the market. The *boro* rice crop, which is harvested during March-April, does not seem to have had a discernible impact. This is predictable since it has contributed only a small fraction (14 per cent) of total rice production (Agriculture Ministry, 1977).

A considerable seasonality in prices is evident. The dominant effect of the *aman* crop is expressed by its impact in pushing down the price of rice over a long period. The slackest season in agricultural work (September-October) unfortunately coincides with one of the highest peaks in rice prices, and this may therefore be a time when the poor are especially vulnerable.

Seasonal Dimensions to Rural Poverty

Wages vary with the seasons partly because of changes in the number of hours worked. In one village, Char-Samraj, labourers worked five hours per day in the slackest season and ten to twelve hours in the busiest time. In the same village, the daily wage rate was found to vary between Taka 3/- in the slack period up to Taka 12/- during busier times (Islam, 1977). The variation in wage rate partly reflects the variation in the number of hours worked per day. However, the higher wage rate during the peak period is also due to a shortage of labour at this time (Habibullah, 1962).

Analysis of time series data on monthly wage rates (without counting

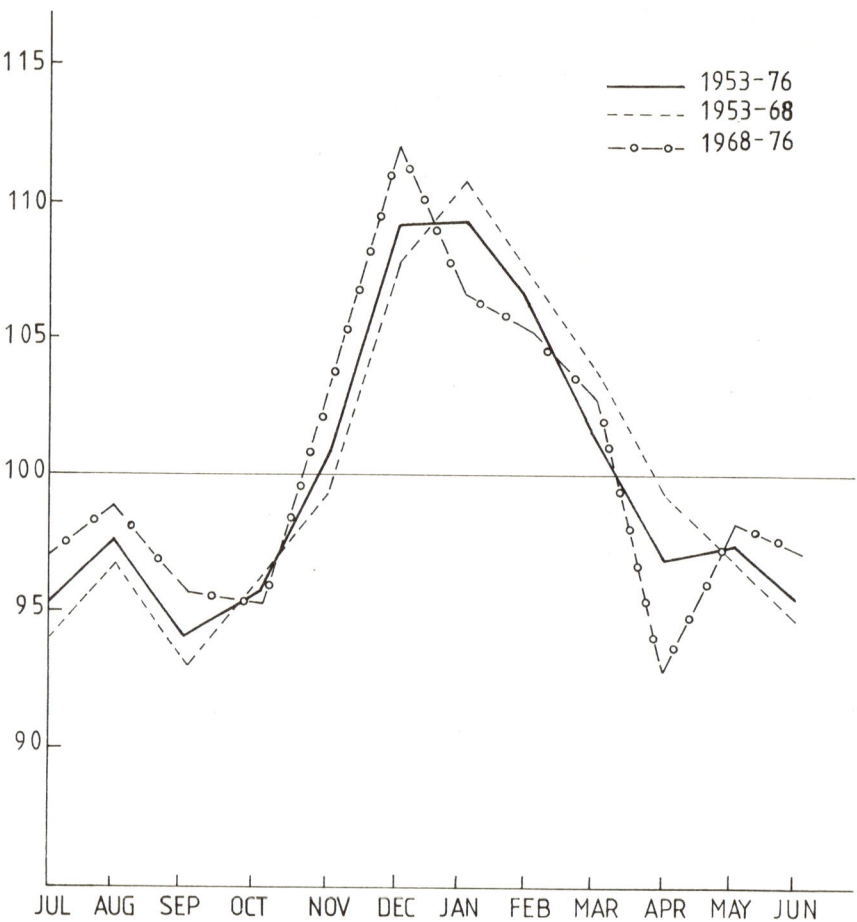

Figure 3·7 An index of real daily wage rates for agricultural labour in Bangladesh. Indices are calculated separately for each time period from raw data from the Bangladesh Directorate of Agriculture, Weather and Crop Report.

payments in the form of food) also indicates a slightly higher daily wage rate during the peak season (especially in May) than the average wage rate for the year (Chaudhury, 1980). However, this rise in wage rate during the peak season of agricultural work is cancelled out by the high price of rice prevailing at that time. Therefore, in terms of real wages, no benefit accrues to the wage labourers during the season of most hectic work, despite longer working hours. The season when the purchasing power of agricultural wages rises is November-February (see Figure 3.7) when food prices are very low.

Adjustment mechanisms

People resort to a number of strategies to adjust to the lean period which include borrowing money or migration in search of work. There is also a strong tendency for the rural poor to combine different occupations, because agriculture cannot guarantee a year-round livelihood. Non-farm jobs include felling trees, cutting firewood, sawing timber, building houses, repairing houses, repairing furniture, boat building, plying boats for trade, and trading in fruit, betel nuts, stationery or groceries. Fishing is an important activity in the period of slack in agricultural work.

Migration is another strategy adopted by the rural poor to offset the worst effects of seasonality in agriculture. Some people migrate to areas with a cropping pattern different from their own, where agricultural work may be available to them at times when it is not available at home. Other people take urban jobs as mill-hands, cooks, domestic servants, taxi drivers, bus conductors, bricklayers, or dock workers (Habibullah, 1962). Although seasonal migration brings some economic relief to those concerned, it has certain negative consequences. There is evidence that migrants are willing to accept wages below the normal market wage rate (Wood, 1977). This has the effect of depressing wage rates for all, and makes it more difficult for local labourers to find work. This process has been noted particularly in parts of Comilla District where 'green revolution' crops are grown (Wood, 1977).

The most desperate survival strategy adopted by the rural poor is to accept a consumption loan from money lenders or big farmers at a very high rate of interest. For example, if a family borrows one maund of paddy during the pre-harvest period, they generally have to pay back one-and-a-half maunds after the next harvest, possibly two months later. Such loans are alleged to be one of the factors responsible for increasing pauperisation and for perpetuating patron-client relationships (Alamgir, 1976). Marginal farmers and landless labourers, knowing full well that they will have to seek help from money lenders during the lean period, try to keep these people in good humour by giving services free or at a wage below the market rate, and also by expressing political or factional allegiance. The money lenders exploit this dependency relationship to the maximum. Exploitation of this kind is so rampant in Bangladesh that there is hardly any need to document it. The poor are very clearly screwed down seasonally into subordinate and dependent relationships.

A number of policy interventions have been suggested to offset the seasonality of agriculture and its effects on the rural poor, of which five are as follows:

(1) land reform aimed at regulating the tide of landlessness and reducing the concentration of land in a few hands;
(2) rural works projects to provide employment during the slack season in agriculture;
(3) introduction of high-yielding rice varieties and other technology to intensify cultivation and bring more land into use during the winter months;
(4) development of small-scale, labour-intensive rural industries based on local resources;
(5) open market purchase and storage of food to control prices, or a food rationing system.

Rural works programmes are currently operative in the dry winter months, and may include irrigation, drainage, land reclamation, and road-building projects, offering employment on a food-for-work basis. Workers participating in these projects are mostly landless (57 per cent) or those who possess very little land (Dacca University, 1978). They are all people who support their families by the sale of their labour. It therefore appears that the works programmes are successful in providing some relief to the poor and those most affected by the seasonality of agricultural labour. However, much of the work done has the effect of improving land, and so offers long-term benefits mainly to the landowners. According to Khan (1976), the 'unearned increment of the landowners was a hundred times more than the wages earned by the labourers'. This effect could be reduced if the costs of projects were paid by a levy on those who benefit. However, these observations also point to the difficulty of tackling poverty in the absence of land reform.

Of the other suggested measures, the ones which would act most directly on prices and wages would be an open market purchasing scheme which could release cheap rice during periods of scarcity and so keep prices down, and also the technological option. The wider use of irrigation technology to expand production during the dry season would both increase production and smooth out the seasonal variations in grain output and employment opportunities. However, detailed studies suggest that although the introduction of high-yielding rice and new technology leads to increased employment in the short-term, its long-term impact on employment generation is not encouraging. This point is taken up in greater detail in the next section.

3.5 Seasonal Patterns of Agricultural Employment In Bangladesh
Edward J. Clay

Introduction

One of the myths about Bangladesh which still persists is that it is a country of peasant owner-cultivators. The most recent information on land occupancy conclusively demolishes this myth. The number of landless rural households owning no land other than their homesteads appears to have doubled since 1960, reaching 30 per cent of all rural households in 1977. The number of effectively landless who were dependent to some degree on wage employment included 48 per cent of rural households in 1977 (Jannuzi and Peach, 1977).

As the agricultural labourer is typically hired only for such activities as transplanting rice, weeding, and harvesting, the seasonal pattern of work determines seasonal patterns of poverty more strongly than in most societies. Agricultural wages, usually paid part in cash and part as food, are close to subsistence levels and leave the labouring household little to carry over into periods of slack activity (Clay, 1976; Bose, 1968; Khan, 1976).

So far, the issue of underemployment has been studied mainly at an aggregate level. An attempt at a more disaggregated analysis was made by Clay and Khan (1977), and this paper makes use of the same methods. Crop labour requirements have been estimated for fourteen separate rice-growing activities and twenty-one other crops. Labour requirements are derived from available farm management data, and are estimated on an operation-by-operation basis distributed over the twelve periods of the Bengali (Saka) calendar. These estimates are intended to represent the probable pattern of labour inputs, not for a specified field but for a region; thus activities such as transplanting are spread over a longer period than they would be if only one plot were considered.

The empirical basis of the present study is fragile and the conclusions reached are tentative. They are, however, thought provoking, especially in the context of this book. Unfortunately, though, space does not permit presentation of all the data and estimates used by the author, for which the reader must refer to the original version of this paper (Clay, 1978).

Labour requirements of some traditional crop rotations

Cropping patterns in Bangladesh reflect a very close adaptation to the existing environment. This has allowed a very large population density to build up, the national average being 580 people per square kilometre of land available for cultivation. The main feature of the rainfall regime is the very wet monsoon period (June-September), which is preceded by several weeks of increasingly frequent rain squalls (March-May). The dry winter season (November-February) includes brief cool spells which halt the vegetative growth of rice.

Apart from these climatic constraints, cropping patterns are strongly influenced by variations in hydrology and flood regimes. Several traditional crop rotations can be distinguished, all with different labour requirements. Where there are important substitution possibilities, such as the choice between jute and B. *aus* rice (for key to abbreviations such as this, see Table 3.5), economic factors also influence labour demand because the substitute crops have slightly different labour requirements. In order to bring out the distinctive characteristics of the major cropping patterns, attention is here focused only on the most widespread sub-type within each crop rotation, and jute is excluded; rotations discussed are listed in Table 3.6 (column A).

The first rotation noted in Table 3.6 consists of a winter *boro* rice crop, with the land left fallow for the rest of the year. This is a traditional cropping pattern on lowland which stays wet during the dry season, or which can be irrigated by traditional lift devices including the *doan* (shute) and the swing bucket.

Large areas of low-lying land in Bangladesh are subject to seasonal flooding, and this accounts for many regional differences in cropping. The

TABLE 3.6. The annual crop labour requirements of selected 'traditional' and 'new' crop rotations in Bangladesh

Rotations		Annual labour requirement		
'Traditional' A	'New' B	A (m-d/acre)	B	Percentage change
1. Local *boro*-fallow (doan irrigation)	Modern *boro*-fallow (low lift pump)	111	109	− 1
2. ditto	Modern *boro*-fallow (*doan* irrigation)	111	144	+ 30
3. B. *aman*-fallow	Modern *boro* (low lift pump)	85	109	+ 28
4. B. *aus*/B. *aman*/khesari	Modern *boro* (low lift pump)	125	109	− 13
5. ditto	B. *aus*/B. *aman*-dwarf wheat	125	156	+ 29
6. Local T. *aman*-fallow	Late *boro* (low lift pump)-Local T. *aman*	64	173	+170
7. Local T. *aus*-Local T. *aman*-fallow	Modern Late *boro*-Modern T. *aman* (dtw irrigated)	142	215	+ 51
8. B. *aus*-lentil	B. *aus*-dwarf wheat (low lift pump/dtw)	91	133	+ 46
9. B. *aus*-mustard	B. *aus*-tobacco (tw irrigated)	93	249	+168

boro-fallow rotation is practised in places where the floodwater is too deep for any crops to be grown in the monsoon season. However, where floods are more moderate, B. *aman* rice, which is a deep-water variety, is important. In places subject to early or rapid flooding, B. *aman* is often the only crop, giving the rotation represented in line 3 of Table 3.6. However, on the less deeply flooded parts of the Brahmaputra and Ganges floodplains, where the floods come late and rise more slowly, it is possible for an *aus* crop to mature and to be harvested before the main part of the B. *aman* growing season. In such areas, the rotation noted in line 4 (Table 3.6) is used: B. *aus* and B. *aman*, followed by a winter khesari crop. The *aus* (early monsoon) and *aman* (deep-water rice) crops are there sown together, with the *aus* crop being harvested before the onset of deep flooding, and the *aman* crop, which is photoperiod-sensitive, being harvested from mid-October to December. Winter or *rabi* crops (such as khesari) are oversown onto the standing *aman* crop or planted after harvest. This rotation has potential for high yield with minimum tillage (Clay *et al.*, 1978).

Analysis of crop labour requirements was restricted to seven administrative Districts representative of the major geo-hydrologic zones, though there is space here to present only selected data. Four of the Districts are Comilla, Dacca, Faridpur and Kushtia, and from the map given in Figure 1.6 it will be seen that these form an east-west transect across the country. Other Districts represented are Sylhet, where the *boro* rice/fallow rotation is common (see

Figure 3.8A), and Patuakhali, where the T. *aman* crop is important (see Figure 3.9B).

Crop calendars and farmers' own notions follow the Bengali calendar, which begins with the month of *Baishakh* in mid-April. This calendar has therefore been used throughout the analysis, and in the diagrams months are numbered from mid-April. Thus Figure 3.8A shows the labour requirements of two rotations in which *boro* rice is the main crop. For both, labour demand is greatest during the time of land preparation and transplanting, and reaches a peak in month 9, the Bengali month of *Pous*, i.e. 17 December to 14 January. The diagram shows that this crop rotation involves a unimodal labour season. However, an inspection of Figures 3.8 and 3.9 reveals significant differences between rotations. For example, the T. *aman* crop rotations have bimodal labour seasons (see Figure 3.9B), with one peak of activity in months 3 and 4 (land preparation and planting) and another in month 9 or 10 (harvest).

The monthly labour profiles also reveal that, within most of the rotations, a time of little activity is always period 6 (mid-September to mid-October), a fact with important implications for the likely seasonal incidence of underemployment.

Technical change and crop labour requirements

A historical review of the development of Bengali agriculture would reveal a continuing sequence of technical innovations over past centuries. The sweet potato was introduced from the New World, and many of the so-called local varieties of rice are selections from research programmes earlier in the century. However, the period since 1960 has witnessed a sequence of technical changes that have had an impact unprecedented in scale and rapidity on the cropping patterns and production of Bangladesh. These innovations include the large-scale introduction of mechanised lift irrigation, many new varieties of rice, and the widespread use of chemical fertilizers. There has been a marked expansion of some minor crops such as potatoes, and also of tobacco for the local cigarette industry.

On higher land where tubewells have been installed for irrigation, or where surface water is available for lifting to higher levels, an irrigated late *boro* or transplanted *aus* crop can be introduced into the T. *aman*/fallow and *aus*/T. *aman* rotations. Within the triple crop rotation which includes *aus, aman* and rabi crops (khesari), rainfed crops of dwarf wheat or potatoes are replacing some of the less productive rabi crops.

Examples of the impact of these and other new crop rotations on labour requirements are presented in Table 3.6, and in Figures 3.8 and 3.9. In most cases, the change in crop rotation is associated with a significant increase in annual labour requirements, ranging from 28 to 170 per cent in the seven examples which involve a positive change in Table 3.6. However, some of the changes in rotation are 'perverse', involving a reduction of the aggregate labour requirement. The two examples of this in the table are both linked with a switch to a single crop of modern *boro* rice. In the first case, this is because the increased labour requirements of modern rice cultivation are outweighed by the reduction involved in switching from a traditional method of irrigation using human labour to a mechanised system. The second case involves a

Seasonal Dimensions to Rural Poverty

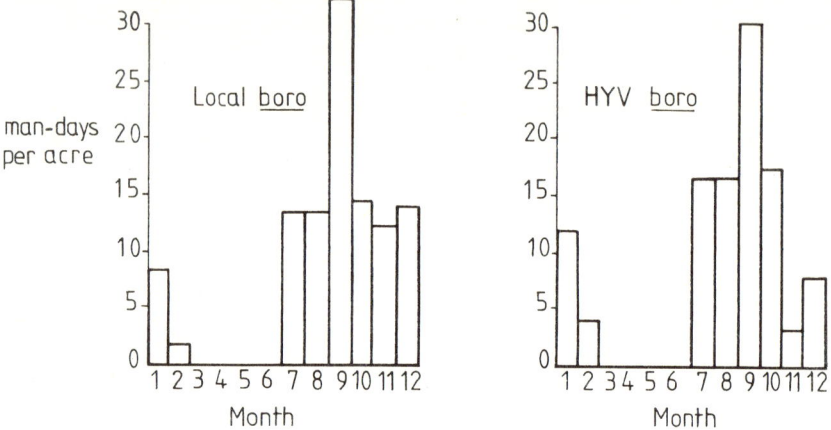

A. From local boro (doan irrigation) to modern (HYV) boro (low lift pump) in Sylhet District.

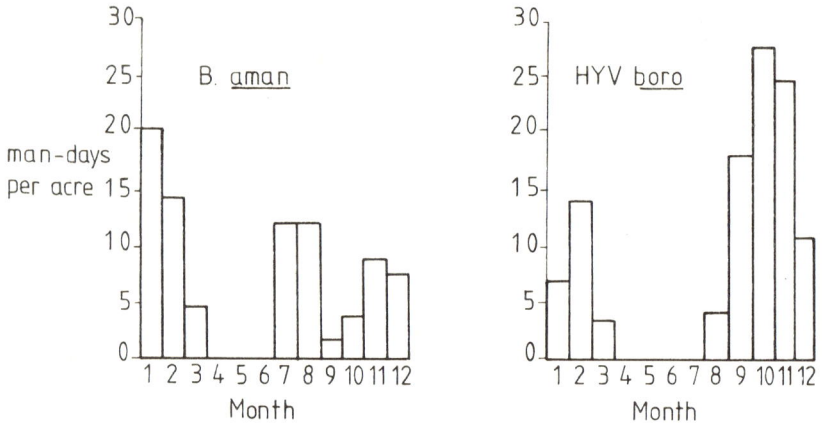

B. From broadcast aman to modern (HYV) boro (low lift pump irrigation) in Dacca District.

Figure 3·8 The impact on labour requirements of changes in cropping patterns. The left-hand diagrams represent the seasonal labour requirements of 'traditional' rotations, while requirements of 'new' rotations are shown on the right.

The two pairs of diagrams refer to the same rotations as lines 1 & 3 in Table. The months (in Figs. 3.8, 3·9 and 3·10) are numbered in the sequence followed in the Bengali calendar, beginning with the month of Baisakh (16 April to 16 May). The data refer to the year 1975-76.

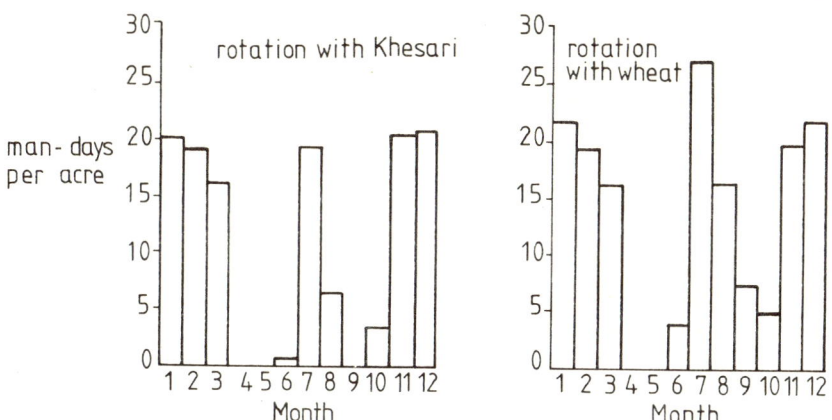

A. Substitution of dwarf wheat for khesari in B. aus / B. aman- - rabi crop rotation in Dacca and Faridpur Districts.

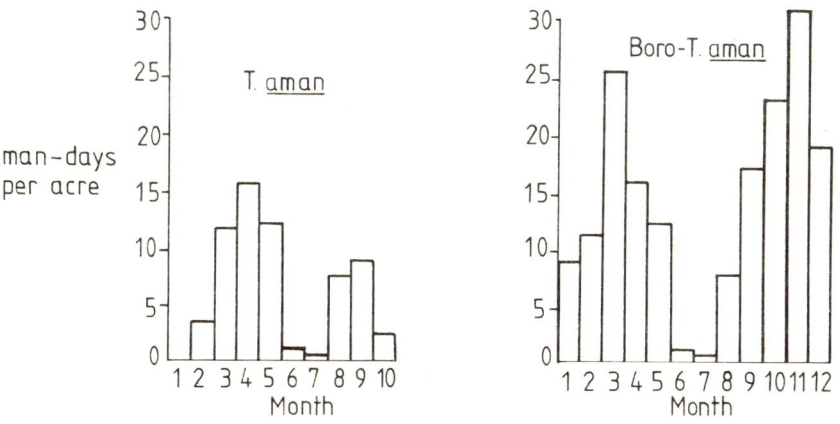

B. Change from T. aman - fallow to modern (HYV) boro - T. aman in Patuakhali district.

Figure 3·9 The impact on labour requirements of changes in cropping patterns. The two pairs of diagrams refer to the same rotations as lines 5 and 6 in Table 3.6.

switch from a mixed B. *aus*/B. *aman* rotation to modern *boro* rice. So far, neither scientists nor farmers have been successful in evolving a rotation which enables irrigated *boro* rice to be combined with a wet-season crop, due to overlap between the growing seasons, so this change involves a switch from multiple cropping to single cropping.

Most of the new rotations involve either a diversion of activity into the winter months, or substantial additional demands for labour in the winter (Figures 3.8B and 3.9B). However, the diagrams show that there is no marked increase in labour demand during the slackest period, around month 6 (September-October). Intensification of crop rotations and the expansion of irrigated cultivation in Bangladesh in most cases significantly increases labour requirements, but does not remove the marked seasonality from crop production work.

Regional seasonality in agriculture

The aggregate crop labour requirements for selected administrative Districts in Bangladesh have been estimated for the agricultural year 1975-6 by multiplying estimates of crop area by data for the various cropping activities such as those presented in Figures 3.8 and 3.9.

Comparing the four central Districts which provide a transect from east to west across Bangladesh, there are marked differences in the peaking of labour requirements within a basically similar bimodal pattern (see Figure 3.10). In each District, the most intense period of activity is in the three months at the turn of the Bengali year (periods 11, 12, and 1; mid-February–mid-May). There is a second, lesser peak in activity at the time of the main *aman* harvest (November-December) which almost disappears in Kushtia, the most western District with the smallest area growing *aman* rice. The seasonal distribution of crop labour requirements is least peaked in Comilla and Dacca Districts, with over 20 per cent of total rice area under *boro*, T. *aman*, and mixed *aus* and B. *aman*. Only in Faridpur and Kushtia Districts could the winter months (December–mid-February, periods 8-10) be said to be a period of relatively less activity.

This analysis of crop labour requirements at District level demonstrates that there is no uniform pattern of agricultural activity throughout Bangladesh, but distinctive regional patterns. In areas which depend on an influx of seasonal labour at peak periods of activity, the patterns of activity complement those of the migrants' home Districts. The dry winter season is a period of less activity only in some Districts (Faridpur and Kushtia). The build-up of activity in land preparation for the *Kharif* season also begins early, so if there is a slack period in winter, it comes early (from mid-December to mid-February). The period of least activity in all Districts is during or at the end of the monsoon months.

Rural poverty and its implications for policy

An analysis of crop labour requirements provides an incomplete picture of the pattern of employment for the rural poor: crop production accounts for an estimated 69 per cent of aggregate agricultural out-of-household employment

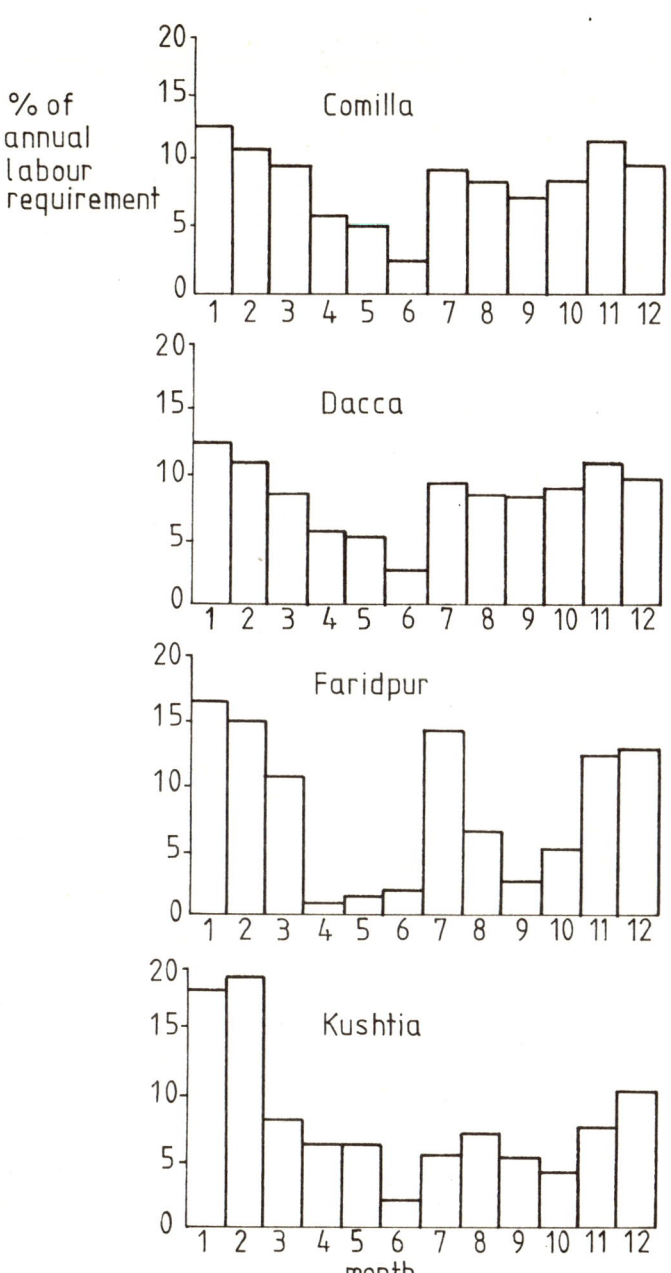

Figure 3.10 Histograms showing the seasonal distribution of crop labour requirements in four administrative districts of Bangladesh.

in 1975-6 (Clay and Khan, 1977). The pattern of other income-earning activities (fishing, forestry) could be complementary to those for crop production. There is, however, little evidence that this is so.

There has been no systematic study of the pattern of in-household processing activities which provide a major source of employment for women (Harriss, 1978; Agriculture Ministry, 1978). The periods of most intense post-harvest processing activity probably occur after the harvesting of the major rice crops, probably from mid-November onwards with the main *aman* crops. Post-harvest processing work may to some extent be complementary with out-of-household agricultural work, but this is a subject which requires further research.

A number of policy interventions which could potentially reduce rural poverty in Bangladesh, particularly in its seasonal aspects, was listed by Chaudhury in the previous paper (Section 3.4). New technology and increased crop production featured among these policies, but Clay and Khan (1977) found that even the most ambitious programmes for expanding production would not reduce the level of aggregate underemployment over the next decade. As illustrated by some of the examples quoted here, the impact of these strategies would also shift the peak in labour demand from the March-June period to the winter months of January-March.

The rural works programme is another policy which in 1977-8 provided 71 million man-days of employment on a food-for-work basis. This is clearly a major contribution, but so far it has proved difficult to devise large-scale projects to provide work during the monsoon season when floods and heavy rain impede earth-moving work.

A food buying and storing operation has been suggested as a way of establishing a more orderly food market, minimising seasonal fluctuations in grain prices (World Bank, 1977). There is little doubt that effective open market operations could reduce the impact of seasonal fluctuations in output. However, the costs of storage alone make it unlikely that seasonal variations in prices could be removed altogether, and the rural poor will remain the most vulnerable to such fluctuations.

It was argued at the beginning of this chapter that seasonality is rarely the *cause* of poverty; the problem is more usually the socio-economic system which confronts seasonal and climatic conditions. In Bangladesh, seasonality brings regular crisis points to the lives of the poor, but the causes of poverty are bound up with the increasing numbers of landless people in rural areas. Rural works or grain purchases which reduce the effects of seasonality merely relieve poverty without attacking the socio-economic causes of landlessness. If the objective is to eliminate poverty rather than alleviate it, there is no satisfactory alternative to assuring the landless a guaranteed share in the income stream from the one basic resource—land.

3.6 References

Agriculture Ministry (1977), *Bangladesh Agriculture in 1978*, Report No. 2-SS/77, Dacca, Bangladesh Ministry of Agriculture.
Agriculture Ministry (1978), *Report of the Task Force on Rice Processing and By-product*

Utilization in Bangladesh, Dacca, Ministry of Agriculture.

Ahmed, I. (1973), 'Employment in Bangladesh, Problems and Prospects', Paper presented at the International Economic Association Conference, Dacca, 6-12 January 1973.

Alamgir, M. (1976), *Bangladesh: a Below Poverty-level Equilibrium Trap*, Dacca, Bangladesh Institute of Development Studies (mimeo).

Bose, S. R. (1968), 'Trend of Real Income of the Rural Poor in East Pakistan: 1949-66', *Pakistan Development Review, 8* (3).

Breman, H., and Cissé, A. M. (1977), 'Dynamics of Sahelian Pastures in Relation to Drought and Grazing', *Oecologia* (Berlin), *28,* pp. 301-31.

Chaudhury, Rafiqul Huda (1980), 'Seasonal Dimensions of Rural Poverty in Bangladesh: Employment, Wages and Consumption Patterns', *Social Action,* 30, Jan.-March.

Clay, E. J. (1976), 'Institutional Change and Agricultural Wages in Bangladesh', *The Bangladesh Development Studies, 4,* 4, pp. 423-40.

Clay, E. J. (1978), 'Environment, Technology, and the Seasonal Patterns of Agricultural Employment in Bangladesh', Paper presented at the Conference on Seasonal Dimensions to Rural Poverty, Institute of Development Studies, University of Sussex, 3-6 July 1978 (mimeo).

Clay, E. J., and Khan, M. S. (1977), *Agricultural Employment and Underemployment in Bangladesh: the Next Decade*, Dacca, Bangladesh Agricultural Research Council, Agricultural Economics Paper 4. (Revised version of Government of Bangladesh and FAO/UNDP Mission, April 1977, Working Paper XI, 'Agricultural Employment in Bangladesh'.)

Clay, E. J. et al. (1978), *Yield Assessment of Broadcast Aman (Deep-water Rice) in Selected Areas of Bangladesh in 1977,* Dacca, BRRI and A/D/C.

Dacca University (1977), *Nutrition Survey of Rural Bangladesh, 1975*, Dacca, Institute of Nutrition and Food Science, Dacca University.

Dacca University (1978), *Economic and Nutritional Effects of Food for Relief Work Projects*, Dacca, Institute of Nutrition and Food Science, Dacca University.

Habibullah, M. (1962), *Pattern of Agricultural Unemployment*, Dacca, Bureau of Economic Research, Dacca University.

Harriss, B. (1978), *Post-harvest Rice Processing Systems in Rural Bangladesh: Technology, Economics and Employment*, Dacca, Bangladesh Agricultural Research Council (unpublished).

Hays, H. M. (1975), *The Marketing and Storage of Food and Grains in Northern Nigeria*, Samaru Miscellaneous Papers No. 50, Samaru, I.A.R.

Islam, Rushidan (1977), 'Approaches to the Problem of Rural Unemployment', Bangladesh Economic Association Conference, 19-21 June 1977.

Jannuzi, F. T., and Peach, J. T. (1977), *Report on the Hierarchy of Interests in Land in Bangladesh*, Dacca, USAID.

Jones, S. M. (1963), *A Study of Swazi Nutrition*, Durban, Institute for Social Research, University of Natal.

Khan, A. R. (1976), 'Poverty and Inequality in Rural Bangladesh', World Employment Programme Research Working Paper, Geneva, International Labour Office.

Norman, D. W. (1972), *An Economic Survey of Three Villages in Zaria Province*, Vols. 1 and 2, Samaru Miscellaneous Papers Nos. 37 and 38, Samaru, I.A.R.

Simmons, E. B. (1976a), *Calories and Protein Intakes in Three Villages of Zaria Province, May 1970-July 1971*, Samaru Miscellaneous Papers No. 55, Samaru, I.A.R.

Simmons, E. B. (1976b), *Rural Household Expenditures in Three Villages of Zaria Province, May 1970-July 1971*, Samaru Miscellaneous Papers No. 56, Samaru, I.A.R.

Swift, J. J. (1977), 'Sahelian Pastoralists; Underdevelopment, Desertification and Famine', *Annual Review of Anthropology, 6,* pp. 457-78.

Swift, J. J. (1979), *West African Pastoral Production Systems*, Ann Arbor, Centre for Research on Economic Development, University of Michigan.

Wood, G. D. (1977), 'The Politics of Rural Development in Bangladesh', Paper for the Bangladesh Agricultural Research Council Seminar on High-yielding Varieties.

World Bank (1977), *Bangladesh: Food Policy Review*, Report 1764-BD, Washington.

Chapter 4
THE SEASONAL ECOLOGY OF DISEASE

4.1 Introduction

Pathogens, vectors and climate

The main climatic factors determining the transmission of infections are rainfall and temperature. They affect disease by way of the breeding of vectors, the survival of pathogenic organisms, and the proliferation rate of microbes in the environment. The human host also plays a large part. Malnutrition may influence susceptibility to infection, while seasonal variations in human behaviour may also have an effect. It is this complex of relationships involving the physical environment, micro-organisms, vectors and human hosts, which justifies the notion of a 'seasonal ecology' of disease.

In many parts of the world, the infections with the greatest regular seasonal impact are malaria, the diarrhoeal and respiratory diseases, and guineaworm. The brunt of the first two falls upon infants, though people of all ages may be affected, and both have a strong interaction with nutritional problems. Indeed, the diarrhoeal diseases have already received some attention in the chapter on nutrition (especially in Section 2.5).

Although these diseases tend to be most prevalent at seasons of peak labour demand, and so exacerbate the problems many families face at this time, generalisations about seasonal impact need to be treated with caution. For example, the ecology of malaria is very complex, and minor differences between local environments can reverse the expected seasonal pattern. With the diarrhoeal diseases, the problem is that many kinds of infection with varying seasonal behaviour give rise to diarrhoea. In addition, its seasonal incidence in a population may reflect the nature of the pathogen and the nutritional status of the population, as well as environmental factors.

4.2 Diarrhoeal Diseases
B. S. Drasar, A. M. Tomkins and R. G. Feachem

Introduction

Diarrhoea occurs in both developed and developing countries in all seasons and among people of all ages. The cause of most of this diarrhoea is unknown though bacterial and viral pathogens are associated with some outbreaks. The enteric fevers, i.e. typhoid and paratyphoid, are considered with the diarrhoeas. Among the acute diarrhoeas it is of value to distinguish the watery diarrhoeas caused by bacteria, such as cholera and enterotoxic *Escherchia coli*, from the bloody diarrhoeas, including the classical bacillary dysentery caused by *Shigella* spp. and those syndromes resulting from infection with enteroinvasive *E. coli*. Infections due to *Salmonella* spp. and intoxications due to the products of other bacteria such as *Staphylococcus aureus, Clostridium perfringens* and *Bacillus cereus* are grouped under the general heading of food poisoning. These categories may include as much as 40 per cent of diarrhoea; the cause of the remainder is uncertain; for no clear reason some investigators have designated it 'viral'. The improvement in bacterial culture methods has resulted in the demonstration that *Campylobacter* spp. are an important cause of diarrhoea. Similarly advances in virology have led to the demonstration of rotavirus in childhood diarrhoea.

Weanling, diarrhoea, summer diarrhoea

The mortality from diarrhoea is much greater in developing than developed countries, but in all areas most of the deaths are among infants and young children. A variety of agents including enteropathogenic *E. coli*, *Shigella* spp., *Salmonella* spp. and several types of virus has been implicated, but the cause of most of the disease remains unknown.

In 1971, Cramblett *et al.* reviewed the various attempts that had been made to isolate pathogenic bacteria and viruses from children with diarrhoea. The proportion of cases from which no pathogen could be isolated varied between 37 and 96 per cent. Since then, *Campylobacter sputorem ss jejunii* and rotavirus have been described as major causes of diarrhoea, and it may be expected that these discoveries will be followed by a reduction in the number of unexplained cases of diarrhoea.

The first of these pathogens is very commonly found in diarrhoea in the United Kingdom, but has not yet been searched for systematically in other areas. Rotavirus infection seems to generally occur as winter infections of young children, as Cutting has described (Section 4.3 below); it has been demonstrated from children in Bangladesh, and in other developing countries. But despite these newly identified pathogens, much diarrhoea remains unexplained — possibly up to half of all cases.

The plan of this paper, therefore, is first to review the seasonal occurrences of some important diarrhoeal syndromes, such as summer diarrhoea, and some specific diseases. Then hypotheses will be put forward to explain why some diarrhoeal diseases are most prevalent at particular times of year.

Current levels of mortality from diarrhoea in developing countries are similar to what was experienced in England and Wales in 1911 (see Table 4.1). Since then, mortality from diarrhoea has decreased by some hundredfold in Britain. In particular, epidemics of 'summer diarrhoea' have disappeared. The reasons for this change are not known but may well be connected with improvements in excreta disposal and infant nutrition. The relationship between environmental contamination and seasonal fluctuations in temperature and rainfall was never exactly determined. Newsholme (1923) stated that, 'The amount of epidemic or summer diarrhoea varies directly with the summer temperature and inversely with the amount of rainfall in the summer months'.

Summer diarrhoea of infants in Britain has been recognised as a major epidemic disease for centuries (Creighton, 1965). Similar epidemics occur in the developing world at the present time. In Guatemala, peak incidence occurs during the rainy season (Scrimshaw *et al.*, 1968), while in Egypt, both

TABLE 4.1. Deaths from diarrhoeal disease at various ages in England and Wales, 1911 and 1971, and in Mexico and Egypt, 1971

	0	1-4	5-14	15-24	25-34	35-44	45-54	55-64	65-74	75 plus
England and Wales										
1971 (pop. 48 million)	320	73	13	4	7	9	17	43	51	78
1911 (pop. 36 million)	31,900	8,483	426	201	302	438	680	1,003	1,596	1,597
Mexico										
1971 (pop. 50 million)	34,859	15,570	3,332	911	885	1,015	1,030	1,449	2,056	3,190
Egypt										
1971 (pop. 34 million)	47,885	41,386	1,832	793	834	1,359	2,029	1,489	824	496

Source: Feachem et al. (1978).

summer and winter peaks occur (Higgins et al., 1955). Peak incidence among Apache children on a reservation occurred while the weather was both hot and wet (Woodward et al., 1974). Feachem et al. (1978) show that in Lesotho, where most rain falls between November and March, diarrhoeal disease peaks markedly in January, while typhoid outbreaks generally occur in March. This period is also, of course, the hot season of the year in southern Africa. Though diarrhoea can occur in all seasons, hot season epidemics are very common. However, this does not mean that environmental temperature is necessarily the main disease determinant.

Adult diarrhoea and food poisoning

Among infants, diarrhoeal disease is often fatal, but among adults, it is usually a self-limiting nuisance. Deaths among adults are most common among the old, but deaths can occur at all ages.

Two types of disease are found among adults. First, there are diarrhoeal diseases to which immunity has not been acquired in childhood, and second, there are diseases to which changes in life-style expose the adult. Epidemics of infantile diarrhoea may be accompanied by infections among adults (Creighton, 1965). Similarly, studies in India have shown that diarrhoea among adults has a similar seasonal distribution to that among infants (Feldman et al., 1969; Kamath et al., 1969; Anjaneyala et al., 1975). Presumably the adults involved in these epidemics did not derive immunity as a result of childhood experience. A further variation results from introduction of adults into an environment to which they have not before been exposed. For example, seasonal epidemics of acute gastroenteritis have been reported among Americans at a military base in the Philippines (Dean and Jones, 1972). This disease, which occurs during the hottest season of the year, but before the heaviest rainfall, had a high attack rate among Americans but a low incidence among the local population.

Food poisoning is primarily a disease of adults and older children, and results from the contamination of foods with bacteria and their growth in the food and ingestion by the patient. Even in England, the main incidence of food poisoning due to all causes, *Salmonella* spp., *Staph. aureus*, and *Clostridium perfringens*, occurs during the warmer months of the year (Wilson and Miles, 1975). *Salmonella* infections in New York and Stockholm also occur during the summer (Cherubin et al., 1969; Hellström, 1975). It seems likely that diarrhoea due to the ingestion of contaminated food is very common in developing countries.

Enteric fever

Typhoid and related enteric infections have become rare in developed countries as a result of improved water supplies and the social imperative to hygiene (Greenwood, 1935). However, infections with *Salmonella paratyphi B* appear to have become common. The disappearance of typhoid fever, and the development of bacteriological surveillance, may have conspired to bring this bacterium into prominence.

Among the developed nations, typhoid fever is usually a water-borne disease, though numerous food-borne epidemics have been observed.

However, the primary transmission route in tropical endemic areas remains obscure. Feachem *et al.* (1978) have presented data which indicate that in one endemic area of Africa (Lesotho), typhoid fever is *not* primarily water-borne. Under conditions of primitive hygiene, direct personal transmission of infection may play an important role, and improved personal cleanliness may reduce transmission (Greenwood, 1935).

In the United States during the period 1920-36, the majority of outbreaks of typhoid occurred in summer and autumn. However, prior to the filtration and chlorination of water supplies, typhoid in the United States had been a winter and spring disease (Gorman and Wolman, 1939). In India, there may be two or three epidemics of enteric fever per year, during the hot dry, hot wet, and cold dry seasons. This same pattern of infection, which persists today, was demonstrated among the British Army in India before 1914 (Roberts, 1906; Mathur and Sharma, 1971; Singh *et al.*, 1965).

Among Yoruba children in Nigeria, exceptionally high mortality occurs despite the most modern treatment. Peak incidence is from May to October. Children under one are most vulnerable to paratyphoid fever, while typhoid kills two-year-olds. The disease pattern in these children seems to have been distorted by malaria suppressing the immune response and reducing the efficiency of treatment (Duggan and Beyer, 1975).

Enteric fever has been controlled in developed countries as a result of environmental improvement. The availability of the pathogen has become the crucial determinant of infection. In endemic areas, seasonal factors are still important but must be considered in the context of the particular society. Although typhoid has been thought of as a water-borne disease, this concentration on water-borne epidemics may be in part a result of the availability of the means for control of water quality and it must not be thought that such unifactorial improvements will necessarily result in reduction in disease incidence (Greenwood, 1935; Feachem, 1977; Feachem, *et al.*, 1978).

Cholera

The reasons for seasonal patterns of cholera in India are not clear. It has been suggested that the incidence of disease in any particular year can be related to the absolute humidity in that year and the failure of the monsoon in the previous year. The failure of the monsoon was thought to aid spread of disease by decreasing the resistance of the population as a result of famine, and to result in their being crowded together in famine relief centres with the resultant increase in disease transmission (Rogers, 1957).

In general, the disease is most prevalent in hot weather when humidity is increased by intermittent rain. In some areas it precedes and in others follows the monsoon rains, and our understanding of the seasonal fluctuations is far from complete. Thus, in Dacca, the cholera season was during the dry winter months (December and January), but in nearby rural areas, a second epidemic could occur during May-July (McCormack *et al.*, 1969; Martin *et al.*, 1969). The position is further complicated by the recent trend of cholera in Dacca to peak earlier (October-November). In the rural areas, the timing of the peak varies each year, but is most usually in the months September-December (see Section 2.5 and Figure 2.6).

Bacillary dysentery

Unlike the other diarrhoeal diseases, infections due to *Shigella* have not declined in the developed nations with the improvement of sanitation and nutrition. However, the types of *Shigella* isolated have changed as sanitation has improved, and *Shigella sonnei* is now the most common. By contrast, among people living in primitive conditions, the variety of *Shigella* isolated includes all species. *Shigella sonnei* is not prominent; *Shigella flexneri* and *Shigella dysenteriae* are common.

A study of diarrhoea among a group of children in Egypt showed that more than 90 per cent had a *Shigella* infection during the year. Three peaks of infection were observed: in spring, in late summer, and in winter (Higgins *et al.*, 1955). In South Africa, among Bantu children, a summer peak was observed (Richardson *et al.*, 1968). In Guatemala, peak incidence occurred during the wet season (Scrimshaw *et al.*, 1968). In all these populations, the people studied lived under insanitary conditions, and all types of *Shigella* were high throughout the year.

Studies among schoolchildren in England show that large outbreaks caused by *Shigella sonnei* occur during the autumn and winter terms, though sporadic cases occur throughout the year (Thomas and Tillett, 1973). It would seem that, as a result of the improvements in sanitation, outbreaks of dysentery caused by organisms other than *Shigella sonnei* are prevented. Further, those outbreaks that do occur tend to be concentrated in the cooler months. Whether the elimination of certain patterns of disease makes winter infections appear more prominent, or whether there is an adaptation of the infection to changed social conditions is not clear.

The 'water-borne' hypothesis to explain seasonal diarrhoea

Many of the best-described outbreaks of diarrhoeal disease have been associated with contamination of drinking water supplies. The compelling logic of the water-borne epidemic has led some investigators to universalise its message, and attempt to explain all periodic outbreaks of diarrhoeal disease as water-borne outbreaks.

In some areas of the world, outbreaks of diarrhoea occur at the same time as the rains. It has been suggested that these outbreaks result from the flushing of faecal material into the water supply. However, a totally opposite water pollution argument can be used: if diarrhoea is occurring mainly in the hot, dry season, it can be argued that the lack of dilution is causing an increase in bacterial concentration in the surface waters.

There are two major shortcomings in what we will call the 'water-borne' hypothesis: we do not know whether seasonal diarrhoea is water-borne, and we do not have much data on the quality of surface water in tropical, rural catchments.

White *et al.* (1972) report data from domestic water sources in East Africa, but do not discuss seasonal fluctuations. Feachem *et al.* (1978) report that mean concentrations of faecal coliforms (FC) and faecal streptococci (FS) are approximately five times higher in the wet season than in the dry season in Lesotho. However, their studies do not clarify the detailed relationship between pollution and particular rainfall events. Moore *et al.* (1965) found that water pollution (total coliform count) rose markedly at the onset of heavy rains in Costa Rica. This effect was largest and most prompt in those water supplies which were most exposed to contamination by surface run-off.

The problem with these few studies from developing countries is that they deal in seasonal or monthly means, and are not intensive enough to reveal the true nature of what are, in all probability, very transient events. More insights are provided by data on water pollution from the Saka valley in the highlands of Papua New Guinea (Feachem, 1974, 1975). There it appeared that FS concentration responded rapidly and dramatically to rainfall on the catchment, while FC concentration, although responding to rainfall, showed other fluctuations also (Figure 4.1).

These studies strongly suggest that rainfall and water pollution are often positively correlated. It is likely that pollution levels rise fairly suddenly after rain, especially if the rain has been preceded by a dry spell. Whether pollution levels will be generally and continuously raised during a rainy season appears much more doubtful.

In seeking to link rainfall and diarrhoeal disease, it is necessary to show that particular rainfall phenomena (e.g. the onset of rains) are followed by a major increase in pollution which can be linked to an increase in diarrhoeal morbidity. Such an association has typically not been demonstrated and does not exist. In Lesotho, heavy rains start in November, whereas diarrhoeal disease does not peak till January, and typhoid till March (Feachem *et al.*, 1978). So there, as in many other places, no clear relationship can be seen between rain, pollution, and disease, and it is necessary to look elsewhere for an explanation of seasonal incidence.

Nutritional factors that may cause seasonal diarrhoea

In some countries, there is evidence of an increase in both gastroenteritis and malnutrition during the rainy season. This is the time of year when food stocks are at their lowest and when there is often a marked increase in the energy expenditure demanded of people through work in the fields (see Chapter 2).

Food shortages and manual work present particular problems for women whose nutritional requirements are increased by lactation. Many studies have documented a severe reduction in breast milk production during maternal malnutrition. This may be a critical factor in the growth failure, and in the increased gastroenteritis among children, which are so often observed during the rains (e.g. in Gambia; see McGregor *et al.*, 1970). However, there may be other factors. In northern Nigeria there is a similar increase in gastroenteritis and malnutrition during the rains, even though energy and protein intakes, of adults at least, are not reduced (Tomkins, 1979). The women have to go out and work in the fields at this season, and it may be this that is the reason for the abrupt weaning practices which are observed in certain tribal groups.

In nearly every community in the world, diarrhoea is more common among bottle-fed than breast-fed infants. A considerable amount of work has defined some of the protective mechanisms of breast milk. Perhaps two of the most

Seasonal Ecology of Disease

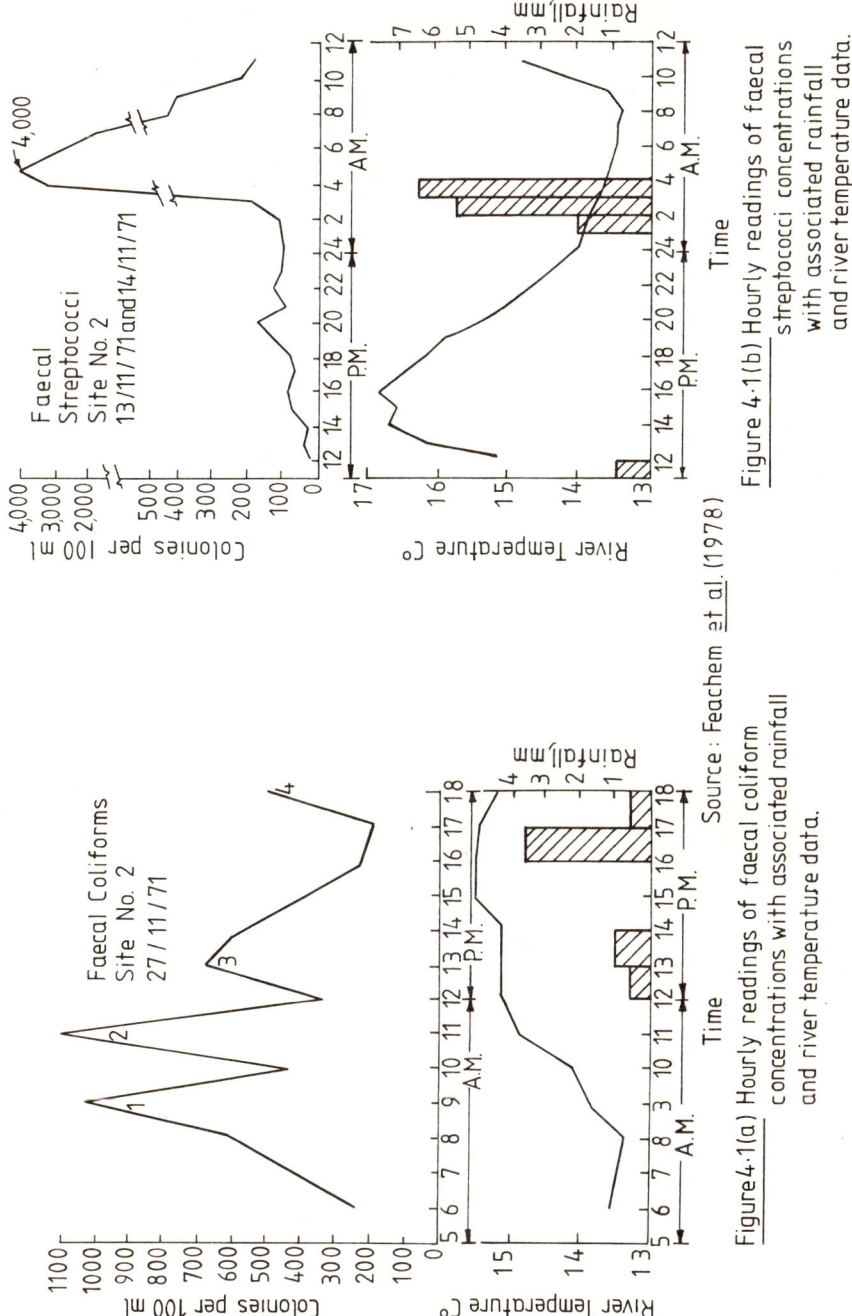

Figure 4·1(a) Hourly readings of faecal coliform concentrations with associated rainfall and river temperature data.

Figure 4·1(b) Hourly readings of faecal streptococci concentrations with associated rainfall and river temperature data.

Source: Feachem et al. (1978)

crucial are the protective effect of maternally derived antibodies secreted in the breast milk, and the inhibitory influence of maternally derived iron-binding proteins. These bind the dietary iron in such a way that it is unavailable for bacterial metabolism. It has also been noted that certain vitamin deficiencies, especially of folic acid, may precipitate diarrhoea. Folate deficiency, affecting the regeneration of cells of the intestine, may be an important factor in the damage and flattening of the lining of the intestine in malabsorption states which follow infective diarrhoea. In northern Nigeria, the dietary folate intake is reduced as fresh vegetables become scarce at the beginning of the rains, and with the sudden withdrawal of breast milk, the folate supply may become critically low. The problem, however, is usually one of multiple nutritional deficiencies and multiple infections. Malaria can cause folic acid deficiency as a result of destruction of red cells by the malaria parasite. This, too, can have a seasonal pattern, with severe anaemia developing in many children.

Another reason why seasonal diarrhoea may be linked with seasonal malnutrition is that gastric acid production, an important defence mechanism, is impaired by malnutrition; this allows live infective organisms to enter the upper intestine. In health, these organisms would elicit a powerful defence response from the paint-like layer of antibodies, especially IgA, which line the intestine, but malnutrition impairs production of these anti-bodies in lacrimal and salivary secretions as well as in the intestine, thereby allowing the organisms to proliferate unopposed at many sites. The precise role that these organisms play in the malnourished host is uncertain, but toxin production, sufficient to stimulate secretion of water and salt into the bowel, may occur.

Finally, some recent studies have described the increase in tropical sprue in Puerto Rico during the months immediately after Christmas (Klipstein *et al.*, 1972). The suggestion is that the prolonged cooking of pork over Christmas by many families produces a marked increase in consumption of long chain saturated fatty acids. The bacterial colonisation of the upper intestine that is stimulated by this dietary regime is quite possibly the cause of the severe diarrhoea and malabsorption that ensues in the New Year.

Diarrhoea as a cause of malnutrition

The preceding paragraphs have discussed ways in which seasonal malnutrition may be a contributory cause of diarrhoea, through problems associated with weaning, and through specific nutrient deficiencies which affect the intestinal tract. Conversely however, there is also much evidence that diarrhoea may contribute to or cause malnutrition. Studies in Central and South America have shown a striking increase in numbers of children with malnutrition after epidemics of diarrhoea (Teruel *et al.*, 1973). This confirmed earlier impressions from studies in a West African village, that gastroenteritis is a major precipitating cause for protein-energy malnutrition (Morley *et al.*, 1968).

The development of techniques for measuring intestinal absorption in children and adults has produced much literature on the disorders of absorptive functions during acute and chronic diarrhoea. Infective agents, particularly certain bacteria, may contribute to a loss of energy in the form of faecal fat, as for instance in the blind loop syndrome, when bile salts, essential for fat digestion, are destroyed by bacterial metabolism. However, the trend at present is to blame the malnutrition on inadequate nutrient intake, because less food is eaten during diarrhoea; anorexia is often part of the syndrome.

Certain cultural conditions are also important. In many countries, there are specific attitudes towards the management of diarrhoea. Some will withold fluids; others will administer fluids in excess accompanied by purgatives. There may often be an inappropriate appreciation of nutrient requirements, especially by the mother about her child. At periods of peak labour requirement in the fields, when mothers need to work long hours, the severe constraint on mother-child contact time may be the major limiting factor in giving an infant sufficient food. Seasonal work patterns and food shortages may combine in several ways, and with several other environmental and social factors, to produce the seasonal outbreaks of diarrhoea that are so often observed.

4.3 Diarrhoeal Diseases: Rotavirus Infection In Children
W.A.M. Cutting*

Viral agents in diarrhoea

For thirty years there has been evidence that some cases of diarrhoea were due to non-bacterial, sub-microscopic agents. Epidemic outbreaks of disease followed patterns suggesting that an agent was transmitted directly between individuals.

Then in 1973, reovirus-like particles were found by electron microscopy (EM) in the duodenal mucosa of children with acute non-bacterial gastroenteritis, first in Melbourne, Australia (Bishop *et al.*, 1973), and almost simultaneously in Birmingham, England (Flewett *et al.*, 1973). Since then, morphologically identical particles have been detected in the stools of children with acute diarrhoea right across the world. A small study from Gambia is a notable exception where none of these particles was seen by EM in the stools of thirty-two children with acute diarrhoea (Rowland *et al.*, 1978).

The virus is spherical with a double-shelled capsid structure. It may have a smooth, sharply-defined, circular outline that looks like the rim of a wheel, hence the name rotavirus. Some particles appear to have lost the outside capsid and have a rough appearance. The smooth particles are about 70 nm in diameter and the rough forms 60 nm. Empty shells are also seen. The particles can only be identified if they reach a concentration of about 10^6 per ml of stool.

In temperate climates, there is a striking seasonal variation in the incidence of rotavirus diarrhoea in children, with a strong predominance of cases in the colder months of the year. A similar pattern has been reported from South India (Mathan, 1978), and from Bangladesh (Chowdhury *et al.*, in Section 2.5 above).

In semi-tropical northern Australia, rotavirus diarrhoea occurred predominantly in the wet rather than the hot season (Walker and Marshall,

---

*The author is grateful to many workers who corresponded about their experience. It has not been possible to make reference to all their contributions. Several are engaged in studies which will be published in the near future.

1978). Of 102 children admitted to the Darwin hospital with gastroenteritis during 1975-77, only nine out of seventy cases seen in the dry months were positive for rotavirus, though in the wet months, seventeen out of thirty-two cases had rotavirus in their stools.

In Guatemala, one study found that 'there was no striking seasonal pattern in the occurrence of diarrhoea associated with rotavirus' (Wyatt et al., in press). However, Mata (1978) reported from Costa Rica that outbreaks of rotavirus diarrhoea were 'concomitant with periods of intense wind and the dry season, but not with high temperature'.

An attempt has been made to correlate numbers of rotavirus diarrhoea cases with temperature, humidity and rainfall, using data from six studies in Britain, North America, and Australia (Cutting, 1978). This has shown a consistent pattern in which rotavirus is more frequently detected in diarrhoea patients in hospital during the colder months of the year. For example, in Washington, D.C., among 143 children with diarrhoea, every case where rotavirus was detected occurred in the winter (November-April), and none at all was seen in summer (Kapikian et al., 1976).

Reasons for seasonal variation

The striking seasonal variation of rotavirus diarrhoea could be due to factors associated with the children infected, or factors associated with the agent, the rotavirus. The virus is excreted in large numbers from persons infected, stools often containing in excess of 10^{10} particles per ml of faeces. Knowledge about rotavirus survival is limited. However, the virus does seem relatively stable. It withstands a temperature of 60°C for one hour, but is inactivated by 30 minutes at 63°C, i.e. pasteurisation. Failure to survive in hot weather does not seem to explain its relative absence then.

Host factors, both biological and social, may also be important. The fact that most infections in new-born babies are relatively benign and usually asymptomatic, suggests some immunological mechanism at work. Possibly infants receive protection from their mothers. Other host-related factors are indicated by the fact that breast-fed neonates are less commonly affected than bottle-fed babies, and when they are infected, they have significantly lower concentrations of virus in the stools (Chrystie et al., 1978). Sociological host factors could be most important. At the coldest times of year, children may be more often gathered together in confined areas, facilitating contact and cross infection. It is just feasible that similar confinement of groups may occur in tropical countries in wet seasons, or even at stormy times of high wind.

4.4 Respiratory Diseases
R.N.P. Sutton

Transmission of virus infections

It is well known that most respiratory disease is caused by viruses. Such diseases include influenza, which affects the whole population in epidemics, and respiratory syncytial virus, which affects infants. Considerable epidemiological work has been carried out on the spread of these diseases, and

Seasonal Ecology of Disease

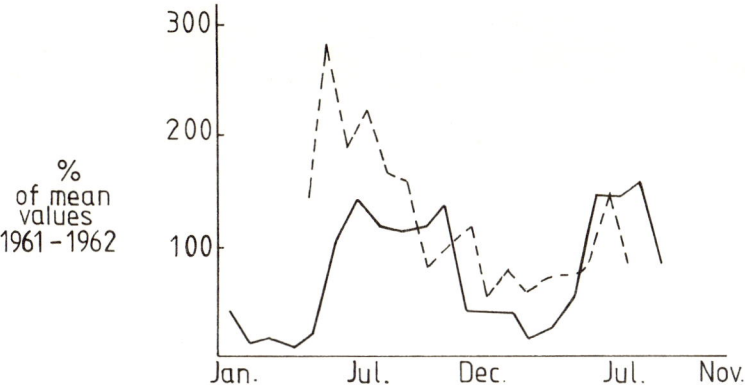

Figure 4.2 Rainfall (full line) and the incidence of respiratory illness (dashed line) in Trinidad; data recorded in 1961-62 (Sutton 1966)

laboratory studies have shown how the inactivation of viruses in the air is more rapid at higher temperatures, and how humidity may also play a part (e.g. Hemmes *et al.*, 1960). Air pollution can also influence transmission and the response of the human body to infection.

One example of the effects of tropical climates on the seasonality of illness caused by viruses was a longitudinal study in Trinidad, West Indies, of minor respiratory illness (e.g. colds, coughs, sore throats). This was compared with a similar study of families in England. The incidence of respiratory illness was the same, but the periodicity differed (Sutton, 1965, 1966). In England, the peak of illness was in November-December. In Trinidad, it was in June (see Figure 4.2), and it was noteworthy that there was a direct relationship between the rainfall and respiratory illness. This could be explained by variations in humidity and the influence of this on virus survival. However, a more plausible explanation was the crowding of people indoors, encouraged by cold weather in England, and by rainfall during the wet season in Trinidad. All types of respiratory virus were present in Trinidad; respiratory syncytial virus was found annually during the rainy season.

Measles

Measles in the tropics is a considerable problem. Morley (1967) has described observations in Ilesha, in western Nigeria, where epidemic measles starts during the dry season and declines in the wet season. Morley attributed this periodicity to the crowding together of people during the festivals which occur in the middle of the dry season, before and after Christmas. During evenings of eating, drinking and dancing, infants are present all the time, securely fastened to their mothers' backs, and there is an increase in droplet infection from one baby to another. The resulting outbreaks of measles affect about one third of infants aged 6-12 months. Infection thus early in life is frequently very severe, and a secondary phenomenon is the effect of measles on the child's nutrition, with a dramatic faltering in the weight gain.

The seasonal incidence of measles is thus influenced as much by social factors as by climate. The peak incidence in West Africa is in the dry season (January-March), but in Zambia, Malawi, and Zimbabwe (Rhodesia), the peak months are in the November-January period, which is the early wet season. In East Africa, the peak month is April.

A group of virus diseases which should be mentioned, although they are not respiratory in nature, are the arthropod-borne virus diseases. These may give rise to mild (but temporarily incapacitating) illness, or to severe illness and death (as in the haemorrhagic fevers associated with dengue virus infection). Changes in land utilisation have on several occasions resulted in changes in the local ecology, with the possibility of changes in the species of the most prevalent mosquitoes. This may result in the spread of virus infections (and malaria) to man where previously such spread might not have occurred (Schaeffer et al., 1959).

The epidemicity of arbovirus infections clearly depends upon fluctuations in the arthropod population as well as, in general terms, the resistance of the human and animal community through which these viruses will pass. Many careful studies, which cannot be detailed here, have been made of the ecology of different arboviruses. Suffice it to say that seasonal and climatic variations will directly (mosquito life cycles) or indirectly (interference with food chains) influence the prevalence of virus vectors (mosquitoes, ticks, sandflies) as well as intermediate hosts (rodents, domestic animals, birds) and hence influence the effect (sometimes important and sometimes marginal) in man. The degree of immunity in individuals will influence the pattern of infection in the community, including the ages at which infection occurs and also (as in dengue haemorrhagic fever) the severity of illness and its economic effect. The proceedings of a workshop devoted to the 1977 pandemic of dengue in the Caribbean (Pan American Health Organisation, 1979) covers all aspects of a typical arbovirus epidemic and could serve as an up-to-date primer on epidemiological, clinical and virological aspects as well as providing critical accounts of practical problems encountered in the field.

4.5 Infectious Skin Diseases
Michael J. Porter

Skin disease in less developed countries

Though there are few data on skin disease, two surveys in Africa have revealed an overall level of skin disease in the community amounting to 26 per cent of the population in Gambia, and almost 40 per cent in Lagos. Such figures would arouse great concern if they referred to more serious illness, but as it is, scant attention is given to the problem (Porter, 1977).

The essential and overwhelming feature of skin disease in the less developed countries is its predominantly infectious origin. Diseases of viral, fungal, bacterial and parasitic genesis comprise up to 90 per cent of total skin disease. This preponderance of infection owes its presence to the same set of determinants as do other kinds of morbidity in less developed countries.

As far as I am aware, only one study has been made to observe skin disease in a community through distinct seasons. By courtesy of the Director of the MRC Laboratories at Keneba, Gambia, and with the cooperation of the people of Keneba, it was possible to carry out a dermatological survey of the whole community at the end of the rainy season in 1976, and at the end of the subsequent dry season (Porter, 1977).

Keneba is one of the case-study areas discussed in several places in this book, and details of its June-October wet season have already been quoted (Table 1.3). The overall prevalence rate of skin diseases was 34 per cent in the rainy season; dropping to 26 per cent in the dry season. The bacterial and some of the fungal diseases showed the biggest interseasonal change. The viral and parasitic diseases showed no variation.

With the bacterial infections, pyoderma chiefly, seasonal changes were confined to children under ten years. Fungal diseases showed the most general seasonal alterations. *Tinea corporis* infection is an adult disease which markedly increased in the rainy season — an unanticipated finding. There were expected and dramatic differences in the prevalence rate for *Tinea versicolor*. The other identified fungal infection, *Tinea capitis*, failed to demonstrate seasonal change.

In Papua New Guinea, with its varied climatic conditions, analysis of health surveys showed that hospital admission rates for infectious skin diseases and tropical ulcers are greater in the lowland than in the highland areas (Bell, 1973; Vines, 1970). While other factors may have influenced this pattern, it appears probable that climatic differences are the source of the change. In the same area, the dermatomycoses clearly show their preference for the higher temperature and humidity of the lowland regions. the close relationship between climatic characteristics and fungal infections was also found in epidemiological studies in Peru (Buck, 1968). Where conditions are hot and humid, fungal infections thrive.

The effect of climate on the skin

Climatic variation affects the prevalence of skin diseases in two ways. First, factors such as wind, temperature and humidity affect sweating and the ability to evaporate water from the skin surface; this affects the hydration of the stratum corneum, and so influences microbial proliferation, and the prevalence of such infections as *Tinea versicolor*.

Second, climatic variation affects insect populations, and this in turn influences the prevalence of pyoderma. Insects proliferate in the rainy season, and children are particularly affected. Young children are sensitive to insect bites, and consequently the effect of the bites is worsened by scratching and secondary infection. Adults are partly desensitised, and experience less irritation.

Climatic conditions exert their influence in other ways. Water availability may vary with season, with an effect on personal hygiene (White *et al.*, 1972).

Activities also vary with season. The rainy period in Keneba is the farming season, and scratches, abrasions, and cuts with secondary infection are more common as a result.

Fortunately, most skin diseases are not so serious as to cause severe debility, although the consequences of some can be serious (e.g. acute glomerulonephritis following streptococcal pyoderma). However, the high levels of infectious skin disease in many countries are sufficient to have a significant economic effect, partly through the time and money spent visiting health centres, and the cost of health care. The solution to this problem in less developed countries is wrapped up with such issues as vector control, water supplies, health education, and better socio-economic conditions.

4.6 Insect-Borne Diseases: Malaria
R. S. Bray

Seasonality and the anopheles mosquito

Among the diseases spread by insects and other arthropods are the virus infection dengue (Section 4.4), some skin diseases (Section 4.5), filariasis (Section 4.7), and kala-azar (Section 4.7). All have seasonal dimensions, if only because the insect vectors are more prevalent in some months than in others. Malaria, the best-known of arthropod-borne diseases, is also profoundly influenced by the effects of the changing season upon its vector, the anopheles mosquito.

As one moves away from the equator, and particularly up the hills, temperature becomes a major determinant of seasonality in malaria (as well as other vector-borne diseases). The cycle is only possible at warm ambient temperatures so that a short warm season — as in Italy and Egypt — is associated with seasonal summer transmission of malaria.

In broadest outline, mosquito numbers are dictated by the availability of water bodies suitable for breeding, and the longevity of the mosquitoes is dependent upon a high relative humidity. A detailed exposition of the effects of climate on all the species of malaria-bearing mosquitoes is impossible, so reference will be made to two main examples: *Anopheles culicifacies*, the great malaria vector of the Indian Subcontinent, and *A. melas*, one of the triad of malaria vectors in West Africa.

A. culicifacies was the cause of the great epidemics of central and northern India before the war, so well studied by Christophers (1911) in the Punjab, and by Covell and Bailey (1930, 1932) in the Sind. During these epidemics, homes and farms were completely abandoned, as happened with outbreaks of no other disease (Sinton, 1935). These disastrous epidemics occurred about every eight years, usually in the autumn of a year of exceptionally heavy monsoon rain. They became a thing of the past following the malaria eradication scheme of the 1950s and 1960s. This campaign is now failing, and *A. culicifacies* is returning to its old haunts. We may therefore expect a return of the old epidemic conditions unless very vigorous and expensive chemotherapeutic campaigns are undertaken to prevent the epidemic.

What happened to cause the epidemics was that if sufficient rainfall occurred to raise the subsoil water level, floods built up on grass plains and around badly drained paddy fields, and *A. culicifacies* requires small open stretches of water for breeding; these were provided in the Punjab by heavy rainfall.

In Ceylon (Sri Lanka), epidemics due to *A. culicifacies* also occurred, and have now returned (Sivagnanasundram, 1971). Here the epidemics followed on the heels of a drought, and in areas normally well watered. In these 'wet areas', the countryside was regularly flooded to a degree not particularly suitable for the breeding of *A. culicifacies*. But in 'drought' years, flooding only occurred to the degree that small pools suitable for *A. culicifacies* breeding were found, particularly as the water receded. So while in the Punjab a wet year was an unhealthy year, in Ceylon a wet year was healthy.

In tropical West Africa, the great malaria vector is *A. gambiae*, though *A. melas* is also important. In Gambia, which has a rainfall of 750-1000 mm, both these mosquitoes are active only in the wet season, so malaria is highly seasonal, with no transmission during the long dry season. During the dry months February-May, malaria density is at a very low level (see Figure 4.3), and malaria prevalence is also lower than during the wet season.

But although *A. melas* is a wet season mosquito in Gambia, in the much wetter climate of Liberia (annual rainfall 4000 mm), it is confined to the dry season. The reason for this is that *A. melas* is a salt water breeder, using a mixture of sea water and fresh water in the pools within mangrove orchards. In Liberia, the correct mixture of waters occurs when the rains lessen and the pools become more brackish with each spring tide. In Gambia, the right conditions are found when fresh water drains into the esturine salt marshes during the rainy season, and the salt is renewed by the spring tides (Giglioli, 1964). So not only do the climatic seasons play a part, but the tides as well.

The malaria parasite and man

So far we have looked only at the mosquito in the complex malaria equation. But what of the other components, parasite and man?

Plasmodium vivax is the agent of benign tertian malaria, and predominates in the temperate and sub-tropical zones. Research has shown this parasite to have a very distinct relapse pattern. Strains from New Guinea have been shown to relapse frequently and at random after the primary attack (Coatney *et al.*, 1950b). Strains from the sub-tropics have been shown to relapse some nine months after the primary attack, and strains from the temperate zones frequently fail to cause a primary attack at all in the weeks following infection by the mosquito, but show a primary attack nine months later (Coatney *et al.*, 1950a).

The selection of these latter strains has obviously been affected by the pressure of climate in non-tropical zones where mosquitoes suitable for transmission are present in sufficient number only for about three months in the year. So the attack, whether it be a delayed primary or a relapse, occurs in the late spring. A week or so later the patient is infective and mosquitoes become abundant and pick up the infection. They transmit it to another person three weeks later. A further two or three weeks later, the new patient has a primary attack. The patient will relapse (or in northern Europe will have a delayed primary) the next spring. Thus seasonal changes have selected the

Seasonal Dimensions to Rural Poverty

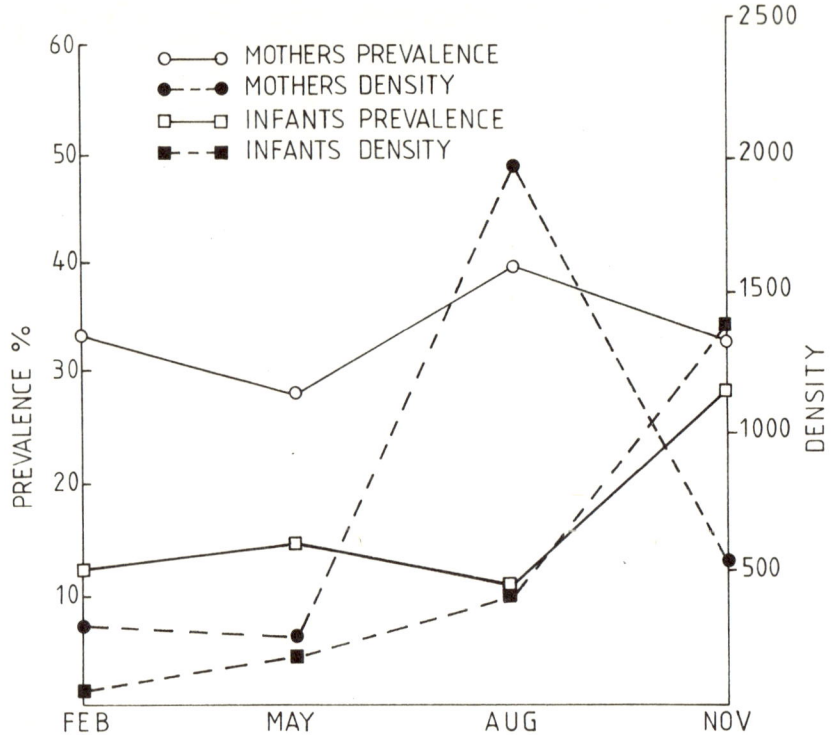

Density is measured in terms of mean parasites per mm³ of blood.
Prevalence is measured in terms of proportion of subjects infected.

Figure 4.3 Malaria prevalence and density among mothers and infants 0-6 months old in Gambia, 1976

primary behaviour pattern of one of the major human malaria parasites.

How is man affected by season in relation to malaria, or by seasonal malaria? Two major activities of man, forced on him by seasonal changes which alter his relationship with malaria, are nomadism and the impounding and usage of water.

The major effect of nomadism is to spread malaria, though this is frequently mitigated in non-tropical zones, such as Afghanistan, where the move is away from malaria. In tropical areas, however, particularly in Africa, the movements in search of grassland tend to follow a rainfall belt which, alas, supports malaria.

The impounding of water, and especially its use in irrigation, has a profound effect upon malaria, though the effect varies equally profoundly from place to place. In Afghanistan, the main source of cereals is the irrigated rice-growing area which also provides the major habitat for all three of the malaria vectors. The situation is reached where malaria is virtually a disease of the rich rice-growing communities — a disease of prosperity.

In the humid tropics, the addition of a few more acres of water to grow swamp rice scarcely makes any difference to malaria endemicity, and in any case, often adds little to the highly selective and favoured habitat of the local *Anopheles* species.

In the savannah areas of West Africa, one may expect irrigation to have a considerable effect. In these areas, malaria is highly seasonal, and what happens when *Anopheles* mosquitoes are allowed to increase markedly, particularly in the dry season, is of considerable interest.

Compare the situation in the sahel savannah, with that which may soon obtain in the Senegal river region if the proposed high dam is built, and intensive irrigation is commenced in the lower reaches. At present, the local population experiences only meso-endemic malaria with an extreme seasonal distribution. The population as a whole builds up little immunity. Here one can predict considerable increase in *Anopheles* populations due to irrigation. Where drainage is poor, conditions will be set up for the breeding of *A. gambiae* and *A. funestus*. What is difficult to predict is the effect upon endemicity of malaria. If dwellings are one mile from the water, it may be that, in the extreme conditions of the sahel dry season, mosquitoes will not be able to survive the journey often enough to transmit malaria. If dwellings are close to the irrigated areas, however, then it seems entirely possible that disastrous epidemics of *falciparum* malaria could occur. They would precede a hyper-endemic malaria situation with greatly increased transmission continuing over a greater part of the year. Complete regular drainage of the irrigated area could control the situation.

Malaria in infants

One complicating factor when considering malaria in young children is the possible effect of seasonal variations in the amount of maternal antibody transmitted to them. Infants are assumed to be protected to some degree from the ill effects of malaria during the first six to nine months of life by the specific anti-malarial immuno-globulin (IgG) received across the placenta from the mother. It is thought that this factor operates in the humid tropics to cause a somewhat lessened prevalence of malaria in infants, as well as to modify the ill-effects of the malaria when eventually acquired. In the drier tropics, this is disputed, and recent results from northern Nigeria seem to show malaria being acquired at the expected rate over the first nine months of life. It is still probable, however, that this malaria is modified in its effect.

It has been hypothesised that seasonal malaria would result in seasonal changes in the levels of maternal antibody available for transmission to the infant (Bray and Anderson, 1979). Thus an infant born at the end of the dry season might receive significantly less antibody than one born in the wet season, but be faced with the full wet season challenge in the succeeding months. Therefore the prevalence and density of *P. falciparum* in pregnant mothers and in infants up to six months of age at four times in the year was examined. At the same time the malarial antibody level in the same subjects and in fifty-two cord bloods collected throughout the year was also investigated.

The graphs (Figures 4.3 and 4.4) show that both prevalence and density of malaria infection rose in the pregnant women in the wet season (August), and

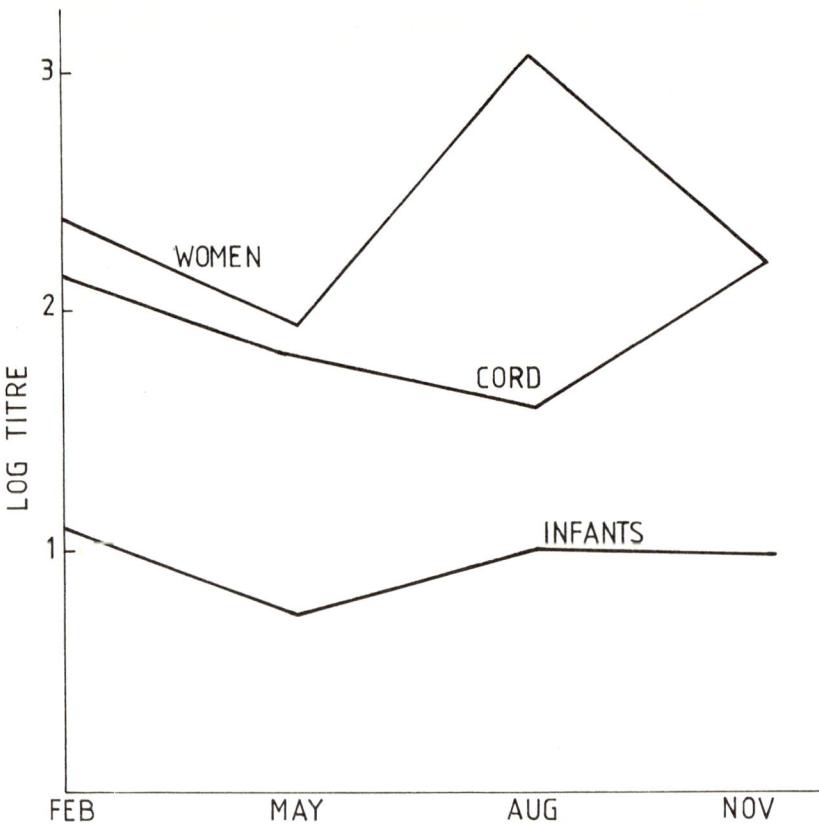

Figure 4·4 Malarial antibody levels in the blood of mothers and infants in Gambia, 1976, and in cord blood samples.

this was mirrored in antibody levels. However, unexpectedly, the wet season antibody rise did not occur in cord blood, and there, antibody levels actually fell. This was interpreted as a block in the passage of antibody across the placenta during the wet season. It could be due to abnormally high levels of IgG in the mother, or to heavy malaria infections in the placenta which blocks, possibly by antigen-antibody complexing, the passage of specific antibody.

In any case, it means that an infant born in the wet season would receive less specific antibody, and the effect of this may be seen in the infant three months later. Again, the graph shows that density and prevalence continue to rise in infants in November, when transmission is known to be dropping. So here is another effect of seasonality — an unexpected one — where seasonal effects on the amount of trans-placental specific antibody received by the infant cause a reverse in the expected fall in malaria in infants at the beginning of the dry season.

4.7 Insect-Borne Diseases: Filarial Infections and Kala-Azar
B. A. Southgate

Bancroftian filariasis

Bancroftian filariasis is a state of infection with the nematode worm, *Wuchereria bancrofti*. The adult worms live mainly in the lymphatic glands and lymphatic vessels. The sexually mature females shed into the bloodstream large numbers of actively motile embryos called microfilariae. These circulating microfilariae are the 'infectious' stage of the worm's life-cycle in man; they are ingested by various female mosquitoes of the family Culicidae during the course of a human blood-meal, and after a period of obligatory development in the mosquito host, they mature into infective larvae which can re-enter the human body via the puncture wound made by the mosquito when feeding. The infective larva develops within man into a sexually mature adult in a period of, typically, eight to twelve months (Sasa, 1976).

Bancroftian filariasis gives rise to a large variety of different symptoms. Early in the course of the disease, its victim may experience fever or various allergies, including asthmatic bronchitis. Later manifestations may include elephantiasis and chronic funiculitis. Many people who are infected do not show any symptoms of disability at all, but serve as a reservoir of infection for the vector mosquitoes. Few people die of the disease, but its manifestations can cause great physical and mental suffering, and lead to partial or complete incapacity for work. The affected person may be an economic cripple for years, and thereby contribute to the impoverishment of the community.

In Upper Volta, two species of mosquito are involved (see Figure 4.5), and their period of maximum activity is related closely to the rainy season. The number of people carrying the microfilariae appears to be constant throughout the year, but as the biting activity of the mosquitoes increases during the rains, so the density of microfilariae per unit volume of blood almost doubles. In Upper Volta, however, there are no marked seasonal variations in symptoms of the disease.

By contrast, there are seasonal patterns in the onset of symptoms in other countries. Napier (1946) records that in Calcutta, there is a tendency for new cases to be diagnosed in the monsoon season (July-September). He points out that the time taken for the development of symptoms is so long and so variable that 'this probably indicates nothing more than a lower resistance on the part of the patient at this time of year'.

In Egypt, symptoms of filariasis, especially fever and scrotal pains, are complained of during the winter (Hassan and Southgate, 1978), but this may reflect either the greater sensitivity of humans to fever in cold weather, or the fact that peasant farmers have time to visit doctors and complain of symptoms only during the winter! Curiously enough, the objective physical signs of filarial disease in Egypt affecting the male genitalia have a very marked seasonal incidence in April, May and June (Ibrahim, 1927).

River blindness

Onchocerciasis, often called 'river blindness', is caused by another

Seasonal Dimensions to Rural Poverty

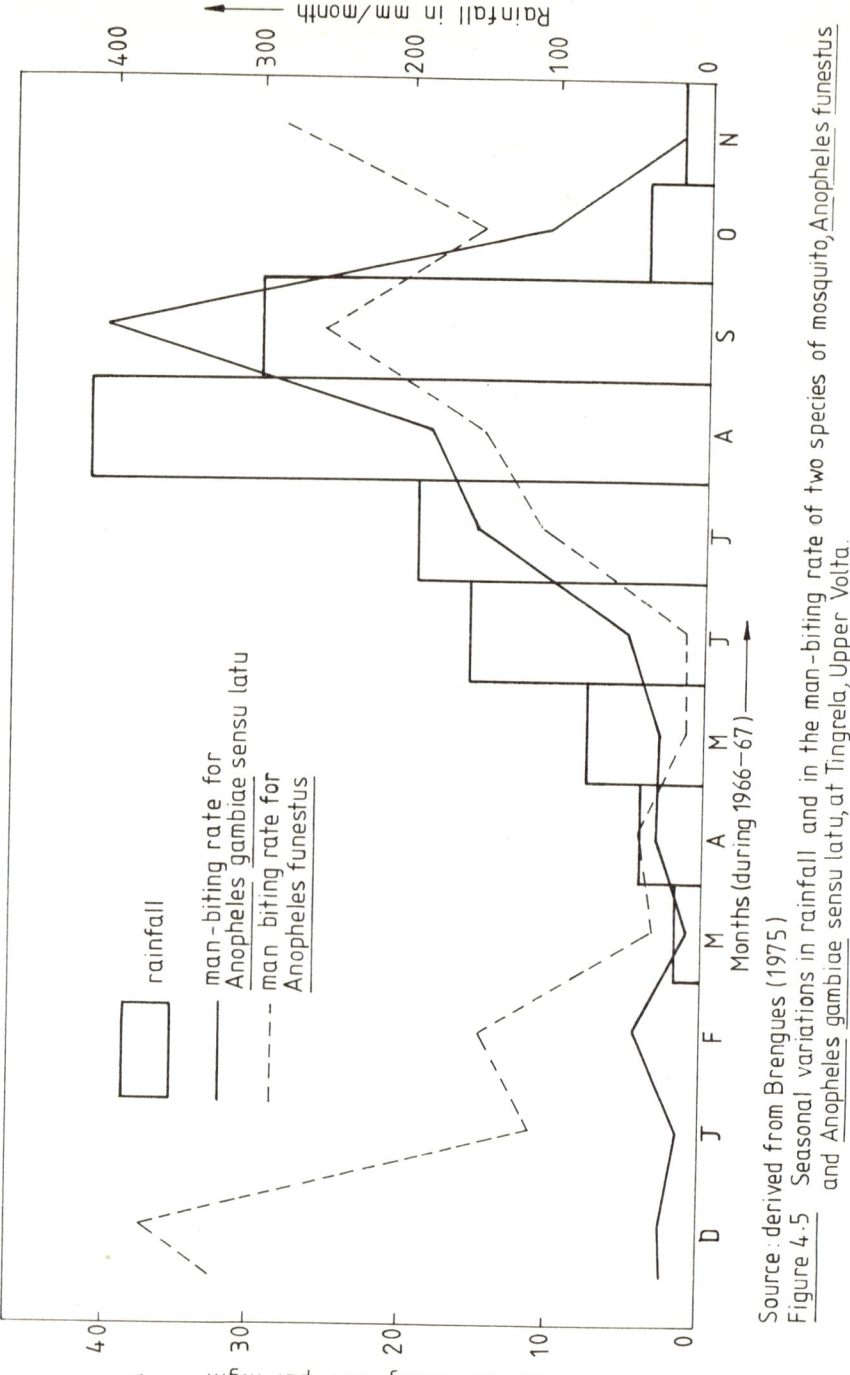

Source: derived from Brengues (1975)
Figure 4.5 Seasonal variations in rainfall and in the man-biting rate of two species of mosquito, Anopheles funestus and Anopheles gambiae sensu latu, at Tingrela, Upper Volta.

Seasonal Ecology of Disease

nematode worm, *Onchocerca volvulus*. This is closely related to the parasite which causes bancroftian filariasis, and has a similar life cycle. However, in the human host, the parasite operates mainly in the skin, and the microfilariae of *O. volvulus* are chiefly to be found there, and not in the blood. It is, indeed, the microfilariae which cause most damage, by their active migrations through the skin, and by their predilection for invading the eye, producing impaired vision and blindness.

Geographically, onchocerciasis has a much more restricted distribution than bancroftian filariasis, with four main endemic zones: West Africa (the largest), East Africa, Central and South America, and North Yemen. Two recent papers have shown that seasonal transmission of the disease strongly influences its intensity (Duke *et al.*, 1975; Fuglsang *et al.*, 1976). The position is worst when transmission is perennial. In a strongly seasonal climate, transmission is generally light, and does not lead to severe eye lesions, at any rate, not in savannah zones of West Africa. Seasonal concentrations of microfilariae in the human skin are highest in West Africa during the rainy season, which is when the insect vector *Simulium* reaches its maximum population.

Comparison with kala-azar

Visceral leishmaniasis, or kala-azar, presents a complete contrast with the two filarial infections discussed. The disease is caused by single-celled protozoa. These parasites are transmitted to man by the bites of sandflies.

The infection gives rise to a slowly progressive disease which rather resembles a long-drawn-out episode of malaria. It is characterised by fever, wasting, anaemia, enlargement of the spleen and liver, and depigmentation of the hair. The incubation period from time of infection to the development of symptoms is about six months, and if left untreated, mortality rates can be as high as 85 to 100 per cent.

Kala-azar had always been considered to have a marked seasonal distribution. Napier (1946) showed that monthly diagnoses of new cases seen in hospitals in Calcutta reached a peak between November and February. Similar data from Kenya (Southgate, 1964) revealed four different monthly patterns in four consecutive years. To try and make some sense of this, studies were made of the relevant insect vector, the sandfly *Phlebotomus martini*. Figure 4.6 shows both monthly rainfall and the monthly abundance of this insect, which are well correlated. The bottom part of the diagram indicates the monthly percentage of the annual totals of kala-azar cases for 1961 and 1962, obtained by monthly clinical and parasitological examinations of the whole population of the area studied. Every case was therefore recorded in the month when he became ill, and *not* in the month when he chose to visit a clinic or hospital, and this gave a far more consistent pattern.

The open bars in Figure 4.6 are simply the solid bars shifted back six months in time, which is the assumed incubation period of kala-azar in this area. They show that there is good correlation between rainfall, sandfly abundance, and the assumed month of infection (Southgate, 1977). This is a more consistent pattern than one usually finds with filarial infections, mainly because the incubation period is more nearly constant.

Seasonal Dimensions to Rural Poverty

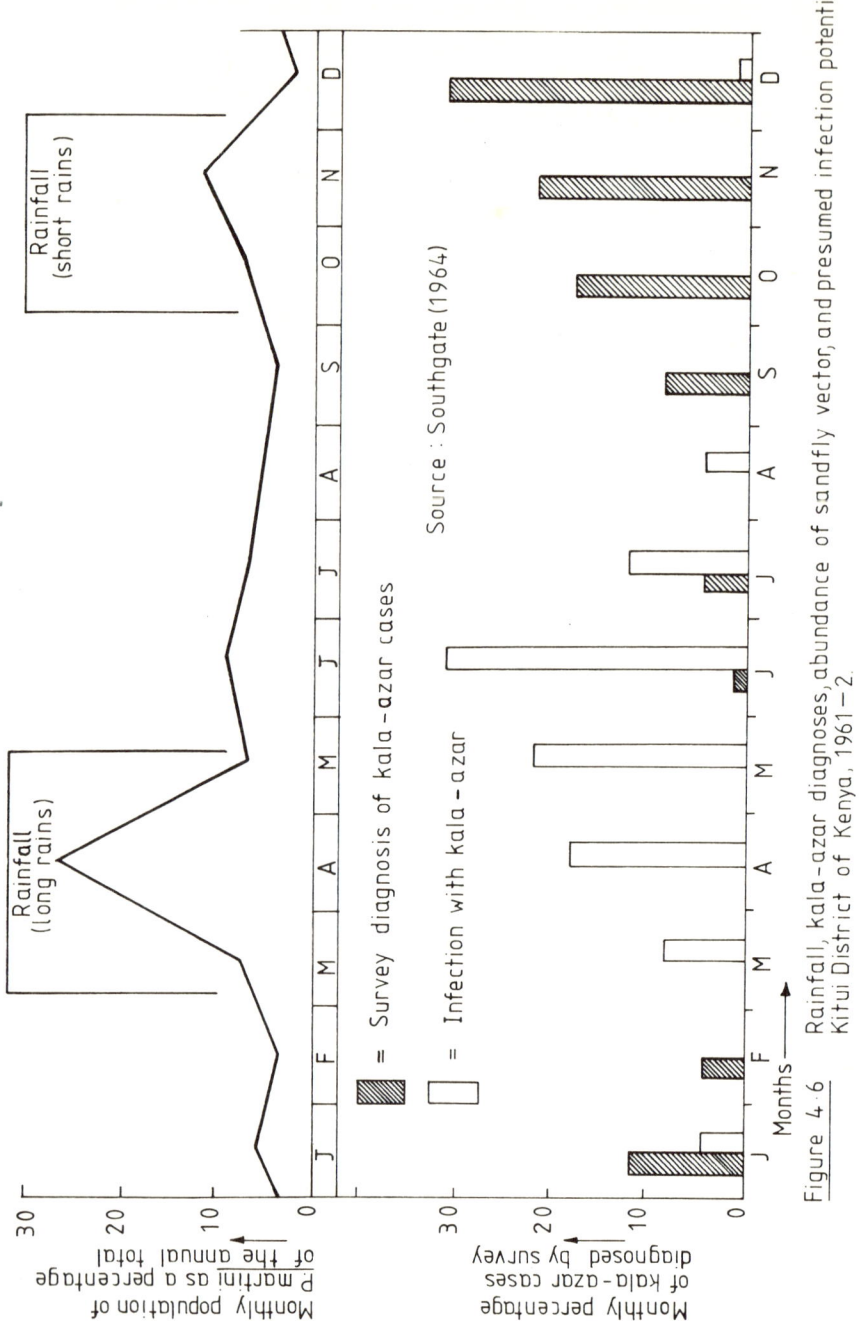

Figure 4.6 Rainfall, kala-azar diagnoses, abundance of sandfly vector, and presumed infection potential, Kitui District of Kenya, 1961–2.

4.8 Guinea-Worm Infection
R. Muller

Introduction

Guinea-worm is a disease that illustrates all too well the theme of this book. Wherever it occurs in the world, it is markedly seasonal in nature. Indeed, few other diseases coincide so closely with peak seasons for agricultural work, and few other diseases have such a disabling effect at this crucial time (Belcher *et al.*, 1975).

The seasonality of infection is bound up with the life cycle of the causative organism, the nematode worm *Dracunculus medinensis*. The worm usually lies under the skin of the leg, and at the beginning of the rainy season, the female worm is ready to produce larvae. It emerges from an abscess in the leg, and releases its larvae into water when the affected part is wetted. The larvae require a period of development in a water-flea, *Cyclops*. Thus about fourteen days must elapse before a person drinking the water containing the Cyclops can be infected.

Infection is likely where water for drinking is taken from still surface water, as in ponds or large open wells. Infection is not associated with running water, nor with wells less than one metre in diameter. Because the female worm takes a year to mature within the human body, the effects of a favourable season for transmission are perpetuated from one year to the next.

In the semi-arid areas of West Africa, Pakistan, and India, the annual rainfall of less than 700 mm is concentrated in three to four months of the year. Thus ponds are dry for much of the time, and drinking water is then obtained from bore wells or other sources. However, pond water is often more convenient to use when it is available, and guinea-worm transmission is thereby encouraged during the five months or so when the ponds contain water (see Table 4.2).

In humid areas of West Africa, ponds may contain water all the year, and infection may be apparent in man for up to eight months in the year (Table 4.2). However, few cases occur in the rainy season because there is then so much surface water that many ponds turn into streams.

Step wells, which provide the main source of drinking water in many rural areas of India, are ideally suited for transmission of guinea-worm. These wells are usually a few metres in diameter, providing good conditions for cyclops to breed. The steps leading down to the water result in affected limbs being immersed as individuals dip their water containers into the well. In these areas, the transmission pattern is similar to that found in the humid areas of West Africa. Little or no disease is found during the monsoon season, when the water level is high, but peak transmission occurs towards the end of the dry season (Table 4.2).

Economic effects of disease

Guinea-worm is very rarely a killing disease and usually results in spontaneous recovery. However, it does cause a degree of disability due to the painful blisters and abscesses on the feet and legs.

TABLE 4.2. Seasonal transmission of guinea-worm infection in various geographical regions

Region	Transmission season	Peak transmission	Length of transmission season (Months)	Rainy season
India				
Rajasthan	June–October	July	5	June–September
Bombay	February–May	March	4	June–October
Mysore	February–July	March–May	6	July–September
Madras	February–June	May	5	July–September
Pakistan				
Sind	June–October	September	5	June–September
Iran				
Larestan	March–August	June	6	November–February
Ghana				
N.W Ashanti	November–June	April	8	May–August
South	July–March	February	9	May–September
Nigeria				
North	June–October	September	5	May–September
South West	October–February	November	5	June–September

Source: Based on information reviewed in Muller (1971).

The age group which is most affected varies from area to area. In many parts of West Africa, the highest attack rate is in adult male farmers, with over three out of four infected in some villages. In India, infection is most common between the ages of six and fifteen years in males, but there is a sharp drop in the attack rate in older men. The infection rate is roughly equal in boys and girls, but does not drop so rapidly in older women (Rao and Reddy, 1965). These differences may be related to the site of infected water sources. In West Africa, some of these are ponds away from the villages, used mainly by working males. In India, they are principally step wells sited in or around the village.

Belcher *et al.* (1975) interviewed twenty men incapacitated by guinea-worm. The average period of complete disability was 5.3 weeks. Patients described three approaches used to minimise the work loss. The first was to shift the work-load onto other members of the family; this had been successful in only two of the families as other members were also infected. The second was to get help from neighbours, but none had been successful in this (cooperative farming was not practised in the area). The third was to employ casual farm labourers. However, such workers are at a premium during the planting season, and although two of the farmers started on this course, neither had the resources to see it through to completion.

One study in villages in western Nigeria showed that almost one-quarter of the working population was incapacitated for at least ten weeks each year (Muller, 1971). In another study, it was reckoned that the period of incapacity of infected individuals ranged from three weeks to nine months (Kale, 1977). In southern Ghana, some farmers lost a major crop as a result of disablement which lasted for over five weeks (Belcher *et al.*, 1975). In both Africa and India, the maximum incidence of disease often coincides with the planting season.

Prospects for control and eradication

Guinea-worm disappears quite quickly when piped water supplies, bore wells, or tubewells are provided and used. However, in many of the poor rural areas where the disease occurs, sophisticated methods of water supply are not feasible. Much can still be done, though, to interrupt transmission of guinea-worm by much simpler means. The most spectacular example was the complete elimination of the disease from Samarkand and Tashkent over forty years ago by the replacement of step wells by draw wells of much smaller diameter. Similar conversions of step wells in a few villages in India lowered the prevalence of disease locally (Rao and Reddy, 1965).

Chemical treatment of ponds and wells with organo-phosphorus compounds with residual action, which can be added to kill cyclops in potable water supplies, is feasible and relatively cheap (Muller, 1979).

Once transmission is interrupted in an area for a single season, infection ceases entirely unless it is reintroduced from outside. The ease with which this might be accomplished is illustrated by experience in the Sind desert area of Pakistan. Infection vanished completely from this region in the early 1930s, following a severe drought when the ponds never filled, and it remained free of disease until 1947, when the disease came back with an influx of people following partition.

4.9 Seasonal Variables In Infective Disease: A Summary
David Bradley

Schistosomiasis and seasonal variables

Schistosomiasis or bilharzia is a disease which illustrates many of the seasonal variables in the transmission of infection which have been discussed in this chapter. The disease is caused by schistosome worms whose life cycle is complex, with 'latent' periods which delay the outcome of seasonal effects.

Paired adult worms in the human body lay eggs which mature in about six days (or more). The eggs then escape via faeces (*Schistosoma mansoni* and *S. japonicum*), or via urine (*S. haematobium*). They hatch at once on reaching water, but can survive in moist faeces for up to three weeks prior to hatching. The larva that emerges has to find an appropriate species of water-snail within a few hours if it is to survive. It penetrates the snail and develops in four to twelve weeks, depending on the ambient temperature and the snail species. It then gives rise to large numbers of cercariae each day, which may survive in the water for up to two days, and penetrate the skin of people coming into contact with the water. Development of such cercariae as enter people's bodies then takes two to three months before the parasites reach maturity and begin laying eggs. The adult worms in the human body may live as long as three to five years, though some have been known to persist much longer.

The most strongly seasonal element in this cycle is related to the water-snails, the size of whose habitat often depends on rainfall. Snail ecology varies with the species, so a range of seasonal patterns occurs. At one extreme is *Biomphalaria choanomphala* living on the bottom of Lake Victoria at a depth where it is protected from much seasonal variation. Not far away, however, is a contrasting situation involving *Bulinus nasutus* in Tanzania. This snail inhabits temporary ponds, often only a few metres across, in a seasonally arid environment. For the latter part of the dry season, the sites of these ponds are marked by depressions lined with dried mud. With the onset of the rains, the ponds fill up and aestivating snails emerge from the mud and begin to lay eggs. When the rains cease, the ponds gradually shrink and the snail population reaches its peak. As the ponds begin to dry up, snails migrate down into the mud again.

If water is continually contaminated, and schistosome eggs enter it at a steady rate, the number of cercariae in the water will depend on the snail population. However, because of the time needed for the organism to develop within the snail, maximum cercarial production lags behind the peak in snail numbers. The development stage within the snail is shortened by high temperatures, but at the same time, the snails may be very short lived in hot weather.

In seasonal habitats such as ponds in Tanzania, or laterite pools in eastern Gambia, the maximum number of *infected* snails is found after total snail population has peaked. Numbers are then soon truncated by the drying of the ponds, so that transmission may be confined to a limited part of the year.

It is evident that schistosomiasis, like other diseases discussed in this chapter, has a varying seasonal pattern of transmission, depending on *local* environmental conditions. Like other diseases also, the determinants of schistosome transmission are not wholly biological, or due to physical conditions. Human factors are important also. Where people defecate near to water sources, infected excreta add to the risk of transmission if rainfall soon washes the schistosome eggs into the water. A more significant seasonal pattern of pollution may occur with *S. haematobium*. Children playing in ponds or streams and urinating while doing so are responsible for much transmission, and when water bodies are shrinking in the dry season, the deposition of parasite eggs may be greatly concentrated.

Human behaviour may thus lead to seasonal variations in the contamination of water. Seasonal variations in contacts made by people with water are more important in relation to infection, however, in two ways. First, the frequency of water contact varies seasonally; children will play in water more in hot weather. Second, and perhaps more significant, the decreasing extent of surface water in the dry season may lead to intensified water contact at those sites and times when cercariae are most likely to be present in the water. Hence, in the absence of irrigation or other artificial conditions, transmission will often peak early in the dry season.

However, the process of becoming infected is very different from illness. What matters most is the insidious effect of a heavy worm-burden, and the

Seasonal Ecology of Disease

progressive consequences of liver fibrosis and renal damage which may result from a heavy infection maintained over years. Seasonal variations in transmission probably lead to rather little seasonality of *disease*. One exception to this is in the condition known as swimmer's itch, where schistosomes of a species which cannot develop in humans die as they enter the skin and cause a nasty rash. There is, as would be expected, a marked seasonal concentration of cases.

Two kinds of seasonal disease

While it would be possible to discuss the seasonality of schistosome transmission in much greater detail, the variables referred to so far are the key ones for general understanding of seasonality in infectious diseases and we now turn to these general issues. The relevant variables include the environmental and human factors already mentioned, and also the time taken for the infective organism to develop through its several stages.

The range of diseases which show some seasonality is great, but all fall into two main groups. For the majority, climatic or related events chance to favour transmission at a certain season, and seasonal outbreaks occur if the progression from infection to manifest disease is short enough for a clustering of cases. Among a minority of diseases, though, regulatory mechanisms defer some disabling stages of illness to a particular season. In the latter, this timing of disease has evolved in relation to the transmission dynamics, and the infection is locked into a seasonal pattern.

The clearest example of an infection 'programmed' to give rise to transmission, and incidentally severe disability, at a particular season is guinea-worm, with its twelve month maturation period (Section 4.8). But there is evidence from India that some hookworm infections may have a seasonal delay in development, or at any rate in egg-laying, which is greatest at a season suitable for transmission. One can see traces of a similar evolutionary path in those strains of *vivax* malaria from Eastern Europe which have an immensely long phase in the liver cells before the red cell infection takes place, and where the primary attack is delayed. This can be viewed as an adaptation of the parasite to a short annual transmission season (Section 4.6).

Among the many seasonally variable diseases less precisely 'locked in' to an annual cycle, the degree of concentration to a particular time of year depends on the way the disease spreads from one person to another, and on the generation time. The latter is the time that elapses between the day on which a case of the disease occurs, and the day on which someone else catching the disease from that first case becomes ill. In respiratory infections and diarrhoea, generation time is rarely more than a few days. In malaria, a month or two is involved, but as the initial case remains infective for several months if untreated, secondary cases may be numerous and spread out in time.

The other feature of a disease that will affect its seasonal concentration is the basic case reproduction rate, or the number of people who can be infected from one case. To get a rapid build-up of disease in a short season favourable for transmission requires either a very short generation time or a very high basic case reproduction rate, or both. Meningococcal meningitis, cholera, and influenza have both these characteristics and therefore tend to occur in epidemic form at seasons favourable to transmission, the epidemics being ended either by environmental factors changing, or by human acquired immunity as the number of susceptible people becomes exhausted.

Environmental and human variables

Because of the delays and latent periods described in previous paragraphs, seasonal disability does not always follow from the seasonal transmission of a disease. Transmission is quite often seasonal, especially under conditions of seasonal rainfall. Vector-borne diseases, in particular, are affected because many insect vectors depend on surface water for breeding. Moist conditions also tend to favour the survival of pathogenic organisms, and surface run-off water during storms may transfer bacterial pollution as well as schistosome eggs into water sources (Section 4.2). High humidity during the rainy season may affect skin flora, and may thereby cause a seasonal increase in infections of the skin (Section 4.5).

Among the human population, if malnutrition is more prevalent in some seasons than others, this may mean that people's susceptibility to infection varies seasonally. There are also seasonal variations in human behaviour which have a large effect: the contact between people indoors during a cold, dry season will facilitate the spread of some respiratory infections.

Among the vector-borne diseases, malaria (Section 4.6), guinea-worm (Section 4.8), and sometimes dengue and other insect-borne viruses (Section 4.4), have the greatest seasonal impact. Schistosomiasis and sleeping sickness may show seasonal transmission but the consequences are drawn out and this is sometimes true of kala-azar and filariasis (Section 4.7). In the savannah areas (e.g. Gambia), malaria transmission increases when the rains begin, following the rise in mosquito population. In some parts of the Indian Subcontinent, malaria is also a disease of the rains, but in others, mosquito breeding is restricted to the dry season when the streams are not in spate.

Diarrhoeal diseases (Sections 4.2 and 4.3) show marked seasonal rises, but against a continuously high background level in many areas. The peak often comes in the hot season and/or the early rains, but detailed analysis shows that differing causes of diarrhoea have staggered peaks. Respiratory infections may resemble the diarrhoeas in their peak season, but this is variable. Cerebrospinal meningitis is spread by the respiratory route. The immense epidemics of the African savannah tend to occur near the end of the dry season, and in a highly predictable manner in any one locality (Section 6.3).

The greatest regular seasonal impact on rural society, then, is often due to malaria, the diarrhoeal diseases, and guinea-worm. The brunt of the first two falls upon infants, though all age-groups are affected. Both diseases have strong interactions with nutrition, and measures that could improve nutrition would reduce the effects of the infections, and vice versa. There is also an obvious connection with maternal care, since all these infections come at a time of peak labour demand.

It is clear that disease is both a cause and a result of poverty. Disease does not appear to be the cause of differential seasonal poverty, except that by adding to the burden of the poorest, it increases the risk that some irreversible downward step will be taken.

4.10 References

Anjaneyulu, G., Banerji, S. C., Indrayan, A. (1975), 'A Study of the Fly Density and Meteorological Factors in Occurrence of Diarrhoea in a Rural Area', *Indian J. Public Health, 19* (3), pp. 115-21.

Belcher, D. W., Wurapa, F. K., Ward, W. B., and Lourie, I. M. (1975), 'Guinea Worm in Southern Ghana', *Amer. J. Trop. Medicine and Hygiene, 24,* pp. 243-9.

Bell, C. (1974), *Diseases and Health Services of Papua-New Guinea,* Department of Public Health, Port Moresby.

Bishop, R. F., Davidson, G. P., Holmes, I. H., and Ruck, B. J. (1973), 'Virus Particles in Epithelial Cells of Duodenal Mucosa from Children with Acute Non-bacterial Gastroenteritis', *Lancet, 2,* pp. 1281-3.

Bray, R. S., and Anderson, M. J. (1979), '*Falciparum* Malaria and Pregnancy', *Trans. Royal Soc. Trop. Med. Hyg., 78,* pp. 427-31.

Brengues, J. (1975), 'La filaroise de Bancroft en Afrique de l'ouest'. Paris: *Mémoires ORSTOM,* No. 79.

Buck, A. A. (1968), *Health and Disease in Four Peruvian Villages,* Baltimore, Johns Hopkins Press.

Cherubin, C. E., Fodor, T., Denmark, L., Master, C., Fuerst, H. T., and Winter, J. (1969), 'The Epidemiology of Salmonellosis in New York City', *Amer. J. Epidemiol., 90* (2), pp. 112-25.

Christophers, S. R. (1911), 'Malaria in the Punjab', *Scientific Memoirs by Officers of the Medical and Sanitary Departments of the Government of India,* New Series No. 46, Calcutta.

Chrystie, I. L., Totterdell, B. M., and Banatvala, J. E. (1978), 'Asymptomatic Endemic Rotavirus Infection in the Newborn', *Lancet, 1,* pp. 1176-8.

Coatney, G. R., Cooper, W. C., Ruhe, D. S., Young, M. D., and Burgess, R. W. (1950a), 'The Life Pattern of Sporozoite-induced St. Elizabeth Strain *vivax* Malaria', *Amer. J. Hyg., 51,* pp. 200-15.

Coatney, G. R., Cooper, W. C., and Young, M. D. (1950b), 'A Summary of 204 Sporozoite-induced Infections with the Chesson Strain of *Plasmodium vivax*', *J. Nat. Mal. Soc., 9,* pp. 381-96.

Covell, G., and Bailey, J. D. (1930), 'Malaria in the Sind', *Rec. Mal. Survey India, 1,* pp. 549-65.

Covell, G., and Bailey, J. D. (1932), 'The Study of a Regional Epidemic of Malaria in Northern Sind', *Rec. Mal. Survey India, 3,* 279-322.

Cramblett, H. G., Azimi, P., and Haynes, R. E. (1971), 'The Aetiology of Infectious Diarrhoea in Infancy', *Ann. New York Acad. Sci., 176,* pp. 80-92.

Creighton, C., (1965), *History of Epidemics in Britain.* 2nd ed. with additional material by D.E.C. Eversley, E. A. Underwood, and L. Ovenall, London, Frank Cass.

Cutting, W.A.M. (1978), 'Seasonal Variations in Rotavirus and Diarrhoea in Childhood', Paper presented at the Conference on Seasonal Dimensions to Rural Poverty, Institute of Development Studies, University of Sussex, 3-6 July 1978 (original version).

Dean, A. G., and Jones, T. C. (1972), 'Seasonal Gastroenteritis and Malabsorption at an American Military Base in the Philippines', *Amer. J. Epidemiol., 95,* p. 111.

Duggan, M. B., and Beyer, L. (1975), 'Enteric Fever in Young Yoruba Children', *Arch. Dis. Child., 50* (1), pp. 67-71.

Duke, B.O.L., Anderson, J., and Fuglsang, H. (1975), '*Onchocerca volvulus* Transmission Potentials and Associated Patterns of Onchocerciasis at Four Cameroon Villages', *Tropenmedizin und Parasitologie, 26,* pp. 143-54.

Feachem, R. (1974), *Environment and Health in a New Guinea Highlands Community,* Oxford, Oxford Microform Publications.

Feachem, R. (1975), 'Faecal Coliforms and Faecal Streptococci in Streams in the New Guinea Highlands', *Water Research, 8,* pp. 367-74.

Feachem, R. (1977), 'Water Supplies for Low-income Communities', in *Water, Wastes and Health in Hot Climates,* eds. R. Feachem, M. McGarry, and D. Mara, London, John Wiley & Sons.

Feachem, R., Burns, E., Cairncross, A., Cronin, A., Cross, P., Curtis, D., Khan, M. K., Lamb, D., and Southall, H. (1978), *Water, Health and Development: An Interdisciplinary Evaluation,* London, Tri-Med.

Feldman, R. A., Kamath, K. R., Rao, P. S., and Webb, J. K. (1969), 'Infection and Disease in a Group of South Indian Families', *Amer. J. Epidemiol., 89* (4), pp. 364-74.

Flewett, T. H., Bryden, A. S., and Davies, H. A. (1973), 'Virus Particles in Gastroenteritis', *Lancet,* 2, p. 1497.

Fuglsang, H., Anderson, J., Marshall, T. F. de C., Ayonge, S., and Fisiy, C. (1976), 'Seasonal Variation in the Concentration of *Onchocerca volvulus* Microfilariae in the Skin', *Tropenmedizin und Parasitologie, 27,* pp. 365-9.

Giglioli, M.E.C. (1964), 'Tides, Salinity, and the Breeding of *Anopheles melas* in the Gambia', *Riv. Malario., 43,* pp. 245-62.

Gorman, A. E., and Wolman, A. (1939), 'Water-borne Outbreaks in the United States and Canada and their Significance', *J. Amer. Water Works Ass., 31,* p. 225.

Greenwood, M. (1935), *Epidemics and Crowd Diseases,* London, Williams and Norgate.

Hassan, Z. A., and Southgate, B. A. (1978), Unpublished observations.

Hellström, L. (1975), 'Salmonella Infections in Stockholm', *Scand. J. Infect. Diseases, 7* (2), pp. 1117-22.

Hemmes, J. H., Winkler, K. C., and Kool, S. M. (1960), 'Virus Survival as a Seasonal Factor in Influenza and Poliomyelitis', *Nature (Lond.), 188,* pp. 430-1.

Higgins, A. R., Floyd, T. M., and Kader, M. A. (1955), 'Studies in Shigellosis', parts I and II. *Amer. J. Trop. Med., 4,* pp. 263 and 271.

Ibrahim, A. (1927), 'The Relation of Funiculitis to Hydrocele in Egypt', *Lancet,* 2, pp. 272-4.

Kale, O. O. (1977), 'The Clinico-epidemiological Profile of Guinea Worm in the Ibadan District of Nigeria', *Amer. J. Trop. Med. Hyg., 26,* pp. 208-14.

Kamath, K. R., Feldman, R. A., Rao, P. S., and Webb, J. K. (1969), 'Infection and Disease in a Group of South India Families', *Amer. J. Epidemiol., 89* (4), pp. 375-83.

Kapikian, A. Z. *et al.* (1976), 'Human Reovirus-like Agent as the Major Pathogen Associated with "Winter" Gastroenteritis', *New England Journal of Medicine, 294,* pp. 965-72.

Klipstein, F. A., Rubio, C., MacDonald, N., and Montas, S. (1972), 'Investigations Concerning the Prevalence of Nutritional Deficiencies and Intestinal Malabsorption among Rural Populations', *Amer. J. Clinical Nutrition, 25,* pp. 1236-42.

McCormack, W. M., Mosley, W. H., Fahimuddin, M., and Benenson, A. S. (1969), 'Endemic Cholera in Rural East Pakistan', *Amer. J. Epidemiol., 89,* p. 393.

McGregor, I. A., Rahman, A. K., Thomson, A. M., Billewicz, W. Z., and Thompson, B. (1970), 'The Health of Young Children in a West African (Gambian) Village', *Trans. R. Soc. Trop. Med. Hyg.,* 64, pp. 48-77.

Martin, A. R., Mosley, W. H., Sau, B. B., Ahmed, S., and Huq, I. (1969), 'Epidemiological Analysis of Endemic Cholera in Urban East Pakistan', *Amer. J. Epidemiol., 89,* p. 572.

Mata, L. J. (1978), Private communication with W.A.M. Cutting.

Mathan, M. M. (1978), Private communication with W.A.M. Cutting.

Mathur, G. M., and Sharma, R. (1971), 'A Study of Typhoid Fever in Jaipur, India', *Trop. Geogr. Med., 23* (4), pp. 329-34.

Moore, H. A., de la Cruz, E., and Vargas-Mendez, O. (1965), 'Diarrhoeal Disease Studies in Costa Rica', *Amer. J. Epidemiol., 82,* pp. 162-4.

Morley, D. C. (1967), in *Modern Trends in Medical Virology,* ed. R. B. Heath and A. P. Waterson, London, Butterworth.

Morley, D. C., Bicknell, J., and Woodland, M. (1968), 'Factors Influencing the Growth and Nutritional Status of Infants and Young Children in a Nigerian Village', *Trans. R. Soc. Trop. Med. Hyg.,* 62, pp. 164-99.

Muller, R. (1971), '*Dracunculus* and Dracunculiasis', *Advances in Parasitology, 9,* pp. 73-152.

Muller, R. (1979), 'Guinea Worm Disease: Epidemiology, Control and Treatment', *Bulletin of the World Health Organisation,* 57, pp. 683-9.

Napier, L. E. (1946), *The Principles and Practice of Tropical Medicine*, New York, Macmillan.
Newsholme, A. (1923), *The Elements of Vital Statistics*, London, Allen and Unwin.
Pan American Health Organisation (1979), *Dengue in the Caribbean*, Proceedings of a Workshop held in Montego Bay, Jamaica, May 1978, PAHO Scientific Publication, Washington D.C.
Porter, M. J. (1977), 'An Epidemiological Approach to Skin Diseases in the Tropics', *Tropical Doctor, 7*, pp. 59-66.
Rao, C. K., and Reddy, G.V.M. (1965), 'Dracontiasis in West Godovari and Kurnool Districts, Andhra Pradesh', *Bull. Indian Soc. Malaria and Communicable Diseases, 2,* pp. 275-93.
Richardson, N. J., Hayden-Smith, S., Bokkenheuser, V., Koornhof, N. (1968), 'Salmonellae and Shigellae in Bantu Children Consuming Drinking Water of Improved Quality', *S. Afr. Med. J., 42* (3), pp. 46-9.
Roberts, E. (1906), *Enteric Fever in India*, London, Balliere, Tindall and Cox.
Rogers, L. (1957), 'Thirty Years' Research on the Control of Cholera Epidemics', *Brit. Med. J., 2,* p. 1193.
Rowland, M.G.M., Davies, H., Patterson, S., Dourmashkin, R. R., Tyrrell, D.A.J., Matthews, T.H.J., Parry, J., Hall, J., and Larson, H. E. (1978), 'Viruses and Diarrhoea in West Africa and London: a Collaborative Study', *Trans. R. Soc. Trop. Med. Hyg., 72* (1), pp. 95-8.
Sasa, M. (1976), *Human Filariasis*, Baltimore, University Park Press.
Schaeffer, M., Gajdusek, D. C., Lema, A. B., and Eichenwald, H. (1959), 'Epidemic Jungle Fevers Among Okinawan Colonists in the Bolivian Rain Forest', *Amer. J. Trop. Med. Hyg., 8*, pp. 372 and 479.
Scrimshaw, N. S., Guzman, M. A., Flores, M., and Gordon, J. E. (1968), 'Nutrition and Infection Field Study in Guatemalan Villages, 1959-64', *Arch. Environ. Health, 16* (2), pp. 223-4.
Singh, B., Sharma, M. D., and Saxena, S. N. (1965), 'Paratyphoid A Fever in Delhi', *Indian J. Med. Res., 53* (10), pp. 938-41.
Sinton, J. A. (1935), 'What Malaria Costs India', *Rec. Mal. Survey India, 5,* pp. 223-64.
Sivagnanasundram, C. (1971), *Dynamics of Malaria in Ceylon*, Ph.D. thesis, University of London.
Southgate, B. A. (1964), 'Studies in the Epidemiology of East African Leishmaniasis', *Trans. R. Soc. Trop. Med. Hyg., 58*, pp. 377-90.
Southgate, B. A. (1977), 'The Structure of Foci of Visceral Leishmaniasis in Northeastern Kenya', in *Écologie des leishmanises*, Colloques Internationaux du Centre National de la Recherche Scientifique, No. 239, Paris, Editions du CNRS, pp. 241-7.
Sutton, R.N.P. (1965), 'Minor Illness in Trinidad: a Longitudinal Study', *Trans. R. Soc. Trop. Med. Hyg., 59*, pp. 212-20.
Sutton, R.N.P. (1966), 'Acute Respiratory Disease and Climate', in S. W. Tromp, and W. H. Weihe, (eds.), *Proc. 3rd Int. Biometeorological Cong. 1963, 2*, 41, Oxford, Pergamon Press.
Teruel, J. R., Gomes, U. A., and Nogueira, J. L. (1973), 'Seasonal Distribution of Deaths Caused by Diarrhoea and Malnutrition in Childhood', *Rev. Inst. Med. Trop. Sao Paulo, 15,* pp. 289-97.
Thomas, M. E., and Tillett, H. E. (1973), 'Sonne Dysentery in Day Schools and Nurseries: an 18-year Study in Edmonton', *J. Hyg. (Camb.), 71* (3), pp. 593-602.
Tomkins, A. M. (1979), 'Folate Malnutrition in Tropical Diarrhoeas', *Trans. R. Soc. Trop. Med. Hyg.* 73, pp. 498-502.
Vines, A. P. (1970), *An Epidemiological Survey of Papua New Guinea*, Port Moresby, Department of Public Health.
Waddy, B. B. (1952), 'Climate and Respiratory Infection', *Lancet, 2,* pp. 674-7.
Walker, A. C., and Marshall, W. C. (1978), 'Rotavirus Infection in Aboriginal Children in Darwin', (in press).
White, G., Bradley, D., and White, A. (1972), *Drawers of Water: Domestic Water Use in East Africa*, Chicago, University of Chicago Press.
Wilson, G. S., and Miles, A. A. (1975), *Principles of Bacteriology, Virology and Immunity* (Topley and Wilson), 6th ed., London, Edward Arnold.

Woodward, W. E., Hirschhorn, N., Sack, R. B., Cash, R. A., Brownlee, I., Chickadonz, G. H., Evans, L. K., Shepard, R. H., and Woodward, R. C. (1974), 'Acute Diarrhoea on an Apache Indian Reservation', *Amer. J. Epidemiol., 99,* (4), pp. 281-90.

Wyatt, R. G., Yolken, R. H., Urrutia, J. J., Mata, L., Greenberg, H. B., Chanock, R. M., and Kapikian, A. Z., (in press), 'Diarrhoeas Associated with Rotavirus in Rural Guatemala: a Longitudinal Study of 24 Infants and Young Children', *American J. Trop. Medicine.*

Chapter 5
SEASONAL PATTERNS IN BIRTHS AND DEATHS

5.1 Causes of Seasonal Fluctuation In Vital Events
Tim Dyson and Nigel Crook*

Demographic interrelationships

The structure and growth of any population is determined by its fertility, mortality, and migration. These variables are linked through the age/sex structure. A change in any one will, after a time, often bring about a change in the other two. Chapter 4 showed that many diseases are seasonal in their impact, and might, therefore, be expected to lead to seasonal variations in mortality. Many other factors, though, lead to seasonal cycles in demographic variables.

In many developing countries, seasonal fluctuations in births bring about corresponding fluctuations in deaths. The probability of dying is highest in the period immediately after birth; therefore a seasonal concentration of births will be accompanied by a seasonal concentration of neonatal deaths. Even if the risk of dying stays the same, the crude death rate will rise due to the seasonally increased number of deaths of the very young.

Conversely, seasonal fluctuations in mortality could induce seasonal fluctuations in fertility. In non-contracepting populations which practise prolonged breast feeding, an infant death may shorten the period of post-partum amenorrhoea, and hasten the resumption of ovulation. If there were a pronounced seasonal peak to early-age mortality, this might lead to a seasonal increase in new pregnancies.

Where short-term migration of members of one sex operates on a seasonal basis, we may expect this to impart a seasonal effect to births. But seasonal patterns of fertility could also induce seasonal short-term migrations. In parts of India, a woman returns to her natal home to give birth; if births occur seasonally, then so will this kind of migration. Seasonal labour migration, discussed in Chapter 7, may well take the fitter persons from a community, leaving the aged and weak in greater danger of sickness and death.

Climate in relation to seasonal fertility changes

Temperature and rainfall are the two climatic variables which, in conjunction with other factors, are most likely to have an effect on fertility. In Figure 5.1, the influence of these variables is seen moving diagramatically from left to right, i.e. from seasonal climatic change to change in the annual tempo of births. In addition we might expect feedback mechanisms to operate, with

---

*In this paper, Tim Dyson takes responsibility for fertility and Nigel Crook for mortality. We acknowledge funding from the Centre for Population Studies and the Institute of Development Studies to cover research assistance. We wish to thank Shan Nicholas, Jane O'Brien, and especially Yolande Jemai, Sue Evans, and Sandhya Dalal for their tremendous help.

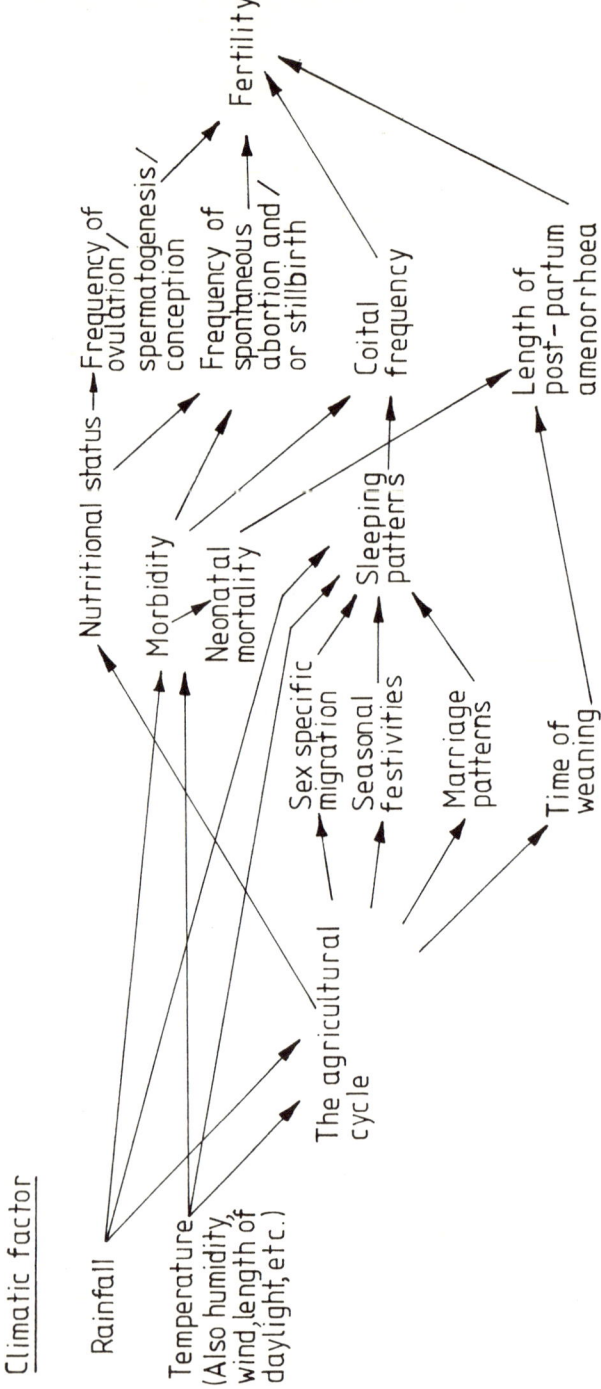

Figure 5.1 A simplified diagram of some of the main interrelationships likely to bring about a seasonal fluctuation in births.

resonance and damping effects. The diagram shows that both biological and social variables affect seasonal fertility variation; further, that any variables bringing about such seasonal changes must operate through one of the following factors:
(1) coital frequency;
(2) variations in ovulation, spermatogenesis, and conception; effects of post-partum amenorrhoea;
(3) the likelihood of successful gestation and parturition.

Perhaps the best documented seasonal association with fertility is that of temperature. Highly significant negative correlations of temperature with the probable number of monthly conceptions have been found in Hong Kong (Chang et al., 1963), Bangladesh (Stoeckel and Chowdhury, 1972), Uganda and Singapore (Parkes, 1976). Below we will show that for most developing countries, the summer months are characterised by a lower than average number of conceptions.

Several physiological mechanisms have been proffered to account for these correlations (Chang et al., 1963). However, the most plausible explanation is that temperature affects coital frequency directly through sleeping patterns and indirectly through intermediate mechanisms related to the agricultural cycle (Figure 5.1). During the heat of summer, people tend to sleep separately — often out of doors in conditions of little privacy; in hot (or humid) conditions, sexual intercourse may be less attractive (Chen et al., 1974a; Takahashi, 1964). Conversely, when temperatures are low, people tend to sleep together for warmth. There is evidence from a rural area of Bangladesh that sexual intercourse is more common during the cool season. Wyon and Gordon (1971) also noted that coital frequency in one part of the Punjab probably varied with the seasons, since couples slept together more often in the winter for warmth (Prasad et al., 1969).

The agricultural cycle in relation to fluctuations in fertility

Temperature and rainfall are perhaps the two most important climatic determinants of the structure of the agricultural year, which in turn has implications for the seasonal pattern of work, migration, sleeping arrangements, festivities, nutrition, marriages, and the weaning of infants. Each of these can be expected to influence the level of conceptions.

Many of the activities affected by the agricultural cycle influence fertility through their effect on coital frequency (Figure 5.1). Coition may take place more often at those relatively easy times of the year when work inputs are lower and food is relatively abundant, i.e. during the 'post-harvest season'; this is a time which is often characterised by many festivities including marriages. In many countries it may also be the coolest time of year. Clearly, both the frequency and length of such periods will depend upon the nature of the particular agricultural system. Several studies in developing countries have found small but significant differences in the seasonality of births between occupation groups, probably related to differences in the annual cycle of work. Labourers and farmers are often away from home during the harvest season and cultivators may decide selectively to sleep out in the fields at this time (Stoeckel and Chowdhury, 1972). Chen et al. (1974a) note that in Bangladesh, fishermen leave home seasonally. In rural Mexico, highly seasonal short-term rural-urban migration was found to have some influence on the annual cycle of births (Thompson and Robbins, 1973). In many countries, seasonal migrants contain a high proportion of young adult males who leave their spouses at home.

Another factor influencing seasonal fertility may be the effect of poor nutrition on ovulation. In a rural area of Bangladesh, Chen *et al.* (1974a) found that a combination of lengthy breast feeding and poor food intake appeared to augment the period of post-partum infertility. Their data indicated a seasonal variation in the onset of ovulation following lactational amenorrhoea. The return of ovulation tended to coincide with and follow the main rice harvest. This might be because the health and nutritional status of the population improves at this time, thereby increasing fecundity; and women may prefer to wean their children during the harvest season because of heavy demands on their time for post-harvest processing work, or because weaning foods become more available. Whatever the reason, this mechanism probably accounts for only a small amount of the total monthly variation in conceptions and the hypothesis is somewhat controversial.

If marriage follows a seasonal pattern, and if it marks the onset of sexual relations, then we would expect this to influence the seasonal distribution of births. Our analysis of monthly marriage data from developing countries indicates that some seasonality of marriage is common. For many countries, the seasonality of births due to the timing of marriages probably accounts for a small proportion of the overall variation, and tends to reinforce other relevant seasonal influences on births. Studies in West Malaysia (Johnson *et al.*, 1975), Japan (Takahashi, 1964), and Bangladesh (Stoeckel and Chowdhury, 1972) indicate that first births (which can be expected to reflect marriages nine months previously) and multiparous births exhibit similar seasonal patterns. This suggests that 'preferred' marriage months often occur at times of year when coital frequency among the already-married section of the population is also above average.

The link between seasonal festivities and increased numbers of conceptions is widely cited. Such festivities may often occur at the most pleasant time of year, and as such, may coincide with other factors making for increased coital frequency (Himes and Malina, 1977). But as with marriages, so also seasonal festivities may be 'detached' from the agricultural cycle — Ramadan is one such example. Moreover, religious festivals such as Ramadan may discourage both marriages and sexual intercourse.

The effect of the agricultural cycle is often that fewer conceptions occur during the busy rainy season, but in very wet climates, the relationship may be reversed. A study in rural Uganda found that rainfall best explained the estimated frequency of monthly conceptions. Thompson and Robbins (1973) write that 'a great deal of time is spent indoors sleeping during rainstorms'. Another study in Ghana also found that the peak period for conceptions was during the rainy season (Holzer, 1968). In contrast, a detailed study of registration data in Maharashtra found that the lowest number of conceptions occurs during the rainy season, because this is the time of planting, and there is less chance of people spending long periods indoors (India, 1973).

Some mention of morbidity (which is certainly affected by both rainfall and temperature variation) is appropriate here. It can plausibly be reasoned that

Seasonal Patterns in Births and Deaths

an increase of sickness in a population would *ceteris paribus* be accompanied by a decrease in coital frequency. People feel much less keen on sexual relations when they are ill; they may believe that sexual activity will make their condition worse; and they may also think that close contact spreads the illness. In Sri Lanka, prior to malaria eradication, estimated conceptions were lowest during the peak period for transmission, whereas after control, the seasonal pattern of births became less pronounced (Newman, 1970). Another effect of illness may be that infection induces excessive foetal loss (Gray and Doyle, forthcoming).

Anthropologists have suggested that people plan conceptions so that births take place at favourable times of year (Nurge, 1970; Cowgill, 1966a, b). In this book, Chapter 3 tentatively suggested that some pastoral communities practise sexual abstinence during the dry season (Swift, Section 3.3). However, we consider it unlikely that such judgements play significant part in determining the seasonality of births in cultivating communities. Indeed, there is evidence that in many places, births tend to occur at the least favourable times of year—for example, in Gambia (Rowland *et al*, Section 6.2). For rural areas of Mexico, Thompson and Robbins (1973) found that more births occurred during periods of heavier work-load. And Himes and Malina (1977) show that births in another part of Mexico actually peak in the rainy season. We can add that it may not be easy to define a single most favourable time of year in which to give birth (though it may be easier to define an optimum time for weaning).

While temperature and rainfall variation are key factors in the seasonality of births, this should not obscure the fact that, as we shall note below, seasonal patterns in births occur in many countries in which there is relatively little obvious climatic change. And while any given seasonal pattern of fertility may result from the interaction of both 'social' and 'biological' variables, most detailed studies conclude that the social kind of mechanisms are likely to be the more important. We can add that the majority of relationships likely to bring about birth seasonality work through coital frequency.

Causes of seasonal fluctuations in mortality

Figure 5.2 traces many of the factors affecting seasonal variations in mortality. Here it is important to note the age distribution of the population under study. The probability of dying is highest at the youngest ages. This must be remembered when comparing the seasonal pattern of deaths of different socio-economic groups (or countries at different stages of development). The *monthly* distribution of ages is most important at very early ages, and this is not always pointed out in the literature: neonatal deaths may peak in a month with a disproportionate number of infants at risk. A further implication is that infants born in certain months of the year have a reduced chance of survival insofar as a critical age coincides with a critical month. Hence our mention of age distribution in Figure 5.2.

The tendency for *temperate* countries to suffer an increase in deaths during the coldest months is well known. The prominence of this phenomenon in industrialised countries is related to eradication of diseases previously prominent at other seasons (so socio-economic and medical rather than climatic distinctions are crucial). Historically, the summer season of diarrhoeal deaths in

Seasonal Dimensions to Rural Poverty

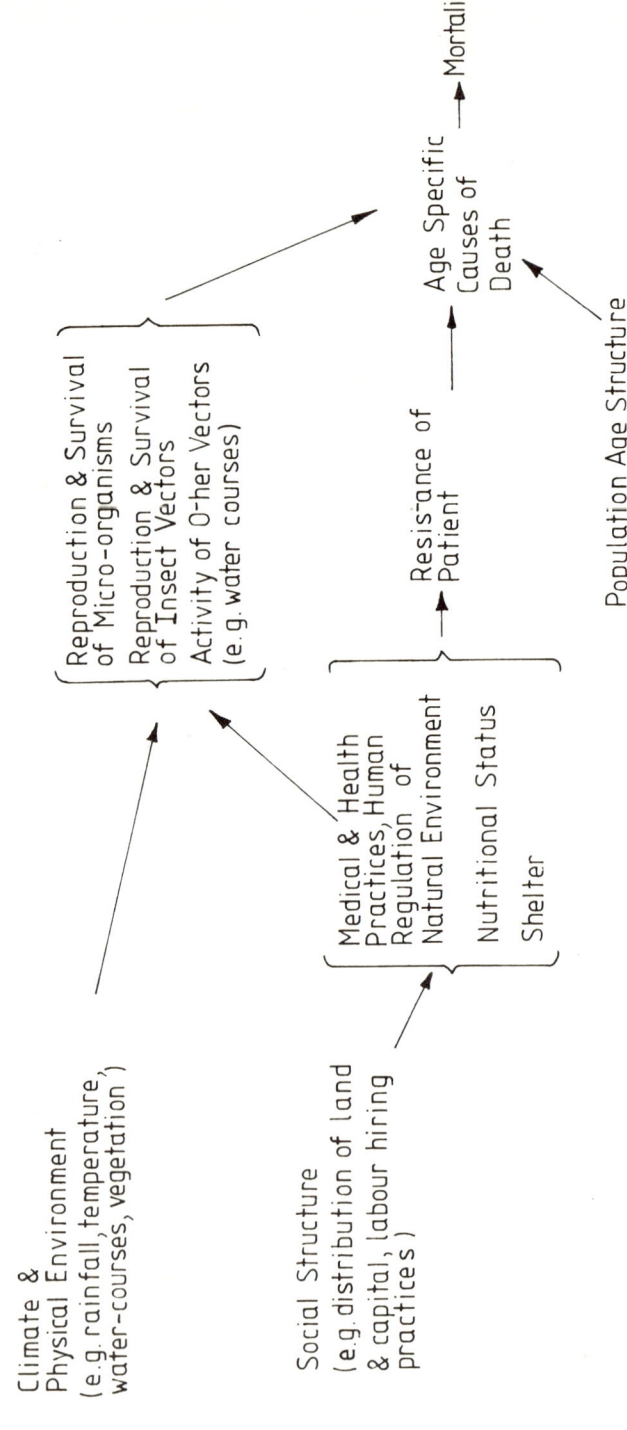

Figure 5.2 A simplified diagram of some of the main interrelationships likely to bring about a seasonal fluctuation in deaths.

children is documented for England down to the early years of this century (Gale, 1959), and until more recently for southern Europe. In the *tropics*, a pioneering study by Hill (1888) showed that smallpox and cholera in North India peaked in the hot months preceding the rains (compare WHO, 1977). Malaria (and also cholera) were observed by Hill to be post-monsoon killers.

Looking at the determinants of death in a broader context, we might schematically divide seasonal factors into three interdependent groups (Figure 5.2): seasonality in the survival of micro-organisms, seasonality in the existence or survival of disease carriers (including animal vectors), and seasonality in the resistance of the human population. These factors are discussed for a number of specific diseases in Chapter 4, where it is noted that a number of diseases flourish during the wet season. A general observation would be that death rates in tropical countries typically peak during or just after the rains.

However, man is himself an intervening variable: the widespread eradication of malaria was due to human interference with the insect vector. The reduction and control of cholera and diarrhoeal diseases is also partly due to human interference with the agent of transmission — water.

Yet another factor is social structure. In an agricultural economy, the most vulnerable groups are the landless and small peasants. Local structures will determine their relative numbers and political weakness: for them, the season of shortage is usually just prior to harvest. The incidence of shortage will be heavily determined by the relative political strengths of those with food-grain stocks versus those without.

We may sometimes find that death rates are 'deseasonalised' as social structure changes. This may happen as shelter from rain and cold improves. The deseasonalising of mortality observed in urban areas may be due both to improved shelter and to the perennial availability of food that accompanies the concentration of the richer classes. It is *not* necessarily true that the deseasonalised pattern will continue indefinitely with improvement in medicine, shelter, or nutrition. The first stages may be the reduction in specific seasonal peaks. But as the overall death rate improves, new peaks emerge. If the population ages, the circulatory and cancerous killers may begin to dominate, and these diseases sometimes have a winter prominence in rich societies (Tromp, 1963).

5.2 Data On Seasonality of Births and Deaths
Nigel Crook and Tim Dyson

Limitations of available data

Almost all relevant statistics are produced by vital registration systems. Yet in developing countries, these are frequently deficient. This need not necessarily matter for the study of seasonality so long as the proportion of events registered remains constant throughout the year, an assumption which, for our general inquiry, we have made here. However, in many countries there is probably some degree of seasonality in the propensity to register, and sometimes this kind of response error may hide real seasonal variations. Regarding deaths, the completeness of registration may also be differentiated by age. With vital registration data, it is also important to distinguish between tabulations based on month of occurrence, from those classified by month of registration. Events registered at the turn of the calendar year must be approached with especial caution; in some countries, a birth occurring in late December will be registered in January (Takahashi, 1964). Moreover, data derived from vital registration systems comes from those people registering an event, and they are often a self-selected and atypical sample.

A related consideration is the 'measure' of seasonality to be used. Ideally we would use *rates*. However, data on the size of the population concerned are usually poor. Therefore we have worked with total numbers of events. We have first computed the number of events occurring in a given month after standardising for length of month. We have then expressed this as a ratio (multiplied by 100) of the average number of events that could have been expected if they had been equally distributed throughout the year.

This procedure gives the twelve monthly columns of data in Appendix Tables 5.1 and 5.2. In addition, it seemed desirable to estimate some kind of 'index' of the amount of variation occurring throughout the year. To provide this index, we have added together the absolute deviations from 100 of the twelve monthly ratios. For example, if one such ratio is 95, the deviation for that month is 5; if the ratio for the next month is 107, the deviation is 7. Adding the deviations for all twelve months gives an index ranging from 30 (where there is little seasonality) to around 200.

Appendix Tables 5.1 and 5.2 present data on the seasonality of births and deaths for a sizeable sample of developing countries. The data collected were those for the last available post-war year, and usually for the one or two years immediately preceding. For each country the table shows (1) the monthly ratios; (2) the mean number of events per month for the year(s) on which the ratios are based; and (3) our index of variation.

On the basis of these tables, two generalisations can be made concerning demographic seasonality. First, the phenomenon can be found in data from all around the world. Second, for any one country there was a considerable degree of consistency in seasonality from year to year, at least in the short term.

Seasonality of births

An important feature to emerge from Appendix Table 5.1 is the existence of distinct 'regional' patterns of seasonality in births in some areas of the world (see Figure 5.3). The countries along the North African coast provide a good example of this; births there regularly peak in the December-February period, and are relatively low between May and September. The seasonal birth patterns in the Caribbean islands are also quite similar; they tend to exhibit two peaks, the first around September and the second four months later. Argentina, Chile and Uruguay also exhibit a common pattern. The main birth peak occurs in September (Figure 5.3) and births are lower than average from March to May.

It appears that those countries which have similar seasonal birth patterns are in regions of the world that are comparatively homogeneous from a socio-economic, cultural, and climatic point of view. Later in this paper we shall indicate that similar regional patterns can be identified in India and Sri Lanka.

Seasonal Patterns in Births and Deaths

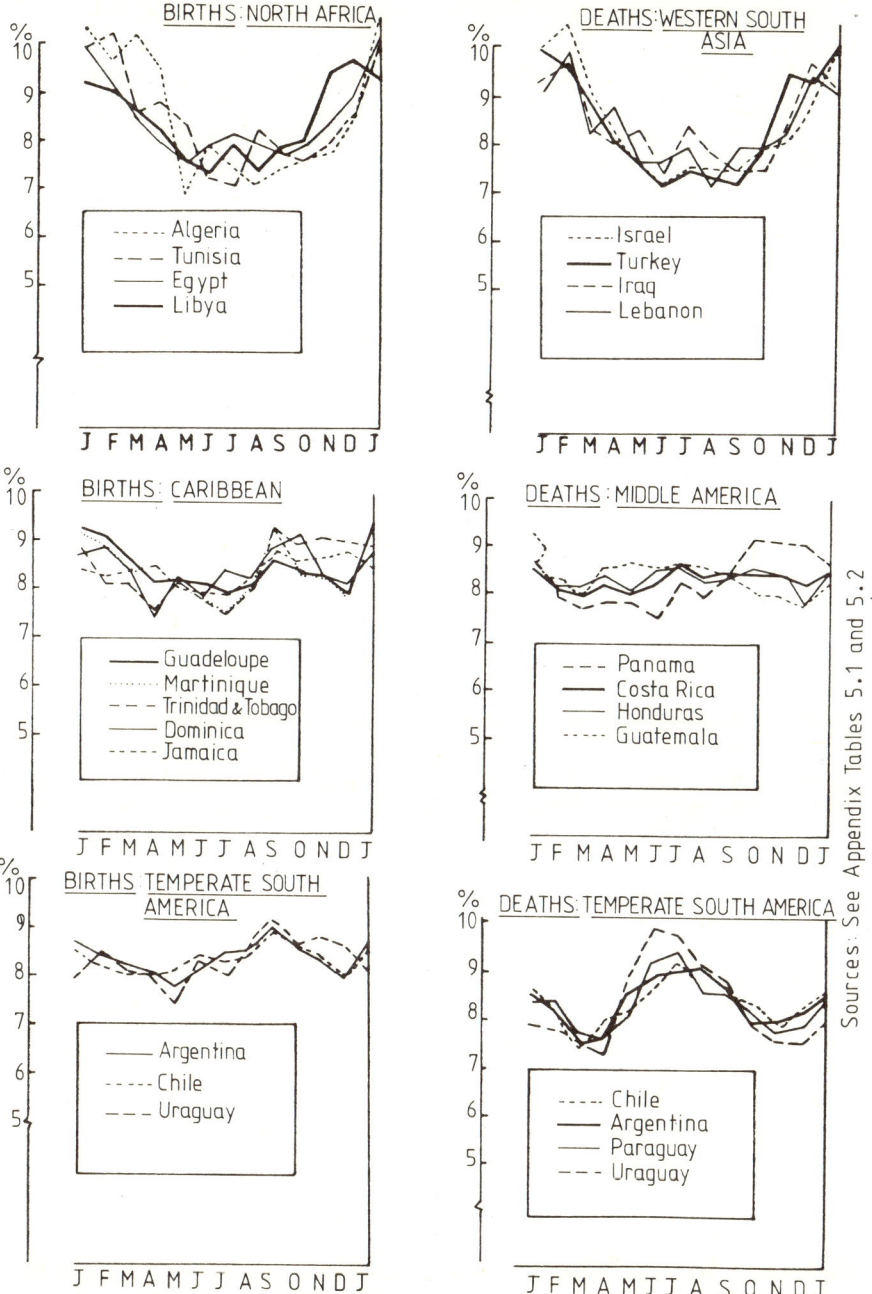

Figure 5.3 Average monthly percentage variation in births and deaths by region.

But in the more heterogeneous and less well documented areas, such as Africa south of the Sahara, regional patterns are not so immediately obvious.

It is sometimes suggested that seasonality of births should be less pronounced in the equatorial zone where annual climatic changes are generally less marked. In addition, it is hypothesised that the seasonal patterns of births in the northern and southern hemispheres should be reversed. These are both attractive ideas, but they are difficult to test on our data, given their poor quality for some countries, different levels of socio-economic development, and the generally inadequate representation of the southern hemisphere in any sample. But we can certainly conclude from Appendix Table 5.1 that many countries near the equator nevertheless do experience some seasonality in their pattern of births, though probably less than those countries further away. A case-study presented later in this chapter (Section 5.4) illustrates such seasonality in an equatorial oceanic region where climatic change is very slight.

One generalisation that can be extracted from Appendix Table 5.1 is that in no developing country north of the equator do the estimated maximum number of conceptions occur in the 'summer' period of June-August. On the contrary, in these countries, the peak months for conceptions almost invariably occur in the period December to May. One may note that these tend to be the cooler, more pleasant months of the year in the northern tropics.

With regard to marriages, we analysed the data for those few developing countries with available monthly distributions, using the same approach as for births. For these countries, the corresponding marriage index is also given in Appendix Table 5.1. It is clear that marriages tend to be far more concentrated into a given month than do births, i.e. the data confirm the existence of favoured 'marriage months'. Again we detected regional patterns. Thus for *all* countries in the Caribbean, Middle America, and South America, the peak month for marriage falls during December to February. Where we had monthly data on marriages, we compared the estimated peak months for conception and for marriage. In the majority of countries, the correspondence between the two was close, and consistent with the view that for similar reasons, marriages and conceptions may both independently occur at the same time of year.

We have argued that seasonal birth patterns are the outcome of an interactive process of many factors: climatic, geographical, and social. The question of change then arises. Several authors have pointed to instances in which the seasonal pattern of births remains the same over very long periods and in the face of considerable socio-economic change. For example, the seasonal pattern of births in England and India has stayed more or less the same for over 100 years. And Chang *et al.* (1963) note for Hong Kong that the seasonal pattern of births has remained constant in the face of considerable fertility decline.

However, analysis of demographic seasonality in South Africa shows a remarkable and systematic change in the birth seasonality of first the white, and then the Asian populations, occurring since the early 1960s (Crook and Dyson, 1980). Prior to the change, the white and Asian birth patterns resembled that of the coloureds today. Only one other documented case of a complete change in the seasonal variation of births is known to us: Cowgill (1964) has shown that between 1941 and 1961, the seasonal pattern of births in Puerto Rico changed regularly from what she calls a 'European' to an

'American' pattern. Systematic changes in birth seasonality may well occur in other populations from time to time.

Seasonality of deaths

Deaths have been treated on the same lines as births, and some regional patterns emerge (Appendix Table 5.2). In West Asia, winter dominates in seasonal mortality, with a minor secondary peak occurring in the hottest months (Figure 5.3). We have seen that this secondary peak was also a feature of temperate (now industrialised) countries in the past.

Sub-Saharan Africa is too poorly represented for any regional patterns to emerge. However, surveys have provided useful information. A study in Senegal showed infant deaths peaking soon after the maximum rains, and Cantrelle (1967) assembled studies and data to show a similar pattern in a number of West African countries, with an additional hot-dry seasonal peak occurring in areas further inland (Cantrelle and Leridon, 1971). The most fascinating data again come from South Africa. One main conclusion from a detailed investigation is that considerable differences in both levels of mortality and age structure among the ethnic groups result in contrasting seasonal patterns: the predominance of diarrhoeal diseases among the coloured and black population leads to a hot-weather mortality peak; the predominance of other diseases among the white and Asian population leads to a cool-weather mortality peak.

Tropical Latin America has a pattern of mortality maxima coinciding with maximum rainfall (and in some cases, preceding the maximum). By contrast (Figure 5.3), temperate Latin America, with a higher life expectancy, displays a cold-weather maximum, and a subsidiary peak in the height of summer. This latter may relate especially to child and infant mortality, particularly among the poorer sections of the population, and is an example of how the monthly pattern of mortality may help in suggesting the underlying cause of many deaths.

Seasonality of births and deaths in India

Almost a century ago, Hill (1888) drew attention to the seasonality of births in India. Writing about data from the North-West Provinces and Oudh, he commented that the minimum number of births is:

. . .in June and the maximum in September — dates which point to a maximum of conceptions in December, and a minimum in September. The latter month is near the end of the long and depressing hot season, when malarial influences are rapidly increasing to a maximum (and) food supply. . . is nearly exhausted. . . . In December, on the other hand, not only is the salubrity of the country greatly increased. . . but food is again cheap and abundant.

Data from the Indian vital registration system for ten major states show that the seasonal pattern of births found by Hill is applicable to most of the states in the north of India today. Births are below average in the first part of the year, and above average for the latter part (Appendix Table 5.3). It is also interesting to note that our index of seasonality is particularly high in Andhra Pradesh, Punjab, Gujarat, and Maharashtra, whereas it is comparatively low in Kerala, Karnataka, and Tamil Nadu. One feature to emerge from a rural/urban breakdown is that in some states (e.g. Andhra Pradesh, Tamil Nadu, West Bengal), the pattern of seasonality between rural and urban areas is quite different. While we might expect birth seasonality in urban areas to be less than in the countryside, Appendix Table 5.3 implies the reverse. In Table 5.1, we present simple correlations between the average monthly distribution of births and the mean minimum temperature nine months previously. It will be seen that the correlation is often closer in the urban areas.

Almost all the coefficients are in the expected direction, and most are significant. The association seems to be strongest in the northern and central states—where of course there are major climatic changes by season. The relationship is clearly shown for the Punjab in Figure 5.4. The seasonal pattern of births in the southern states is more complex. In Kerala, the distribution of births is fairly uniform throughout the year except for a pronounced peak in June and July. In this respect the Kerala pattern is quite similar to that exhibited in Sri Lanka.

Another tentative implication is that in most states, temperature is more closely related to conceptions in urban areas. Is it possible that temperature affects the frequency of conceptions in urban areas directly through sleeping patterns, whereas in rural areas the influence of temperature is dampened by other factors? Or does the difference between rural and urban areas also reflect seasonal irregularities in the registration of births in rural areas?

It is clear from Appendix Table 5.3 that August to October is the peak period for births in most states. Yet from information on work inputs, this appears to be a time of increased labour input connected with the major harvest (Chattapadhyay, 1977). So in India, births tend to occur during a period when women's labour may be subject to increased demand, and in turn this may be reflected in an increased risk of infant and child mortality.

The connection between mortality and rainfall can be traced geographically from state to state, and like the rains, maximum deaths occur later in the south (Figure 5.5). The peak months of births, infant deaths, and overall deaths frequently coincide, as in Bihar, but infant deaths are only 8 per cent of all registered deaths, strongly suggesting that the seasonality in deaths is not simply due to the seasonality in births. In general, we also found reduced seasonality of deaths in urban areas, in contrast with the case of births. With better food supply in urban areas, this is to be expected.

Shifting patterns of disease alter the seasonal maximum in overall deaths. Smallpox tended to peak in the hot dry months, and when the disease was prominent, it affected the overall seasonality. As late as 1958, a smallpox outbreak in Bihar resulted in a bimodal peak in deaths. Hill (1888) commented on the double peak in northern India at the end of the last century. In Punjab, Wyon and Gordon (1971) observed only a pre-monsoon peak, at a time when acute diarrhoeal disease was at its maximum. But tetanus peaked in October and November, which is expected if neonatal tetanus is a major component, because births also peak at that time. The Punjab is a relatively prosperous state. One does not expect crises in food availability and hence the links with harvest may be weaker than elsewhere.

No one would deny that seasonal deaths must relate to crop failure, given a serious enough failure. Yet the issue is obscured since deaths are usually

Seasonal Patterns in Births and Deaths

TABLE 5.1. Correlations between the average monthly distribution of births and the mean minimum temperature nine months previously, 1962-4

	Urban correlations	Rural correlations
Central and northern States of India		
Gujarat	-0.950^a	-0.862^a
Madhya Pradesh	-0.897^a	-0.786^b
Maharashtra	-0.888^a	-0.598^c
Punjab	-0.988^a	-0.917^a
Uttar Pradesh	-0.955^a	-0.764^b
West Bengal	-0.771^b	$+0.066$
South India		
Andhra Pradesh	-0.753^b	-0.786^b
Kerala	-0.519	-0.337
Tamil Nadu (Madras)	-0.421	-0.449
Karnataka (Mysore)	-0.505	-0.403

Notes: a denotes $p < 0.001$
b denotes $p < 0.01$
c denotes $p < 0.05$

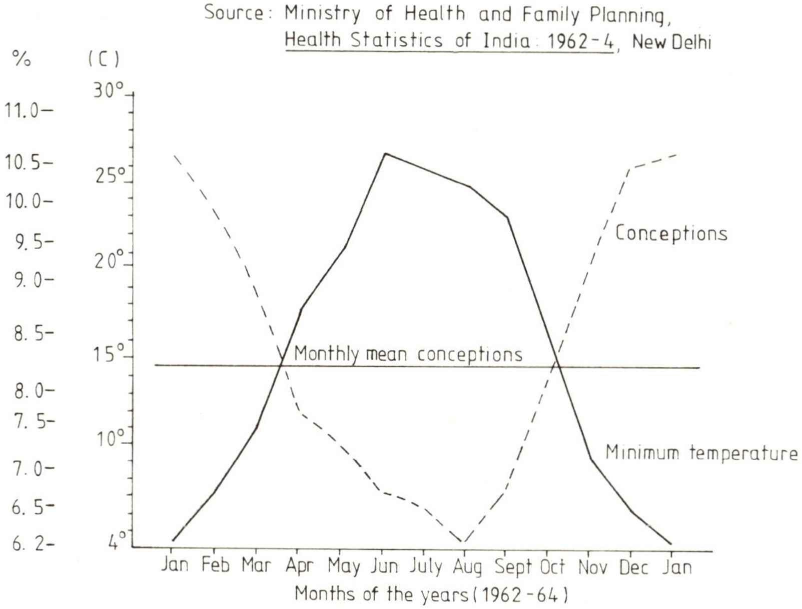

Figure 5.4 The monthly percentage distribution of 'conceptions' and the mean minimum air temperature for the urban population of the Punjab, over a three-year period (1962-64)

147

Seasonal Dimensions to Rural Poverty

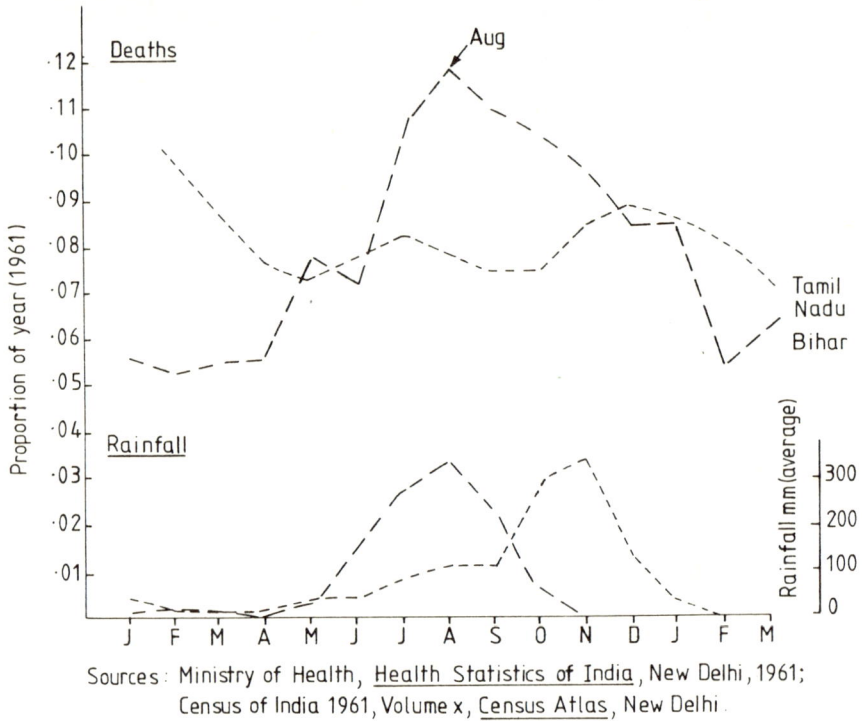

Sources: Ministry of Health, Health Statistics of India, New Delhi, 1961; Census of India 1961, Volume x, Census Atlas, New Delhi.

Figure 5.5 Deaths and rainfall in two Indian states

registered as due to a particular disease rather than a lack of food. Seasonal resistance to disease is clearly exemplified by the Bengal famine of 1943 as shown by the sequence of events (Sen, 1977). The winter rice crop of 1942 was very poor. A failure to import, a failure to distribute, and a failure in the incomes of some of the landless community resulted in widespread starvation. This generated a mortality peak in December 1943, well in excess of that for the average of the years 1938-42. It was recorded as a dramatic increase particularly in cholera and malaria, with smallpox peaking the following year.

In Maharashtra, a severe shortfall in both rice and jowar occurred in both 1965 and 1966, with major repercussions, again of a complex kind, in 1966 and 1967: the first year was characterised by cholera, the second by a smallpox outbreak, and both by distress migrations to the towns. The August and September incidence of infant deaths was greater than usual, and adult deaths also increased (to a lesser extent). The effect was greater in the rural than the urban areas.

Of course, these examples mask the details by aggregating over age groups, socio-economic status, and different food grains. They suggest, however, that research could be directed toward discovering how far food availability is a significant determinant of pre-harvest deaths in non-catastrophic years, for particular age groups and classes.

Some implications

It is worth emphasising the potential of examining monthly variation as a way of unravelling the effects of different variables on fertility and mortality. The study of seasonal determinants can direct our attention to commonly neglected variables, which directly or indirectly not only affect the seasonal distribution of events, but also help determine their *levels*. Thus it is not always acknowledged that there may be any connection between variations in climate on the one hand, and different mortality levels on the other. Of course, this should never obscure the fact that social and medical changes can and will bring about major improvements in mortality in developing countries. Nevertheless, climatic factors may make the task that bit harder.

Many of the approaches to data collection in developing countries are based on retrospective questioning. It should be recognised that the responses obtained will often be the product of the *interaction* of seasonal effects and memory errors. With a strong seasonality, the total number of events recorded as occurring during a year prior to a survey can therefore be expected to vary according to the timing of the survey, even though the number of events in any twelve-month period remains the same. With a pronounced seasonal variation in the frequency of events, any attempt to detect short-term trends must be based on measures relating to the same point in time of the calendar year. Thus a recent interpretation of a sudden fall in crude birth rates during 1973 and 1974 by India's Sample Registration System (SRS) failed to take this into account (India, 1975). For those years, the SRS estimates are based on the first six months of the year alone rather than all twelve. But as we have seen, births in India during the first part of the year always fall well below the annual average.

Finally, a possible policy implication arising from the phenomena of demographic seasonality might be that health planners step up some of their efforts during certain months. In any case, one can argue with regard to some policies, that they are more effective if staged from time to time, than if operated continuously throughout the year. Another implication of our study is that births sometimes occur at an unfavourable time of year, from the point of view of susceptibility to disease, food supply, and alternative demands on the mother (a point explored by Schofield [1974]). That both births and deaths in many developing countries do exhibit a pronounced and predictable change with the seasons is therefore something that should be known to all groups concerned.

5.3 Seasonal Patterns of Vital Events In Matlab Thana, Bangladesh
Stan Becker and M. A. Sardar*

Introduction

This paper discusses seasonal patterns of demographic events in Matlab

---

*This project has involved many people in the International Centre for Diarrhoeal Disease Research, Bangladesh: Md. Mohashin tabulated births, deaths and migrations; Kashem Sheikh adjusted the raw monthly data; Mizanur Rahman performed the trigonometric regressions; Mr. Bhuiyan and Sayedur Rahman programmed the matching of census and death records; Saleha Begum drew the diagrams; and Pamela Kelly and Judy Chowdhury did the typing.

thana, Comilla District, Bangladesh, a case-study area previously discussed in Chapter 2 (Section 2.5). Matlab is a rural area with a population (in 1974) of 265,000 in 228 villages. There has been vital registration since 1966 under the aegis of the Cholera Research Laboratory, now the International Centre for Diarrhoeal Disease Research, Bangladesh (ICDDR,B), and censuses were conducted in 1966, 1970 and 1974 in one group of villages (Old Trial Area), and in 1968 and 1974 in the remaining group (New Trial Area). The details of the censuses and registration system have been described elsewhere (Cholera Research Laboratory, 1978; Ruzicka and Chowdhury, 1978). For this analysis, the time period January 1972 to mid-1974 was selected. This period was chosen because it was a relatively stable time between the disruptions of war in 1971 and famine in late 1974.

With much of the data, trigonometrical regression analysis has been used in order to detect seasonal cycles and their peaks and troughs more precisely; the method has been discussed by Bloomfield (1976). Where this has been done diagrams show the fitted curve against a scatter of the actual data points.

Births and deaths in Matlab thana

The marked seasonal pattern of births in Matlab has been documented in several earlier publications (Mosley *et al.*, 1968; Stoeckel and Chowdhury, 1972; Chen *et al.*, 1974a). Figure 5.6 (i) shows the births by half-month intervals from January 1972 to December 1974. The peak is clearly October-December and the trough occurs in May-July. The number of births varies up to 30 per cent above and below the mean. The peak of fertility curve is estimated as 5 December.

Several pieces of information that help explain the seasonal pattern are now available, though the relative contribution of each factor has not been determined and the possibility of other factors is not ruled out. First, Chen *et al.* (1974a) showed that the seasonal absence of husbands (especially for fishing) explains part of the seasonal variation in conceptions. Second, Huffman *et al.* (1977) have shown that after a birth, a significantly larger number of women resume menstruation in the month of November than in other months, which makes the number of women at risk of conception higher in the early months of the year.

Figure 5.6 (ii) shows the monthly numbers of *deaths* for all age groups (in the Old Trial Area). As with births, a distinct seasonal pattern is found, and the pattern appears to be 'in phase' with the pattern of births. The question that arises, then, is whether the peak of deaths in November-December is merely due to the large number of neonatal deaths which follow the large numbers of births in those months.

There are several ways of looking at this question. For example, we can examine monthly deaths in a straightforward fashion for children aged one year and above. We then find that the marked seasonal pattern seen in Figure 5.6 (ii) is not evidenced. Other methods of analysis confirm that the most significant cause of the seasonal pattern of deaths is the seasonal birth pattern and the corresponding large number of neonatal deaths.

Marriage data has only recently (since late 1975) been collected for Matlab. However, it is possible to study the pattern of marriage in the earlier periods via migration records. Marriage almost always involves a change of residence

Seasonal Patterns in Births and Deaths

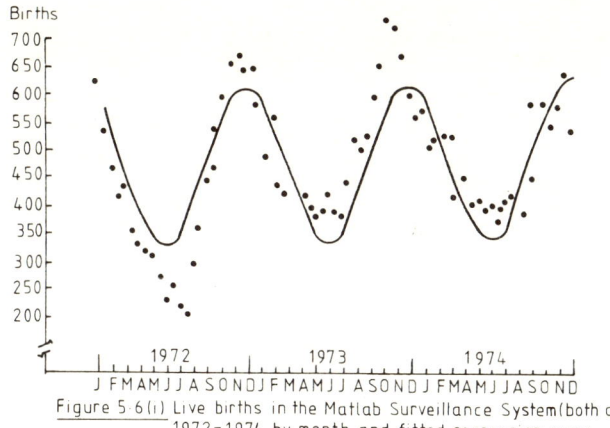

Figure 5.6(i) Live births in the Matlab Surveillance System (both areas) 1972-1974 by month and fitted regression curve.

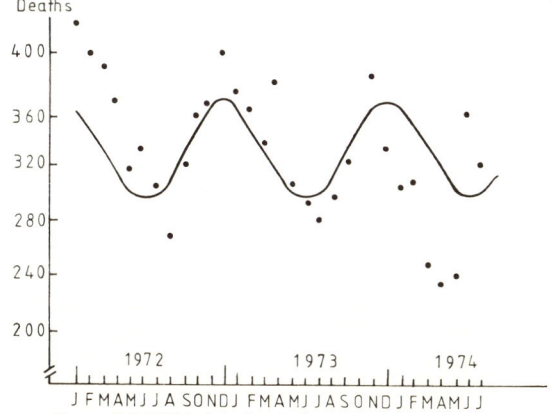

Figure 5.6(ii) Total deaths in the Matlab Surveillance System (both areas) 1972-1974 by month and fitted regression curve

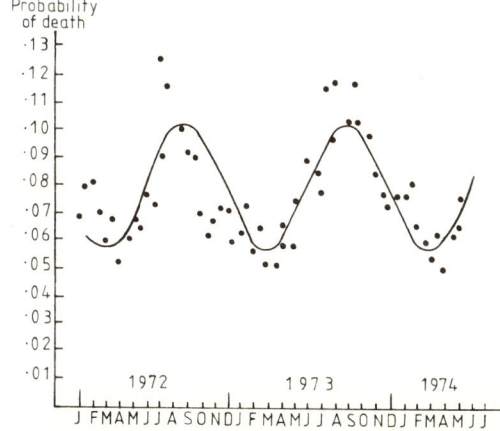

Figure 5.6(iii) Neonatal mortality rates in the Matlab Surveillance System (both areas) 1972-1974 by month and fitted regression curve.

for the female. Thus information is available for those women whose marriage led to out-migration from or in-migration to the surveillance area. Study of these data has led to two peaks being identified: one in January-February, and the other in June-August. The same pattern is observed in the actual marriage data collected in the surveillance system in 1976 (Ruzicka and Chowdhury, 1978). The reason for these peaks is not precisely known. Their coincidence with the times of harvest of the *aman* and *aus* rice crops may be an indicator of the better general financial condition in those months. Religious customs are also important determinants, e.g. marriages of Muslims are not held during Maharram month.

Deaths: a closer analysis

We have seen that the number of neonatal deaths has a definite seasonal pattern because of the pattern of births. We now examine the *risk* of neonatal death. Death rates can be estimated from data on numbers of deaths of infants under one month old, and from data for births (Figure 5.6 [iii]). An interesting finding emerges. Though the numbers of neonatal deaths peak in December, the risk of neonatal mortality has a definite seasonal pattern with a peak in September. The same pattern has been observed in neonatal death rates from the surveillance data of 1975 and 1976 (Ruzicka and Chowdhury, 1978).

The causes of this pattern are not definitely known, though two avenues for further exploration can be noted. First, in another account of the Matlab case-study area earlier in this book, it was shown that the body-weights of mothers tend to fall to a minimum in September (Figure 2.4), that breast-feeding tends to be reduced, and children may be losing weight (Chowdhury, Huffman, and Chen, Section 2.5). The second line of investigation is through data on reported causes of death (Table 5.2). These data show that neonatal tetanus is the most important cause of death in infants under one month old, and this reaches a peak in August and remains high to the end of the year.

Among children between one and four years old, there appears to be a peak in deaths in March-April. However for children over four, and for adults in the fifteen–forty-four age group, there is no seasonal pattern. We might expect a peak in deaths among adult women in November due to the seasonal pattern of births and maternal mortality. Yet the risk of maternal mortality is relatively low (5.7 per thousand live births, Chen *et al.*, 1974b), so the overall monthly series is not affected.

In the over-forty-five group, the same seasonal pattern is apparent for both males and females, with a peak in mid-December.[1]

Deaths and socio-economic status

For the three age groups which show a marked seasonality of deaths (< 1 mo., 1-11 mo., and 45 yrs. and above), the same series are examined by socio-economic status. Three socio-economic variables (education of head of household in which the death occurred, occupation of household head, and type of housing in which the household resides) derived from the 1974 census have been studied.

For neonatal deaths there are no differences in the seasonal pattern by education, occupation group, or type of housing in which the family resides.

Seasonal Patterns in Births and Deaths

TABLE 5.2. Percentage distribution of leading causes of death for infants under one month old and adults over forty-five years in Matlab DSS, 1972–73

Cause of death	Month											
	January	February	March	April	May	June	July	August	September	October	November	December
						age 0–29 days						
Number of deaths	654	569	548	547	482	509	490	476	548	685	620	610
Fever (%)	18	13	20	19	20	22	11	13	17	16	12	13
Dysentery (%)	22	18	22	26	21	22	23	16	16	19	19	20
Respiratory[a] (%)	7	7	10	9	9	8	7	9	8	7	8	6
Tetanus (%)	32	34	24	25	28	30	28	42	38	39	37	37
Other[b] (%)	22	28	24	22	21	18	26	20	21	20	25	25

Notes: a Respiratory includes colds, coughs, TB, etc.
b Other includes dropsy, asthma, rheumatism, etc.

For post-neonatal deaths there are no differences in seasonal patterns by type of housing of the household but there are differences by both education and occupation. In households in which the head had no formal education or Maktab (religious school) only, the peak is in April but for those households in which the head had some education, no seasonal pattern of the trigonometric is observed.

In the occupation groups the seasonal patterns of post-neonatal deaths in households where the head belonged to the owner-worker or 'other' group are the same as the overall pattern for the age group. The deaths in households of the labourer/sharecropper group do not fit this pattern; however, deaths in this group are far below the expected level in May and far above the expected level in October.

There are no differences in the seasonal patterns of deaths of persons forty-five years of age and above according to educational status of the household head or type of housing structure. Again differences did appear according to occupational group however—the owner-worker group and 'other' groups show the expected pattern with a peak in December but the labourer/sharecropper group did not have this pattern. In the latter group deaths are considerably above the expected levels in April and September and below the expected level in November.

Conclusions

It is clear that all demographic events in Matlab, Bangladesh, have seasonal patterns. The causes of these patterns are more difficult to pinpoint. The patterns themselves are interrelated; in explaining the wave of total deaths, the seasonal pattern of births is the most important factor.

The age groups with the most marked seasonality of death are those in which the overall risk of death is high, i.e. persons in these age groups are most vulnerable to start with. Within these age groups families which are landless seem to be the most vulnerable to sharp fluctuations in deaths, perhaps reflecting their very precarious financial position in slack months prior to harvests.

5.4 Seasonality of Births In the Solomon Islands
Sheila Macrae

Climate

The Solomon Islands have a population of 197,000 (1976 census) which is predominantly Melanesian (93 per cent) and Polynesian (4 per cent), and where the growth rate is 3.4 per cent per annum. A scheme for the notification of births was introduced in 1966, and data for the monthly number of births notified are available for the years 1967-75.

The islands lie in the equatorial oceanic and tropical oceanic climatic zones. There are no seasonal patterns in temperature, which varies little throughout the year. In many areas, monthly mean maxima and minima seldom vary by more than 1°C, averaging around 27°C for the islands as a whole. In addition, there is little diurnal variation in temperature except in the vicinity of high mountains. Rainfall is also seasonally uniform in most of the islands, with averages of between 2000 and 5000 mm per annum. Rain falls everywhere almost daily, but the coasts exposed to the rain-bearing south-east trade winds experience the highest rainfall. The trade-winds season (May–October) consists of gentle breezes and only occasional storms on the exposed south-east coasts, whereas the season of north-westerly winds (November–April) often produces severe squalls.

Although winds are seasonal, temperature, humidity, and rainfall vary little throughout the year, and the difference between the two wind seasons is much less marked than that between seasons in many other countries. Overall, climatic seasonality is slight, and does not greatly influence the lives of the people.

Another possible seasonal influence is the agricultural cycle. However, the majority of islanders in the rural areas do not depend on a single crop, but cultivate mixed gardens of several root vegetables. Some of these crops (e.g. yams) are seasonal, but some (taro) can be planted and harvested continuously. There are thus no periods in the year when all islanders are either harvesting their one staple crop or experiencing a lean period of food intake. In fact, the ease of cultivation of several root crops and the additional adequate supply of various fruits and nuts, and occasionally fish, pigs, and poultry, means that most people have a well balanced and sufficient diet throughout the year.

Seasonality of births

Despite the absence of seasonal variations in weather and agriculture—variations which are usually offered as explanations for the seasonal distribution of births—there is a distinct seasonal pattern in the number of births notified each month in the Solomon Islands. The seasonal pattern is especially apparent if the data are adjusted to allow for the fact that a steadily increasing proportion of all births are being registered each year. It was found that, with the exception of 1969, each year clearly showed a maximum proportion of births in the third quarter (July–September). Standardisation for length of month did not alter the pattern, which was confirmed from calculation of a seasonal index using the basic data for all the years combined.

Explanations for this seasonal pattern of births cannot be found in factors relating to temperature, rainfall, agricultural activities, or nutrition. Malaria was the most prevalent disease prior to recent eradication programmes, but with regular rainfall, that is equally common in all months of the year. No other disease is so prevalent, and none shows any seasonal pattern.

Yet the seasonality of births is too striking and regular over a period of nine years to be dismissed as a matter of chance or as a consequence of some artefact of the data. Hence the explanation, if indeed there is an explanation at all, should be a social or cultural one. There is some inter-island mobility, and there is also migration from the rural areas to the only urban area, the capital Honiara, on Guadalcanal. These migration patterns are not seasonal, although there is increased movement around the Christmas holiday period. In the Solomon Islands, the people are mainly Christian, though with a nucleus of traditional belief on one large island, Malaita. The Church calendar mainly influences the weekly rather than the seasonal habits of the people, with the exception of Christmas, which is regarded as a special festival. Granted that this is so, could a single social occasion explain a seasonal rise in births? Births do not peak sharply nine months after Christmas, but a higher birth rate is general through most of the third quarter of the year. Actual dates of birth and mean length of pregnancy in Melanesian women need to be known for dates of conception to be studied in more detail. Although there may, in some areas, still be taboos on intercourse at certain times (e.g. immediately post-partum), there are no seasonal sexual taboos practised generally throughout the islands.

Clearly, then, no satisfactory explanation has been found for the seasonal pattern of births in the Solomon Islands. This conclusion may perhaps serve as a warning that explanations of demographic seasonality based on weather or agriculture may not be the whole story; there may be other factors, as yet undiscovered, and coincidence of peak numbers of births with particular points in the agricultural cycle may be fortuitous.

5.5 Births, Work and Nutrition In Tamil Nadu, India
S. Rajagopalan, P. K. Kymal and Pu-ai Pei

Effects of agricultural seasonality*

The two previous case studies include one example where the seasonality of births appears to be closely linked to the agricultural cycle, and another where no such link exists. Our final case-study, based on the State of Tamil Nadu, India, is one where a clearly defined climatic and agricultural cycle does appear to have an obvious (but not simple) influence on births.

Rainfall seasonality is very pronounced on the Tamil Nadu coast, particularly in the Old and New Delta areas (see Figure 5.7); the Walsh seasonality classification for this region, defined in Chapter 1, is E4. Further inland, rainfall is less sharply seasonal, and in North Arcot District, the Walsh class drops back to D3. In this area, rainfall is less than on the coast, but the wet season begins as early as May or June and lasts until November-December (Figure 5.7). In favourable conditions, it is possible to grow some crops in the early rains (pulses, groundnuts or rice), and then to transplant the main *samba* rice crop in September, though irrigation is usually required for double cropping.

Small-scale irrigation from wells, tanks and weirs has long been practised to supplement the rainfall, and sometimes makes possible a third short cropping period in December-March. High-yielding rice varieties tend to do best in this season since low humidity favours them. In the delta areas, large dams and irrigation canals allow two crops per year to be grown over wide areas.

In most of Tamil Nadu three growing seasons are recognised by farmers (Figure 5.7). One survey of North Arcot District found that 45 per cent of cultivators grow some crops in all three seasons, and 56 per cent use at least part of their land for two crops per year (Chinnappa and Silva, 1977). Despite this reduced seasonality in agriculture, however, the *samba* rice crop, grown in the rainiest of the three seasons, is by far the most important, and dominates the pattern of labour demand. The months for transplanting and harvesting this crop—September and January—are the two months when most agricultural labour is required. Work done by women—chiefly transplanting, weed-

---
*The first part of this paper is contributed by Pu-ai Pei.

Seasonal Patterns in Births and Deaths

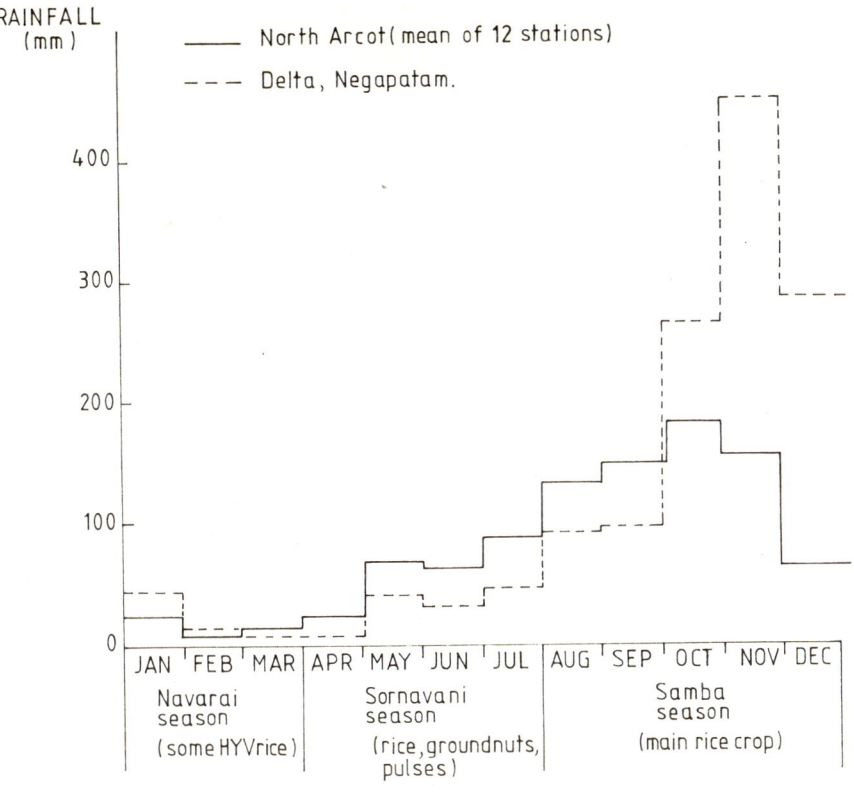

Source: Chinnappa and Silva (1977)

Figure 5.7 Climatic seasonality and agriculture in Tamil Nadu

ing and harvesting—is more sharply seasonal than male employment, and shows the two peaks caused by the *samba* crop very clearly (see Figure 5.8).

A consideration of the agricultural tasks undertaken by women is particularly relevant in a study of social and demographic events, and we may note three periods in the year which are of particular importance:
(1) April and May tend to be the hottest months; March and April are among the driest, and are a time of little agricultural work;
(2) September provides women with maximum work, transplanting rice;
(3) in December-January, the *samba* rice harvest causes a second labour peak; a preferred season for marriages follows in January-March.

Seasonality of births and deaths

The peak period for births in Tamil Nadu varies greatly as between urban and rural areas, but in all parts of the state, the probable number of conceptions is very obviously at its lowest in April and May (Figure 5.8). This conforms with the general finding of Crook and Dyson (Section 5.2) that almost

157

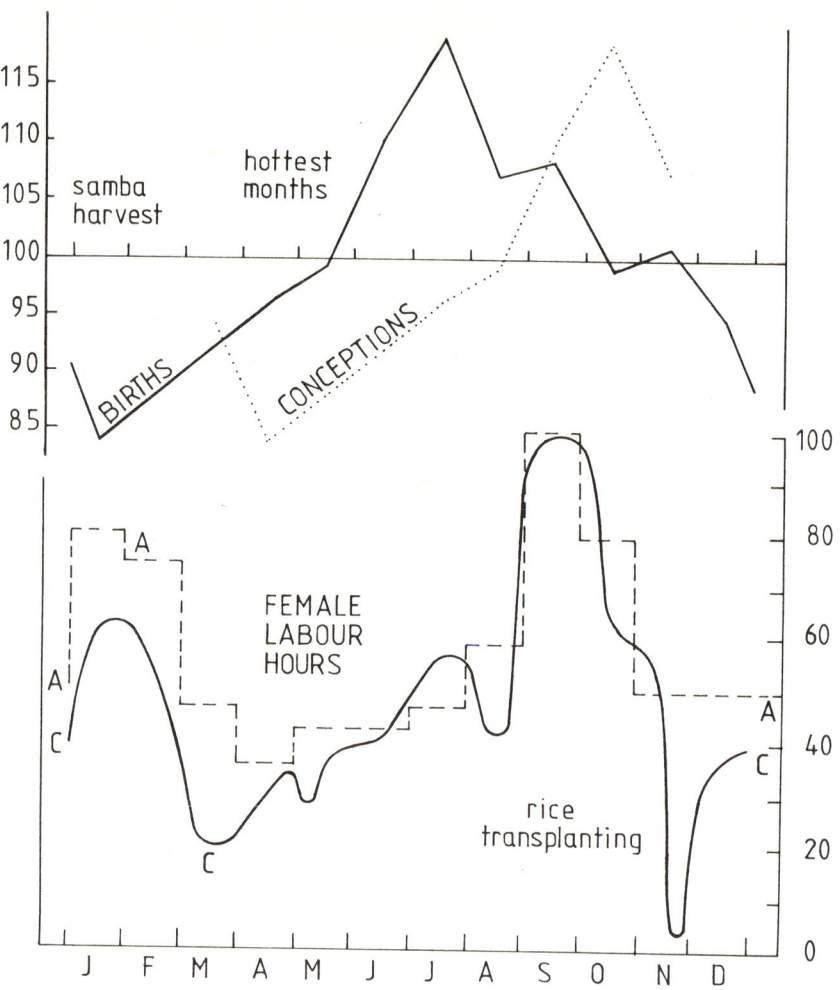

Figure 5.8 The seasonality of births and conceptions in rural Tamil Nadu (top), and the seasonality of women's agricultural work in the North Arcot District of Tamil Nadu (bottom).

Data on births are from Appendix Table 5.3 and are expressed as percentages of the mean figure; data on women's agricultural work are expressed as a percentage of the maximum number of woman-hours worked. The two sets of data for women's work output are: (A) author's estimates of all women's agricultural labour (based on data from Chinnappa and Silva, 1977); (B) Harriss's (1980) observations of casual labour by women in 'Randam' village.

Seasonal Patterns in Births and Deaths

everywhere, conceptions are reduced in hot weather. In Tamil Nadu, this seasonal trough in conceptions means that the number of births is a minimum in January.

In *rural* areas, the peak number of births is in July (Figure 5.8), during the early rains, and the trough in the birth rate coincides with the main rice harvest. This timing contrasts markedly with the situation found in several other countries where the peak birth rate is near to harvest, and where many women are pregnant during a period of heavy work and food shortage. In Tamil Nadu, pregnancies of women in the 'peak group' are over before the heavy work begins; this should be easier for the women, but may affect infants adversely by limiting the time available for breast-feeding once rice transplanting begins. Older babies may well be weaned at this time while the newborn get less than the optimum time at the breast.

It should also be noted that, although the peak number of births occurs in July, births are still above average in September, probably creating great difficulties for women who need the income they can earn that month transplanting rice. In North Arcot District, at least, a very large proportion of the women who take on this work are casual wage labourers and not family labour (Chinnappa and Silva, 1977).

The July peak in rural births corresponds to an October (or November) peak in conceptions. This is difficult to account for if preferred months of marriage are taken as a guide to likely times for increased coital frequency; however, the brief slack period between transplanting and harvesting in the *samba* season could be a relevant factor. It is obviously impossible to draw firm conclusions without birth data and agricultural work data from precisely the same areas. Figure 5.8 does not provide this, though it does usefully raise some relevant questions. It is consistent, for example, with the notion that the peak in births may be connected with a tendency to wean infants when the heaviest agricultural work begins. Where that does happen, then ovulation in the women concerned may resume soon after the main rice transplanting period. A similar mechanism was suggested in the Bangladesh case-study (Becker and Sadar, Section 5.3), but much further work is needed to decide whether it operates in Tamil Nadu.

We are now able to construct a tentative hypothesis to account for the different seasonality of births in rural and urban areas. If weaning at the time of rice transplanting influences peak conceptions in rural areas, that would not apply in the towns. The December peak in urban births implies a peak in conceptions in March. This could be explained in terms of conceptions following marriage, since it comes just after the preferred marriage season; and in terms of cool weather encouraging and permitting more sleeping indoors and perhaps coital frequency.

Data on deaths during 1961-2 in Tamil Nadu were presented in Figure 5.5. Two peaks can be observed, in December-February and in July. The July peak coincides with the peak in rural births, and is undoubtedly affected by infant mortality. The larger winter increase follows on from the wet-season period of increased illness, and can be compared with the wet-season peak in mortality found elsewhere in India (Figure 5.5) and Bangladesh (Figure 5.6 [ii]). Winter is also the season for the maximum number of urban births, so the peak death rate at that time may include many infant deaths.

Nutritional conditions*

Enormously detailed data on nutrition covering an eight-year period (1966-74) have been collected by the Tamil Nadu Nutrition Project, but have not been analysed on a seasonal basis. The data point to a rather low level of energy intake (8.71 MJ/person/day on average, equivalent to 2083 kcal/person/day). Possibly more serious is the finding that in nearly 56 per cent of the rural population, consumption of vitamin A is less than 10 per cent of need. Protein requirements are generally fulfilled wherever energy intake is adequate.

More significant than these general statements is the information obtained on food distribution *within the family*. This indicates that the energy and protein need of the vulnerable segments of the population, namely pregnant and lactating mothers and pre-school children, is not fully met. This is true in all households irrespective of income and size.

Data from the separate administrative Districts of Tamil Nadu were analysed in order to identify 'high risk' Districts where food shortages were most common. The two most at risk were found to be Ramanathapuram and North Arcot, while not surprisingly, the areas least at risk were the irrigated delta lands of Thanjavur District. This contrast between North Arcot and Thanjavur is referred to again in Chapter 7, in a discussion of seasonality, labour demand and dependence (Harriss and Harriss, Section 7.4).

Nutrition-related morbidity in Tamil Nadu was studied by analysing the records of hospitals, dispensaries, and primary health centres. The proportion of children below six years who are victims of nutrition-related morbidity is very conspicuous but varies from region to region. The nutrition-related morbidity pattern observed in different regions is in consonance with the food behaviour and environmental sanitation in those areas. Besides protein-energy malnutrition (which is partly seasonal in incidence), it was noticed that children are suffering from nutritional anaemia and vitamin A deficiency. The latter is often so serious that seasonal improvement in the availability of vegetables and milk has only a slight impact. There is also unmistakable evidence that environmental sanitation is a prerequisite for the success of any feeding programme.

A survey of the food processing industry demonstrated the magnitude of nutrient loss during processing. In particular, the huge loss of protein in oil mills calls for a strategy to recover as much protein as possible from oil cake for human consumption. The quality of the processed foods could also be improved. In well-controlled systems, processed and semiprocessed foods can help in improving the quality and quantity of nutrients available at low cost. One such processed food was prepared by the Project using extruder plant and field-tested in feeding programmes.

Conclusion

The one topic in this case-study which most stands out as needing further investigation is the early peak in births in rural areas of Tamil Nadu, with the

---

*This section is contributed by S. Rajagopalan and P. K. Kymal; see also Rajagopalan and Kymal (1978).

Seasonal Patterns in Births and Deaths

largest number occurring in July. The relationship of this peak period to activities in the agricultural cycle needs to be investigated, region by region, to discover in which places the season of maximum pregnancies and births is separated from the season of maximum agricultural labour. Figure 5.8 implies that most babies are born before the start of the main season for transplanting rice. If this is confirmed, it would be important to compare the welfare of the mothers and children affected with welfare in areas where pregnancy more often coincides with heavy agricultural or crop processing work by women.

Such a study would also need to look at seasonal variations in food availability and nutritional status, paying particular attention to the finding of the Tamil Nadu Nutrition Project that 'nearly 40 per cent of the morbidity in children under one year in rural areas relates to nutritional problems' (Rajagopalan and Kymal, 1978).

Apart from the timing of the peak in rural births, Tamil Nadu conforms to the pattern which this chapter has identified in many countries: conceptions are fewest in the hottest months and deaths tend to increase towards the end of the rains.

Note

1. Comparison with West Bengal: Before the partition of India in 1947, Bangladesh and West Bengal were parts of one state; their climate and culture have many similarities. Data for the seasonality of births in West Bengal are presented in this chapter (Appendix Table 5.3), and it is interesting to note that in both rural and urban areas there, births tend to peak in November-December. A low point in numbers of births is reached in June-July. This pattern corresponds closely with the seasonality of births identified in the Matlab case study.

5.6 References

Bloomfield, P. (1976), *Fourier Analysis of Time Series: an Introduction*, New York, John Wiley & Sons.
Cantrelle, P. (1967), 'Mortalité Facteurs', in INED, *Afrique Noire, Madagascar, Comores: démographie comparée*, Paris, Délégation Générale a la Recherche Scientifique et Technique.
Cantrelle, P., and Leridon, H., (1971), 'Breast Feeding, Mortality in Childhood, and Fertility in a Rural Zone of Senegal', *Population Studies, 25,* 2, pp. 503-33.
Chang, K.S.F., Chan, S. T., Low, W. D., and Ng, C. K. (1963), 'Climate and Conception Rates in Hong Kong', *Human Biology, 35.*
Chattapadhya, M. (1977), 'Some Aspects of Employment and Unemployment in Agriculture', *Economic and Political Weekly,* September 1977, (Review of Agriculture), pp. A66-A76.
Chen, L. C., Ahmed, S., Gesche, M., and Mosley, W. H. (1974a), 'A Prospective Study of Birth Interval Dynamic in Rural Bangladesh', *Population Studies, 28,* pp. 277-97.
Chen, L. C., Gesche, M. C., Ahmed, S., Chowdhury, A. I., and Mosley, W. H. (1974b), 'Maternal Mortality in Rural Bangladesh', *Studies in Family Planning,* 5, pp. 334-41.
Chinnappa, B. N., and Silva, W.P.T. (1977), 'Impact of the Cultivation of High-yielding Varieties of Paddy on Employment and Income', in *Green Revolution?,* ed. B. H. Farmer, London, Macmillan, pp. 204-24.
Cholera Research Laboratory (1978), *Demographic Surveillance System, Matlab,* Volume 1: Methods and Procedures, Dacca.
Cowgill, U. M. (1964), 'Recent Variations in the Season of Birth in Puerto Rico', *Proc. National Acad. Sci., 52.*
Cowgill, U. M. (1966a), 'The Season of Birth in Man', *Man,* 1966.
Cowgill, U. M. (1966b), 'The Season of Birth in Man: the Northern New World', Kroeber Anthropology Society Papers, No. 35, Berkeley, California.
Crook, N., and Dyson, T. (1980), 'Variations saisonières des événements démographiques ·

naturels en Afrique du Sud: contrasts entre les races', *Population, 35,* 3, pp. 691-7.
Gale, A. H. (1959), *Epidemic Diseases,* Harmondsworth, Penguin.
Gray, R. and Doyle, P. (forthcoming), *The Epidemiology of Human Pregnancy,* ed. S. L. Barron, London, Academic Press.
Harriss, J. (1977), 'Implications of Changes in Agriculture for Social Relationships at the Village Level: The Case of Randam' in *Green Revolution?,* ed. B. H. Farmer, London and Basingstoke, Macmillan, pp. 225-45.
Hill, S. A. (1888), 'The Life Statistics of an Indian Province', *Nature, Lond.*.
Himes, J. H., and Malina, R. M. (1977), 'Seasonality of Births in a Rural Zapotec Municipio, 1945-70', *Human Biol., 49,* 2.
Holzer, J. (1968), 'The Seasonality of Vital Events in Selected Cities in Ghana', in *The Population of Tropical Africa,* ed. J. C. Caldwell and C. Okonjo, London, Longmans.
Huffman, S. L., Chackroborty, J., and Mosley, W. H. (1977), 'Nutrition and Postpartum Amenorrhoea in Rural Bangladesh', Paper for annual meeting of Population Association of America, St. Louis, Missouri.
India (1973), 'Seasonality in Vital Events and Rates', Sample Registration System, Analytical Series, No. 5. New Delhi, Office of the Registrar General.
India (1975), *Sample Registration Bulletin,* Volumes 9 and 10 for 1975-6, New Delhi, Office of the Registrar General.
Johnson, J. T., Ann, T. B., and Palan, V. T. (1975), 'Seasonality of Births for West Malaysia's Two Main Racial Groups', *Human Biology, 47,* 3.
Mosley, W. H., Chowdhury, A.K.M.A., Aziz, K.M.A., Islam, M. S., and Fahirruddin, M. (1968), *Demographic Studies in Rural East Pakistan,* Dacca, Cholera Research Laboratory.
Newman, P. (1970), 'Malaria Control and Population Growth', *J. Development Studies,* 6 (2), pp. 133-58.
Nurge, E. (1970), 'Birth Rate and Work Load', *American Anthropologist, 72.*
Parkes, A. S. (1976), 'Seasonal Changes in Sexual Activity and the Birth Rate', in *Patterns of Sexual Equality and Reproduction,* London, Oxford University Press.
Prasad, B. G., Srivastava, R. N., Bhushan, V., and Jain, V. C. (1969), 'A Study of the Seasonal Variation of Births at Maternity Hospitals of Some Medical Colleges in India', *Indian Journal of Medical Research, 57,* 4.
Rajagopalan, S., and Kymal, P. K. (1978), 'Findings of Tamilnadu Nutrition Project', Paper for Conference on Seasonal Dimensions to Rural Poverty, Institute of Development Studies, University of Sussex, 3-6 July 1978.
Ruzicka, L. T., and Chowdhury, A.K.M.A. (1978), *Demographic Surveillance System—Matlab,* Volume 2: *Census;* Volume 4: *Vital Events and Migration;* Volume 5: *Vital Events, Migration and Marriage,* Dacca, Cholera Research Laboratory.
Schofield, S. (1974), 'Seasonal Factors Affecting Nutrition in Different Age Groups and Especially Pre-school Children', *J, Development Studies,* 11 (1), pp. 22-40.
Sen, A. (1977), 'Starvation and Exchange Entitlements: a General Approach and its Application to the Great Bengal Famine', *Cambridge Journal of Economics, 1,* p. 1.
Stoeckel, J., and Chowdhury, A.K.M.A. (1972), 'Seasonal Variation in Births in Rural East Pakistan', *Journal of Biosocial Science, 4,* pp. 107-16.
Takahashi, E. (1964), 'Seasonal Variation of Conception and Suicide', *Tohoku Journal of Experimental Medicine.*
Thompson, R. W., and Robbins, M. C. (1973), 'Seasonal Variation in Conception in Rural Uganda and Mexico', *American Anthropologist,* 75, 3, pp. 676-86.
Tromp, S. W. (1963), *Medical Biometeorology,* London, Elsevier, Part IV, pp. 179-676.
WHO (1977), *Smallpox Eradication in Bangladesh,* World Health Organization with the Government of Bangladesh.
Wyon, J. B., and Gordon, J. E. (1971), *The Khanna Study,* Cambridge, Mass., Harvard University Press.

Chapter 6
FAMILY HEALTH AND SEASONAL WELFARE

6.1 Introduction

Poverty and health

The effects of climatic seasonality on human communities may be studied in several different dimensions — in food supplies and nutrition, in prices and wages, in the prevalence of disease, and in birth and death rates. Previous chapters have looked at these subjects separately. The purpose of this chapter is to present case-studies which bring the different aspects of seasonality together, and which attempt a more comprehensive view of welfare and quality of life among the rural poor.

Poverty is often thought about in terms of low income, and may be defined according to whether incomes fall below a specified subsistence level. What is more significant, though, is the kind of deprivation to which poverty leads. In the rural communities discussed in this book, which depend on their own production as much as on money incomes, deprivation can take the form of a food shortage, or it can be caused by excessively hard work, as when mothers are forced to wean their babies early in order to spend more time working in the fields.

Poverty leads to deprivations of many different kinds, and these cannot be measured on a single, income-related scale. Inadequate food, clothing and housing may be the visible and outward signs of deprivation, but malnutrition, high child mortality, and the diseases associated with bad environmental conditions are its more fundamental effects. To discuss the quality of life of the rural poor is therefore to discuss their health and the welfare of their children.

This implies a rather different approach to health from that presented in Chapter 4. The emphasis there was on specific diseases and their seasonal variation. Some of them, including guinea-worm and malaria, were diseases which tend to cause poverty by disabling adults at the time of year when crops should be planted or weeded. In this chapter, by contrast, we are concerned with diseases which can be seen as resulting from poverty. In particular, we are concerned with diseases which are the outcome of a community's life-style, and which indicate the particular forms of deprivation or hazard which that life-style involves.

Thus Tomkins (Section 6.4) compares the seasonal incidence of disease among different social groups in the same district, and relates his observations to their nutrition, water supplies, and social customs; Waddy (Section 6.3) shows how different types of housing and different levels of impoverishment affect the incidence of meningitis; and Rowland *et al.* (Section 6.2) refer to a wide range of conditions relevant to the welfare of children, including food availability, water supply, and the heavy farm labour undertaken by women.

In all these instances, seasonal changes in the pattern of deprivation are reflected in seasonal changes in family health and welfare. Of course, different social groups have different ways of coping with seasonal hardship. Thus, in one comparison of pastoralists and cultivators in the same district, Ndagala (Section 6.6) indicates that the cultivators are more vulnerable to seasonal stress and climatic variability, and so are more prone to malnutrition and its consequences.

In studying disease as a contributory cause of poverty, one's attention is directed toward the economically productive members of the community, and the interruptions to their work caused by illness. When studying ill-health which is the outcome of poverty, however, it makes more sense to concentrate attention on the very young. This is because it is only a relatively rich community that can devote ample care and resources to its most weak and vulnerable members, its children and old people. A poor community, in contrast, is one where the weak and the vulnerable must sometimes be neglected in the struggle to produce food or other necessities. There, the needs of children may have to take second place to the daily labour of their parents in the fields. One may learn much about the meaning of poverty by attention to the welfare of children, and for that reason parts of this chapter focus sharply on child health and growth.

Another feature of this chapter is that it is much concerned with African case-study areas: in Gambia, northern Nigeria, and Tanzania. Case-studies from Bangladesh described elsewhere in the book portray a somewhat different situation, in that many of the rural poor in Bangladesh are landless, and dependent wholly on what wages they can earn. Poverty there has therefore much more to do with low wage rates and unemployment than in Africa. For that reason, the seasonal dimensions of rural poverty in Bangladesh have been discussed at length in the chapter on economics (Sections 3.4 and 3.5) rather than here. It is relevant to observe, however, that extreme poverty in Bangladesh, as in Africa, involves a struggle for survival that often entails neglect of weaker members of the family. According to Chowdhury et al. (Section 2.5), adult men receive the largest share of family food, and babies are suckled for shorter periods during seasons when the women are heavily engaged in crop processing work. The hypothesis was suggested, therefore, that seasonal reductions in total food availability may be disproportionately absorbed by the more vulnerable family members, amplifying the deleterious impact of seasonal scarcities. In Bangladesh, as in Africa, selective deprivation of this type seems to be characteristic of the life-styles forced on the very poor.

6.2 Seasonality and the Growth of Infants In a Gambian Village
M.G.M. Rowland, Alison Paul, A. M. Prentice,
Elisabeth Müller, Melanie Hutton, R.A.E. Barrell,
and R. G. Whitehead

Introduction
The lives of the rural poor are dominated by changes in the seasons affecting their activities, comfort, and well-being. This is well illustrated by the seasonal

Family Health and Seasonal Welfare

changes in mortality described in Gambian villages by McGregor, (1976) and McGregor *et al.* (1961). These workers described a village situation in which the neonatal death rate was fifty-four and the infant death rate was 134 per 1000 live births. Such figures were typical of many other developing African countries (WHO, 1976). They highlighted the peak in child mortality which occurred between nine and fourteen months of age and the fact that children born in the first half of the year (dry season) were less likely to die at that age than those born in the second half of the year, interpreting this as a result of interplay between waning protection from maternal antibodies and the largely seasonal onslaught by infectious diseases. Half of the deaths in late infancy and early childhood occurred mainly at the height of the rainy season, during the months of August, September and October.

Gambian studies also revealed seasonal variations in disease patterns and prevalence (Marsden, 1964; McGregor *et al.*, 1970). Similarly, weight gain and growth faltering in children varied according to the time of year (Marsden & Marsden, 1965; McGregor, 1976; McGregor *et al.*, 1968; Billewicz, 1967).

Since 1974, members of a multidisciplinary team from the Dunn Nutrition Unit, Cambridge, have been carrying out an indepth longitudinal survey in Keneba, documenting simultaneously growth performance, dietary intake and disease patterns in early childhood. This paper describes some of the interrelating seasonal variations found.

The environment

Keneba (population 900) is a small isolated village situated in the West Kiang Peninsula in Gambia (Fig. 1.9); this is an area of orchard savannah of 750 sq km bounded on three sides by brackish tidal rivers, there being no natural surface source of fresh water. The rains are unimodal, falling between June and October, the annual rainfall totalling 1000 mm, 1084 mm, 939 mm and 570 mm in 1974 through 1977 respectively. These marginal conditions have meant that crops have been vulnerable to spacing of rainfall as well as to the total amount.

The indigenous Mandinkos are largely subsistence farmers and the seasonal nature of their activities is illustrated by a simple annual events calendar (see Table 6.1).

Housing is typically of the mud brick variety, though temporary dwellings may be constructed of grass or cereal stalks. Traditional grass roofs have largely been replaced in recent years by sheet corrugate, partly as a result of the activity of expatriate workers. Houses are grouped in compounds, accommodating extended families of between seven and ninety-five people (Tully, 1978).

Water supplies come from six wells from 15-19 m deep, situated within the village. Two only are lined and in five there is some protection in the form of a surrounding concrete plinth.

Water is withdrawn by rope and bucket and stored in households in large unglazed earthenware pots. Sanitation is virtually non-existent; defecation in the bush is sometimes practised on a systematic basis as a way of preparing ground just before the farming season.

Medical care is provided by a government dispenser who is resident in

Seasonal Dimensions to Rural Poverty

TABLE 6.1. Simplified annual events calendar for the Gambian village of Keneba

Month	Weather	Activity	Food availability	Other
Dec Jan Feb	Dry and largely cool	Tail end of harvest Trade	All food good	Easiest time of year
Mar Apr May	Increasingly hot	Building (men) Little burning off and clearing	Dwindling stocks but can buy food	Cash in hand, little illness
Jun Jul Aug	Start of rains and peak	Intensive clearing findo and ground-nuts, planting rice	Poor stocks and money shortage	Some Co-op loans and government handouts of food
Sep Oct Nov	Fall off and cessation of rains	Weeding Guarding crops Harvesting	Improving with early harvesting of maize and findo	Peak of child morbidity and mortality

Keneba, and responsible for primary care for most of the 10,000 inhabitants of the peninsula. Government field workers in community health and agriculture are present either in Keneba or neighbouring villages, but material inputs are hampered by the ever-present problems of transport availability heightened by the lack of all-weather roads during the wet season. Two small schools exist in neighbouring villages, but none of the older villagers is literate (in English or Mandinka), though some basic literacy in Arabic exists among the menfolk by virtue of Koranic teaching.

The survey

The Dunn Nutrition Unit longitudinal survey was started in March 1974 and concentrated initially on children in the six to thirty-six month age group, previous work by McGregor having shown this to be the group in whom the most marked growth and disease problems occurred (McGregor *et al.*, 1968, 1970).

In a second phase of work starting two years later the study was intensified in the zero to eighteen-month age group. In 1977 this included all pregnant mothers and nursing mothers in the first three months of lactation. Some of these it was possible to follow through pregnancy and during the subsequent period of breast feeding of the infant, who also fell within the scope of the survey.

A monitored food supplementation programme was also introduced in Phase II (1976 onwards), in which a fortified gruel was made available twice daily, five days per week, to all Keneba children aged between three and twelve months (Rowland, in press). Data collection has fallen into four main categories: anthropometric, food intake, disease patterns, and environmental hygiene.

Growth of children has been monitored on a regular monthly basis in all children between zero and three years; weight, height, mid-upper-arm circumference and skinfold thickness were the main measurements made (Rowland et al., 1977; Whitehead et al., 1977).

Since 1976 birth weights have been obtained within twenty-four hours of birth by a trained midwife, using a Salter spring balance. During this period a range of anthropometric measurements was carried out on pregnant mothers from fourteen weeks onwards and during the first three months of lactation (Paul et al., 1979). Limited activity studies were also carried out on these women, using a minute-by-minute diary record.

Breast milk intake has been measured from two months until the end of lactation (usually at eighteen months or later) in a 50 per cent sample of children using a monthly test weighing technique (Whitehead et al., 1978). Intake of home weaning foods, traditionally introduced between three and six months of age, was measured by direct weighing and chemical analysis of samples in the same group of children for six days in every month. This technique was also used to determine the dietary energy intake of a sample of pregnant and lactating mothers during 1977.

During the period of the supplementary feeding programme introduced by the Medical Research Council (MRC) accurate measurement was also made of all food consumed from this source.

Children were examined clinically and investigated when necessary on a monthly routine basis and were encouraged to attend whenever sick at a regular outpatient clinic held for six days in every week. Care was taken to make a precise diagnosis with an assessment of duration of illness, confirmed by laboratory tests where possible. The appropriate treatment was given in all cases. Diseases were grouped into eleven categories described in detail elsewhere (Rowland et al., 1977).

Because of the importance of water-related disease, a longitudinal bacteriological study was undertaken of water sources, i.e. the six village wells and also water storage pots. Similar studies were carried out on children's food at different times of the year and at various intervals after cooking. Bacteriological methods have been described in detail elsewhere (Barrell & Rowland, 1979 a, b).

Growth and diet

Birth weight and birth season have a profound effect on subsequent progress of the child. Babies born in the months December-June had a significantly higher birth weight (3.12 kg and 2.80 kg) than those born July-November (2.91 kg and 2.69 kg for boys and girls respectively).

The average growth rate in Keneba infants during the first three months of life is good. Thereafter a marked fall-away from international standards (Jelliffe, 1966) occurs, which persists until three years of age (Whitehead et al., 1977). When two groups of children are distinguished by season of birth, a marked difference in early growth performance is observed (see Figure 6.1). Seasonal variation in subsequent growth is illustrated by the fact that in October 1977 about 70 per cent of survey children aged three to eighteen months

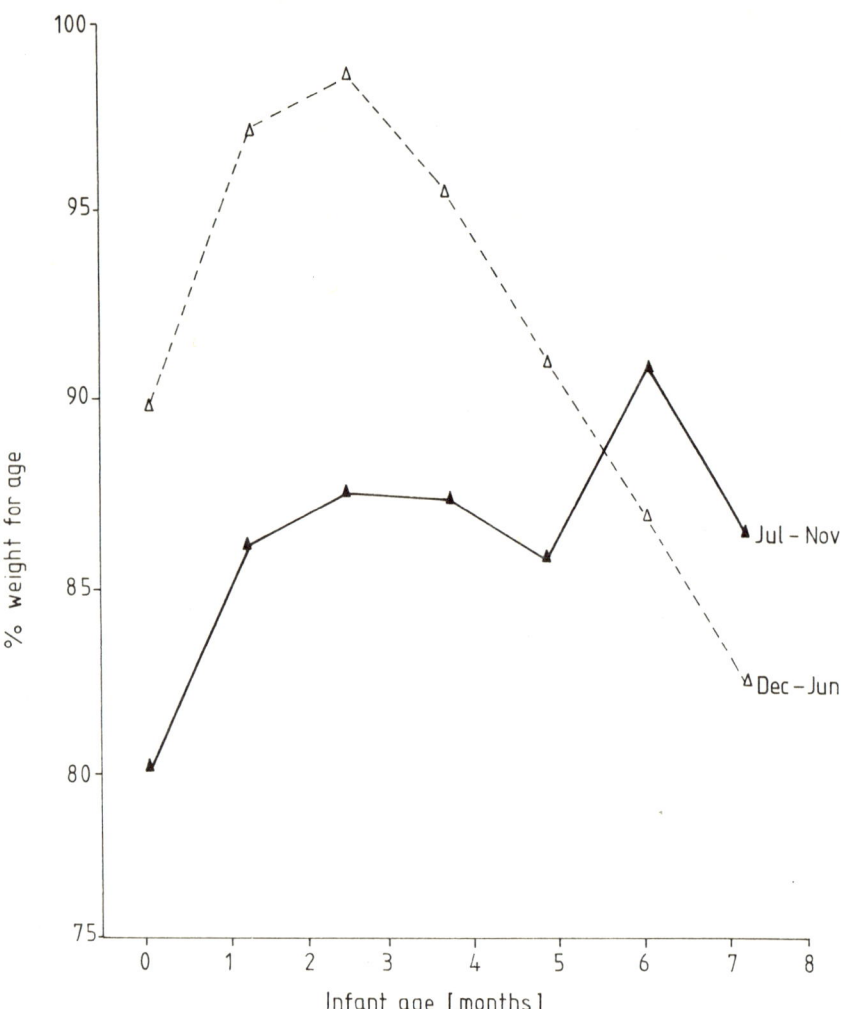

Figure 6.1 Contrasting growth in Gambian children born in different seasons. The full line refers to children born in the wet season; the dashed line to those born in the dry season.

The data shown are partly cross sectional from a sample size of between 20 and 25 in each group, and refer to Keneba village.

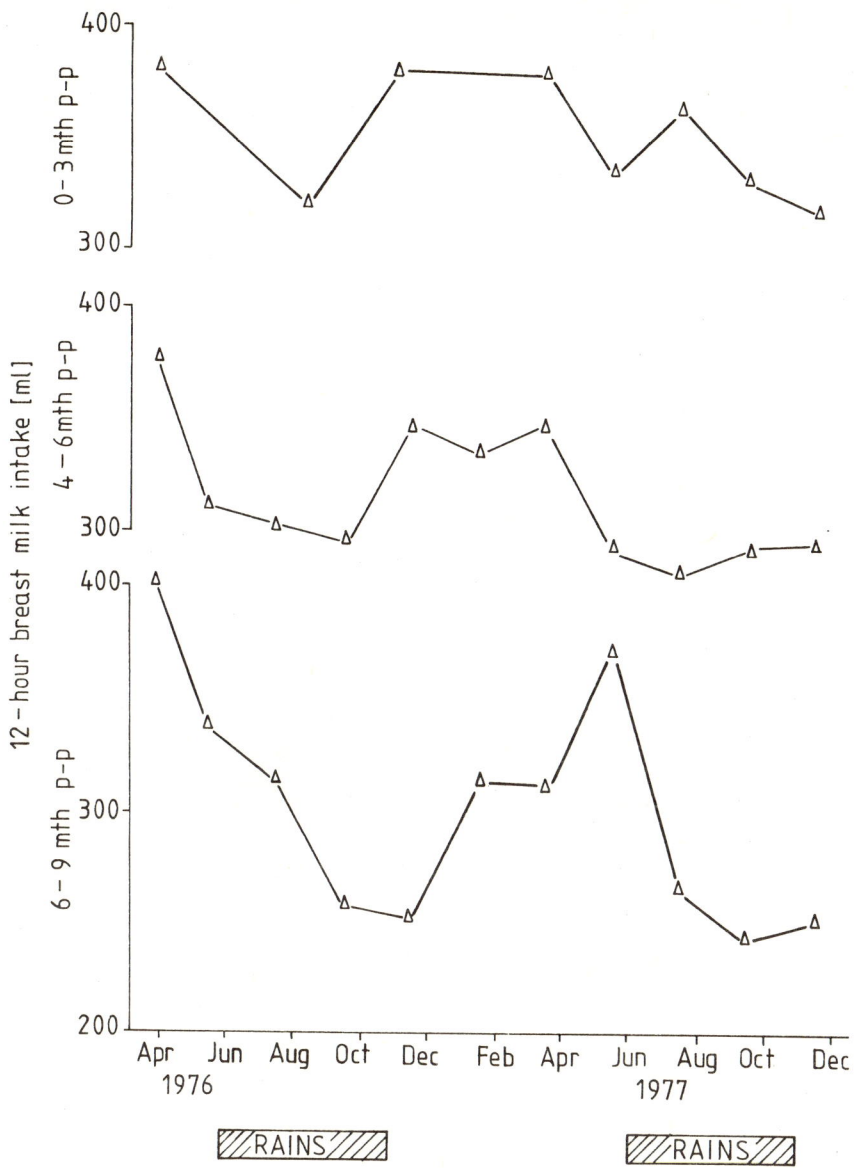

Figure 6·2 Seasonal variations in breast milk intake for babies at Keneba, Gambia.

were less than 80 per cent of the standard for age (Jelliffe, 1966) compared with only 30 per cent in March. For an explanation of this growth pattern it is logical to look first at dietary intake.

Figure 6.2 illustrates the mean twelve hours breast milk intake at various stages during infancy. This correlates well with total daily intake (Whitehead *et al.*, 1978). The values are highest during the first six months of life and the seasonal effect is relatively small. Thereafter volumes fall markedly during the rainy season.

A very similar pattern was found when the energy intake from traditional local weaning foods was considered. On an age basis, as with the breast milk data, there is a much more marked seasonal effect from the second half of infancy onwards.

When recording the amount of MRC food supplement (wheat soy blend, dried skim milk, groundnut oil and sugar) consumed, two effects were observed. First there was a steady increase in uptake through 1976 into 1977, probably due to the gradual accommodation of the intervention in the villagers' daily routine activities. In both years, however, there was a fall-off in consumption during the rainy season despite the uniformly ready availability of this food throughout the year.

Pregnancy and lactation

Variation in breast milk output raised the question of energy intake during pregnancy and lactation. Figure 6.3 shows that pregnant and lactating women have intakes considerably below the normally accepted range (WHO/FAO, 1973). This effect was most marked during the rainy season and the deficit was even greater if one considered the very high energy expenditure associated with farming activities during that period (Paul *et al.*, 1979).

The pattern of weight gain in these women is shown in Figure 6.4 and fits well with the above observations. Pregnant and lactating women lost weight during the middle of the rainy season, though the former group at least would have been expected to gain. The relationship between the pattern of breast milk output and the energy intake of mothers during the first six months of lactation was also striking.

It is well known that infections have an important modifying effect on growth in infants and young children. Figure 6.5 shows seasonal variations in prevalence of some of the major diseases categorised during 1974 and 1975.

Multiple regression analysis showed that gastroenteritis and malaria had marked effects on growth but that children suffered about thirteen times as much with diarrhoeal illness as they did with malaria, the former having a correspondingly greater impact on growth. Not only did diarrhoeal illness show marked variation in seasonal prevalence, but the effect on growth also varied with season. Fitted regression slopes were used to predict the possible weight gain at various periods of the year if diarrhoea could be eliminated. These results are presented in more detail elsewhere (Rowland *et al.*, 1977; Whitehead *et al.*, 1976). The nature of the diarrhoeal illness has also been described (Rowland & McCollum, 1977; Rowland *et al.*, 1978b).

In attempting to highlight relevant aspects of environmental hygiene, levels of contamination of the village wells were monitored during wet and dry

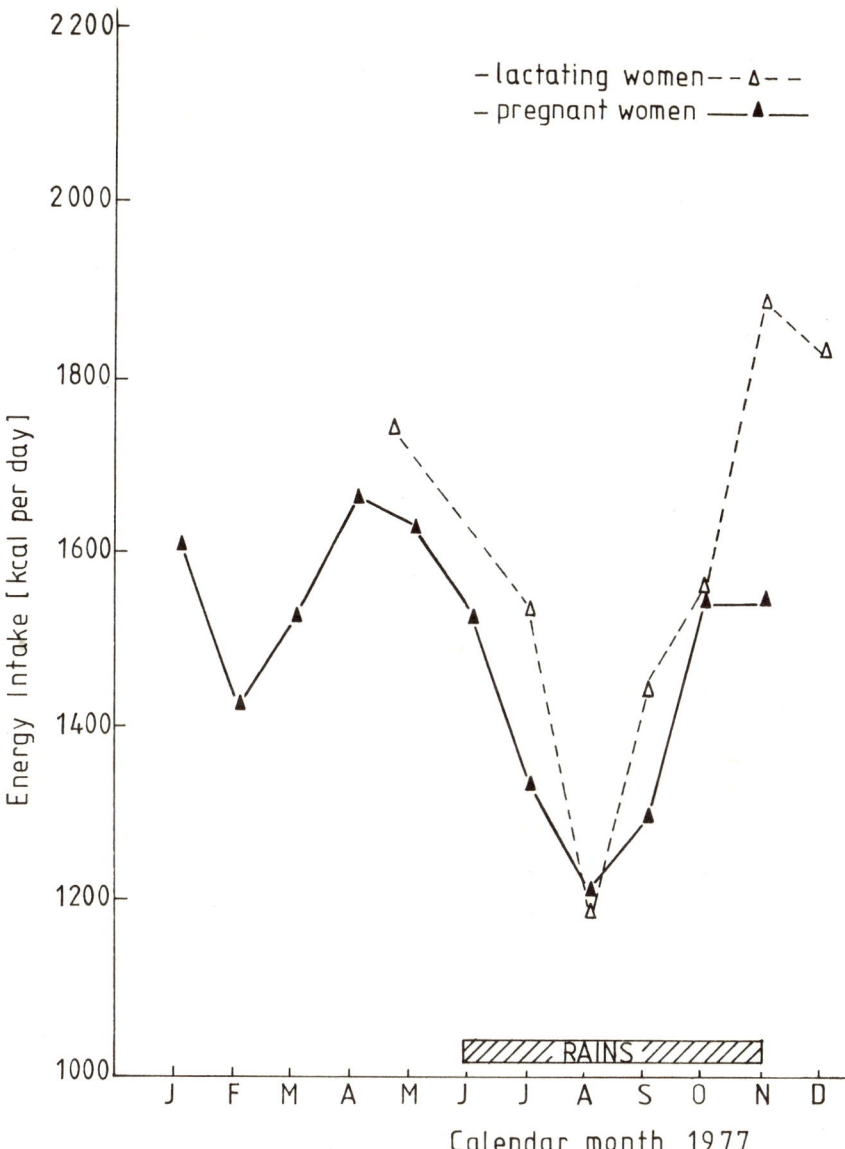

Figure 6.3 Seasonal variations in energy intake of women in Keneba, Gambia.

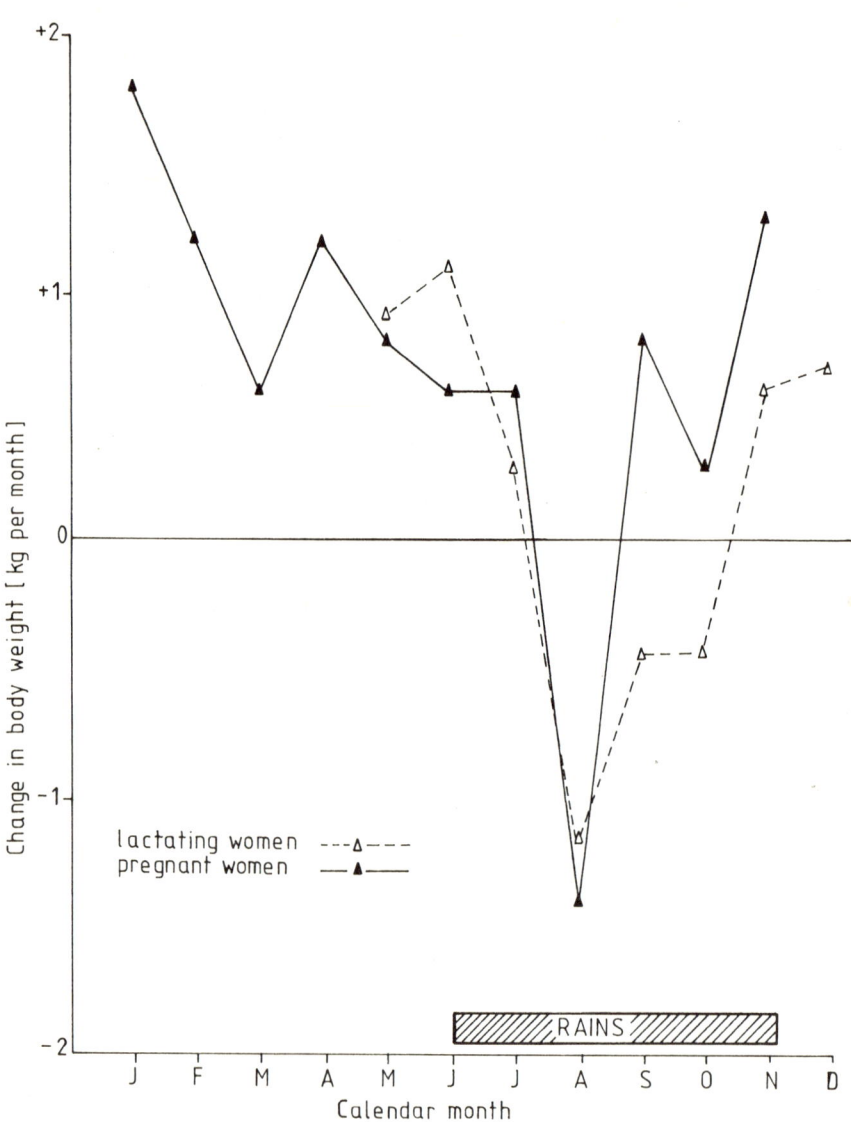

Figure 6·4 Gambia: weight loss and gain among women in Keneba, showing that even pregnant women lose weight during the rains.

Family Health and Seasonal Welfare

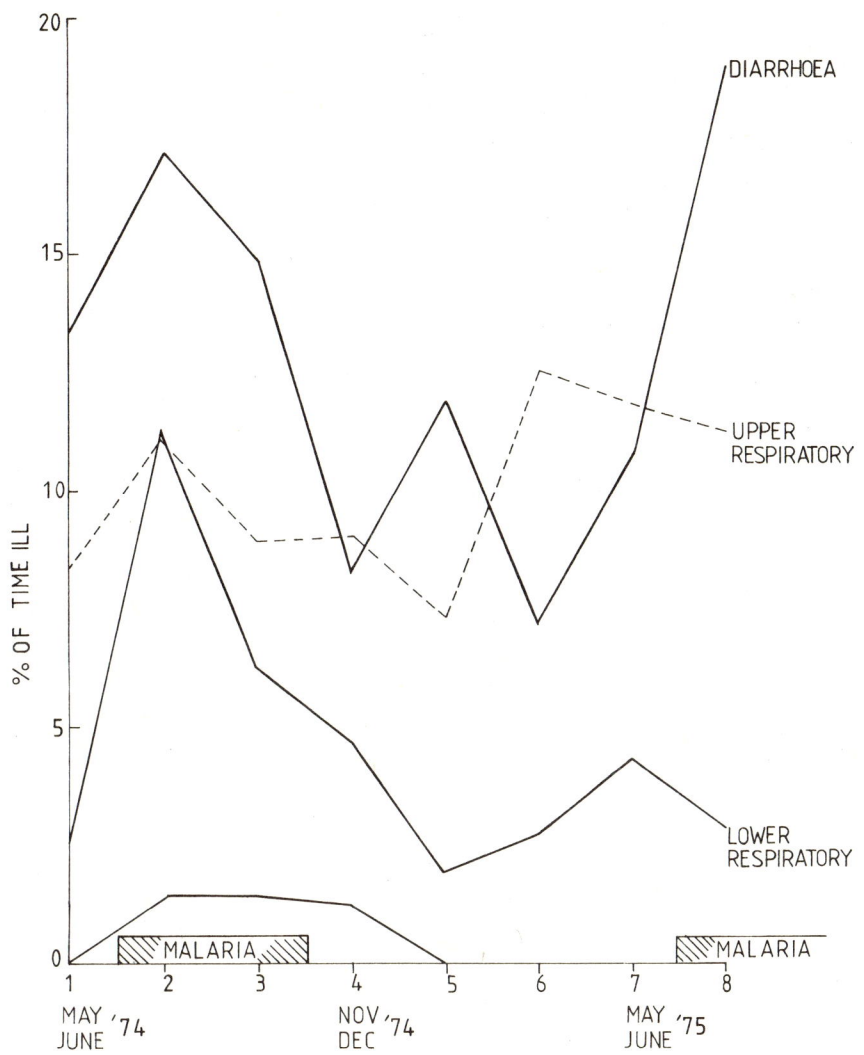

Source: Rowland et al. (1977); Whitehead et al. (1976)

Figure 6.5   Gambia: seasonal changes in disease prevalence, Keneba village.

seasons, concentrating mainly on levels of faecal coliforms and faecal streptococci. Shortly after the onset of the rains there was a ten to one hundredth-fold increase in levels of faecal contamination. Little protection appeared to be conferred by lining the wells in our particular survey village (Barrell and Rowland, 1979b).

This increase in water contamination is one factor leading to a significant increase in food contamination during the rains, with five times as many food samples exceeding the maximum recommended levels of pathogens (International Commission on Microbiological Specifications for Food, 1974), as in the dry season foods within one hour of preparation. There is also a very considerable increase in the degree of bacterial overgrowth of food if meals are not consumed soon after preparation. In fact, the pressures on the mothers during the rainy season tend to lend to increasing delay in consumption of infant foods after cooking, thus compounding the problem (Rowland *et al.*, 1978a; Barrell and Rowland, 1979a).

Discussion

The environmental conditions seen in Keneba and neighbouring survey villages are typical of many of the rural areas of the developing countries (Mata, 1976, 1977; Gordon *et al.*, 1964). The childhood mortality rates in Keneba are characteristic of underprivileged communities in rural areas (WHO, 1976). The occurrence of a nutritional crisis early in infancy is recognised increasingly (Waterlow & Rutishauser, 1975). Diarrhoeal illness has long been known as a scourge of the children in the third world (Elliott, 1976). This pattern of morbidity and mortality is usually seen in situations with a common denominator — poverty. It is impractical to invoke a global remedy for the problem. Interventionists must seek specific areas within their respective fields of expertise in the hope that a limited input may have some effect on overall health and well-being.

This paper has demonstrated some of the closely interrelated factors which exist even within the limited field of health and nutrition. We have shown that many of the adverse factors operate mainly during one period of the year, the rainy season. The mother who produces her child at this time will have suffered more weight loss herself during pregnancy, producing a smaller child who then gets less breast milk and cannot 'catch up'. The weaning period is always hazardous and the food supplementation requirements of growing infants are less effectively met in these same children, though food availability does not appear to be the sole responsible factor.

Diarrhoeal illness is related to the appalling environmental hygiene. Food contamination is almost inevitable and poor food handling is caused by unduly arduous work pressures on the village mothers. The heaviest seasonal work commitments contribute to the highly unfavorable energy balance seen in the rainy season in pregnant and lactating mothers, with a direct bearing on birth weight, milk production and subsequent mortality in their offspring.

Before effective intervention is possible one must first try to define various problems as accurately as possible; such an assessment must be of sufficient duration to encompass seasonal variation.

Short-term interventions (dietary supplementation, for instance) may well be best applied during the relatively 'benign' season in order to build up subjects to better withstand the inevitable rigours of the wet season. The immediately obvious solution of intervening during the rainy season may be logistically far more difficult. Another consideration arises; a birth regulation system which selectively reduced the number of babies born in the wet season might effect some improvement in infant welfare. Such approaches, however, are largely palliative and long-term interventions are likely to involve fairly fundamental changes affecting environmental conditions and use of local resources.

6.3 Poverty, Housing and Disease
B. B. Waddy

Cerebrospinal meningitis in Africa

Cerebrospinal meningitis (CSM) is an epidemic disease caused by an organism (the meningococcus) which is spread via the respiratory route. It causes a transient, symptomless infection in the nasal passages of many more people than succumb to the disease, and these people act as carriers. The meningococcus has virtually no survival time outside the human body in moist air, and it is also killed by ultraviolet light. CSM is therefore a disease of the dry season, and it is spread from one person to another exclusively in dark, interior conditions.

The disease occurs mainly in a sub-Saharan savannah belt that crosses Africa roughly between latitudes 10° and 15°N (Waddy, 1957). Within this belt, some areas are particularly susceptible, and have suffered devastating epidemics in every epidemic cycle. Other areas seem to escape completely, or to get off lightly. In northern Ghana, the north-west was overwhelmingly affected in every cycle, while in the more densely populated north-east, there has only been one great epidemic in all the cycles, namely in the dry season of 1948 (Grene and Waddy, 1954). This relative immunity or susceptibility seems to depend on the type of dwelling. One type consists of thatched rondavels: a whole house or curtilage may contain 100 or more of these, but each one has its own outside door. The other type has mud walls and roofs, and has numerous rooms opening internally one off the next. I know one such house with over 300 rooms (admittedly, not all of them open from the one door). In the interior, darkness was absolute, and it is in areas with this type of house that the really great epidemics occur.

It was always probable that (as with so many diseases) a slight rise in the general standard of living would cut CSM down to size. The main reason for the magnitude of the epidemics of previous decades was that people had no blankets. In the cold nights of the dry season, they slept close together to retain the warmth that they could not afford to lose, because they did not have the surplus food energy to replace it. The standard of living in north-west Ghana began to rise at the end of the 1940s, and there has not been a comparable cycle of huge lethal CSM epidemics since.

Nevertheless, CSM is by no means a spent force, even if it is no longer likely to kill off 15 to 25 per cent of a population. There is disturbing evidence that resistance to sulphonamide therapy is becoming increasingly common. In recent years highly specific vaccines have been developed from the capsular polysaccharides of group A and C meningococci. The great epidemics have been due mostly to group A strains, and there is an obvious case for organising mass vaccination. This was used with good results in Brazil, where 81 million doses were given in less than ten months in 1975 (a feat made possible by the use of electrically operated jet injectors; Brazil Ministry of Health, 1976).

Poverty and disease

The farming season begins when the first rainstorm softens the ground, and in the six weeks that follow, the farm land must be broken up and planted. This is the most vital period in the farming year. CSM is a disease of the dry season, but in the sub-Saharan region, the epidemic was still at its height when the first rains fell in April. Thus, although the disease was often a symptom of poverty, associated with housing conditions and lack of blankets, it immobilised and killed active workers at a crucial time of year. It thus depressed farming output and created more poverty in its wake.

In this respect, CSM may be compared with a range of other diseases, of which there are several that attack man at the very moment when the first rains fall. Guinea-worm infection, by its nature, cripples its host at this time, and I have seen an entire village immobilised by guinea-worm just when they should have been planting their farms. Yaws, the rheumatism of the tropics, was exacerbated by the rise in humidity. In the pre-penicillin era, a man who could not bend down to use his hoe, and had to go to the hospital to have two or three weekly injections, lost that amount of planting time — a third or more of his year's productive work. The annual attack of malaria fever was likely to coincide with the first rains, and wherever streams began to run, the annual ordeal due to the attentions of immense swarms of *Simulium* flies, which, in addition to carrying the mass blinding disease onchocerciasis, are without compare the worst insect pests in the world, soon followed.

I saw the north-west Ghana community at a level where death by starvation was always a real possibility. Villages were sometimes so reduced by the inadequacy of last year's harvest that they had no strength left to plant their crops for a new harvest. Even worse, I have seen a village starving for lack of the residual energy to harvest the little crop that they had planted. I also saw, in north-west Ghana, the effect of removing just some disabilities. In four or five years, lives were revolutionised for the better. There have been other spectacular gains in public health since then. Local people would probably say that the advent of penicillin and the defeat of yaws were the greatest, but I have good reason to know that no village in the region has forgotten the difference between epidemics of CSM before and after the advent of the sulphonamides.

CSM, like most of the mass diseases, is as much the result of poverty as its creator. The development of even a very small-scale money economy, just enough to enable a man to buy a blanket or two to keep himself and his family warm at night, was enough to demote CSM from its former status. I have known yaws to disappear from an area, long before the penicillin era, apparently because of an improvement in the water supply. A little soap, a little water, and a little health education must break the transmission cycle of contact diseases. There is evidence from East Africa that even malaria carried by *Anopheles gambiae* declines in correlation with a rise in the standard of living — and it is clear that this is not achieved by residual insecticides.

Campaigns against individual mass diseases must obviously continue. But it is clear also that development which reduces poverty throughout a community may be equally or more important in the conquest of disease.

6.4 Seasonal Health Problems In the Zaria Region
Andrew Tomkins

Introduction

Twelve years ago, a Faculty of Medicine was established at the Ahmadu Bello University, Zaria. Careful studies of disease patterns which were made there showed very definite seasonal variations (Sibellas, 1975). Such findings were not surprising, given the sharp contrast between the long dry season and the shorter rains in this savannah region. However, the study had a high degree of urban bias, and the population concerned included many immigrants from other areas.

It became possible to study the health problems of a more typical rural community when a 'bush' hospital was opened at Malumfashi, and associated with it, an Endemic Diseases Research Unit (established in 1974 by the Institute of Health, Ahmadu Bello University, and the Liverpool School of Tropical Medicine, United Kingdom). The Unit has concentrated on certain diseases of considerable importance locally; it has also collected demographic data in selected villages in the Malumfashi area. Much of its material is still being analysed, and this paper is therefore an interim and descriptive account rather than a completed, quantitative study. A further data source is the published reports of the Finnish Field Services Paediatric Unit, which has established maternal and child welfare clinics in several villages in the Malumfashi area.

Seasonal influence on biological events in health

By amalgamating the various reports and data resources, it is possible to classify, albeit crudely, many of the common health problems into a wet season and dry season categorisation (see Table 6.2). The dry months of December-March favour diseases of mucosal surfaces exposed to air. The devastating annual epidemics of CSM are typical of such diseases in which climatic factors influence infection. Similarly, the changes in bacterial and viral flora of the respiratory tract may account for the peak of respiratory diseases such as pneumonia and measles which occur at this time.

Water-related diseases such as typhoid, cholera and gastroenteritis appear to peak during the rainy season, as described in many developing communities. Guinea-worm infection, probably the result of increased use of surface water during the dry season, may critically affect farming activity (Section 4.8).

The peak incidence of peripartal cardiac failure during the wet season is a feature peculiar to this region. It appears to be due to the custom of recumbence in the post-partum period on couches by wood fires. The humid

TABLE 6.2. Diseases of particular prevalence in the Zaria region of northern Nigeria

Common in dry season	Common in wet season
Measles	Malaria
Cerebrospinal meningitis*	Peripartum cardiac failure
Pneumonia	Typhoid
Tetanus	Gastroenteritis
Scabies	Guinea-worm
Vitamin A deficiency	Protein-energy malnutrition
	Folate deficiency anaemia

Note: *Epidemics occur in February/March.

conditions during the rains prevent adequate heat loss through sweating, and body temperatures rise. The problem is exacerbated by high salt intake in the diet; fluid retention occurs and heart failure develops (Parry et al., 1977).

It is perhaps surprising that protein-energy malnutrition (PEM) should appear on a list of health problems in a community with such rich agricultural resources (documented by Simmons, Section 3.2). There is little information on the nutritional status of adults, though the severe weight loss of pregnant women observed in Gambia (Figure 6.4) is certainly not an overt problem. But PEM among children, especially pre-school infants, is of major concern, whether viewed as a predisposing factor to infective disease, as a limitation in vaccination programmes, or as a cause of infant mortality.

A nutrition survey of pre-school children at the end of the dry season showed that stunting (chronic long-term malnutrition affecting height/age ratios) is present in about 30 per cent of a pre-school village population (Tomkins et al., 1978). These children may be compared with those from an élite urban Nigerian group whose height/age ratios were indistinguishable from Harvard standards. Perhaps of greater importance was the finding that up to 40 per cent of pre-school children in some areas had wasting (acute short-term malnutrition affecting weight/height).

The peak of admissions to hospital for clinically severe PEM during the rainy season is characteristic for this area. However, severe PEM (kwashiorkor and marasmus) is only the tip of the iceberg, representing 2-4 per cent of the pre-school children in this area. Although precise figures for causes of PEM are not available on a seasonal basis, it is likely that this peak of admissions in the wet season is the result of the sequelae of measles occurring at the end of the dry season and gastroenteritis at the beginning of the wet season.

The nutritional anaemias, mainly due to iron and folate deficiency, become more common in the rainy season. This is probably because of the lack of foods containing folate at the end of the dry season. With the onset of malaria, the replacement of damaged red blood cells is critically limited by the availability of dietary folate. The tendency to wean infants off the breast at the beginning of the rains may limit the supply of folate to infants (see Figure 6.6).

Family Health and Seasonal Welfare

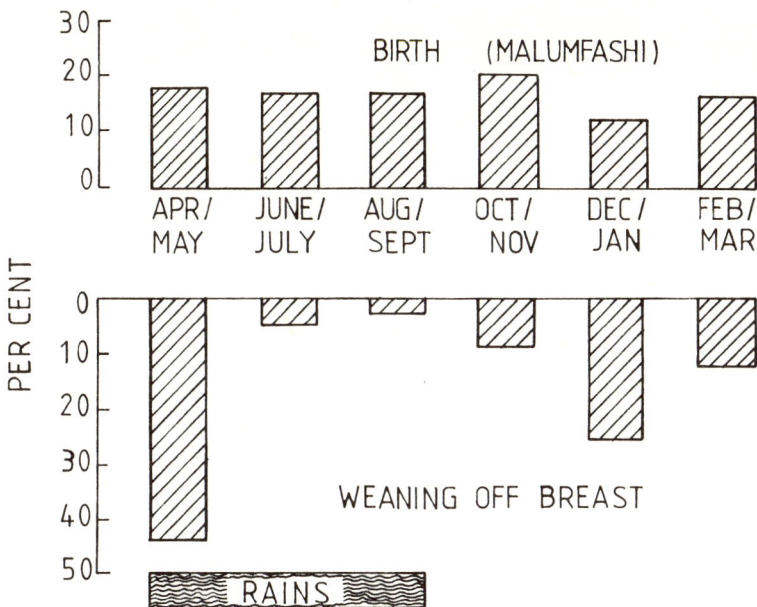

Figure 6.6 The time of year at which babies are completely weaned off the breast in the Malumfashi area, northern Nigeria. Births are distributed fairly evenly through the year but weaning is most common in the early rains (Tomkins et al.,1979)

There is little information about vitamin A deficiency or its significance for eye disease. Ocular lesions are seen during the dry season, but this may be due to secondary infection of the cornea during measles. The latter is probably the major cause of blindness among children in the region.

Cultural influences on seasonal health patterns

During the dry season, when agricultural activity is slack, there is considerable movement of people as they attend weddings, naming ceremonies, and family gatherings which are most common at this time. The social interaction in these meetings, and in crowded places such as markets, encourages the spread of disease by droplet infection (e.g. measles, Section 4.4), such factors acting in association with the climate. The onset of the rains heralds the start of marked activity on the farms, and population movement is rapidly reduced almost overnight.

The family's fields are usually adjacent to the dwelling, and in general the

TABLE 6.3. Diseases of particular prevalance among different population groups within one village area in Zaria region of northern Nigeria

Central hamlet agriculturists (Hausa)	Scattered agriculturists (Maguzawa)	Pastoralists (Fulani)
Gastroenteritis	Gastroenteritis	Gastroenteritis
Cerebrospinal meningitis	Malaria	Guinea-worm
Measles	Skin infections	Malaria
Malaria	Protein-energy malnutrition	Folate deficiency anaemia
Protein-energy malnutrition		Protein-energy malnutrition
(Problems of maternal neglect; baby minding)		(Problems of access to health care)

crops grown require only modest energy expenditure for planting and weeding. In recent years, the plough has been introduced, but the hoe remains the most commonly utilised means of tilling the soil. The main crops are cereals such as guineacorn (sorghum), millet, and maize. This contrasts with the considerable energy expenditure necessary for rice cultivation in other savannah areas (e.g. Gambia, Section 2.2). The tendency for Moslem women in the Hausa majority to stay within the compound rather than to work in the fields may also explain the absence of overt 'hungry season malnutrition'.

The majority group of Hausa farmers lives in centralised hamlets, and is more prone than other social groups to diseases which require a significant population density for transmission, including measles and CSM (see Table 6.3). Malaria and gastroenteritis also present problems, particularly during the rainy season when the extent and availability of surface water increases. Among pre-school children, it is evident that there are significant differences in nutritional status between children from hamlets with different kinds of water supply. It is not certain whether these differences are the direct result of an increased incidence of gastroenteritis in hamlets with contaminated water, and of a related link between gastroenteritis and malnutrition; the matter requires further investigation.

A second social grouping of Hausa, the Maguzawa, is either pagan or Christian, and encourages its women to work in the fields. Mothers take their infants into the fields with them, and prop them up between furrows while they dig. This avoids the need for baby minding, which is often associated with malnutrition in both developed and developing countries. The Maguzawa live in more isolated circumstances than the Hausa, and so are less prone to measles and CSM (Table 6.3). However, they have severe difficulties in obtaining a satisfactory water supply, and are potentially subject to a higher incidence of gastroenteritis. They tend to use surface water for drinking, particularly during the dry season, and guinea-worm is a factor which seriously affects their health.

A third group, the pastoralist Fulani, pauses in its migrations during the rainy season and cultivates some crops. Meaningful comparisons of its nutritional status with the Hausa and Maguzawa are difficult because of different ethnic background. However, there are problems of nutritional anaemia (folate deficiency, Table 6.3); and intake of vitamin-containing foods is limited because of limited utilisation of fresh vegetables. The greater need for such a migrant group to make use of surface water increases the risk of guineaworm. And close association with cattle renders them susceptible to brucellosis.

One further factor which is inextricably linked with seasonal patterns of health is the attitude of people towards the value of individuals within the community. The conservatism and fatalism of the Hausa in this region results in characteristic attitudes towards health, disease, and everyday events. Even when provided with access to clinics and rural hospitals, there is frequently considerable reticence in using the system. This is especially so if the health of the community member is regarded as less important than continuing agricultural activities. The value of the pre-school child in the community is relatively 'low' and steps to alleviate or prevent illness are not rapidly taken. This has a particular seasonal importance because it is when activity is at its busiest, as during farming in the early rains, that the pre-school children have least chance of obtaining medical care.

It is frequently claimed that such attitudes reflect the result of centuries of disease and high infant mortality. And at the beginning of this chapter, it was suggested that one aspect of rural poverty is that vulnerable members of the community often have to take second place in the struggle to provide the community's basic subsistence. It is therefore interesting to note the greater enthusiasm of the Maguzawa for medical facilities such as immunisation and maternal/child care services. The migrant pastoralist is least able of all to avail himself of primary health care services, but little is documented on the attitudes of this group. It is not certain, therefore, whether the failure of this group to attend village clinics is due to attitudes, or to evident problems of access.

The access of all patients to health facilities is more difficult in the rains than in the dry season, because rising rivers and streams hinder travel. Vaccination programmes can only be effectively carried out during the dry season.

In the preceding paragraphs, classification has moved from pathology and taxonomy to social and human factors, and to the major theme of this chapter, the relationship between life-styles and health. However, we have remained within the general areas of recognised disease patterns, and pathological states. We may compare incidence of any of these diseases on a seasonal basis with results from other areas of the world, but if we remain within the strict area of pathology and biology, then we will be omitting the vital consideration of what 'illness' is, as actually perceived by the sick people themselves. Limited but very useful information on attitudes towards disease is becoming available from Hausa village studies (Last, 1970). Central to these is an understanding of a person's attitude towards his own body and a greater appreciation of local concepts of 'health' as necessary in future planning of primary health care facilities.

6.5 A Study of Childhood Disease In Tanzania
James P. Goetz

Bagamoyo District

The previous section made comparisons between the life-styles of different social and tribal groups in northern Nigeria as they correlate with disease. This paper and the one that follows (Section 6.6) raise the prospect of a similar comparison in the Bagamoyo District of Tanzania. However, with less data than was available for Nigeria, the material on life-styles, economy, and health problems cannot be so completely integrated.

Bagamoyo District is a rural area in the Coast Region of Tanzania, lying 70 kilometres north of Dar es Salaam. It has a population of approximately 120,000 people, and covers an area of 9000 square kilometres. There are two tarmac, all-weather roads, and several dirt roads, many of which are impassable during the long rainy season. One railroad and two rivers also pass through the district.

The area has a bimodal climate with two distinct rainy seasons: the long rains occur from mid-March to mid-June, and the short rains come in September-October. The average annual rainfall is from 750-1000 mm, and average temperatures range from 22-23°C (June-July) to 33-34°C (December-January).

Although agriculture is the occupation of the majority of the people, fishing along the coast and cattle-raising inland are also practised. In the next section, comparison is made between the life-styles and economies of pastoralists and agriculturists occupying an inland part of the district. This paper, however, is based on data collected at Bagamoyo District Hospital, which is situated on the coast, in Bagamoyo town (population 10,000). The population represented by these data is predominantly one of cultivators, though there is some urban bias due to the presence in the sample of patients from the town.

In order to gain a reasonably precise picture of the pattern of childhood disease in the area, it was planned that every child under the age of fifteen years admitted to Bagamoyo District Hospital during 1976 would be examined by a paediatrician. Some 92 per cent of all admissions of children less than fifteen were actually seen in this way; the remaining patients were discussed with the Medical Assistant responsible for the ward before his diagnosis was accepted as correct. Hospital statistics may not exactly reflect the health problems of the community, as many decisions are made between the onset of illness and admission to hospital by both the patient and the hospital personnel. However, hospital data are at present the most reliable information available on rural health in Tanzania, as in many other developing countries.

Seasonal variations in hospital admissions

The total year's intake of children under fifteen amounted to 907 patients during 1976, an average of 76 per month. The lowest numbers of admissions were recorded in January (56 patients), February (61) and December (60). The number increased markedly in March (to 96), remained relatively high

Family Health and Seasonal Welfare

TABLE 6.4. Diseases of particular prevalence in Bagamoyo District, Tanzania

Common in long rains (mid-March–June)	Common in other seasons
Diarrhoea*	Lower respiratory tract diseases (bronchitis, pneumonia)++
Protein-energy malnutrition*	
Malaria*	
Anaemia*	Measles+
Typhoid	

Notes: *With these diseases, there is also a peak of admissions to hospital in August, during the dry period between the long and short rains.
+Peak incidence in October.
++High incidence during the dry season and into the first month of the long rains.

through April and May and, except for a remarkable increase in the number of admissions in August (to a peak of 108), decreased almost linearly until December. It is apparent that the greatest number of admissions was coincident with the long rainy season (March–June). August, the month with greatest number of admissions, stands as an enigma: during this month there were no striking outbreaks of disease; food and water were plentiful and, furthermore, there was no concomitant increase in patient visits either to the hospital outpatient department, or to health centres and dispensaries in the district. However, admissions by Rural Medical Assistants in training at the hospital may have artificially increased the number of admissions in this month. As we shall see, the diseases which accounted for the increased admissions were mainly diarrhoea, protein-energy malnutrition, malaria/fever, and anaemia.

The most prevalent diseases, and the seasons when they tend to be most common, are listed in Table 6.4. The seasonal pattern is complicated by the bimodal rainfall regime, and by the August peak just noted. Even so, several diseases tend to be associated either with the long rains, or with the longer of the two dry seasons, and in these instances, as the table shows, there is quite close similarity with the corresponding results for northern Nigeria (Table 6.2).

Lower respiratory tract infections and measles

Lower respiratory tract infection (including bronchitis, bronchopneumonia, bronchiolitis and pneumonia) was the most common cause for admission of children to the hospital, accounting for 151 out of 907 admissions (16.6 per cent). Almost equally prevalent was measles, with 150 admissions.

With the lower respiratory tract infections, there is a statistically significant trend ($p < 0.05$) towards a higher number of cases in the early months of the year, with a peak in April and a second, smaller peak in November–December. The period when these infections are most common is thus mainly the dry season, but with the peak occurring early in the long rains (see Figure 6.7).

Seasonal Dimensions to Rural Poverty

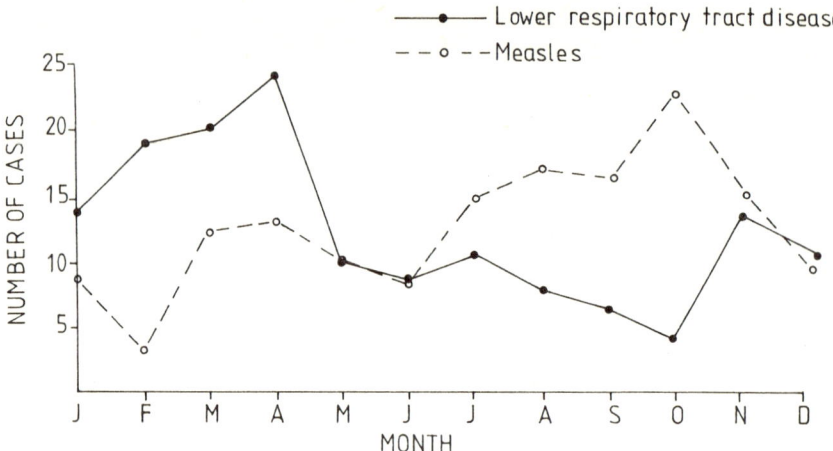

Figure 6.7 Monthly occurrence of cases of lower respiratory tract disease (full line) and of measles (dashed line) in children under 15 years admitted to Bagamoyo District Hospital, Tanzania, 1976.

With measles, there was a statistically significant trend towards an increasing number of cases in the latter half of the year. A similar pattern was observed in 1974 and 1975, and it would appear that 'epidemics' of measles occur at yearly intervals in Bagamoyo during September-December. In 1976, the peak came in October (Figure 6.7) and was due to an epidemic in Bagamoyo town; 86 per cent of patients with measles came from the urban area during that month instead of the more normal 50 per cent.

Measles might have been expected to show a similar seasonal pattern to the lower respiratory tract infections, since both are transmitted via the airborne route, and both tend to spread when people are crowded together. The fall in levels of respiratory tract infections during the busiest time of year may perhaps reflect the fact that families are then dispersed at their fields or 'shambas', sometimes even camping there in simply constructed huts. As people gather together and communities have large celebrations during the Moslem holiday of Id in September, it might be anticipated that a more highly contagious disease such as measles would show a peak during September/October whereas lesser contagious droplet-spread diseases may not demonstrate a rise.

Diarrhoea, malnutrition and malaria

Diarrhoea (defined as six or more watery stools, with or without blood, per twenty-four hours), often associated with vomiting, was the third most common diagnosis, accounting for 115 out of 907 admissions (12.7 per cent). There was a very erratic occurrence of diarrhoeal disease during the year with three distinct peaks in March, May and August (see Figure 6.8). However, the long rainy season of March-June did have a statistically significant greater

Family Health and Seasonal Welfare

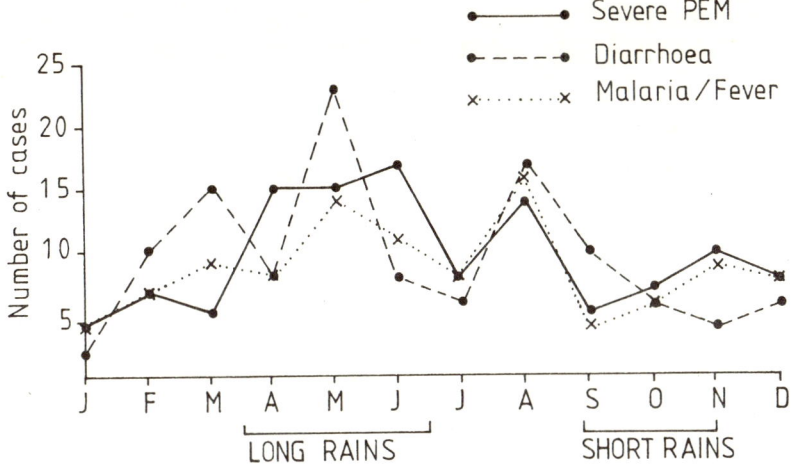

Figure 6.8 Monthly occurrence of cases of severe protein-energy malnutrition (PEM), diarrhoea, and malaria/fever in children under 15 admitted to Bagamoyo District Hospital, Tanzania in 1976.

incidence of cases of diarrhoea than the rest of the year ($p < 0.05$).

Most children admitted with diarrhoea were under two years of age, and it is this age group which both plays and defecates around the house. During the long rainy season, the ground turns to mud, and children not only are more difficult to keep clean, but they may have a greater chance of coming into contact with faecal material as well.

There is a constant water supply throughout the year in Bagamoyo town, based on three deep wells. Two separate student research projects in December 1975 and April 1976 demonstrated that these wells, and others in the town, were contaminated with coliforms to an unsatisfactory degree.

Two-thirds of the cases of typhoid fever occurred in the three-month period March-May. Peak incidence in May coincided with the peak for diarrhoeal disease, and seems to reflect a generally increased transmission of diseases spread by the faecal-oral route during the long rains. As with diarrhoea, there was no clustering of cases in any one locality, and no suggestion of a common-source outbreak.

Severe protein-energy malnutrition accounted for 115 admissions of children to the hospital. Cases were most numerous during April-June, the months immediately preceding harvest, and therefore the months with the least food available. This peak also generally coincided with the time of peak incidence of both diarrhoea and malaria/fever (Figure 6.8), and all three kinds of illness showed a further peak in August. These similar patterns in the seasonality of diseases suggest a connection between malnutrition and infectious disease as discussed in Chapter 4 (Section 4.2).

Malaria/fever accounted for 104 out of the 907 children admitted to

Bagamoyo Hospital during 1976. Peak mosquito density was calculated from the average number of anopheline mosquitoes per room determined by pyrethrum spray knock-down in thirty houses in Bagamoyo town. These estimates were made twice a month throughout the year, and maximum mosquito density was found to occur during May-July. The number of patients with malaria was high during most of the May-August period, but with a puzzling drop in July and a peak in August (Figure 6.8). However, in a holoendemic area such as Bagamoyo, there is a high incidence of malaria throughout the year.

Among thirty-five cases of anaemia seen, the greatest number occurred in the months May-August, with a decided peak in August. The increased prevalence of protein-energy malnutrition and malaria during May-August may well have contributed to the striking increase in admissions of anaemia during these months.

Implications for health services

Seasonal variation in the occurrence of particular diseases can lead to an understanding of both the pathogenesis and control of those diseases. With regard to control, preventive measures include environmental sanitation, immunisation, residual insecticide spraying, and better methods of food storage. Such measures should be implemented in ongoing programmes throughout the district, but with special emphasis in the few months preceding and during the expected seasonal increases in the related diseases. Increased efforts in educating the people about prevention and early treatment of diseases should be timed to coincide with the season when the disease is most prevalent.

Perhaps most important, it is necessary that health personnel at hospitals and dispensaries maintain accurate records regarding disease incidence on a longitudinal basis, in order to detect any changes in the seasonal pattern which may call for a modified approach to disease control.

6.6 Pastoralists and Cultivators In Bagamoyo District
D. K. Ndagala

Crop production

In order to understand more fully problems of poverty in Bagamoyo District, Tanzania, we now turn from discussion of disease to a consideration of contrasting life-styles, concentrating particularly on the area that lies between the Wami and Ruvu Rivers (see Figure 1.8).

Water resources are one severe constraint on production and on human welfare in that area. Dry-season drinking water is obtained mainly by digging holes in dried-up river beds. However, the area along the Ruvu River supports rice cultivation, and cassava, cashew and pineapples are grown. Further inland, where the rainfall is less, crops include maize, cassava, and sisal.

Land preparation on the farm plots or shambas begins in February before the long rains begin. Land clearing is undertaken then, planting starts as soon as the rains set in, and once the crops begin to grow, there is weeding to be done and there are marauding birds and monkeys to be driven off.

After harvest, most families sell some grain. There are crop-buying posts which handle maize, rice, peas, and beans. There are also middlemen from Dar es Salaam and Morogoro who buy crops directly from peasant cultivators at low prices, and re-sell them in the towns at a very great profit. Perishables such as pineapples are a particular advantage to these middlemen as there are no official crop-buying posts for these commodities.

At the end of the dry season, when people have exhausted their domestic grain stocks, they buy food supplies from neighbours and from shops. Prices are now high, and a family's cash savings may be quickly spent. Having sold a 90 kg bag of maize after harvest for Shs. 76/-, they now buy a 90 kg bag of maize flour (equivalent to 100 kg of unmilled maize) for Shs. 157/-. Thus cultivators sell maize in one season only to buy it back later at twice the price. Very often, and especially when the rains are delayed, extra cash for buying food has to be raised by selling small stock, or by seeking employment. Government supplies of free food must sometimes be called on and, as already noted, there is a significant rise in the incidence of malnutrition among children from April onwards (Figure 6.8).

Pastoralists

The Ilbaraguyu is a minority group of pastoral stock owners in Bagamoyo District. For them, peak labour requirements are experienced in the dry season, and it is at this time that cultivators can often obtain paid work as herdsmen (Ndagala, 1975; Beidelman, 1960).

Parts of Bagamoyo District are supplies with dams and permanent wells where cattle may be watered; elsewhere, pastoralists must depend on the rivers. Land use is complex, with scattered shambas and larger farms, forests near the rivers, and more open bush elsewhere. One head of cattle needs 2-4 hectares of grazing to sustain it. But since the animals do not occupy all this area at any one time, large tracts may appear to be unused, and are encroached on by the cultivators. Thus small areas of land are constantly being withdrawn from the pastoralists' use.

The division of labour among the pastoral stock owners is based on age and sex. Men look after cattle, while small boys look after sheep and goats. Women assisted by girls look after sick cattle and calves. They have to do the milking every morning and evening, and they have to count the cattle as they enter and leave the kraal each day. Until now, women have been the builders of houses, but this task is currently being transferred to men from the cultivating communities who are paid in cash or in kind, and are mainly employed in the dry season.

It becomes very difficult, during the dry season, to find the extra grass and water needed by the cattle. Herdsmen have to travel to distant water points and ungrazed stretches of land. Most streams and water holes dry up, and water levels in the permanent rivers fall. During the dry season, the cattle are mostly distributed along the Ruvu and Wami Rivers, though in some localities the herdsmen water their cattle from wells and water holes reserved for human use. This often causes quarrels between pastoralists and cultivators.

One way of looking at the economics of pastoral production is to say that while the amount of grass and water available during the wet seasons is determined by the rains, the amount available in the dry season is determined by the amount by labour and hardship the pastoralists are prepared to suffer (Monod, 1975). The value attached to three items, grass and water for cattle, and milk for the pastoralists themselves, is highest during the dry season. The pastoralists will do almost anything to get grass and water, so tension with cultivators over land use is common. Celebrations and rituals during times of drought are accompanied by the slaughter and eating of stock, and simultaneously relieve anxiety and ameliorate food shortages (Rigby, 1976). Similar meat-eating festivities during periods of prolonged drought are practised by the Twareg of northern Mali, as was noted in Chapter 3 (Section 3.3).

The Ilbaraguyu practise an effective two-pasture rotation system. Immediately after the first rains, as the land turns green, the herds are driven away from their dry season grazing near the rivers to wet season pastures away from permanent water supplies. Temporary ponds are used, thus sparing the pastures around permanent water sources for grazing during the dry season. The production of milk increases greatly during the rains with the abundance of water and grass. Families obtain enough for their needs, often with immense surpluses.

It is probable that growing demands for goods and services by the Ilbaraguyu pastoralists will encourage the expansion of surplus production. Currently, surplus milk is sent to market by the women and the money obtained is used to buy grain, flour, and other agricultural products which are increasingly becoming part of the pastoral diet. Substantial amounts of milk destined for the market go bad before they can be sold due to lack of an appropriate means of storage, and improvements in hygiene are also necessary if the sale of milk is to be more successful.

To pastoralists, milk is a necessity. Children have first priority in milk consumption. It is drunk in various forms, fresh or curdled, and butter is eaten as well as being applied as a cosmetic. Almost all the products from livestock are used. Meat is eaten; hides are made into sleeping 'mats', bags, or sandals; droppings are used in plastering houses and as fuel; horns are used as containers. Decisions as to the sale or slaughter of cattle are made by the head of the household. If an animal is sick and cannot be cured, it is killed and eaten. Old animals are sold for slaughter.

Relationships between cultivators and pastoralists

Cultivators and pastoralists all look upon the long rains with hope and anxiety. The rainy season is the bridge between famine and plenty. However, seasonal labour requirements are quite different for the two occupational groups. While the cultivators spend as much time as they can in the fields during the rainy season to make sure they produce enough food for the rest of the year, the pastoralists take time off, since during the rains, water and grass are abundant. One group toils while the other is relaxing. The position is reversed in the dry season. After harvest the cultivators have enough to eat, and since nothing will grow during the dry season, their work is shelved.

Two factors govern the interaction between the communities of Central Bagamoyo. One is the disputes which occur about the use of land and of water

Family Health and Seasonal Welfare

sources, and about cattle straying onto shambas. The other is connected with the seasonal differences in labour and production. The dry season creates a greater labour demand for the pastoralists than can be supplied by some pastoral families. The shortage is filled by employing cultivators as herdsmen, and at the same time, the pastoralists supplement their diminishing milk supply by purchasing agricultural products from the cultivators.

When the dry season is longer than usual or the rains fail, both occupational groups may be unsuccessful in meeting their subsistence needs. If famine develops, the cultivators depend for relief on supplies from the government. The pastoralists, however, are able to survive by selling a few head of cattle using the cash thus obtained to purchase food.

Storage of produce is a problem throughout the area. The cultivators sell all the crops which they consider to be over and above their subsistence requirements. Since most of the marketed produce is taken to the cities and stored there, when there are food shortages, there is considerable difficulty in bringing sufficient supplies back into the area. The people are now being urged to retain a larger proportion of their produce, and to build larger household granaries.

Better storage of milk or butter would enable pastoralists to sell more and waste less during seasons of surplus production. However, the pastoralists' greatest assets are stored 'on the hoof', and in times of food shortage can be turned into meat or sold for cash.

Population growth on a fixed area of land, with few accompanying improvements in technology, poses a threat to both cultivators and pastoralists. On the shambas, periods of fallow are being shortened and soil fertility is declining. On grazing areas, the two-pasture rotation system is being constrained by the expansion of cultivated areas. With increases in livestock numbers, from 33,000 head in 1965 to 70,150 head in 1971, there are dangers of over-grazing and consequent soil erosion. This can be averted to some extent by clearing areas of tsetse-infested bush to make new grazing lands. The pastoralists are thus in a better position than the cultivators to improve their production, and their increasing cattle herds relative to a slow-growing human population is evidence of their success in doing so.

Conclusion: perspectives on poverty

The economy of Central Bagamoyo depends greatly on the rhythm of the seasons. With existing technology, and with local ecological conditions, all activities must conform to a seasonal framework of opportunities and constraints.

Peasant cultivators in the tropics are said to be on holiday for a great part of the year, during the long dry season. But the cultivator lacks the ability to vary the regularity and duration of this 'holiday'. It is also wrong to think of the pastoralists as 'wanderers' who simply enjoy nomadism. The rotation of herds is a necessary feature of livestock keeping. Paddocks, for instance, are but 'capital-intensive nomadism'. The rotational grazing system as practised by the pastoralists offers optimum resource utilisation given the prevailing low degree of capital intensity.

As these communities confront seasonal change, their experience is that whatever is accumulated during the rainy season is consumed during the dry season. There is very little margin to cope with emergencies, or to provide a surplus for investment. But the seasons are not by themselves the cause of poverty. Two other factors are local exchange relations and the production of export crops. The role of middlemen in buying from farmers cheaply and selling dear in the towns has already been mentioned. Whether the product is meat, or maize, or pineapples, selling prices are typically twice or three times what the farmer receives. Export crops such as sisal and cashew nuts occupy many hectares of good land. They absorb much labour and other inputs. Yet the prices of these products and the amount that can be sold are determined by consumers abroad. The result is the paradox of a predominantly agricultural country that is short of food while it has many tons of 'export' crops unsold for lack of markets.

These are among the causes of poverty. But as was pointed out at the beginning of this chapter, the meaning of poverty for the very poor has many dimensions. This paper has showed that in Central Bagamoyo, cultivators are more vulnerable to seasonal stress, and have a smaller margin than pastoralists to cope with a bad season. If *vulnerability* is taken as a criterion of poverty, then the cultivators are the poorer of the two groups. Their inadequate grain storage arrangements serve to reduce their subsistence margin, while the pastoralists maintain a considerable reserve in the form of livestock. If *material possessions* are taken as criteria of living standards, then again the cultivators may be regarded as the poorer of the two groups. For example, pastoralists all have footwear, and they have donkeys to carry goods and do not have to resort to head-loading.

However, the main theme of this chapter has been *health problems* as indicators of poverty. Such data as exist for cultivators in Bagamoyo District were discussed in the previous section. The seasonal incidence of malnutrition and of related infections (e.g. diarrhoea) during the long rains was particularly noted (Figure 6.8).

An impression is that malnutrition and anaemia are more common among cultivators than pastoralists with this difference being accounted for by the improved milk and the intake of meat by pastoralists' children. On the other hand, eye disease and tuberculosis seem to be more common among pastoralists. As the houses' of pastoralists have few or no windows, the extension of droplet-spread diseases such as tuberculosis is enhanced. Furthermore, as the majority of cooking is done in the house, eye irritation from smoke predisposes to eye infections such as conjunctivitis. As cultivators tend to live in larger villages or towns with central or at least deep well water supplies, diarrhoea is less common than in pastoralists who often drink from the same water supply (unprotected ponds) as their cattle. The material presented earlier on pastoralists and neighbouring cultivators in northern Nigeria suggests a range of other comparisons that might be made between the corresponding groups in Tanzania (Table 6.3).*

Poverty has many faces. Two of the most distressing, and two criteria by which the extent of poverty might be judged, have been discussed in this

---

*Comparative material in these last paragraphs has been added by the editors.

Family Health and Seasonal Welfare

chapter. First, the point was made that the very poor are those least able to protect their most vulnerable members from the hazards of infection and malnutrition; this led to the discussion of child health in Sections 6.2, 6.4 and 6.5. Second, though, and in this last section, it was seen that the very poor are those with the smallest margins to cope with climatic variability — with failure of the rains and with consequent food shortages. The poor are the most vulnerable to irregularities in the seasonal pattern, and among the poor, children are the most vulnerable of all.

6.7 References

Barrell, R.A.E., and Rowland, M.G.M. (1979a), 'Infant Foods as a Potential Source of Diarrhoeal Illness in Rural West Africa', *Trans. Roy. Soc. Trop. Med. Hyg., 73,* pp. 85-90.

Barrell, R.A.E., and Rowland, M.G.M. (1979b), 'The Relationship between Rainfall and Well Water Pollution in a West African (Gambian) Village', *J. Hyg. (Camb.)* 83, pp. 143-50.

Beidelman, T. O. (1960), 'The Baraguyu', *Tanganyika Notes and Records, 55,* pp. 245-78.

Billewicz, W. Z. (1967), 'A Note on Body Weight Measurements and Seasonal Variation', *Human Biology, 39,* pp. 241-50.

Brazil Ministry of Health (1976), Meeting on Meningococcal Meningitis, Annex 1, Cerebrospinal Meningitis in Brazil, PAHO/WHO.

Elliott, K. (1976), in *Acute Diarrhoea in Childhood,* CIBA Foundation Symposium 42 (new series), Amsterdam, Elsevier/North Holland.

Gordon, J. E., Guzman, M. A., Ascoli, W., and Scrimshaw, N. S. (1964), 'Acute Diarrhoeal Disease in Less Developed Countries', *Bull. Wld. Hlth. Org., 31,* pp. 9-20.

Grene, J. D., and Waddy, B. B. (1954), 'A Cycle of Cerebrospinal Meningitis in the Gold Coast', *Trans. R. Soc. Trop. Med. Hyg., 48,* pp. 64-72.

International Commission on Microbiological Specifications for Foods of the International Association of Microbiological Societies (1974), *Micro Organisms in Foods: 2. Sampling for Microbiological Analysis,* University of Toronto Press.

Jelliffe, D. B. (1966), 'The Assessment of the Nutritional Status of the Community (with Special Reference to Field Surveys in Developing Regions)', Wld. Hlth. Org. Monographs, Ser. 53, p. 271.

Last, M. (1970), Text of talk given to the clinical meeting of the teaching hospital, Ahmadu Bello University, Zaria.

McGregor, I. A. (1976), 'Health and Communicable Disease in a Rural African Environment', *Oikos,* Copenhagen, *27,* pp. 180-92.

McGregor, I. A., Billewicz, W. Z., and Thomson, A. M. (1961), 'Growth and Mortality in Children in an African Village', *Br. Med. J.,* pp. 1661-6.

McGregor, I. A., Rahman, A. K., Thompson, B., Billewicz, W. Z., and Thomson, A. M. (1968), 'The Growth of Young Children in a Gambian Village', *Trans. R. Soc. Trop. Med. Hyg., 62,* pp. 341-52.

McGregor, I. A., Rahman, A. K., Thomson, A. M., Billewicz, W. Z., and Thompson, B. (1970), 'The Health of Young Children in a West African (Gambian) Village', *Trans. R. Soc. Trop. Med. Hyg., 64,* pp. 48-77.

Marsden, P. D. (1964), 'The Sukuta Project: a Longitudinal Study of Health in Gambian Children from Birth to 18 Months', *Trans. R. Soc. Trop. Med. Hyg., 58,* pp. 455-89.

Marsden, P. D., and Marsden, S. A. (1965), 'A Pattern of Weight Gain in Gambian Babies during the First 18 Months of Life', *J. Trop. Paediatrics,* pp. 89-99.

Mata, L. J. (1976), 'The Environment of the Malnourished Child', in *Nutrition and Agricultural Development,* ed. N. S. Scrimshaw and M. Behar, New York, Plenum Press, pp. 45-60.

Mata, L. J. (1977), 'Environmental Determinants and Origins of Malnutrition', in *Malnutrition and the Immune Response,* ed. R. M. Suskind, New York, Raven Press, pp. 9-19.

Monod, T. (ed.) (1975), *Pastoralism in Tropical Africa,* London, Oxford University Press.

Ndagala, D. K. (1975), 'Social and Economic Change among the Pastoral Wakwavi

and its impact on Rural Development', Unpublished M. A. dissertation, University of Dar es Salaam.
Parry, E.H.O., Davidson, N. McD., Ladipo, G.O.A., and Watkins, H. (1977), 'Seasonal Variation of Cardiac Failure in Northern Nigeria', *Lancet, 1,* pp. 1023-5.
Paul, A. A., Muller, E. M., and Whitehead, R. G. (1979), 'The Quantitative Effects of Maternal Dietary Intake in Pregnancy and Lactation in Rural Gambian Women', *Trans. R. Soc. Trop. Med. Hyg.* 73, pp. 686-92.
Rigby, P. (1976), 'Olpul and Entoroj: the Economy of Sharing among the Pastoral Baraguyu of Tanzania', Paper presented at the 12th annual social science conference of East African societies.
Rowland, M.G.M. (in press), 'Malnutrition: Prevention or Cure', *Trop. Paediatr. Env. Child Hlth.*
Rowland, M.G.M., Cole, T. J., and Whitehead, R. G. (1977), 'A Quantitative Study into the Role of Infection in Determining Nutritional Status in Gambian Village Children', *Br. J. Nutr., 37,* pp. 441-50.
Rowland, M.G.M., and McCollum, J.P.K. (1977), 'Malnutrition and Gastroenteritis in The Gambia', *Trans. R. Soc. Trop. Med. Hyg., 71,* pp. 199-203.
Rowland, M.G.M., Barrell, R.A.E., and Whitehead, R. G. (1978a), 'Bacterial Contamination in Traditional Gambian Weaning Foods', *Lancet, 1,* pp. 136-8.
Rowland, M.G.M., Davies, H., Patterson, S., Dourmashkin, R. R., Tyrrell, D.A.J., Matthews, T.H.J., Parry, J., Hall, J., and Larson, H. R. (1978b), 'Viruses and Diarrhoea in West Africa and London: a Collaborative Study', *Trans. R. Soc. Trop. Med. Hyg., 72,* pp. 95-7.
Sibellas, M. (1975), 'Outpatient Studies in Zaria', M. D. thesis, University of London.
Tomkins, A. M., Drasar, B. S., Bradley, A. K., and Williamson, A. (1978), 'Nutritional Status and Water Supply in Rural Northern Nigeria', *Trans. R. Soc. Trop. Med. Hyg., 72,* pp. 239-43.
Tomkins, A. M., (1979), 'Folate Malnutrition in Tropical Diarrhoeas', *Trans. R. Soc. Trop. Med. Hyg.* 73, pp. 498-502.
Tully, Maura (1978), 'Nursing with a Research Unit in Africa', *Nursing Times, 74,* pp. 401-5.
Waddy, B. B. (1952), 'Climate and Respiratory Infection', *Lancet, 2,* pp. 674-7.
Waddy, B. B. (1957), 'African Epidemic Cerebro-spinal Meningitis', *J. Trop. Med. Hyg., 60,* pp. 179-80 and 218-23.
Waterlow, J. C., and Rutishauser, I.H.E. (1975), *Malnutrition in Man,* ed. G. Blix, Swedish Nutrition Foundation Symposium 12.
Whitehead, R. G., Coward, W. A., Lunn, P. G., and Rutishauser, I.H.E. (1977), 'A Comparison of the Pathogenesis of Protein-energy Malnutrition in Uganda and The Gambia', *Trans. R. Soc. Trop. Med. Hyg., 71,* pp. 189-95.
Whitehead, R. G., Rowland, M.G.M., and Cole, R. J. (1976), 'Infection, Nutrition and Growth in a Rural African Environment', *Proc. Nutr. Soc., 35,* pp. 369-75.
Whitehead, R. G., Rowland, M.G.M., Hutton, M. A., Prentice, A. M., Müller, E., and Paul, A. A. (1978), 'Factors Influencing Lactation Performance in Rural Gambian Mothers', *Lancet, 2,* pp. 178-81.
WHO/FAO (1973), *Energy and Protein Requirements,* Wld. Hlth. Org. Tech. Rep. Ser. No. 522, FAO, Nutr. Meetings Rep. Ser. No. 52.
WHO (1976), *Food and Nutrition Summaries for Countries in the African Region,* 2 vols., Brazzaville, WHO Regional Office for Africa.

Chapter 7
THE SOCIAL DISTRIBUTION OF SEASONAL BURDENS

7.1 Social and Familial Inequalities

Introduction

There is a tendency in all rural societies for seasonal burdens to be transferred from dominant to weaker groups: from landowners to the landless, from employers to labourers, and from men to women and children. The better-off farmer can solve his seasonal labour problems by hiring others to do the work; but in doing this he may greatly increase the burden of peak labour requirements among those he employs. Within the family, men often eat better than women and children, and avoid onerous seasonal tasks (e.g. weeding) through the 'custom' that it is the women's role to undertake such work.

Such inequalities in the community and in the family are mentioned frequently in this book, and it has been argued, especially in Chapter 3, that the development of modern cash economies may be increasing the uneven distribution of seasonal work. In this chapter, one case-study clearly shows that increasing monetisation and increasing stress on export crops has created 'new forms of indebtedness' (Watts, Section 7.3).

What this chapter tries to do is to shed light on these questions by distinguishing between inequalities in seasonal burdens which are due to *social structure,* and newer forms of inequality arising from the *economic relations* of production (Watts, Section 7.3). The point of this distinction is that the money economy provides an impersonal means of exchange carrying no responsibility.

Inequalities based on social structure may arise through the exploitation of the weak by the strong. But their distinctive feature is the awareness among dominant groups that the community has to survive as a unit. Peasants may be placed under all kinds of obligation to their superiors; they may be screwed down by over-work in every hungry season. But there is no point in having them mortgage their labour or land in such a way that they are driven out of production, because that impoverishes the whole community.

Historically, therefore, many traditional social structures existed in which mechanisms that reinforced the dominance of leading members of the community were partly off-set by redistributive mechanisms which cushioned the poor against seasons of particular hardship. Simmons (Section 3.2) has shown that in northern Nigeria, large amounts of grain are still redistributed through gifts and tithes; more is said about this case-study area in the present chapter (Section 7.3). Comparable redistribution occurs in pastoral communities, and Swift (Section 3.3) has described customs whereby the owners of large herds will lend lactating cattle to the poor, to give them a milk supply.

It should be noted that in all these instances, the receipt of gift grain, loaned animals, or other redistributed resources entails obligations to the wealthier members of the community responsible, and thereby reinforces their social dominance. However, as long as such a system is effective in insuring the poor against bad harvests or difficult seasons, it is unlikely that they will rebel against the inequalities and obligations placed on them. However, where economic relations have become monetised and are more subject to market forces, traditional relationships begin to disintegrate. In Bangladesh,

> the decline of the traditional system and the rise of the market economy has led to a dramatic polarization in rural society. In the decade since 1966, about 15 per cent of households have increased their income, while . . . real agricultural wages have declined by nearly half, and nutritional standards have fallen drastically (Briscoe, 1978).

In such a situation, with the rich feeling less responsibility towards the poor, and with fewer traditional ties to hold the community together, agrarian unrest is obviously more likely. The question of seasonality then arises in a new context: if the poor suffer greater hardship in regions with highly seasonal climates, one might expect to find that agrarian unrest is also more common. This point is discussed in relation to South India later in the chapter (Section 7.4).

Seasonal burdens within the family

If, as seems often the case, the exploitation of the poor which takes place within stable social structures is modified by redistributive mechanisms (and some sense of responsibility) such as are absent from purely economic relations, it seems worth enquiring whether this model can be applied also to the inequalities of distribution which occur within families. If it does, then work burdens and food will be shared within families in a way which reflects the interests of dominant members, but which simultaneously favours the survival of the whole group as a family. In other words, the self-interest of dominant family members will be expressed, but will also be tempered by some responsibility, and indeed, affection.

With regard to children, who may be malnourished while their parents still appear to be eating fairly well, it has to be recognised that the survival of the family as a whole may sometimes depend on the adults keeping up their strength to plant the household's crops. Field workers *must* have sufficient energy for this task, whatever the consequences for children. Where the children suffer during seasons of peak agricultural activity, then, as Chapter 6 argues, this may be taken as a clear indicator of the family's serious poverty. Schofield (1974, p. 26) suggests that the problem of certain family members being under-fed probably varies, 'with income levels, in that only the poorest families distribute food in relation to the earning potential of members'. It follows that relief programmes which focus on child welfare without simultaneously taking action to reduce poverty are attacking symptoms without tackling the underlying disease.

When it comes to the position of women in relation to men, it often seems that men do not act in the way the model suggests, but assert dominance without a corresponding measure of responsibility, leaving women with excessive work burdens and sometimes inadequately fed (Palmer, Section 7.2).

The model may, perhaps, break down because of differences in the way men and women perceive what is necessary for the family's survival. Men are often unaware of the problems of pregnancy, child care, breast-feeding and nutrition, and sometimes show their lack of awareness by resisting developments that would aid women. In a part of Swaziland where women spend about an hour each day carrying water, some men 'resent water supply improvements which liberate their women-folk, asking what the women will do with their time when relieved of water-carrying duties' (Farrar, 1974, p. 193).

The division of labour within families tends to be quite different in Moslem communities than elsewhere because of the religious requirement that women should keep seclusion. In two of the case-study areas described in this book, this is a major factor. In northern Nigeria (Simmons, Section 3.2) and in Bangladesh (Chowdhury *et al.*, Section 2.5), some women do not work in the fields but do various jobs at home. Often these entail heavy crop processing work, but tasks that will bring in some income may also be important. In Hanwa village, northern Nigeria, work of the latter kind often takes the form of preparing cooked food for sale (Simmons, 1976c).

Monetisation of traditional economies may be a factor distorting relations between men and women. In parts of Africa, men grow cash crops while the women are left to grow 80 per cent of the family's food. Agricultural extension services reinforce this division of labour by encouraging the cultivation of export crops and by ignoring the women farmers who are so important for food production (Pacey, 1978). Agricultural economists add to this bias against women, partly by making an unjustifiable division between 'production' and a number of other forms of work which are also vital for household subsistence, such as processing harvest produce for immediate consumption. These latter activities are given subordinate status as 'housework'. Yet agricultural development and farm mechanisation can affect women's work quite fundamentally, and in ways that have serious effects on family welfare.

7.2 Seasonal Dimensions of Women's Roles
Ingrid Palmer

Introduction
Study of the seasonality of women's roles reveals far more about problems of quality of life in the whole community — men included — than the year-round observation of men's activities. Women's roles include production, maintenance, and reproduction, and even within these three areas their function can be diverse. Within reproduction, for instance, carrying a foetus to term is a different 'activity' than breast-feeding in terms of a woman's strength, nutritional requirements, and labour availability. Because reproductive functions are sex-determined, and production and maintenance tasks are gender-determined, women are obliged, when facing time or energy constraints, to trade off the benefit of one of their functions against the others, largely independently of what their husbands are doing or not doing. In fact, children's labour, especially daughters', is usually more significant than husbands' in easing a work bottleneck for women.

It can sometimes be argued that household labour is rationally allocated in terms of maximising income. However, no such rationality can be assumed with regard to conserving bodily resources and meeting individuals' bodily needs. Economists have been content to study development in terms of the first kind of rationality. But health and family planning workers are coming to see the fundamental irrationality of the sexual division of labour, and of current relations of exchange between the sexes. These, indeed, are major obstacles to development.

Seasonality of births and deaths and women's roles

If there is seasonality in vital events, whatever its causes, then women have the overwhelming responsibility to meet its demands on the family. Conception and birth inevitably have consequences mainly for women. But deaths do too, because of women's roles as nurturers and household nurses, and because when a breast-fed infant dies, the woman becomes more vulnerable to conceiving again.

In Chapter 5, Dyson and Crook point to evidence that conception tends to peak in the dry season, after harvest, and they suggest that sexual activity may be concentrated in the colder, drier months — though a few countries, including Ghana, provide contra-indications. Chapters 2 and 6 point to nutritional problems in certain seasons affecting the growth of children in Ghana (Longhurst and Payne, Section 2.4), affecting breast-feeding (Onchere and Slooff, Section 2.3; Chowdhury *et al.*, Section 2.5), and most notably, in Gambia, causing pregnant and lactating women actually to lose weight due to a combination of low food intake and high energy expenditure (Rowland *et al.*, Section 6.2). It is clear in most of these instances that the seasonality of reproduction and the seasonality of women's productive labour are in conflict. High expenditures of energy as labour worsen the effects of food shortages and are reflected in reduced breast milk for the infant, and hence reduced growth. In India, the sexual division of labour and the seasonal scarcity of food may differ in the wheat and rice belts. It would be instructive to compare the seasonal pattern of births, nutritional problems and mortality in the two areas.

The evidence presented in this book leaves many unanswered questions. Some authors (e.g. Bayliss-Smith, Section 2.1) have demonstrated the problems of peak energy expenditures without even mentioning the sexual division of labour, and the fact that these peaks may be borne disproportionately by women. Of greater interest, though, are a number of questions concerning the relationships between the seasonal food and *energy* balance experienced by women, and their seasonal *time* balance. Data from Bangladesh and Nigeria suggest that babies are often weaned off the breast because the mother has other demands on her time during busy seasons of the year (Chowdhury *et al.*, Section 2.5; Tomkins, Section 6.4).

Thus in Bangladesh, the total incidence of infants coming off the breast, due to the sum of infant deaths, women's time balances and energy problems, is greatest around December. This is a time when women are very busy with post-harvest rice processing. The result of so many babies being weaned then is that many women resume ovulation in January-February. This leads to a peak in conceptions by March, and a peak in births nine months later. Hence the cycle in which child care and agricultural work compete for the mothers' time and energy is perpetuated.

Much remains to be elucidated about such problems. We clearly need to know whether there is an in-built mechanism arising from the seasonality of women's energy and time balances coupled with the 'unnatural' onset of ovulation, and whether this causes the reproductive timetable to share a misfit relationship with the agricultural timetable. And if this is true, does it also mean a faster reproductive cycle for women than if natural means of child spacing were maintained? And how do higher yielding crops and other means of agricultural intensification affect the energy and time balances?

The impact of agricultural intensification on women

To answer the latter question, we need to distinguish differing circumstances in which agricultural intensification may take place. For instance, when rice is introduced as a new crop, as in certain projects in Gambia or Kenya, total labour demand in agriculture undergoes a sharp rise, with seasonal peaks reaching new records. But where rice cultivation has long been established, as in Malaysia or the Philippines, intensification starts at a high base level. Then the introduction of higher yielding crops and chemical inputs is likely to bring about a more modest increase in both labour demand and in its seasonal distribution. Indeed, where higher incomes from the new crop varieties are invested in mechanisation, either on farms or at mills, there may be some reduction in labour requirements. But there is nothing in these processes that tends to rationalise the sexual division of labour, nor are the heaviest work-loads necessarily eased first. Where a peasant class exists alongside a substantial landless class which offers a cheap supply of labour, the new technology can be such that those in greatest need of employment may be the first to be redundant.

Except among secluded women, transplanting rice, weeding, and processing are the usual female-typed tasks. The traditional sex composition of harvesters can vary from mainly men in the Philippines to mainly women and girls in Java. Intensification of agriculture brings sharper seasonal labour peaks to all these tasks, and where new irrigation facilitates double-cropping for the first time, more frequent seasonal labour peaks result.

Thus the effect of introducing higher yielding crop varieties and irrigation is, prior to mechanisation, to increase the annual work increment on women who must add their home and child-care responsibilities to the new agricultural schedule. The working day for women is certainly longer during seasonal peaks, so their time-balance problems will be even more acute at some stages of the agricultural cycle. Whether their seasonal energy balance suffers in the same way must depend not only on their greater energy expenditure but also on whether the new levels of output have improved or worsened the year-round supply of food.

In Java, rice production was already highly labour-intensive at the time of the introduction of the latest high yielding varieties around 1968. Even before the Second World War, pre-harvest tasks required an average of 151 work-days per hectare (Vink, 1941); an average of an additional 98 work-days per hectare were needed for harvesting. The initial impact of the post-1968 intensification was variable, but it seems likely that more labour was used (Palmer, n.d.). Collier and Sajogyo (1972) quoted survey results which showed that 229 work-days were needed for pre-harvest activities on local varieties and 284 work-days were needed for the highest yielding varieties. While there was no break-down by sex, the average number of hours per day worked by family men and women in the paddy fields did not change but remained at 6.1 and 4.6 hours respectively. What is apparent from the reports of the Agro-Economic Survey is that the amount of family labour used tended to remain constant over a wide range of farm sizes, and that any change in labour requirements was absorbed by hired labour.

But since the early 1970s, changes in work methods have reduced labour use. In 1978, Collier concluded that the new varieties had not perceptibly increased the demand for labour. Greater potential requirements had been more than cancelled by changes in technology, both before and after harvesting. Hand weeding is increasingly giving way to rotary or toothbed weeders; human and animal power to tractors for ploughing; the traditional flat harvesting knife to the sickle; and hand pounding of paddy to hulling machines. The corollary has been that large mixed groups of harvesters have given way to a much smaller hired gang of males. So, as of 1978, the innovations adopted most widely have concerned weeding, harvesting, and hulling—all tasks formerly dominated by women's labour.

Transformation of tasks through technology not only causes labour redundancy. If the increase in labour productivity is substantial enough to change social relations governing the work, then there may also be a reversal of gender-typing. Harvesting in Java has switched from being mainly a female task to being the work of hired men—involving a decline in workers from perhaps 184 to 80 per hectare (Collier *et al.*, 1973). Most of the jobs in the rice mills are taken by men, whereas hand-pounding was clearly women's work. And the majority of the labour force for these two tasks was previously landless women.

A peculiarity of the situation in Java is that about 85 per cent of all labour requirements for paddy production used to be hired labour (male and female), even on very small farms (less than 0.5 ha). While farming households occupy themselves with the better-remunerated off-farm opportunities, it pays them to hire very cheap labour on their own land. And when labour-displacing technologies are available, there is less of a dilemma about whether to use them because they will displace hired wage labour rather than 'zero cost' family labour.

Hence household labour allocation is not only determined by size of farm, but by relative asset status and by the social relations of production both in the agricultural sector and in non-agricultural rural employment. So after an initial intensification of agricultural methods which involves more hired labour, it is relatively attractive to adopt labour-saving technologies.

It is unclear what the final results will be for the agricultural work of women of farming households. If hired labour is shed, these women may be left with tasks which have not been affected by technological innovations, and they may also continue with their off-farm occupations. It is reasonable to assume, however, that seasonal stress will be moderated for them.

For *landless* women, however, seasonal demands for their labour will be drastically reduced and perhaps eliminated. They will become more dependent upon non-agricultural employment which is characterised by low productivity and very low wages.

If landless women are experiencing longer hours of work for the same income, or less income for the same amount of work, then their increasing poverty could mean that all that has been said of seasonal stress on women will become year-round phenomena. That seasonal stresses have been moderated should not lead to complacency about the health of women and infants. Time and energy imbalances of women will become unremitting.

Java may be the most advanced instance of finely graded access to employment by class, and of intensified work for the same or lower incomes, but if rural poverty and landlessness increase in other countries, it could be regarded as the model of ultimate convergence. Because women in Bangladesh are subject to a high degree of seclusion, their redundancy in processing the rice harvest must mean that they lose opportunities to contribute to their households' income. Unlike their sisters in Java, landless women in Bangladesh might not suffer time imbalances, but through their reduced income they could be subject to harsher energy imbalances year-round and even more acute seasonal energy imbalances when there is a seasonal rise in the price of food.

Obstacles to amelioration of women's work-loads

Relief for women from seasonal work stresses and time imbalances can come from a combination of changes in gender-typing of production and maintenance work, the judicious application of technology for these tasks, and the use of more hired labour to help peasant women who work intensively on their family farms. To a pragmatic person, there are obvious ways of helping women during their seasonal peak work periods. One would be appropriate technology for transplanting and post-harvest processing; another would be a revised organisation of work allowing for breast-feeding and child care.

But gender-typing of tasks and the sexual division of labour are determined by relations of exchange of economic power between men and women within the household. Much of the literature on peasant communities uses explicit or implicit assumptions about the rationality of labour allocation and of 'self-exploitation' within families (Chayanov, 1966). This has even been applied to the unequal distribution of food between men and women, which supposedly reflects the heavier (though more intermittent) work done by men. To imply a rational basis for this is a mischievous idea which takes no account of the exploitation of women by men.

Family patriarchy has to be recognised as the main obstacle to securing a fairer distribution of work and food. It requires more than the usual economic analysis to devise means of encouraging male heads of households to surrender to women some of their power to allocate work and to decide where investment in more productive methods should be made. The International Labour Office (1976) pointed out that, in rural areas, 'most women in developing countries are overworked rather than underemployed, and a more appropriate technology for the tasks they perform implies labour saving. . . rather than employment creation'. However, the document fails to address itself to intra-household decision-making powers to invest in higher productivity methods in women's work. Instead, it takes refuge in arguing for what is mostly extra-household investment when it states that there is 'much scope' for relieving the lot of women, 'by the provision of accessible water points, rural electrification, and simple technological improvements in the processing and preparation of food...'.

By failing to recognise the problems of family patriarchy, this document does not explain how peasant women found themselves in a position of over-work in the first place when their husbands were unemployed. Nor does it say anything of the power relations behind gender-typing the total household work-load, or how altering this might also contribute to ameliorating women's work burdens.

The standard forms of agricultural modernisation tend to strengthen patriarchy. When land reform is introduced as part of the package of agricultural modernisation, land title is invariably conferred on male heads of household. When farming cooperatives are established to channel credit and such inputs as seed and fertilizer to farmers, male heads of household normally become the members of the cooperatives and are therefore seen as the representatives of the farming household with powers of allocating family labour and income. Inevitably men become the entrepreneurial managers of the family's production, leaving their wives in the position of bonded labour.

Gender-typing of tasks is not as sacrosanct in local cultures as might be supposed from its observed rigidity. In many countries, when there are large rises in labour productivity due to mechanisation, a task which was formerly done by women is taken over by men. The new harvesting practice in Java is one example. The change from hand-pounding rice to milling rice in Bangladesh and Java is another. The latter, at least, is an example of an investment decision taken above the household level and one which was subject to planning at the highest national level. But it led to a change in gender-typing of a task such that women lost the opportunity to enjoy higher productivity methods in their original work.

Policy implications

Pervading all discussions on farming, women's ability to negotiate an easier workload and to demand appropriate technology is dependent on their access to resources and to membership of institutions (which in turn confer rights to resources including income). Reform of rural institutions, especially of farming cooperatives, to allow women full membership rights and direct access to the returns to their households' labour is essential. Without it, women cannot be expected to overcome their subordinate labour position. This kind of intervention in intra-household relations of exchange does no more than correct past interventions which have made the male head of household the managerial entrepreneur as the family unit has moved increasingly into the market economy.

The function of a farmers' cooperative could also be extended to imposing a levy on household income from the sale of produce to finance investment in some technology which reduces women's work-load in unremunerated tasks. If, as is frequently asserted, the farming household is an integrated unit whose members work in a complementary manner, then this measure can only reinforce that structure.

Granting women full membership rights to cooperatives becomes even more imperative when it has been found impossible to grant women equal rights with men in land reform. This may be the case where planners fear that population density will lead to fragmentation of small farms if all children enjoy equal inheritance rights. But where land scarcity is not a problem, there is no reason why women's access to resources should not be strengthened by granting them equal rights to land with men.

The income-gaining opportunities of landless women are seriously threatened by the kind of technology being introduced into many rural areas, because of the changed gender-typing of jobs after mechanisation. Relief for such women will only come from an expansion of properly-remunerated non-agricultural employment in the rural economy.

In planning for all these situations, it has to be clearly understood that one cannot gain an objective view of work stresses on women simply by looking at measurable conditions in the locality. Data on size of land-holdings, the extent of landlessness, and the average size of family labour forces are not enough. One must also look at the social relations of production between men and women, and between landed and landless.

7.3 The Sociology of Seasonal Food Shortage In Hausaland
Michael Watts[*]

Introduction

In her treatise on peasant inequality in a Hausa village, Polly Hill (1972) took the ability to withstand the shock of a late or poor harvest as a criterion of what she loosely described as the farming unit's standard of living. This criterion is particularly relevant for the poor peasantry in highly seasonal biomes such as the West African savannah (Adeoye, 1976). The purpose of this paper is to enlarge on the social, political, and economic context of pre-harvest hunger in that region. In doing so, it draws on archival sources, and on my own field experience in a large Muslim Hausa village north of Katsina on the Nigerian side of the frontier with Niger. The location is indicated by the map in Figure 1.9, which also shows its proximity to other northern Nigerian case-study areas in this book.

We should beware of sliding into a naive environmental determinism. There is no inevitability about seasonal food shortages, just as there is no predetermined relationship between drought and famine. The connections that do exist between seasonal food scarcity and the environment are mediated by the political and economic relations of a society. Raynault (1976), working in Niger, suggests that the character of seasonality has changed historically with the transformation of the relations of production, and the generation of

---

[*]I should like to acknowledge the generous support, during the period of field research (1976-8), of the Social Science Research Council, the Wenner-Gren Foundation for Anthropological Research Inc., the National Science Foundation, and Resources for the Future. This paper is something of a collaborative effort; I have learned much from Bill Freund, Bob Shenton, Richard Palmer-Jones, Louise Lennihan, and Sam Jackson.

new types of social inequality. The break-up of traditional farming units, the growing commercial use of land, the increase of hired farm labour, and the deepening of merchant relationships has actually increased the vulnerability of the poorest to seasonal oscillations in the environment. This perspective is important, because any ahistoric analysis of contemporary seasonality runs the risk of assuming that the character of pre-harvest hunger is static and unchanging. This paper therefore includes a rather summary discussion of changes which have occurred in Nigerian Hausaland since the end of the nineteenth century.

The basic unit of production in the nineteenth century was the household, perhaps embracing sons, clients and slaves (Shenton and Freund, 1978; Usman, 1974). Households were often subsumed in communities controlled through the agency of village heads whose responsibilities extended to land sales and village adjudication. A proportion of the peasant surplus was expropriated by a ruling class (*sarauta*) in the form of labour, grain, or cash. Though the *sarauta* usually resided on private estates worked by slave, client and hired labour, they could also demand corvée labour (*gayya*) from villages within their jurisdiction. Slave labour, though crucial to the large estates operated by the ruling class, was not a dominant characteristic of the productive system. Craft production and petty commodity production generally within individual households was, conversely, a widespread phenomenon in Hausaland. The state apparatus controlled the means of coercion, provided protection for the peasantry (*talakawa*) and for travelling merchants, organised large-scale labour projects, and acted as a guarantor in times of need. Within this social formation, the nature of seasonal scarcity was modified by (1) the redistributive social matrix, and (2) a comprehensive and articulated series of coping mechanisms capable of accommodating the effects of food shortage — what has been called a 'moral economy'.

Traditional redistribution and coping mechanisms

Marcel Mauss (1954) has shown that for many non-capitalist societies, the logic of the gift operated simultaneously as a kind of language and as a means of cementing the social fabric. The spirit of the gift mediates against accumulation through an ideology which stresses redistribution. Referring to Hausaland, Raynault (1976) points out that, 'the possibility of accumulation... has an institutional counterpart in the obligation to redistribute'. This acts, to some extent, as a mechanism for collective security.

In a society where redistribution is emphasised, the gift is an investment both as a means of gaining prestige and as a security to guarantee subsistence should hard times arise. To a certain extent, the *biki* system in Hausaland (Hill, 1972), which exists today in modified form, operates in this way. The extent of the gifts made at marriages and naming ceremonies within one community near Zaria was documented earlier in this book (Simmons, Section 3.2). Among the non-Muslim Hausa, the Maguzawa, the family group referred to as a clan segment or *gida* functions so that 'when the grain stores of one household are exhausted, its head may borrow grain from another *gida* household and repay that grain at harvest without interest' (Faulkingham, 1971).

At an ideological level, the redistributive ethic was reiterated through the Muslim dogma which saw gift-giving as obligatory for the rich and for the *sarauta* (Nicolas *et al.*, 1968). At another level, other formal institutional mechanisms incumbent on the rich served to free resources for the peasantry or *talakawa*. The *gayya* or communal work group is a case in point, in which foodstuffs are released during the critical pre-harvest period (Raulin, 1964).

In a society based on an absolute hierarchical segmentation between classes—between *talakawa* and *sarauta*—it is hardly surprising that the upper echelons were expected to act as the ultimate buffers for the village-level redistributive operations. The responsibilities and obligations of the village heads were quite clear in this respect, and when their capabilities were overridden in cases of extreme seasonal hardship, the next level of the hierarchy, that of the *hakimi* or fief-holders, was activated (Raynault, 1975). In Katsina emirate, for example, the *hakimi* often kept grain at several centres throughout their district, particularly in villages where they may have acted as patron to a number of clients. Ultimately, extreme situations could involve the state structure itself, which used the grain tithe (*zakkat*) in central granaries for organised distribution during famine periods (Palmer, 1910; Smith, 1967).

Alongside the redistributive system was a sequence of graduated coping mechanisms, some of which are still extant in Hausa society. These include (1) agronomic measures, (2) the use of famine foods, (3) crop storage, and (4) seasonal migration. The principal agronomic measure is the mixed cropping of millet and sorghum, so that if the rains partially fail, the millet will still produce a crop. Famine foods include wild plants which can be employed as supplements to the basic diet. More fundamental were the very efficient traditional techniques of grain storage:

> the seed destined to be planted the next year as well as the quantity of grain necessary for the subsistence of the group during the planting season were placed by the clan head in a large granary which could not be opened until after the first rains (Raynault, 1975).

When the granaries were sealed during the post-harvest period, the adult males frequently departed on migration to corvée labour or state-sponsored (defense) projects. During the wet season, hardship could be partly alleviated by short-distance migration to make use of the differential onset of the rains and hence the local variation in the timing of agricultural operations.

All this is not to suggest a Rousseauian pre-capitalist bliss: serious famines did occur in nineteenth century Hausaland (Watts and Shenton, 1978). But given the technological limitations, food shortages were accommodated reasonably well; the social formation as a whole was able to limit the extent to which seasonality was a 'problem'.

Effects of monetisation

The arrival of British colonial forces around 1900 heralded a new era; the new administration sought, through taxation, to divert to their own coffers as much as possible of the surplus formerly extracted by the *sarauta*. More traumatic than increases in tax was the move to collect the tax in cash rather than grain. Effected by 1910, not only did this undermine the grain reserve based on tithes (*zakkat*), but did much to extend the modern money economy

(Raynault, 1977; Shenton and Freund, 1978).

Unlike the indigenous Hausa fiscal system, colonial taxes were regular and inflexible, taking no account of late rains, poor harvests, and an environment subject to locust invasions and epidemics. Though far from innocent of extortion, the old system had attempted to graduate taxes according to circumstances (Palmer, 1908a). Colonial taxation was also designed to promote the extension of commodity production and cash cropping, and groundnuts were the principal tax-paying crop in northern Hausaland.

More generally, the groundnut revolution meant a decrease in the area devoted to food grown for local consumption; it also meant increased subjection to the vagaries of the world commodity market and the ever-present threat of indebtedness at the hands of middlemen. Thus the nature of seasonal hunger changed in its dynamics, and also in the predicament it placed on those who found themselves short of food. The result tended to be that seasonal shortages more easily evolved into full-scale famine, as happened in 1913-14 and has been repeated regularly since.

In these changed circumstances, it is hardly surprising that new forms of indebtedness arose. This is especially so with the evolution of a new group of middlemen, the *'yan baranda*. These men received cash advances from European firms via their buying agents. The money was in turn lent directly to the producer, who pledged his crop to the middleman and indirectly to the buying agent responsible. The interest on such loans was frequently around 100 per cent, and for the producer, was the initial step into a cyclical debt trap (Giles, 1934). The lower-order middleman actually exploited seasonal variations and the pre-harvest need for cash, and it is precisely in this manner that urban and merchant capital penetrated the countryside.

The deepening involvement with commodity production and cash crops naturally impinged upon the social organisation of agricultural production itself. Raynault (1976, 1977) has shown how, in the groundnut zone of Niger, this has taken the form of the dissolution of traditional estates, escalation in land sales, and increases in the hiring of farm labour. These changes, and the growth of indebtedness, imposed strains on the corporateness of the rural world. The old responsibilities and obligations became less binding and less able to buffer individuals in times of stress. In the densely settled areas, extreme land shortages heralded larger food deficits and heightened vulnerability to seasonal crises.

In short, the social nature of the subsistence system was disrupted in the sense that the distribution and production of foodstuff was no longer based upon old, socially established norms. Reciprocity and solidarity had gone, and hence the nature of inequality itself had changed. Of course, Hausa society prior to the arrival of the British had emphasised hierarchy and inequality. But the appearance of new inequities was founded, not on *social structure*, but on changes in the *relations of production*.

The implications of these changes for seasonal hunger are thrown into relief by the incidence of famine in Hausaland since 1900. In Katsina, famine occurred in 1906, 1913, 1920 (partially), 1927, 1931 (partially), 1942, 1950, 1959 (partially) and 1974 (Watts, 1976). The frequency is itself astonishing, but more to the point are the mechanics by which seasonal hunger assumed

Social Distribution of Seasonal Burdens

famine proportions. The 1950-51 famine, for example, was precipitated by buying agents who foresaw a mediocre harvest and demanded that mortgaged cash crops be redeemed with subsistence foodstuffs. With a high tax burden and little grain in their bins from the poor harvest of 1949, the peasants were extraordinarily vulnerable. The colonial administration, still without a policy on food reserves, was therefore faced with the choice of buying grain for relief from local wholesalers at inflated prices, or purchasing elsewhere and paying high freight rates (Katsina, 1952). The experience shows how erroneous it would be to assume that seasonal scarcity is a 'natural' if lamentable feature of Hausaland.

The village-level study

The village in which I worked, which I shall call Sabo, is a compact, formerly walled settlement of just under 4000 persons, situated on a minor road to the north of Katsina. The climate is of E5 type on Walsh's classification (Chapter 1), with a pronounced wet-dry season dichotomy corresponding to discrete periods of social activity.

In 1900, Sabo district contained much uncultivated upland, but now farmland is almost impossible to buy, and population densities have risen sharply. The result has been a decline in the average size of farm holdings which, in conjunction with the relatively poor quality of the soil, has meant that the poorer peasantry are increasingly incapable of fulfilling basic biological requirements in most years.

The grains trade is principally organised through complex patron-client chains which connect the urban dealer with the hamlet-level producers; the same patron-client chains also operate the system of village-level credit. The poor peasantry often need credit in the dry season (e.g. for marriages), or in the pre-harvest period (to buy food), and have to sell grain at harvest to pay back their debts, but while prices are still low. An initial grain loan during the dry season, repaid at harvest with 100 per cent interest, may escalate over a period of several years into land pledging, mortgaging, and possibly outright sale of land. Thus indebtedness tends to increase seasonally through a kind of ratchet mechanism.

Dry-season irrigation is one way of reducing pre-harvest scarcity, but a chronic shortage of suitable *fadama* land has prevented access for a large proportion of farmers. However, *fadama* land differs from the upland fields in that almost 50 per cent of it is rented. Interestingly, the payment of rent is frequently denied, as the arrangement is conceived as a 'borrowing' agreement (*aro*). Such a conception appears to suppress potential class conflict. However, those of the poor who can gain access to *fadama* land with a view to overcoming seasonal shortages tend to repay the additional debts with their labour power. This creates immense scheduling problems, frequently culminating in the debtor postponing his own planting or weeding activities.

The development and security of the household consists of the reproduction of the domestic means of production, and takes three forms: (1) the extension of the household to ensure the necessary labour power, (2) the creation of alliances through marriage and ceremonial exchange, and (3) the production of commodities and the sale of labour. Clearly, then, obligatory ceremonial expenditures, especially on marriage, assume great social importance. However, they are now extraordinarily expensive in relation to the annual income of the poor. Marriage cost ₦ 2-5 in the early 1940s, but had inflated to ₦ 60-80 by 1966-7, and a staggering ₦ 350 in Sabo by 1978 (Salifou, 1973; Hill, 1972). In addition, *annual* ceremonial expenses such as naming ceremonies and gift exchange usually amount to more than ₦ 50 for the middle peasantry. These expenditures frequently necessitate large-scale borrowing, and it is not surprising that one of the principal motives for land sales and pledging is to cover marriage expenses. Such expenditures, being more frequent in the dry season, complicate the seasonal vulnerability of the peasant quite significantly.

Conclusion

Landlessness and class differentiation have not developed so far, nor so starkly, as in parts of Asia. But Wood's (1978) description of class formation in Bangladesh has much in common with the situation in parts of Hausaland, particularly the close-settled zones:

> Indebtedness abounds and the small peasant's land is gradually expropriated. . . so he is transformed into a sharecropper. . . a dependent labourer; an insecure peripatetic trader. . . a migrant labourer; a hopeful on the urban labour market or a vagrant. (p. 42)

Not only is peasant differentiation thus related to the hiring of land and labour, usury and commodity production, but the problems which arise from seasonality are also inseparable from it. Seasonal food shortage can neither be understood nor resolved unless we accept that things would be very different if, as Hill (1972) says, there were none too poor to farm. The village social ethic among the Hausa places a premium on assisting poor households in time of dire need. But one should not let these collective responsibilities, such as they are, obscure the predicament of the poor peasantry (Palmer-Jones, 1978). Seasonal hunger may be a silent problem, and hence it often goes unperceived, but it is no less real for those who suffer from it.

7.4 Seasonality and Dependence In South Asia
John and Barbara Harriss

The scenario of seasonal dependence

In his introduction to this book, Robert Chambers identifies the hungry season at the beginning of the rains as a time when the poor 'are screwed down seasonally into subordinate and dependent relationships in which they are open to exploitation'. This far-reaching statement, which we see as key, generates some issues which we can examine in the context of South Asia. In particular, it implies a causal correlation between low seasonality and a low frequency of vertical dependence or of patron-client relationships. Areas of low seasonality might also show a strengthening of the economic power of poor groups.

There is some indirect evidence from South India and Sri Lanka to support this idea. The states in that region all have relatively high agricultural growth rates, with relatively low fluctuations in agricultural output as compared with

Social Distribution of Seasonal Burdens

TABLE 7.1. Seasonality in selected South Asian regions

Region	Climatic seasonality (Walsh classes*, see Chapter 1)	Agricultural seasonality (number of cultivation seasons per year**)
Sri Lanka		
north	D3)	
south-east	D2)	2
south-west	C2)	
Kerala (India)		
Alleppey area	C3	2
Tamil Nadu (India)		
North Arcot District	D3	(1–2
		(2–3 irrigated
Thanjavur District		
(1) Old Delta (west)	E4	2–3 irrigated
(2) Old Delta (east)	E4	1–2 not irrigated
(3) New Delta	E4	2–3 irrigated
Andhra Pradesh (India)	D4	2–3 irrigated
Bihar (India)	D4	1–2
Madhya Pradesh (India)	E5	1–2
Punjab (India)	E4	2–3 irrigated

Notes: *C2, C3, and D2 denote relatively low seasonality; D3, D4, E4, and E5 denote relatively high seasonality.
**These are typical figures only; local variations must be expected, depending especially on the extent and type of irrigation.

the rest of South Asia (Jose, 1977). However, climatic seasonality varies greatly from area to area within the region (see Table 7.1) and makes some instructive comparisons possible.

First, in Tamil Nadu, the agricultural poor, notably landless labourers, have been provoked to protest in regions where, despite high climatic seasonality, irrigation has most reduced the seasonality of agriculture. Examples are to be found in the rice bowls of Thanjavur and Chingleput Districts (Frankel, 1971). There is also a long history of greater rural equality and more accumulation by the poor peasantry in some of the irrigated areas compared with the dry areas of more seasonal agriculture (Washbrook, 1973). Further debate on the latter point has queried some details (Kumar, 1976), but Baker (1976) concludes that dry and highly seasonal Districts were absolutely poorer; they had higher numbers of pauperised cultivators and a small class of wealthy usurer-traders. In contrast, irrigated areas with low seasonality of agricultural production such as Thanjavur District supported a much larger number of people in rural trade and workshop industry, among whom there was less differentiation by wealth.

As a second, more geographically extended comparison, we may contrast the relative absence of agrarian reform measures in Tamil Nadu as a whole with the more considerable achievement with redistributionist land reforms, and the long history of the organisation of landless labour in Kerala to the west which has a less seasonal climate (Jose, 1977) — although seasonality may have relatively little to do with these changes. In Aleppey, for example, rural politicisation has spread from the highly unionised labour extruded from bankrupt coconut and coir factories, and there is a long history of organised labour (from 1939) and of rural protest. However, more recent agricultural development has led to an increase in agrarian inequality, with farmers benefiting from rising paddy prices, but with rising unemployment among labourers.

In contrast to these cases, which support our initial thesis, we can set micro-level evidence from villages in the North Arcot District of Tamil Nadu, a region where farmers increasingly have their own electric pump-sets for well irrigation. Here, strong client-patron dependence is significantly more in evidence in villages where agricultural production is relatively independent of climatic seasons, and where the demand for labour is well spread through the year (Chambers and Harriss, 1977; J. C. Harriss, forthcoming, 1980).

Second, we can note the existence of 'abject dependency' relationships between small farmers and landowners and traders as well as the absence of any strong movements of protest indicative of a breakdown of dependency relationships in Sri Lanka, where with two cultivation seasons, the influence of seasonality is as low as in Kerala, and the commodity and money markets are comparatively highly controlled (Dias and Wickremanayake, 1976; Harriss, 1976).

Third, Oomen (1971), in discussing rural agitation, remarks on the fact that the States with the largest number of organised protests in the late 1960s were Bihar and Madhya Pradesh (States with strongly seasonal and uncertain agriculture), rather than Punjab or Andhra Pradesh, where farmers have generally greater control over their production environment, and where there is more demand for labour.

Tamil Nadu case-studies

So far we have simply recorded some instances of crude co-variation, and have not attempted to explain the role that seasonality plays. Tamil Nadu is one of the case-study areas for this book (see Chapters 1 and 5) and offers more detailed insights.

For a start, Beteille (1974) reminds us that Thanjavur District is by no means ecologically homogeneous and that there are important differences between the Old and New Deltas. In the west of the Old Delta, despite the highly seasonal E4 climate (Table 7.1), there is low agricultural seasonality and a long history of irrigated and intensive agriculture, high population density, a high degree of tenancy, and 'elaborate patterns of social stratification'. The east of the Old Delta has very seasonal agriculture (still one crop a year in places), high population density, and extreme economic polarisation. By contrast, the New Delta has only relatively recently been endowed with major irrigation systems, and is in process of being made less seasonal by the use of energised well irrigation. Here, the population and resource endowment resembles the dry district archetype with low pressure of population on land and less economic polarisation. Here dependency relations are little changed.

Beteille's argument for the breakdown of dependence and the evolution of rural protest among the landless stresses that in the Old Delta, an untypically high proportion of the rural population is landless (60 per cent—twice that of the New Delta). The landless are wage labourers, socially homogeneous (harijan) and geographically segregated in their settlements, and thus 'easily organised into a class for political action'. This has also been encouraged by the polarisation between landless people and secure tenants caused by State tenancy legislation since 1952. A further factor has been the reduction in the time span of seasonal labour peaks, associated with an increase in multiple cropping and in overall labour demand. This has provided a catalyst for agitation by the organised landless.

The North Arcot evidence underlines the reciprocity of patron-client relationships. In a sample of twelve villages, attached employment was found to be most common in two villages where labour demand was relatively evenly spread round the year and where wages for the landless were highest, reflecting seasonal labour shortages (Chambers and Harriss, p. 316). The poor may depend on patrons for the 'right to subsistence', but these patrons also depend on the poor for their labour (Scott, 1972). This may explain the North Arcot situation: in villages with highly seasonal labour demands, patrons may not welcome clients who may make demands on them through parts of the year when there is no work; in contrast, where labour demand is more evenly spread and where labour is seasonally short, patrons may seek to acquire and maintain clients in order to assure themselves of a continuous, timely and reliable source of labour.

This is an important point of quite general validity: that the existence of dependency relations mediated through paternalism depends upon the dominant partner's needs for clients—and this may be stronger in areas of low rather than of high seasonality.

Conclusion

The crucial difference between communities where low seasonality is associated with mobilisation of the poor and improvement in their condition and communities where it is not would seem to be the combination of other factors affecting political mobilisation. As the Kerala example showed, political organisation may spread from an urban industrial situation. It may also be restricted to areas where oppressed groups have considerable economic and cultural unity. There are many other factors which may play a part, none of them sufficient on its own; such factors include high population density, high levels of landlessness, and changes in the demand for labour arising from agricultural intensification. The idea that low seasonality implies a particular pattern of poverty and authority cannot go without question. In Thanjavur District, both the Western Old Delta and the New Delta are now of low seasonality with respect to agricultural production, but their historical evolution has involved different demographic and agrarian structures as well as different patterns of economic exploitation of the poor.

Whether or not the poor 'are screwed down seasonally into subordinate and dependent relationships' seems to depend on factors not included in the model, such as the relations of the poor to the means of production, the particular history of political mobilisation, and finally, the action of the State. For instance, the tenancy legislation specific to Thanjavur District was catalytic in leading to the organisation of labour and the breakdown of relations of dependency.

Yet another factor is the variation of food and produce prices. It is often argued that a potent mechanism for rural impoverishment is the necessity for poor peasants to sell subsistence crops cheaply after harvest, and then later, to buy food dearly (Harriss and Harriss, 1978). In South Asia, the mechanism is a good deal more complex than usually supposed. For example, in Sri Lanka, controlled paddy prices over a long period have not prevented the intensification of dependency. And purchases of agro-chemicals, for weed control, perhaps, when labour for weeding is short, can greatly alter the peasant's seasonal costs.

Thus the real world of South Asia is complex, and our vision is correspondingly blurred. Paraphrasing Beteille (1974, p. 169), a social fact such as the seasonal dimensions of poverty, 'has many causes and the same cause produces different results at different places because it never acts in combination with the same factors everywhere'.

7.5 Seasonal Out-Migration and Rural Poverty
Henry Rempel

Definition

In this survey of published data on the interaction between climatic season, rural out-migration and poverty at the migration source, I have adopted Goddard's (1974) definition of 'seasonal labour circulation'. This he describes as a movement of labour that is 'characteristically short term, repetitive or cyclical in nature, and adjusted to the annual agricultural cycle'. Such a definition limits the study to persons 'absent from their permanent homes through a particular season(s) of the year' (Gould and Prothero, 1975), but absent for less than a year. Circulation is an appropriate term as it designates the permanent home as one end of the movement cycle.

This definition eliminates from consideration the large amount of labour circulation in Africa which typically is not defined in terms of an annual agricultural cycle (Mitchell, 1959, 1962, 1969; Gulliver, 1955; Southall, 1962), even though in some studies such movement is called seasonal migration (e.g. Todaro, 1976). However, longer-term migration may have distinct seasonal dimensions. For example, longer-term migrants may decide to leave after the peak in the agricultural cycle, time their eventual return to coincide with the beginning of the peak season, or attempt to obtain their annual leave at the time of the peak season.

Locations of seasonal labour circulation

The geographic location where seasonal labour circulation has been particularly evident is West Africa (Gould and Prothero, 1975; map, Udo, 1974). Because much of the movement crosses national boundaries, it is more easily identified than most seasonal movement, though seasonal movement from north to south within Ghana and Nigeria has received attention in the literature also.

Based largely on data sources from the early 1960s, Amin (1974) estimates an annual flow of seasonal migrants of 120,000 from Upper Volta; 200,000 into the coffee-cocoa belt of southern Ghana and the Ivory Coast; 20,000 from Togo; 259,000 from Sokoto Province in Nigeria; and a total within and from Nigeria of 500,000.

Udo (1974) identifies 'thousands of Hausa workers' moving annually into the cocoa belt of south-western Nigeria. Further, he identifies an annual flow of 75,000 seasonal migrants into the groundnut area of Senegal and Gambia. Most are said to come from Mali and Guinea, though in contrast, Amin (1974) says that the flow from Mali and Guinea was at a peak of 60,000 in 1935 and had largely disappeared by the 1960s. Finally, Beals and Menezes (1970), on the basis of 1960 census data, estimate that more than half of the working-age males in northern Ghana must have been involved in seasonal circulation to the south at some point in their lives.

A much smaller seasonal circulation in Africa is documented in Kenya, where Gwyer and Ruigi (1971) identified some migrants from the Rift Valley to Tetu (Nyeri District), and some movement from Machakos District to Mbere (Embu District). Gwyer (1971) also found some seasonal migrants from Machakos District seeking employment at the Kindaruma dam construction site.

One labour circulation that has received particularly careful attention from scholars is the movement from Mexico to part of the United States (e.g. Hancock, 1959; Wiest, 1973). In addition, labour circulation is reported for Guatemala and Brazil (Miracle and Berry, 1970); Peru (Doughty, 1968); Uganda (Hutton, 1973); Turkey, India, and Taiwan (Connell *et al.*, 1976); Bangladesh (Sections 3.4 and 3.5 above); Vietnam (Oshima, 1971); the Solomon Islands (Connell *et al.*, 1976); and Alaska (Van Stone, 1960).

The determinants of seasonal migration

Of the migration flows identified explicitly above, most of the source regions fall into a 'one rainy season' category. The notable exception is the out-migration from Machakos District in Kenya. The bimodal rainfall regime of this area was discussed in Chapter 2, where it was stated that 10 per cent of the economically active population may be involved in migration. Probably in most bimodal regions, the length of employment involved is too short to make lengthy journeys worthwhile. But information on the subject is lacking, and this must be considered merely a hypothesis.

In order to understand seasonal labour circulation, we need to ask, is a seasonal demand for labour sufficiently strong to explain the movement that occurs? For the flow from Mexico to the United States, the answer is probably in the affirmative. The income differential is so large that permanent movement of families and longer stays would have been common if this had been legally possible. Because longer-term movement is limited by United States immigration laws, an adequate supply has been available on a seasonal basis at the time required by the United States agricultural cycle.

In Africa, by contrast, the mere existence of a seasonal demand for labour has not by itself generated adequate in-migration, even though widespread unemployment exists. Some specific examples of available seasonal employment which has difficulty attracting labour are given by Gwyer (1972) and Wasow (1973). Gwyer and Ruigu (1971) report on a situation in Nyeri District, Kenya, where there is difficulty in attracting seasonal labour because potential workers are busy on their own plots at the relevant time. In a somewhat similar situation in Egypt, Byerlee and Eicher (1972) cite seasonal variation in agricultural wages to induce an adequate labour response from small farmers during peaks in the agricultural cycle.

These experiences suggest that seasonal dimensions in the source area play a dominant role in the seasonal movement of labour. Connell (1973) puts forth the general proposition that: 'The longer the growing season in the labour-supplying villages and the greater the number of crops that can be grown per year, the greater the potential production foregone as a result of migration is likely to be'.

The validity of this hypothesis is borne out by several studies. For Sokoto (Nigeria), Goddard (1974) found that cash cropping on *fadama* farms and local employment were competitive with out-migration as a use of labour. Labour circulation was most evident in the 'remote village' and least evident in the 'riverine village' which provided opportunity for wet farming all year round. Also, the length of the temporary absences was found to vary inversely with the opportunities for wet farming. Adomako-Sarfoh (1974) provides supporting evidence as well in stating that irrigation projects in northern Ghana have served to reduce the supply of seasonal labour available to the south.

One would expect seasonal migration to be most evident where the timing of seasons in the sending and receiving regions complements one another. Such complementarity is claimed to exist in the movement from north to south in West Africa (Adomako-Sarfoh, 1974, but see Miracle and Berry, 1970). And the United States demand for seasonal labour coincides largely with the Mexican dry season.

Among other factors which may affect out-migration from the source area, landlessness is not usually one (Poupart, 1965; Goddard, 1974). It is their rights to land that give seasonal migrants their main reason to return; the landless are likely to move permanently with their households to a new area if they migrate at all. For those with land, the absence of a market for cash crops may be one incentive for seasonal migration, for this can provide an alternative way of securing some money income (Byerlee and Eicher, 1972; Goddard, 1974).

Another factor seen as relevant in some cases is the role of women in agriculture. Both among the Mossi of Upper Volta (Miracle and Berry, 1970) and among the Moslem residents of Sokoto province (Goddard, 1974), there are social sanctions against women engaging in heavy farm work. Similarly, among the Eskimo of Point Hope, Alaska, women do not participate in certain aspects of fishing and hunting (Van Stone, 1960). This may reduce the opportunities for men to leave the area except where it is customary for male kin to undertake labour for households where the male head is absent. Their attitudes to the role of women in agriculture may explain why the people of Sokoto and the Mossi of Upper Volta engage in seasonal labour circulation rather than longer term migration.

These points can be summarised by saying that those involved in labour circulation are typically people with land whose exploitation of their land is held down either by the lack of a market for cash crops, or by a seasonal rainfall regime and a lack of irrigation which make year-round farming impossible. The role of women and other family commitments also affect the timing of migrations. Households with less than three adults typically do not send out-migrants (Wiest, 1973). Finally, no doubt, there are regions that meet the conditions for seasonal out-migration but where people regard earning possibilities elsewhere as too low relative to the cost of moving.

The effects of seasonal labour circulation

If people seek to supplement their income by seasonal migration, they are clearly not satisfied with current earnings. But it is not usually the poorest people who migrate. It is not the landless, and it is not those dependent on landlords and money-lenders, who are not usually so free to consider seeking work elsewhere (Connell *et al.*, 1976). Both Wiest (1973) for Mexico and Van Stone (1960) for Alaska report that the poorer families are the ones who do not participate in the seasonal labour circulation.

The production effects of out-migration from an area are seen to be detrimental in that area, but the magnitude is hard to measure. Several sources mention a more general negative effect in the form of neglected maintenance and production of social overhead capital (Miracle and Berry, 1970; Amin, 1974). More significant is perhaps that the seasonal absence removes pressure to transform local production methods as a means of maintaining living standards. Indeed, Gugler (1976) cites evidence that efforts to introduce cotton production in Upper Volta failed where it interfered with the existing pattern of seasonal labour circulation.

More favourable production effects may occur where the migration experience provides people with ideas about the kind of improvements that are potentially possible (Hancock, 1959; Keyes, 1966; Poupart, 1965), or where the income generated is invested productively in the migration source area. However, most experience is that earnings are used for consumption items or taxes (Hancock, 1959; Goddard, 1974). With reference to migration as a means of obtaining new technology, ideas, or skills, Miracle and Berry (1970) hypothesise that the effect will vary directly with the degree of similarity between the activity done elsewhere and local production. Hancock (1959) assesses the Mexico-United States flow as generating useful technological changes for Mexican agriculture.

In addition to such economic effects of seasonal labour circulation, one would expect social effects as well, but there is not much discussion of these in the literature surveyed. Van Stone (1960) notes that summer employment opportunities have resulted in 'atomisation of the individuals within the family' and parental authority is undermined. The hypothesised negative effect on the work-load of women while the men are absent seems to be associated more with the longer-term circulation. When the circulation is seasonal only, the men return for the main period of activity. Finally, frequent movement of people among regions raises the potential of disease being spread geographically. To my knowledge, this is not discussed in the literature.

In conclusion, then, seasonal labour circulation appears to be an effective adaptation to a particular economic, environmental and historical situation. It does not appear to be associated with the extremes of rural poverty, nor are the worst negative impacts typically associated with migration particularly evident in seasonal labour circulation. Similarly, the potential benefits that could transform the local situation into a better place for living, without the need for out-migration, are also seen to be limited. It is likely that the seasonal circulation of labour contributes to the regional disparity of income and wealth because the receiving area probably gains more than half of the net benefits associated with labour circulation. One relevant policy might be a redistribution of investment away from the labour receiving areas to the regions of out-migration, so that labour no longer has to move. But whether this would generate a more 'optimal' development path for a country as a whole is not easily measured. Such an exercise is beyond the scope of this paper.

7.6 References

Adeoye, K. B. (1976), 'A Note on the Reliability of Rainfall at Samaru and Kano, Nigeria', *Samaru Miscellaneous Papers*, No. 54, Ahamadu Bello University, Zaria.

Adomako-Sarfoh, J. (1974), 'The Effects of the Expulsion of Migrant Workers on Ghana's Economy', in *Modern Migrations in Western Africa*, ed. Samir Amin, London, Oxford University Press.

Amin, S. (1974), Introduction, in *Modern Migrations in Western Africa*, ed. Samir Amin, London, Oxford University Press.

Baker, C. (1976), 'On Guessing Who Controlled How Much Land in Madras', Cambridge, Centre of South Asian Studies (mimeo).

Beals, R. E., and Menezes, C. F. (1970), 'Migrant Labour and Agricultural Output in Ghana', *Oxford Economic Papers*, 22, pp. 109-27.

Beteille, A. (1974), *Studies in Agrarian Social Structure*, London, Oxford University Press.

Briscoe, J. (1978), 'Labour and Organic Resources in the Indian Subcontinent', in *Sanitation in Developing Countries*, ed. A. Pacey, Chichester and New York, John Wiley & Sons.

Byerlee, D., and Eicher, C. K. (1972), *Rural Employment, Migration, and Economic Development*, African Rural Development Paper No. 1, Department of Agricultural Economics, Michigan State University, East Lansing.

Chambers, R., and Harriss, J. C. (1977), 'Comparing Twelve South Indian Villages in Search of Practical Theory', in *Green Revolution?*, ed. B. H. Farmer, London, Macmillan.

Chayanov, A. V. (1966), *The Theory of Peasant Economy*, ed. D. Thorner, B. Kerblay and R.E.F. Smith, Homewood, Richard D. Irwin Inc.

Collier, W. L. (1977), 'Technology and Peasant Production: a Comment', *Development and Change*, 8 (3), pp. 351-62.

Collier, W. L., and Sajogyo (1972), 'Employment Opportunities Created by the High Yielding Rice Varieties in Several Areas on Java', *Ekonomi dan Keuangen Indonesia*, 20 (2).

Collier, W. L., Gunawan Wirandi, and Soantoro (1973), 'Recent Changes in Rice Harvesting Methods', *Bulletin of Indonesian Economic Studies*, 9 (2).

Connell, J. (1973), 'Migration and the Rural Job Situation: the Evidence from Village Studies', *Discussion Paper* 26, Institute of Development Studies, University of Sussex.

Connell, J., Dasgupta, B., Laishley, R., and Lipton, M. (1976), *Migration from Rural Areas: the Evidence from Village Studies*, Delhi, Oxford University Press.

Dias, H. D., and Wickremanayake, B.W.E. (1976), 'The Gambara System', in *Agriculture in the Peasant Sector of Sri Lanka*, Ceylon Studies Seminar, Peradeniya.

Doughty, P. L. (1968), *Huaylas: an Andean District in Search of Progress*, New York, Cornell University Press.

Farmer, B. H. (ed.) (1977), *Green Revolution?*, London, Macmillan.

Farrar, D. M. (1974), 'Aspects of Water Supply and Conservation in Some Semi-Arid Regions of Africa', Unpublished Ph.D. thesis, University of Manchester Institute of Science and Technology.

Faulkingham, R. (1971), 'Political Support in a Hausa Village, Niger', Unpublished Ph.D. thesis, Michigan State University.

Frankel, F. E. (1971), *India's Green Revolution*, New York, Cornell University Press.

Ghatak, S. (1975), 'Rural Interest Rates in the Indian Economy', *J. Development Studies, 11*, pp. 190-201.

Giles, R. (1934), 'Co-operation in a Hausa Village', Unpublished manuscript, Rhodes House Library, Oxford.

Goddard, A. D. (1974), 'Population Movements and Land Shortages in the Sokoto Close-settled Zone, Nigeria', in *Modern Migrations in Western Africa*, ed. Samir Amin, London, Oxford University Press.

Gould, W.T.S., and Prothero, R. M. (1975), 'Space and Time in African Population Mobility', in *People on the Move: Studies on Internal Migration*, London, Methuen.

Gugler, J. (1976), 'Migrating to Urban Centres of Unemployment in Tropical Africa', in *Internal Migration: The New World and the Third World*, ed. A. A. Richard and D. Kubat, London, Sage Publications.

Gulliver, P. H. (1955), 'Labour Migration in a Rural Economy', East African Studies, No. 6, Kampala, East African Institue of Social Research.

Gwyer, G. D. (1971), 'The Agricultural Labour Markets for Two Smallholder Areas of Kenya', Staff paper No. 94, Institute for Development Studies, University of Nairobi.

Gwyer, G. D. (1972), 'Trends in Kenya Agriculture in Relation to Employment', Discussion paper No. 153, Institute for Development Studies, University of Nairobi.

Gwyer, G. D., and Ruigu, G. (1971), 'Some Preliminary Findings on the Agricultural Employment Situation in Selected Areas', in *Strategies for Improving Rural Welfare*, Nairobi, Institute for Development Studies, University of Nairobi.

Hancock, R. H. (1959), *The Role of the Bracero in the Economic and Cultural Dynamics of Mexico*, Stanford, Hispanic American Studies, Stanford University.

Harriss, J. C. (1976), 'Aspects of Rural Society in the Dry Zone', in *Agriculture in the Peasant Sector of Sri Lanka*, ed. S.W.R. de A. Samarasinghe, Ceylon Studies Seminar, Peradeniya.

Harriss, J. C. (forthcoming), *Capitalism and Peasant Farming*, Bombay, Oxford University Press.

Harriss, J. C., and Harriss, B. (1978), 'Seasonal Dimensions to Rural Poverty: the Vision through Southern South Asian Eyes', Paper prepared for Conference on Seasonal Dimensions to Rural Poverty, Institute of Development Studies, University of Sussex, 3-6 July 1978 (mimeo).

Hill, P. (1972), *Rural Hausa: a Village and a Setting*, Cambridge, Cambridge University Press.

Hutton, C. (1973), *Reluctant Farmers? Unemployment and Planned Rural Development in Uganda*, Nairobi, East African Publishing House.

International Labour Office (1976), *Employment, Growth and Basic Needs: a One-world Problem*, Geneva, ILO.

Jose, A. V. (1977), 'Growth and Fluctuations in Indian Agriculture, 1956-7 to 1972-3', Working Paper No. 58, Centre for Development Studies, Trivandrum.

Katsina (1952), Famine Relief and Corn Reserves, File no. 2/3, 403, Katsina Native Authority.

Keyes, C. F. (1966), *Peasant and Nation: A Thai-Lao Village in a Thai State*, Unpublished Ph.D. thesis, Cornell University.

Kumar, D. (1976), 'Landownership and Inequality in Madras Presidency: 1853-54 to 1946-47', *Indian Economic and Social History Review, 12*, 3, pp. 229-61.

Mauss, M. (1954), *The Gift*, Glencoe, Ill., The Free Press.

Miracle, M. P., and Berry, S. S. (1970), 'Migrant Labour and Economic Development', *Oxford Economic Papers, 22*, pp. 86-108.

Mitchell, J. C. (1959), 'Migrant Labour in Africa South of the Sahara', *Bull. Inter-African Labour Institute, 6*, pp. 12-47.

Mitchell, J. C. (1962), 'Wage Labour and African Population Movements in Central

Africa', in *Essays on African Population,* eds. M. K. Barbour and R. M. Prothero, New York, Praeger.
Mitchell, J. C. (1969), 'Structural Plurality, Urbanization, and Labour Circulation in Southern Rhodesia', in *Sociological Studies 2: Migration,* ed. J. A. Jackson, Cambridge, Cambridge University Press.
Nicolas, G., Doumesche, H., and Mouche, M., (1968), 'Étude socio-économique de deux villages Hausa', *Études nigériennes,* No. 22, Paris, CNRS, p. 126.
Oomen, T. K. (1971), 'Agrarian Tension in a Kerala District: an Analysis', *J. Industrial Relations,* 7 (2), pp. 229-68.
Oshima, H. T. (1971), 'Seasonality and Underemployment in Monsoon Asia', *Philippine Economic Journal, 10,* pp. 63-97.
Pacey, A. (1978), *Gardening for Better Nutrition,* London, Intermediate Technology Publications.
Palmer, H. R. (1908a), Changes in Taxation in Katsina Division, Kaduna archives, NAK, Katprof. 1289.
Palmer, H. R. (1908b), Minutes of Evidence, Northern Nigeria Lands Committee, HMSO, Cd. 5103, p. 69.
Palmer, H. R. (1910), Kano Annual Report, 1910, National Archives Kaduna, NAK, SNPIO, 951p/1911.
Palmer, I. (n.d.), *The New Rice in Indonesia,* Geneva, UNRISD.
Palmer-Jones, R. (1978), 'Rural Differentiation in Hausaland', Unpublished manuscript.
Poupart, R. (1965), *Report to the Government of Thailand on Internal Migration,* Geneva, International Labour Office.
Raulin, H. (1964), 'Techniques et bases socio-économique des sociétés rurales nigériennes', *Études nigériennes,* No. 12, Paris, CNRS, p. 71.
Raynault, C. (1975), 'Le cas de la region de Maradi (Niger)', in *Sécheresse et Famine du Sahel,* ed. J. Copans, Vol. 2., pp. 5-42, Paris, Maspero.
Raynault, C. (1976), 'Transformation du système de production et inégalité économique: le cas d'un village haoussa', *Canadian J. African Studies, 10,* pp. 279-306.
Raynault, C. (1977), 'Circulation monétaire et évolution des structures socio-économique chez les haoussas du Niger', *Africa, 47,* p. 163.
Salifou, A. (1973), 'Le Damagaram ou Sultanat de Zinder au XIX Siècle', *Études nigériennes,* No. 27, Niamey, IRSH, p. 180.
Schofield, S. (1974), 'Seasonal Factors Affecting Nutrition in Different Age Groups and Especially of Pre-school Children', *J. Development Studies,* 11 (1), pp. 22-40.
Scott, J. (1972), 'Patron-client Politics and Political Change in S.E. Asia', *American Political Science Review, 66,* pp. 91-113.
Shenton, R., and Freund, W. (1978), 'The Incorporation of Northern Nigeria into the World Capitalist Economy', 23rd Congress of the Historical Society of Nigeria, Zaria, 1978.
Simmons, E. B. (1976c), 'Economic Research on Women in Northern Nigeria', OLC Paper, No. 10 (September 1976), Washington D.C.
Smith, M. G. (1967), 'A Hausa Kingdom', in *West African Kingdoms in the Nineteenth Century,* ed. D. Forde and P. Kaberry, London, Oxford University Press.
Southall, A. W. (1962), 'Population Movements in East Africa', in *Essays on African Population,* ed. M. K. Barbour and R. M. Prothero, New York, Praeger.
Todaro, M. P. (1976), *Internal Migration in Developing Countries,* Geneva, International Labour Office.
Udo, R. K. (1974), 'Rural Migration and the Problem of Agricultural Labour in Western Tropical Africa', in *Spatial Aspects of Development,* ed. B. S. Hoyle, London, John Wiley & Sons.
Usman, Y. B. (1974), *The Transformation of Katsina 1796-1905,* Unpublished Ph.D. thesis, Ahmadu Bello University, Zaria.
Van Stone, J. W. (1960), 'A Successful Combination of Subsistence and Wage Economies at Village Level', *Economic Development and Cultural Change, 8,* pp. 174-91.
Vink, G. J. (1941), *The Basis of Indonesian Farms,* Wageningen, H. Veenman and Sons.
Washbrook, D. (1973), 'Country Politics: Madras 1880-1930', *Modern Asia Studies,* 7 (3), pp. 475-531.
Wasow, B. (1973), 'Regional Inequality and Migration in Kenya', Working Paper No. 125, Institute for Development Studies, University of Nairobi.

Watts, M. (1976), 'Pre-disaster Planning and Drought in Nigeria', Paper presented to the Conference on the Aftermath of Drought and Famine in Nigeria, Bagauda, Kano.

Watts, M., and Shenton, R. (1978), 'Capitalism and Hunger in Northern Nigeria', Seminar Paper, Department of History, Ahmadu Bello University, Zaria.

Wiest, R. E. (1973), 'Wage-labour Migration and the Household in a Mexican Town', *J. Anthropol. Research, 22,* pp. 180-209.

Wood, G. (1978), 'Class Formation and "Antediluvian" Capital in Bangladesh', *IDS Bulletin, 9* (3), pp. 39-43.

Chapter 8
CONCLUSIONS AND PRACTICAL IMPLICATIONS

8.1 Seasonality In Rural Experience*
Robert Chambers, Richard Longhurst, David Bradley and Richard Feachem

The seasonal dimension

The objectives of rural development are many. The definition given by the World Bank is

> a strategy designed to improve the economic and social life of a specific group of people—the rural poor. It involves extending the benefits of development to the poorest among those who seek a livelihood in the rural areas. The group includes small-scale farmers, tenants and the landless. (World Bank, 1975, p. 3)

Accepting this definition, analysis of the seasonal experience of rural poverty adds an extra dimension and helps clarify objectives. Thus one major objective can be seen as enabling poorer rural families to secure adequate stocks and flows of food and cash *around the whole of the year.* Then by concentrating on times of the year when food stocks and cash flows are inadequate, and when poor families fall below an acceptable threshold, we may be able to direct attention to more cost-effective interventions. More may be achieved in action against poverty by enabling poor families to rise above these thresholds at bad times of the year than by trying to generate entirely new year-round livelihoods.

In order to see how this approach might be applied, we will first review conclusions from earlier chapters about the way seasons affect experience of poverty. In regions without marked seasons, the poor may have a hard grind all the year round, with no sharp crises, but no let-up either. But where there are sharp seasonal contrasts, there are times each year when life is relatively easy (usually in the early dry season) and times when the experience of poverty reaches crisis point (usually during the rains and up to the harvest).

For pastoralists, the seasonal crisis tends to come earlier than for cultivators. During the late dry season, the work involved in drawing water for animals is at a peak, but milk supplies are very low. Soon after the rains come there is less work and more milk (Swift, Section 3.3; Ndagala, Section 6.6).

For cultivators, the most critical period begins with the rains. Future food supplies and cash income depend upon timely planting of crops. Poorer farmers are often delayed by lack of inputs—whether seeds, fertilizers, irrigation water, or draught power. Draught animals, for those farmers who use them, are weak after the dry season. Some farmers have to delay preparing

---
*Much of this material originally appeared in *Discussion Paper* 142, Institute of Development Studies, University of Sussex.

Conclusions and Practical Implications

their own fields and planting while they earn some money labouring for better-off farmers. For most rural people, heavy and urgent energy demands have to be met. Labourers benefit from being able to get work, but many people are in energy deficit and lose weight (Chapter 2).

The rainy season is also often the least healthy time of year. Diseases differ in their seasonalities, but some of the more serious and debilitating peak during or just after the rains (Chapter 4). These often include malaria, diarrhoeal diseases (the latter especially where the wet season is also a hot season), guinea-worm disease, dengue fever, infections of the skin, and even snake-bite (Warrell and Arnett, 1976). This is also a time when the development of protein-energy malnutrition and perhaps other stresses contribute to low immune response.

The rainy season is a bad time for mothers and children. Anticipating hard work, mothers wean their infants or, if they continue to breast-feed, may only be able to do so less regularly (Chapters 2 and 6) and less milk may be consumed at each feed (Whitehead *et al.*, 1978). Food preparation becomes more hurried and the diet less adequate, varied and nutritious (Schofield, 1974). There is more bacterial growth in food left standing in humid conditions (Barrell and Rowland, 1979). Late pregnancy is common and births peak, but body weights of mothers and birth weights of babies are both low, and the rate of neonatal mortality rises (Chapter 5). Child care is neglected by mothers who have to work. Pregnant and lactating women are weakened by disease and work, and those in the poorer, smaller families are especially vulnerable because of the need to work when work is available; one instance is of a Gambian village where women in the last trimester of pregnancy were observed to lose an average of 1·4 kg of weight during the worst month, August (Whitehead *et al.*, 1978; see also Figure 6.4 here).

In highly seasonal conditions of the sort described, being poor means being vulnerable, at the end of every dry season, to any lateness or inadequacy of the rain; and then, in every wet pre-harvest period, being short of food and being forced to obtain it on adverse terms. Food prices are high. Those who are less poor have better food stocks and can anyway afford the higher prices. But the poorer people are often driven to borrowing under duress or to distress sales. They sell or mortgage assets, or their future crops or labour. They eat less than they need at this time of hard work, and they lose weight. Any sickness has a crippling effect on a family's independence. Poor people are hyper-vulnerable to contingencies. Before harvest is a time when dependent and exploitative relationships are likely to begin and to be reinforced and deepened.

With harvest, food is abundant. Debts are repaid, but often at high rates of interest, especially when the money must be raised by selling food crops when the prices are low. But food intake recovers in both quantity and quality. Body weights rise, there is less illness and mortality rates decline. There are celebrations and marriages. There is a peak in rates of conception. And then gradually as the dry season progresses, food becomes scarcer, cash reserves diminish, and the cycle begins all over again.

Case-studies

In this book, the examples of the case-study areas may help to give clear individual pictures of what seasonality may mean and also to show how the generalised description of seasonal factors given above has to be modified for individual locations. A crude but telling way of summarising findings is by means of Tables 8.1 and 8.2 which compare the case-study areas in Bangladesh and Gambia. ('Bangladesh', 'Gambia' and 'northern Nigeria' as used below refer only to the case-study areas.) Climatic seasonality is greater in Gambia, where there is only one cultivation season, from June to October. In Bangladesh this is slightly less marked with a longer, wetter rainy season: agricultural seasonality is further reduced by irrigation and high water tables. The information that can be summarised in these two tables is obviously limited: both tables support the findings of the general scenario but different socio-economic conditions lead to qualifications about the distribution of seasonal stress. In Gambia, the main farming load is taken by the women who grow swamp rice while the men cultivate the less labour-intensive millets. However, in Bangladesh, women have less responsibility for field work; in many families, their main agricultural work is the post-harvest processing of rice. Another contrast is that the rural population of Gambia is still dependent on subsistence crops grown on their own land, while in Bangladesh, many of the rural poor are landless labourers, dependent on wages and the purchase of food. Thus Table 8.2 includes columns representing wages and food (rice) prices, factors which have a very strong influence on the plight of the poor in Bangladesh.

It cannot be emphasised too strongly that, notwithstanding the findings reported in this book, each environment should be examined independently. This will reveal many different patterns and will in time lead to a more subtle and varied classification of seasonal types, as can be illustrated by three points.

First, a major qualification to the scenario and generalisations applies in much of northern India where there are three main seasons — hot wet, cold dry, and hot dry — and where, with irrigation, stresses of heat, work and sickness occur together in the hot dry season.

Second, even where rainfall is bimodal, or where there is more complex cropping under irrigation, seasonal peaks and stresses still occur. In the East African cases, for example, although bimodal rainfall has smoothing effects, there remain marked peaks in labour demand for agriculture.

Third, despite climatic similarity between Gambia and northern Nigeria, there are many differences, attributable to four factors. The first is in the division of labour; in rural northern Nigeria the wives of the settled cultivators (of child bearing age) are secluded. Men carry out the bulk of the farm work and this implies that the energy expenditure of women here is less than that of Gambian women. The second difference appears in the energy returns of crops: compared with sorghum in northern Nigeria, rice in Gambia probably has a far lower ratio of calories gained in the crop yield to calories expended as human energy input. Sorghum is grown in Gambia but because of poor soils yield only one-third to one-quarter of that grown in the Zaria area. Third, northern Nigeria has a shorter period without a staple crop than has Gambia; rice also stores less well than sorghum. Finally, farmers in northern Nigeria have more opportunities to earn off-farm income than their Gambian counter-

TABLE 8.1. The variation of various factors by month in Gambia

	Rain	Infant deaths	Agric. work	Birth weight	Child weight gain	Breast Milk intake	Child nutrient intake	Energy intake Preg. lact. women	Body weight Preg. lact. women	Disease prevalence Diarrhoea	Lower respiratory	Malaria
Mar			L		H		H					
Apr			L		H		H					
May					H		H					
Jun	H		H		H					H		
Jul	H	H	H	L	L	L	L	L	L	H	H	H
Aug	H	H	H	L	L	L	L	L	L	H	H	H
Sep	H	H	H	L	L	L	L	L	L	H		H
Oct	H	H	H	L	L	L	L	L	L	H		H
Nov			H	L		L			L			H
Dec												
Jan												
Feb			L				L					

Notes: H and L denote high and low levels for the factor. The main harvest is in November.
Source: Rowland *et al.* (Chapter 6); Haswell (Chapter 2).

TABLE 8.2. The variation of various factors by month, in Matlab, Bangladesh

	Rain	Flood	Mothers ill in month %	Fathers/ mothers % days ill in bed	Births	Body weight of mothers at birth	Neonatal mortality rate	Deaths of persons aged 45+	Child weight gain	Breast-feeding time	Labour demand in agriculture	Daily wage rates	Rice price	Household food stocks >2 Acres	Household food stocks Landless
Mar	H					H	L				H	H		L	
Apr	H					H	L				H	H			H
May	H		H								H				
Jun	VH												H		
Jul	VH	H								H			H	H	
Aug	VH	H	H	H		L	H		Lose			L	H		
Sep	VH	H	H	H		L	H				L		H		
Oct	H		H	H	H	L				H	L	L	H	L	Nil
Nov	H		H	L	H	L		H	Lose		H		L		H
Dec					H			H		L			L	H	
Jan			L	L				H			L				
Feb				L							L				L

Notes: VH, H, and L denote very high, high, and low levels for the factor respectively. The main harvest is in November–December.

Source: Becker and Sardar (Chapter 5); Chowdhury, Huffman and Chen (Chapter 2); and personal communication with E. J. Clay (compare Chapter 3).

Conclusions and Practical Implications

parts. Overall there appears to be greater food availability in northern Nigeria with less of a hungry season than in Gambia, although undoubtedly there are still individuals at risk. Greater poverty and seasonality in Gambia appear to push people into short-term strategies; in northern Nigeria, despite similar problems of labour demand, a better food production position allows more room for manoeuvre.

Qualifications and implications

While the case-studies confirm that many of the adverse factors initially described do indeed operate together in the wet season, at least in the case-study areas, three qualifications are in order.

First, care is needed in assessing whether and to what extent seasonality can be regarded as a cause of rural poverty. The conclusion of this book is that seasonality presents contexts which bring poverty to periodic crises. It provides conditions which enable other forces which create and sustain poverty to act more powerfully. There are thus obvious senses in which tropical seasons, as described, help to keep poor people poor. One can even go further and suggest that unimodal seasonality may, other things being equal, provide a context in which exploitation of the poorer by the richer is made easier than in bimodal or non-seasonal climates. Seasonality here is a cause of poverty in the sense that if it were removed, the other forces which create and sustain poverty would be less powerful. Reducing or eliminating adverse seasonal effects would reduce the vulnerability of poor people, and might strengthen their hand. But it would not remove poverty which would continue to be sustained by other stronger forces.

Second, failure of the rains — an irregular occurrence — may be more significant than the regular rhythm of the seasons. We have distinguished two types of process: first, seasonal 'screws' — seasonal cycles with repeated but usually reversible hardship; people are pressed down on a regular basis but the cycle allows some recovery. And second, 'ratchets' — more irreversible effects where disability or misfortune (such as sickness, flood, famine, pregnancy, or death), often linked with erratic climatic occurrences, force a downward shift from which recovery is much more difficult. Seasonal screws have symptoms such as losses of body weight and temporary indebtedness; ratchets, in contrast, most commonly take the form of mortgaging or sales of assets — land, livestock, trees, jewelry, tools, pots and pans, furniture, and future crops and labour. Screws may lead to ratchets; but ratchets are usually provoked by contingencies such as failures of seasons.

Third, seasonal stress and crises vary between different social and economic groups in the same environment. Some may have access to off-farm or non-agricultural employment and income sources which will have smoothing effects on adverse seasonality. Others are affected in different ways by the agricultural cycle. The pre-harvest crisis may sometimes be more acute for self-provisioning small farm families than for landless labourers. The small farm families rely on their harvest for food and income, and may be driven to employ labour at a time when they are very short of money. In contrast, landless labourers who can get work at this time will, if they are remunerated immediately, have a source of food and/or income. For some of them the worst time may be the dry season when there is little work. These examples emphasise the dangers of unsubtle generalisation about seasonality, and the importance of breaking down the analysis not only by environment and by time of year but also by socio-economic group.

Thus far, the main focus of this book has been on analysis rather than policy. But at different points, contributors have pointed to practical implications, and yet others can be derived. Most of these require implementation by government departments or agencies, although non-government agencies also have a part to play. It is sobering, then, to start with a sceptical view of the capacity of government organisations to implement counter-seasonal programmes.

8.2 Government Perceptions and Responses
Ian Carruthers

Rural sector problems
Rural development is inherently difficult to sustain because of the many complex and interacting factors that affect agricultural production. These may be categorised as the biological nature of production, the dispersed character and small scale of the production units, their peculiar investment requirements, the traditional set of institutional arrangements, and in some instances, the lack of a well-tested theoretical framework or detailed technical knowledge (Barter, 1962).

The biological nature of the production process is the essence of the seasonality issue. Not only does it create difficulties through the periodic nature of production and work and the long interval between harvests, but these difficulties are added to by climatic irregularities, by insect pests, and by the limited life of the products in storage. These biological rhythms can also change as technical progress creates new opportunities involving new demands for labour or other inputs. For example, in Madhya Pradesh, April-May is a slack, dry period and the socially accepted period for marriages. But new agricultural opportunities relating to well irrigation, kharif cropping, weed control and soil conservation are now making this a potentially rewarding work period. One wonders what is the lag between discernment of opportunity and changes in current social customs.

Considerable though seasonal complexities may be, there are still the several other factors to examine. For example, the *dispersed nature of production units* over varying terrain with a varying resource base makes planning difficult, not least because data are expensive to collect: compare the data problems from an administrator's viewpoint of five fertilizer factories and 500,000 small farmers. The *smallness of operations* creates other problems too — serving such farmers via an extension service is costly in relation to the value of their production; and they are weak bargainers with government unless there is a collective interest and some form of effective, democratic organisation. Yet further complications arise from *institutional factors* which include land tenure, credit systems, and marketing arrangements. All play crucial roles in influenc-

Conclusions and Practical Implications

ing the relative success of the various possible patterns of production.

Seasonality, though a prominent factor, is only one dimension among many special problems confronting the rural sector. And such is the complexity of these many dimensions that only an elaborate form of management can hope to succeed in planning and implementing fully comprehensive rural development. It may therefore be useful to turn from general areas of government action to fairly specific dimensions, such as seasonality, where action should be more feasible.

Inter-seasonal variation

In this book, the main emphasis has been placed upon seasonal rhythms, and the stresses they create. Less emphasis has been placed upon inter-seasonal variation, although it is this which dominates most farmers' decision-making. It is the odd season that frustrates public policies for agricultural credit, buffer stocks, crop storage, public works and so on. It is the problems posed by the 'bad' year that must be solved if regular measures to tackle the more regular seasonal strains are to succeed.

Perhaps the most important prerequisite for coping with the 'bad' year is an early warning system. Whether this should come from a scheme based on local administrators, from remote sensing techniques, or from some combination, is unclear. One valuable practical proposal for an information system to give advance warning of drought is Sandford's (1977) study dealing with drought and livestock in Botswana.

What seems certain is that few governments know at an early enough stage precisely what are the circumstances in their rural areas. Furthermore, few administrations are geared to the flexible action that such information would prompt. However, knowledge of impending disaster is only a necessary condition for avoiding the effects of an extremely poor season. Recent experience in Ethiopia and elsewhere suggests that knowledge is not a sufficient condition to generate feasible avoiding action or preventive measures.

Public sector capacity constraints

It is conceivable that failure to recognise the special nature and needs of the rural sector accounts for some of the difficulties highlighted in this book. More plausible, perhaps, is that governments lack the capacity to react to the complicated problems presented by agriculture and other activities influenced by the seasons. Even without tackling seasonal variations and needs, governments often face grave difficulties in implementing rural development projects and programmes. An indication of the range of obstacles is given by a Pakistan Government form (code PC-IIIC) for quarterly reporting which lists no less than ninety-five possible bottlenecks.

I am attracted by the ideas of Ilchman (1972) who vividly illustrates the problems of government responding to areas of difficulty such as seasonality by an agricultural analogy. He suggests that the public services in India are like peasant farmers (p. 226):

> Given the inputs at their disposal and the margin next to which they live, they are among the most rational allocators in existence — efficient, though not effective; able by one miracle to produce the irreducible

minimum; unable, by any technique of social organisation, to raise the level of output by more than five or ten per cent.

If this is the case, recognition by government of seasonal problems is not an issue, in that there are no major returns to be expected from government action. What is required is rather a massive increase in administrative capacity so that relevant programmes and policies can be effectively devised and implemented. What is required, indeed, is 'an administrative equivalent of the Green Revolution' (Ilchman, 1972).

8.3 Practical Implications
Robert Chambers and Simon Maxwell*

Counter-seasonal measures

Seasonal analysis has many practical implications. To what extent 'an administrative equivalent of the green revolution' is needed before they can be followed through is open to debate. Many counter-seasonal measures are already implemented; some rural administrations have a greater capacity than others for implementing them. Administrative capacity itself evolves over time, not least in response to the articulation from below of seasonal demands — for public works, for health services, for agricultural inputs, for credit and so on. The measures outlined below will vary, place by place, in their appropriateness and implementability. They are listed here as a start with a counter-seasonal repertoire from which practitioners can select to match need and opportunity.

A. The timing of administration

Seasonal analysis has many implications for the timing of activities in government and voluntary agency administration, among which the timing of *the financial year* is one of the most basic. Two common features may be noted. First, the release of funds for rural projects and programmes is often delayed after the start of the financial year. Second, funds are often exhausted towards the end of the financial year. Thus there may be a regular, seasonal financial famine for some months on either side of the start of the financial year, and, conversely, a regular seasonal period when funds are available. To the extent that this occurs, the question is then whether the availability of funds coincides with the time of greatest need.

In agriculture, health and construction, the timing of need is roughly the same. In all cases, funds are needed in advance of the rains: in agriculture, to enable the timely purchase and supply of inputs and credit before cultivation; in health, to make possible the purchase of drugs and their distribution to rural areas before the rains; in construction, for the purchase and delivery of materials before communications become difficult. There will be other considerations; but to the extent that these points apply, it would seem best if

---

*Part B of this paper is by Simon Maxwell; the rest is by Robert Chambers, who wishes to acknowledge ideas contributed by the other editors and by many others in discussion and correspondence.

financial years began well before the main rainy season.

Seasonal labour constraints can be eased by deliberate government action, particularly in adjusting the school term so that children can help at peak periods, as with the cotton harvest in Uganda, rice-cultivation on the Mwea Irrigation Settlement in Kenya, and even potato-picking in rural Britain during the Second World War. Similarly, granting leave to small farmer employees during the agricultural peak seasons can be recommended, especially with employees in tropical tourist industries which have a slack season during the rains.

Tax collection is usually timed for post-harvest periods, and collection at other times might lead to disproportionate hardship. With larger farmers subject to income taxes, there may also be a case for ensuring that their main crop falls within a single accounting period.

Rural campaigns — for adult education, family planning, immunisation, and the like — are often best carried out in dry seasons, for reasons of ease of communication, lack of competing demands from work, and general level of well-being and receptivity.

B. The role of public works

Public works, especially in the off-season, are often cited as a counter-seasonal measure to help the poorer people. However, with the possible exception of China and some other socialist countries, public works programmes have fallen far short of expectations in most places where they have been organised (Maxwell, 1978; IBRD, 1976; USAID, 1977). Far from acting as major catalysts of rural development, public works programmes have more often than not degenerated into inefficient and unproductive soup kitchens, costly to organise and supervise. Most important of all, public works programmes have shown themselves to be subject to the same political constraints as underlie much rural poverty, and which have stymied attempts to tackle the problem by other routes; they may even tend to worsen the distribution of asset ownership, with the rich benefiting disproportionately from the type of works undertaken (Grissa, 1973; Sobhan, 1968). The latter point has been made in this book with particular regard to Bangladesh (Chaudhury, Section 3.4), even though public works provide a vast amount of seasonal employment there (Clay, Section 3.5).

Why, then, bother with public works? There are three obvious reasons. One is that 'soup kitchens' in themselves have some value: public works employ people who would otherwise be unemployed. In one area of South India, workers derived 40 per cent of their income from public works (Donovan, 1973), and for some workers in Morocco, the figure was two-thirds (Andriamananjara, 1971). Nevertheless, in his study of public works in Bihar, Rodgers (1972, 1973) was able to conclude that 'in all cases where distribution of consumption was an objective, it was at least partly successful'.

A second reason why it may be worth bothering with public works is that opportunities exist to make them more productive (Lewis, 1972; WFP, 1976b). For example, one study indicates that the provision of spades and wheelbarrows on public works in India increased output by between 30 and 100 per cent (Costa, 1973). Other observers have stressed the value of higher wages and piece work (IBRD, 1976), or the value of agrarian reform as an incentive (Tiano, 1972). Greater benefits could also be obtained from the assets created if complementary inputs were provided and if maintenance were better; 'greater production is not guaranteed by the earthworks themselves' (WFP, 1976a). It is necessary to match irrigation facilities with better seeds and more fertilizer, and also to set up a reliable maintenance system which will keep the channels open.

A third reason for not discarding public works programmes is that, despite poor productivity and political limitations, they do manage to create a certain amount of long-term employment. How much employment varies greatly from country to country, though, and from project to project. The permanent employment created tends to be less on works which are highly labour-using in construction than on those which are not, so that the long-term and short-term objectives are to a certain extent in conflict (IBRD, 1976). This contrast is one reason behind the general disapproval in the public works literature of road construction projects which meet the short-term objective of employing large numbers of people, but are seen to have little long-term impact (UN, 1975; IBRD, 1976).

In considering the contribution that public works might make to the easing of seasonal problems, it is important to look, not simply at the employment created, but at the assets produced. A part — and sometimes a large part — of the seasonal problems faced by a community may be of a kind that public works are well suited to tackle: flooded roads making it difficult to bring food into a village; poor drainage and sanitation encouraging the breeding of mosquitoes and flies in the rainy season; price fluctuations and food shortages due to lack of storage facilities. There is also obvious scope for closer complementarity between different works schemes, and for closer integration between schemes planned and carried out at the village level (often with a large voluntary contribution) and those organised at higher levels in the administrative hierarchy.

To the extent that an awareness of the seasonal dimension suggests action at the community level, it may be possible to avoid some of the conflicts of interest which bedevil public works schemes. This is a hypothesis which requires testing, since it is likely that someone always benefits from disaster, but prima facie, public works aimed at lifting particular seasonal constraints which affect everybody seem well placed to attract support from the community as a whole and to benefit everybody equally. The control of mosquitoes might seem a candidate for projects of this sort, and there must be other examples. The point is that the basic needs planner may find in seasonality a path to the avoidance of conflicts (Maxwell, 1978).

Where conflicts or political problems relating to the assets being created cannot be avoided, it may be necessary to focus more simply on the employment created. Here a crucial problem arises: seasonal poverty is the result of lack of income at particular times of year, and public works provide incomes, but the two are not necessarily at the same time. Seasonal hunger is not at its worst during the slack season in agriculture, but at the time when the land is being ploughed and planted before a new harvest, when every available man and woman is busy in the fields. To the extent that the public works literature discusses seasonality at all, it assumes that poverty and unemployment are

Conclusions and Practical Implications

temporally co-existent. But if public works provide incomes at a time when they are less urgently needed, then the problem of savings and storage arises, which involves questions of institutions, the role of money-lenders, and control over markets. Public works in January do not guarantee that saving will take place to meet consumption needs in July. Public works projects may therefore need to be treated as an integral part of a wider attack on the problems of seasonality.

Finally, however, if public works are able to help lift seasonal constraints, then it may be that their value has been underrated in the literature. Most cost-benefit analyses fail to count as a benefit the consumption of the labourers during the construction period, the exception being Rodgers (1972). If, however, such aspects of poverty as malnutrition and child mortality are heavily influenced by seasonality, and if public works projects are able to tide families over the hungry season, then the value of works is not to be measured simply in terms of short-term consumption, but in the longer term as improved health, productivity, receptivity to education, and so on. The weight given to consumption by public works participants, to take only one aspect, could vary according to the month in which public works take place.

Such refinements require more empirical data. It is by no means clear that the poor track record of public works can be remedied, nor that the seasonal problem is particularly amenable to solutions which include public works. But to be realistic does not preclude being optimistic: public works are a flexible tool and with the right political support can be extremely powerful. As the seasonal dimension becomes better understood, public works certainly deserve to be kept in mind.

C. Agriculture, food and nutrition

There are many ways in which *farming systems* can be adapted and developed to reduce adverse seasonality. One approach is to introduce techniques which make lower energy demands at peak periods, though a danger here is that employment and incomes for the landless may be reduced. Another is to develop sequences and mixes of land preparation and crops (minimum tillage, inter-cropping, serial cropping, fodder crops such as the tree legume Leucaena (NAS, 1977), etc.) which reduce risks and spread both labour demands and flows of food and income from harvests. In particular, short-duration food crops such as quick-maturing millets, even if not high-yielding, can help by giving farming families a food supply before the main harvest. Nor should cash crops be unthinkingly condemned as they sometimes are; they may, more often than not, give families reserves of cash and of purchased food which they could not have obtained with food crops on the same land. Livestock, too, can have important smoothing and buffering effects, providing milk, meat or cash at otherwise lean times. Smallstock (sheep, goats, pigs, ducks, hens, etc.) are often important buffers against hunger and permanent impoverishment. The main point is that the farming system should be seen in terms of family livelihoods and food security round the whole year, and modified where possible to improve these, with especial attention to the most difficult times.

Irrigation increases productivity, reduces risk and increases employment in ways that are very well known; it also contributes greatly to the productivity of the seed-fertilizer combinations of the green revolution. Less well recognised is its value to families, whether small-farming or landless, in spacing food and income flows round the year. Irrigation may lift families above the thresholds of adequate livelihoods by filling in an annual trough of lack of food and income. Where it generates employment all round the year it may also attract families for permanent quasi-urban settlement in rural areas (Chambers and Harriss, 1977). Where irrigation is not possible, techniques of water harvesting such as contour ridging and ploughing to reduce run-off losses, and dryland farming methods which conserve soil moisture (Arnon, 1972; NAS, 1974), may have similar if less dramatic effects. But of all the counter-seasonal strategies which do not involve a redistribution of the means of production, irrigation is probably the most powerful.

In the improvement of *nutrition,* timing appears to be crucial in policy design. Feeding programmes — the most direct form of intervention — may well reduce body weight loss if administered at any time of the year. There may, however, be some times of the year when they will be more effective than others. For example, fewer leakages of food to uses other than consumption may occur in the wet season. Optimal timing for a food-for-work programme may depend on balancing considerations such as the availability of labour (in slack seasons) against the need of poor families for calories (at times when they have other work). Such programmes may also shield families from the ratchet effects of unforeseen contingencies if they contribute to food supplies at the most vulnerable times of year. A balance of considerations also applies with strategies to reduce the energy expenditure of farm families. One way of improving their nutritional security is to reduce the energy required when energy demand is high and food supply is low. Such a strategy may reduce human energy expenditure through mechanisation, chemical weed control, or even the introduction of varieties for which operations are less time-constrained. But care has to be taken in assessing who gains and who benefits. If all are small farmers, then all may gain. But if there are poorer people who need to sell their labour, innovations of this sort may deprive them of their livelihoods. As with other counter-seasonal strategies, account has to be taken of local conditions and of the interest of different groups.

D. *Storage and savings*

To even out the seasonality of food supply, many *storage techniques* can be used: crops may be grown which store well in the soil, such as cassava (manioc); fruits, vegetables, fish and meat may be dried in the sun; fish and some vegetables can be salted; and most commonly crops are stored in silos, bins, and family grain stores.

Studies of on-farm grain storage in Africa and Asia have shown that traditional technology can be very efficient. In Andhra Pradesh, a careful study found losses of only about 4 per cent in farm-level paddy stores (Boxall *et al.,* 1978) and village-level post-harvest losses in rice in Bangladesh have been found to be only 5-8 per cent (Greeley, 1980), far less than earlier estimates (under a variety of definitions) ranging from 10 per cent to 38 per cent (*ibid*).

Improvements are nonetheless possible. Despite the low losses in storage in Andhra Pradesh, there are still high rates of return on improvements to tradi-

Conclusions and Practical Implications

tional stores. (Boxall *et al.*, 1978). The deterioration of grain in storage is often not due to deficient technology but to poor maintenance and poor hygiene. Before newly harvested grain is placed in a store, it should be cleaned, and cracks in the walls filled in with mud plaster to prevent reinfestation through the eggs and larvae of insect pests. A problem here is that cleaning and maintenance are required when stores are empty which may be just when people are busy in the fields. Absence on migration may also hinder construction of necessary new storage capacity (Section 7.5). In some communities it might be worth devising programmes which would encourage people to spend more time working on their own household storage facilities, perhaps compensating them in some way for wages lost by not participating in public works or migratory employment.

Government purchases of grain can reduce seasonal hardship by maintaining prices at harvest, and then through releases of grain on the market at times of shortage, by keeping prices down. This requires the maintenance of adequate buffer stocks in official storage. The issues of government intervention, procurement, pricing, storage, and subsidy are not simple (Harriss, 1977, 1978) and perverse outcomes can occur. It is enough to note here that if the desired effects can be achieved—maintaining floor prices at harvest, and restraining price rises in the lean season—the poorer people will benefit disproportionately. At harvest, small farmers and sharecroppers who have to repay loans in cash will benefit because they will get more for their crop; and in the lean season, all those—landless labourers and small farmers alike—who are short of food will benefit through having to pay less for it. An even stronger counterseasonal strategy is to provide free or subsidised food to the poorer people all round the year, as practised in Sri Lanka with the rice ration and other food subsidies, and in Kerala through the fair price shops which, exceptionally for India, are found throughout the rural areas. The very high life expectancies and low fertility of Sri Lanka and Kerala are usually attributed to education, health services, and late marriage. It is at least possible that a major factor is the exceptional food security of poor families in those two regions.

Village savings clubs or cooperatives may provide a form of storage without wastage. In one African country, village savings clubs have been particularly effective in enabling poor farmers to buy fertilizer and to obtain it in bulk at a reduced price (Oxfam, 1975). In West Bengal, a system called *dharmagola* helps landless labourers and poor farmers. They deposit what they can in grain or cash at good times, and are then allowed to withdraw twice that amount in lean times, repaying again at the next good time. In tackling seasonal deprivation and dependence, perhaps especially in Asia and West Africa, consumption credit for the lean season appears a high priority.

E. *The family, women and children*

The experience of poverty is both shared and distributed within families. All suffer, but some suffer more than others. Each case deserves to be examined in its own right, but privation is often especially experienced by women; and Chapter 6 suggests that a symptom of extreme poverty is the way children have to be neglected as parents struggle to secure future food supplies for the family. Much evidence can be adduced of the seasonal stress on women and children in particular. In thinking about policies for food production and health services, family welfare is a central consideration, not so much in immediate action as in ultimate goals. Programmes which concentrate action on child welfare and disregard all else are usually treating symptoms rather than causes, and may even do harm by distracting women from essential production activities. Even more serious, however, are programmes for improved food production which do not consider the problems of women and children at all, and which damage the welfare of families by imposing excessive burdens on women. Palmer (Section 7.2) has made the point that agricultural planners habitually forget the effect on women of the 'green revolutions' they organise.

One important goal is to lighten the *disproportionate work burdens* that fall on women, especially during times of peak labour demand. Palmer discusses various possibilities in Chapter 7, and others have suggested 'equity-oriented technologies' which reduce the work of women (or of the poor generally) and which are not likely to have the benefits captured by the better-off (Oxfam, 1976). Examples are improved water supplies which relieve women of long journeys carrying water, and improved hoes which reduce the energy used in weeding (Section 2.6), and techniques to reduce the drudgery of food processing, such as peeling cassava, pounding yams and grinding millet.

If such innovations apply to unpaid tasks, they may not deprive women or others of income. The danger often is that innovations transfer traditional women's work to machines, men and urban factory workers. For example, the livelihoods of very poor rural women in Bangladesh who have relied for much of their income on laborious foot-pounding to husk rice, or who have been employed in manual threshing, are threatened by power hullers for husking and by new threshing machines. Some of these changes appear unavoidable. What is vital is to see what seasonal sources of income they remove from whom, and to seek to provide alternatives. This may be especially important where women earn money at times when their husbands are seasonally unemployed, and where women's earnings, as seems often the case, are spent more responsibly on family needs than those of men.

Small families, and especially *female-headed households* where the male has deserted or is a migrant, are especially vulnerable. Seasonal conflict between agricultural activities and child care is most acute in these small families and there is less family labour to deal with contingencies. Agricultural research and extension are almost invariably directed towards families which are stronger and which command more resources. Measures to be recommended here include careful analysis of the activities and constraints of small and weak families, the development of innovations designed for them, and agricultural extension services specifically for women (Pacey, 1978).

Child care facilities in seasons of stress may be arranged to ease the seasonal burden on families and risks to children. Two possible measures are the provision of day-care in villages during periods of peak labour demand in the fields, and the provision of food for the most vulnerable groups at times of food shortage. These two measures may be linked since the season when day-care is most needed is usually also the time when food is most short and when children are most likely to have been recently weaned. The day-care facility may thus be a suitable location for seasonal child-feeding.

Conclusions and Practical Implications

One final and much more problematic factor on which action may possibly be considered to ease the seasonal stress for women concerns the *timing of pregnancy and birth*. The conjunction often observed of late pregnancy and birth with periods of peak labour demand, food shortage, and high exposure to infection appear bad, linked as it is to low birthweights, high neonatal mortality, and poor prognoses for babies (Chapter 6). But the notion of family planning aimed at an optimum season of birth seems nowhere to have been adopted in modern societies. There are dangers of oversimplifying here; and Schofield has shown how complex are the pros and cons of different seasons of birth for the prospects for the first two years of life (Schofield, 1974). Experience of the acute seasonal stress in late pregnancy in Gambia has led Rowland *et al.* (Section 6.2) to suggest that seasonal birth regulation aimed at avoiding births during the rains might be of some value. Elsewhere, without prejudging whether or when there might be an optimal time for birth, this question, raised with rural women, might provide a good point of entry for discussions about family planning. Rural women may have well-founded views about the best time to give birth, in which case a discussion of this could lead logically into questions of how to time and control conceptions.

F. Health services

The importance of seasonality seems to have been largely lost sight of in the planning of modern health services. Attention has concentrated on location rather than timing. Seasonality is recognised mainly in terms of constraints: when rains come and roads become impassable, villages served by mobile clinics are cut off, and mass immunisation programmes in rural areas may have to be suspended (Tomkins, Section 6.4). The costs of sickness — in terms of losses of family food and income, of losses of body weight reserves, and of national agricultural production foregone — are both high and very seasonal. Sickness in an agricultural slack season entails suffering; but its social and economic costs may be far less than those of sickness in an agricultural season which directly prevents work to earn income or grow food. There are arguments, on both welfare and economic grounds, for special attention to health care during the agricultural seasons, and to those diseases and complaints which are most likely to incapacitate at that time (Chambers, 1979). There is here a strong but little recognised complementarity between health services and agriculture.

Six measures can be proposed:

(1) *seasonal stocking of rural clinics.* It is rare for rural clinics and health posts to be stocked with medicaments to meet seasonal needs. This is, however, a need where disease is seasonal and where clinics are cut off during rains and floods.

(2) *preventive and curative priority for diseases of the wet (and agricultural) seasons.* This applies especially, depending on local conditions, to the diarrhoeas, malaria, skin infections, guinea-worm disease, and dengue fever. It also applies to whatever diseases and complaints most incapacitate and weaken at these periods of peak agricultural activity. Malaria is a notable case where much may sometimes be achieved for low cost and with enthusiastic public support. An example is seasonal anti-malarial

chemoprophylaxis combined with other preventive measures in Raigarh District, Madhya Pradesh, where in two years an incidence believed to have been about 95 per cent was brought down to almost nil, with poor people prepared to pay for their pills (Sister Lorraine Ryan, personal communication). The cost-effectiveness of chemoprophylactic antimalarial programmes can also be increased by shifting from year-round to seasonal implementation, as in some parts of Mozambique where action is being concentrated on the seasons of highest incidence (Malcolm Segall, personal communication).

(3) *locating health services according to seasonal needs.* A case can be made for concentrating health services in those areas where the incidence and cost of sickness in the wet and agricultural seasons are highest.

(4) *caution in introducing mobile clinics.* Mobile clinics have been questioned on other grounds. The additional seasonal argument is that they may be unable to reach the more remote people who are often poorer and more vulnerable to adverse seasonality; and that during the rains, when health services are most needed in less accessible places, mobile clinics will be at their least mobile, often confined to tarmac roads, if not to garages.

(5) *seasonal staffing.* This involves the timing of leave, or shifting staff from one area to another to ensure high coverage at the times of greatest need. This may, however, be a difficult refinement to implement. It has been tried in Matlab thana in Bangladesh, for which Chen *et al.* (1979, p. 186) report that

> ... the annual epidemic of diarrhoeal diseases ... places enormous stress on the Matlab health care delivery system for three months of the year. To meet such stress, shift of facilities and staff may be required. Preventive work and nonseasonal curative services such as family planning, may be deferred to slack seasons, so that resources can be focused to meet peak service demands. It should be pointed out, however, that this increase of staff efficiency may be achieved only at the cost of increased program complexity. Shifting of staff requires more training, supervision, and other program support services.

(6) *selecting community health workers who do not have farming obligations.* There is a danger that primary health care workers in villages will themselves be farmers or have farming obligations, and will be distracted from health work at the times of greatest need. Seasonal analysis leans here against that conventional wisdom which holds that community health workers should be part-time farmers, typical members of the community, and unpaid. If a community faces a seasonal crisis simultaneously in cultivation and in health, a community health worker in a farming family will be torn between conflicting obligations, and those of cultivation for the family may prevail over those of health for the community. In planning primary health care, and in selecting community health workers, this is a factor to be borne in mind.

G. Seasonal analysis and action

As noted in the introduction, the perceptions of urban-based professionals are distorted by biases so that they either underestimate or fail to recognise

Conclusions and Practical Implications

seasonal linkages and seasonal deprivation. This failure of perception presents an opportunity. It is precisely because seasonality has so often been missed as a link between health, agriculture, nutrition and poverty, that there is so much scope for counter-seasonal programmes and measures such as those outlined above.

One major problem is identifying the types of counter-seasonal programme appropriate for each environment. This can be approached in two complementary ways.

The first, top-down, approach involves seasonal mapping. At an early stage in planning counter-seasonal strategies, this means mapping the spatial and seasonal distribution of adverse factors and their linkages. What can be done will depend on what data and knowledge are available. At the very least, maps indicating the agricultural peak seasons and the seasonal incidence of rural diseases could be matched and analysed to identify zones of adverse health-agricultural linkages. This could be deepened with other data — on seasonal births, deaths, body weights, malnutrition, wage rates, indebtedness and food prices — as available. Any such approach should quite quickly point to certain zones deserving closer analysis at certain seasons.

The second, bottom-up, approach, would rely heavily on local knowledge. Official statistics are often misleading, and need correction at the lowest level, implying decentralisation. One approach is a required procedure for local-level staff to carry out seasonal analysis. Health and agricultural staff can be required jointly with each other and with rural people to identify seasonal linkages between health, nutrition, agriculture and poverty and in the areas where they work. Particular attention might be paid to the views and experience of those poorer rural people most adversely affected. The incentives to staff can be enhanced by workshops with their colleagues from other areas to which their findings are reported, and then by together working out and agreeing proposals for action. Such joint analysis and action can be suggested for the district and subdistrict level. This procedure should heighten awareness of seasonal problems leading to health programmes and other interventions better geared to the seasonal needs of agriculture and of the poorer people.

But implementation, as argued by Carruthers (Section 8.2), is the crux. Good ideas which are not implementable are bad ideas, at least for the time being. The best way forward may be to develop methods of seasonal analysis and a repertoire of interventions which are simple, manageable, replicable and effective, and which involve rural people as partners. Analysis is the easier part; the greater challenge is action. Ways forward may be sought through combinations of decentralised seasonal analysis, action programmes, evaluation, and then training and replication. Such measures might restrain processes of impoverishment, increase agricultural production, and benefit those who are poorer and weaker. This might be achieved, moreover, without significant loss, and often with gains, to those rural people who are less poor and more powerful. The local political obstacles which so often impede and subvert programmes intended to benefit the rural poor should therefore be less serious than usual, and may not appear at all. Seasonal analysis and action should, then, benefit those most in need, making things better for them at the times they find worst.

Conclusion

This book has been mostly concerned with trying to understand in factual terms what seasonal influences bear most strongly on the welfare of poor rural people in tropical countries. Many of the papers have, however, followed through to practical implications, and this chapter has illustrated how seasonal analysis can stimulate interdisciplinary thought about the choice, design and above all timing of rural development activities. For the practitioner Table 8.3 provides a checklist of policy implications that have been discussed in the text.

Seasonal analysis and measures to relieve seasonal problems do not require complex or large-scale research. What they do require is an interchange of knowledge and ideas between rural people, doctors, agriculturists, social scientists, planners, administrators, and politicians. Since each environment is in some respects unique, it requires that this analysis and exchange of ideas occur at the local level. Each type of environment will require its own mix of measures and its own priorities. In one place, tackling a disease which has a crippling effect in the wet season may be a higher priority than modifying farming systems; in another, changing farm technology of the farming calendar to enable smaller poorer farmers to obtain an earlier food crop, or higher yields, may be more important. But in all environments, there are likely to be seasonal links between health, nutrition, agriculture and poverty which, when examined, will suggest new programmes or new timing and emphases in existing programmes.

The benefits from this approach may be especially high where the poorer rural people are able to sustain an adequate livelihood for most of the year, but are highly vulnerable or unable to support themselves during a lean period. If a government objective is the provision of basic needs and an adequate livelihood to all citizens, then a focus on the lean period may often have higher returns in terms of livelihoods created — helping many people over the threshold — than attempts to create fewer entirely new livelihoods around the year. Complementary or alternative to this approach is raising food and income floors at other times and improving savings and storage in order to enable the poorer rural people to tide over the lean periods. Off-farm employment, whether through migration, public works, small-scale industries, or other means, is a major source of smoothing and may have to be a more prominent component in future counter-seasonal strategies to secure adequate livelihoods.

In recommending seasonal analysis and counter-seasonal programmes, three reservations must be made.

First, rural poverty has international aspects. The temptation is to conclude, from a seasonal analysis, that the measures needed are only internal to third world countries. This is not so. Rural poverty is linked with unequal exchange between rich and poor countries, to commodity prices, and to other concerns of the North-South dialogue. The seasonal mode of analysis should not divert attention from these international aspects but should rather, by exposing more of the scale, nature and dynamics of rural poverty, show up even more clearly the relevance of international action to redress the inequalities of trade and economic relations.

Conclusions and Practical Implications

TABLE 8.3. Checklist on the policy implications of seasonality

Policy area and implication	Sections in this book where discussed
Government technical services	
(1) long-range weather forecasting	8.2
(2) monitoring drought/food situation	8.2
(3) agricultural services for food crops	
(4) agricultural services for women	8.3
Government social policies	
(5) social education in the off-season	
Government food policy	
(6) maintenance of buffer food stocks	8.3
(7) food price regulation/market intervention	3.4, 3.5
(8) decentralise food stores to vulnerable areas	
Government administrative changes	
(9) timing of tax demands	7.3, 8.3
(10) timing of end of financial year	8.3
(11) timing of school and other holidays	8.3
Seasonal employment	
(12) careful and selective use of public works	8.3, 3.5,
(13) small-scale industry in rural areas	3.4
Women's employment	
(14) fuller recognition in agricultural planning	7.1, 7.2
(15) tools and techniques to relieve drudgery (water supply, hand tools)	2.6, 7.2, 8.3
(16) agricultural services for women	8.3
(17) day-care facilities for children	7.2, 8.3
Family welfare	
(18) seasonal food supplies for vulnerable groups	8.3
(19) explore seasonal birth regulation	6.2, 8.3
Health services	
(20) plan for diseases with critical seasonal peaks (malaria? guinea-worm?)	6.5, 8.3, 2.5
(21) regulation of staff leave, drug issues	8.3
(22) concentration on seasonally vulnerable people	8.3
(23) timing of health education work	2.5, 8.3
Agriculture	
(24) use of irrigation to extend growing season	2.1, 2.6, 8.3
(25) use of dryland farming methods	8.3
(26) technology to reduce labour peaks	2.6
(27) inter-cropping as a safeguard against climatic variability	7.3
(28) effect of new crop varieties	3.5
(29) crop breeding for drought resistance	
Savings and credit	
(30) village savings clubs	8.3
Crop storage	
(31) construction of food stores	8.3
(32) operation of family grain stores	7.3, 8.3
(33) crops that store in the soil (cassava)	8.3
(34) need for milk/cheese/butter storage	3.3, 6.6

Second, the question—who benefits?—must always be asked. We have argued that counter-seasonal measures may differentially benefit the poorer rural people. But the extent to which this is so depends on the nature of the programme and the local social and political structure. Seasonal supplies of drugs may be available only to those who are more influential. Public works may create facilities for the richer farmers. The effects of relief food vary: the famine of 1972 in the highlands of Papua New Guinea was relieved by moving food into the area; but in 1974 food was moved into Assam and West Bengal and the famine there was not relieved. Papua New Guinea had a relatively undifferentiated social hierarchy, so that all had access to the food; whereas in Assam and West Bengal, the local hierarchy enabled those who were powerful to benefit while the poorer people did not, or benefited much less. Counter-seasonal programmes can, as in this example, be subverted. But more generally they may benefit the poor precisely because the powerful have less need of them and less to gain from them.

Finally, seasonal analysis should not divert attention from more basic issues. Those who are less poor are much less vulnerable to seasonal afflictions and stress. The most effective counter-seasonal measure is to remove extreme poverty, and this could often best be done by redistributing land and water. Where such reform is not yet feasible, other counter-seasonal measures may appear palliatives or diversions. But this need not be so. We have seen the close links between seasonality, poverty and dependence. If counter-seasonal programmes can enable the poorer rural people to gain more adequate flows of food and income and to become less vulnerable and less dependent, they may then be more able and ready to assert themselves. More food and better health may provide the physical and psychological preconditions for political organisation and pressure to achieve reforms. If, after such reforms, the poorer families have direct control of adequate means of production, and if they receive adequate returns for their labour, they will then be much less vulnerable to adverse seasonal effects. Seasonally-oriented programmes will still be needed; but the need will be less acute.

8.4 References

Andriamananjara, R. (1971), *Labour Mobilization: the Moroccan Experience*, Discussion Paper No. 15, Centre for Research on Economic Development, University of Michigan.

Arnon, I. (1972), *Crop Production in Dry Regions*, 2 vols., London, Leonard Hill.

Barrell, R.A.E., and Rowland, M.G.M. (1979), 'Infant Foods as a Potential Source of Diarrhoeal Illness in Rural West Africa', *Transactions of the Royal Society of Tropical Medicine and Hygiene*, 73, 1, pp. 85-90.

Barter, P.G.H. (1962), 'Special Problems of Agricultural Planning', *Monthly Bulletins of Agricultural Economics and Statistics*, 2, 6.

Boxall, R. A., Greeley, M., and Tyagi, D. S., with Lipton, M., and Neelakanta, J. (1978), 'The Prevention of Farm-level Food Grain Storage Losses in India: a Social Cost-benefit Analysis', *IDS Research Report*, Institute of Development Studies, University of Sussex (October).

Chambers, Robert (1979), 'Health, Agriculture and Rural Poverty: Why Seasons Matter', *IDS Discussion Paper* No. 148, Institute of Development Studies, University of Sussex (December).

Conclusions and Practical Implications

Chambers, Robert, and Harriss, John (1977), 'Comparing Twelve South Indian Villages: in Search of Practical Theory', in *Green Revolution? Technology and Change in Rice-Growing Areas of Tamil Nadu and Sri Lanka,* ed. B. H. Farmer, London and Basingstoke, Macmillan.

Chen, Lincoln C., Alauddin Chowdhury, A.K.M., and Huffman, Sandra L. (1979), 'Seasonal Dimensions of Energy Protein Malnutrition in Rural Bangladesh: the Role of Agriculture, Dietary Practices, and Infection', *Ecology of Food and Nutrition, 8,* pp. 175-87.

Costa, E. (1973), 'Maximising Employment in Labour-intensive Development Programmes', *International Labour Review,* 108, p. 5.

Donovan, W. G. (1973), *Rural Works and Employment: Description and Preliminary Analysis of a Land Army Project in Mysore State, India,* Occasional Paper No. 60, New York, Department of Agricultural Economics, Cornell University.

Elliott, K. (1975), *The Training of Auxiliaries in Health Care* (an Annotated Bibliography with Project Descriptions), London, Intermediate Technology Publications.

Godbole, A. (1973), 'Productive Relief Works for the Rich', *EPW, 8,* 17 (28 April).

Greeley, Martin (1980), 'Rural Technology, Rural Institutions and the Rural Poorest', *Discussion Paper,* Institute of Development Studies, University of Sussex.

Grissa, A. (1973), *Agricultural Policies and Employment: Case Study of Tunisia,* OECD Development Centre Studies, Employment Series, No. 9, Paris, OECD.

Harriss, Barbara (1977), *Piecemeal Planning in Rice Markets: the Effects of Partial Government Intervention on Marketing Efficiency in a South Indian District,* Monographs in Development Studies No. 1, School of Development Studies, University of East Anglia.

Harriss, Barbara (1978), 'Allocation, Location and Dislocation in Non-market Rice Distribution', *Journal of Development Studies, 15* (1) (October), pp. 87-105.

IBRD (1976), *Public Works Programmes in Developing Countries: a Comparative Analysis,* World Bank Staff Working Paper No. 224, Washington, IBRD.

Ilchman, W. F. (1972), 'Decision Rules and Decision Roles', *African Review,* 2 (2), pp. 219-46.

Lewis, J. P. (1972), 'The Public Works to Low-end Poverty Problems', *J. Development Planning,* No. 5.

Lewis, J. P. (1975), 'Designing the Public Works Mode of Anti-poverty Policy', Princeton University, Brookings Institute (mimeo).

Malawi (1973), *A Guide to the Safe Storage of Cereals, Oilseeds and Pulses,* Lilongwe (Malawi), Extension Aids Branch, Ministry of Agriculture.

Maxwell, S. (1978), 'Food Aid, Food for Work, and Public Works', *Discussion Paper* No. 127, Institute of Development Studies, University of Sussex.

NAS (1974), *More Water for Arid Lands,* Washington, National Academy of Sciences.

NAS (1977), *Leucaena: Promising Forage and Tree Crop for the Tropics,* Washington, National Academy of Sciences.

NIAE (1974), *Botswana Dryland Farming Project,* Wrest Park, Bedfordshire, National Institute of Agricultural Engineering.

Oxfam (1975), *Saveway Clubs,* Oxford, Oxfam (booklet and kit).

Oxfam (1976), *Field Directors' Handbook,* Oxford, Oxfam. (See especially Sections 4, 18, 19 and 34; 1976 ed. only).

Pacey, A. (1978), *Gardening for Better Nutrition,* London, Intermediate Technology Publications.

Rodgers, G. B. (1972), *Poverty and Policy: the Impact of Rural Public Works in the Kosi Area of Bihar, India,* Unpublished D. Phil. thesis, University of Sussex.

Rodgers, G. B. (1973), 'Effects of Public Works on Rural Poverty', *EPW* Annual Number, *8,* (4-6), Bombay (February).

Ruttan, V. W. (1977), 'Induced Innovation and Agricultural Development', *Food Policy,* 2 (1), pp. 196-296.

Sandford, S. (1977), Report to UK Ministry of Overseas Development (May).

Schofield, Susan (1974), 'Seasonal Factors Affecting Nutrition in Different Age Groups and Especially Pre-school Children', *Journal of Development Studies, 11* (1), pp. 22-40.

Sobhan, R. (1968), *Basic Democracies, Works Programmes and Rural Development in East Pakistan,* Dacca, Oxford University Press.

Stevens, C. (1977), *The Uses of Food Aid in Lesotho,* ODI Working Paper No. 4,

London, Overseas Development Institute (mimeo).
Tiano, A. (1972), 'Human Resources, Investment and Employment Policy in the Maghreb', *International Labour Review, 105* (2).
UN (1975), *Poverty, Unemployment and Development Policy,* New York, UN/ST/ESA/29.
USAID (1977), *Creating Rural Employment: a Manual for Organising Rural Works Programmes,* J. W. Thomas and R. M. Hook, Washington.
Warrell, David, and Arnett, Charles (1976), 'The Importance of Bites by the Saw-scaled or Carpet Viper (*Echis Carinatus*): Epidemiological Studies in Nigeria and a Review of the World Literature', *Acta Tropica, 33,* 4.
WFP (1976a), *Interim Evaluation Report Bangladesh 2197 Q. Relief Works Programme for Land and Water Development,* Rome, WFP/CFA 2/12-A Add C23.
WFP (1976b), *The World Food Programme and Employment Report,* by the Executive Director, Rome, WFP/CFA: 1/15-A.
Whitehead, R. G., Rowland, M.G.M., Hutton, Melanie, Prentice, A. M., Muller, Elisabeth, and Paul, Alison (1978), 'Factors Influencing Lactation Performance in Rural Gambian Mothers', *Lancet,* 22 July, pp. 178-81.
World Bank (1975), *Rural Development Sector Policy Paper,* Washington, World Bank.

APPENDIX TABLE 5.1. Seasonal measures of births (and marriages) by month of birth, for countries with available data, grouped into regions*

Month of occurrence/registration 'Estimated' month of conception	Jan Apr	Feb May	Mar Jun	Apr Jul	May Aug	Jun Sep	Jul Oct	Aug Nov	Sep Dec	Oct Jan	Nov Feb	Dec Mar	Mean no. of events per month	Birth index	Marriage index
AFRICA															
North Africa															
Algeria (1969)	124	116	123	113	83	95	89	85	88	91	92	100	47459	153	n.a.
Egypt (1954/55/56)	119	110	101	98	90	95	97	95	93	95	99	108	78991	78	216
Libya (1972/73/74)	111	108	103	98	91	87	95	88	94	97	113	115	8775	105	360
Tunisia (1958/59/60)	119	123	103	105	100	87	84	99	91	92	95	103	14621	105	251
Sub-Saharan Africa															
Ghana (1976)	88	91	96	94	103	111	104	104	107	103	106	94	13962	75	n.a.
Mauritius (1974/75)	105	94	93	111	102	105	102	94	99	110	93	90	1851	72	n.a.
Mozambique (1971/72/73)	70	80	80	77	93	99	134	133	123	107	111	93	11508	216	n.a.
South Africa (Asian) (1973/74/75)	101	115	104	101	103	102	88	95	101	96	99	95	1763	54	159
South Africa (Coloured) (1973/74/75)	97	95	99	98	98	96	100	104	113	102	99	98	5903	39	179
South Africa (White) (1973/74/75)	103	109	106	105	104	100	92	96	96	97	98	94	7067	54	166

APPENDIX TABLE 5.1. (continued)

Month of occurrence/registration 'Estimated' month of conception	Jan Apr	Feb May	Mar Jun	Apr Jul	May Aug	Jun Sep	Jul Oct	Aug Nov	Sep Dec	Oct Jan	Nov Feb	Dec Mar	Mean no. of events per month	Birth index	Marriage index
LATIN AMERICA															
Caribbean															
Barbados (1957/58/59)	112	110	103	102	103	92	95	106	118	113	107	38	553	149	454
Dominica (1960/61/62)	103	106	99	89	98	94	100	98	106	109	99	97	8873	50	126
Jamaica (1959/60/61)	101	99	100	101	96	95	94	99	105	102	104	105	5512	35	n.a.
Trinidad & Tobago (1972/73/74)	106	97	97	91	97	93	90	96	111	107	108	108	2234	79	n.a.
Guadaloupe (1973/74/75)	111	108	102	97	98	97	95	97	102	100	99	94	736	46	n.a.
Martinique (1973/74/75)	109	107	101	102	96	94	90	96	110	100	100	96	604	57	n.a.
Middle America															
Costa Rica (1973)	113	107	111	105	103	100	97	99	104	104	99	58	4127	94	178
Guatemala (1958/59)	106	105	95	96	94	90	100	103	106	100	103	100	14775	48	n.a.
Mexico (1973/74/75)	95	96	96	99	94	94	99	110	103	107	111	95	197738	63	105
Panama (1971/72/73)	103	101	99	100	99	93	91	94	105	106	108	103	4500	50	126
Temperate South America															
Argentina (1958/59/60)	105	100	99	97	93	98	102	102	109	102	99	95	39506	59	210
Chile (1967/68/69)	103	100	97	97	97	102	100	100	107	104	101	94	20787	32	109
Uruguay (1958/59/60)	96	102	97	95	88	99	96	103	109	105	106	103	2057	57	196
Tropical South America															
Ecuador (1964/65/66)	96	92	92	93	101	104	107	106	108	104	103	95	18505	65	99
Venezuela (1971/72/73)	95	100	102	95	103	98	97	104	98	101	110	98	33852	39	142
Bolivia (1944/45)	99	97	91	99	94	96	101	102	105	105	105	108	9646	50	n.a.

APPENDIX TABLE 5.1. (continued)

Month of occurrence/registration 'Estimated' month of conception	Jan Apr	Feb May	Mar Jun	Apr Jul	May Aug	Jun Sep	Jul Oct	Aug Nov	Sep Dec	Oct Jan	Nov Feb	Dec Mar	Mean no. of events per month	Birth index	Marriage index
ASIA															
East Asia															
Japan (1971/72/73)	102	103	98	101	98	97	103	103	102	98	95	99	170350	29	401
Middle South Asia															
India (1969/70/71)	92	93	96	92	90	97	103	109	111	106	108	103	696935	80	n.a.
Sri Lanka (1964/65/66)	97	105	105	103	105	110	95	94	96	94	97	99	30579	56	n.a.
Eastern South Asia															
Malaysia (1973/74)	110	97	99	102	103	101	100	98	101	104	97	88	25644	42	n.a.
Philippines (1972/73/74)	104	97	95	95	94	91	94	95	104	114	108	110	86048	79	276
Singapore (1974/75/76)	94	97	97	98	98	99	99	101	107	109	102	99	3500	38	202
Thailand (1970/71/72)	103	108	101	105	105	101	91	98	102	93	95	98	98711	50	n.a.
Western South Asia															
Cyprus (1974/75/76)	105	116	105	91	103	95	98	101	99	99	94	94	830	60	463
Iraq (1958)	96	100	101	76	80	78	82	113	116	107	117	134	6471	176	n.a.
Israel (1974/75/76)	101	99	96	93	92	97	98	104	109	106	103	104	7987	52	266
Lebanon (1963/69/70)	118	113	107	110	100	97	98	92	96	95	89	84	6237	97	n.a.
Jordan (1972/73/74)	107	118	106	103	99	97	95	93	91	89	98	105	6761	77	n.a.

Note: * Copies of the data sources from which our measures of both birth and death seasonality are derived, are obtainable from the authors upon request.

APPENDIX TABLE 5.2. Seasonal measures of deaths, by month of death, for countries with available data, grouped into regions

	Month of occurrence/registration												Mean no. of events	Index	Life expectancy*
	Jan	Feb	Mar	Apr	May	Jun	Jul	Aug	Sep	Oct	Nov	Dec			
AFRICA															
North Africa															
Egypt (1954/55/56)	87	86	84	89	103	127	134	124	100	90	88	88	33021	176	53
Libya (1972/73/74)	129	121	105	90	89	94	97	91	96	93	84	112	1627	133	50
Tunisia (1958/59/60)	106	102	86	90	88	88	90	98	107	116	115	114	3173	120	55
Sub-Saharan Africa															
Ghana (1976)	92	97	100	99	99	107	107	101	102	89	101	106	2992	48	48
Mauritius (1974/75/76)	95	90	94	104	97	106	106	114	108	98	96	93	555	75	66
Mozambique (1971/72/73)	103	99	99	95	101	102	98	100	96	103	109	95	1214	36	43
South Africa (Asian)(1973/74/75)	96	93	88	98	109	124	108	102	97	98	91	97	399	85	64
South Africa (Coloured) (1973/74/75)	100	107	107	108	105	106	105	98	93	87	88	95	2377	77	56
South Africa (White)(1973/74/75)	90	91	93	95	103	119	117	114	103	97	90	90	2881	110	72

APPENDIX TABLE 5.2. (continued)

	Month of occurrence/registration												Mean no. of events	Index	Life expectancy*
	Jan	Feb	Mar	Apr	May	Jun	Jul	Aug	Sep	Oct	Nov	Dec			
LATIN AMERICA															
Caribbean															
Barbados (1957/58/59)	99	104	103	96	97	102	102	102	112	120	92	73	184	88	72
Dominica (1960/61/62)	111	107	99	95	94	105	106	99	97	97	96	93	2095	59	65
Jamaica (1959/60/61)	107	103	97	100	107	105	97	96	95	95	97	103	1252	48	70
Trinidad & Tobago (1972/73/74)	118	98	99	95	96	92	97	95	102	100	99	110	588	59	69
Middle America															
Costa Rica (1965/73)	113	104	105	106	94	91	102	100	102	102	95	85	775	67	69
Honduras (1971/72/73)	100	98	99	101	98	102	103	100	100	103	102	94	1747	22	51
Guatemala (1958/59)	98	101	96	104	104	103	105	102	101	96	96	93	5778	41	54
Mexico (1973/74/75)	110	110	96	95	95	94	100	100	98	98	101	103	35470	48	64
Panama (1971/72/73)	104	96	93	94	95	91	100	94	101	111	110	110	780	73	67
Temperate South America															
Argentina (1958/59/60)	102	98	90	91	102	106	108	109	104	95	96	98	14410	63	68
Chile (1967/68/69)	104	95	89	97	99	105	110	103	103	101	96	99	7154	51	63
Uruguay (1958/59/60)	95	94	90	88	105	119	117	110	105	94	91	91	985	113	70
Paraguay (1971/72/73)	100	101	92	91	97	111	113	103	103	99	94	94			
Tropical South America															
Ecuador (1964/65/66)	106	110	106	100	98	97	102	98	97	94	95	97	4969	48	59
Venezuela (1971/72/73)	103	101	96	94	97	96	101	101	101	102	103	105	6151	34	66
Bolivia (1944/45)	109	100	92	94	93	95	95	97	101	104	115	106	4230	69	47
Colombia (1968/69)	106	106	104	107	107	105	107	101	97	86	88	84	13460	88	61

APPENDIX TABLE 5.2. (continued)

	Month of occurrence/registration												Mean no. of events	Index	Life expectancy[*]
	Jan	Feb	Mar	Apr	May	Jun	Jul	Aug	Sep	Oct	Nov	Dec			
ASIA															
East Asia															
Japan (1971/72/73)	110	116	114	99	95	90	93	92	88	95	100	109	57751	97	73
Middle South Asia															
India (1969/70/71)	97	95	92	94	96	99	101	108	112	102	102	101	293255	53	51
Pakistan (1968/69/71)	86	85	82	99	93	123	82	87	111	86	120	144	41885	198	54
Sri Lanka (1964/65/66)	100	105	97	95	97	102	97	98	100	100	104	105	7831	32	65
Eastern South Asia															
Hong Kong (1971/72/73)	112	115	106	96	91	97	95	94	91	93	97	111	1752	90	71
Malaysia (1973/74)	102	102	96	97	102	101	98	100	97	99	102	102	5387	24	60
Philippines (1972/73/74)	107	97	90	88	93	96	103	109	110	110	101	97	23691	79	59
Singapore (1974/75/76)	103	100	96	100	113	108	96	95	93	98	95	102	966	53	70
Thailand (1970/71/72)	98	99	103	101	102	101	102	100	100	98	100	95	19460	19	62
Western South Asia															
Cyprus (1974/75/76)	121	115	114	86	81	82	119	116	86	88	92	101	665	171	72
Iraq (1959/60)	112	116	99	97	100	88	100	94	89	90	100	116	2410	87	54
Israel (1974/75/76)	120	126	109	97	92	87	91	90	90	93	97	108	2023	126	73
Lebanon (1969/70)	109	119	98	106	92	92	94	85	95	95	100	114	1051	97	61
Turkey (1971/72/73)	119	115	107	98	92	86	90	87	86	94	114	112	9020	134	57
Jordan (1972/73/74)	120	124	107	90	94	90	93	90	96	92	94	109	531	121	55

Sources: Data on life expectation are from Office of Population Agency for International Development, *Annual Report*, Washington, 1974, and for South Africa, Department of Statistics, *S. African Statistics*, Republic of South Africa, 1976.

APPENDIX TABLE 5.3. Comparison of state urban and rural birth indices of seasonality for ten states, by month, India 1962–64

Month of occurrence/registration		Jan	Feb	Mar	Apr	May	Jun	Jul	Aug	Sep	Oct	Nov	Dec	Average	Index	Index rural + urban
'Estimated' month of conception		Apr	May	Jun	Jul	Aug	Sep	Oct	Nov	Dec	Jan	Feb	Mar			
STATE																
Andhra Pradesh	Rural	89	83	82	84	89	107	120	123	117	109	104	92	35514	155	142
	Urban	95	84	86	89	90	94	110	113	108	105	110	114	13904	122	
Gujarat	Rural	94	89	85	84	81	99	109	119	120	105	109	104	34193	144	132
	Urban	97	87	88	84	83	91	102	111	125	113	111	104	15151	136	
Kerala	Rural	96	104	102	99	101	107	109	99	97	99	94	95	27311	44	46
	Urban	83	86	94	87	102	113	118	107	90	94	110	115	6441	131	
Madhya Pradesh	Rural	86	86	90	98	95	102	111	114	107	105	107	100	38934	91	89
	Urban	89	95	88	97	90	89	102	109	117	111	107	105	8856	103	
Madras (Tamil Nadu)	Rural	84	88	92	96	99	110	119	107	108	99	101	95	44456	92	83
	Urban	80	87	93	97	99	97	102	98	97	101	109	136	28280	100	
Maharashtra	Rural	84	90	92	92	87	95	107	123	118	111	103	97	72941	125	128
	Urban	91	90	89	89	87	96	102	106	119	117	119	94	29562	127	
Mysore (Karnataka)	Rural	91	100	100	94	92	103	109	112	110	104	97	88	26335	76	59
	Urban	98	102	100	97	95	100	101	104	103	101	101	97	12170	29	
Punjab	Rural	104	102	92	85	80	86	94	106	114	115	113	107	47898	124	133
	Urban	93	89	83	80	75	82	99	115	126	127	119	110	11102	196	
Uttar Pradesh	Rural	100	102	99	90	87	95	95	102	114	103	104	105	79009	64	80
	Urban	98	89	89	85	83	87	95	109	121	114	115	114	20578	147	
West Bengal	Rural	85	105	112	107	97	94	82	90	97	95	112	122	41197	118	100
	Urban	93	93	93	87	88	83	90	106	108	113	130	117	11729	147	

Source: Ministry of Health and Family Planning, Health Statistics of India: 1962–4, New Delhi.

Appendix
ODE TO THE SEASONS CONFERENCE

Assembled here in sunny Brighton
we hope our meeting will shed light on
seasons. Is this good or bad?
Another conference? One *more* fad?

The answer is we're in a trap
we don't have seasons on our map
Our disciplines aren't trained to see
the range of seasonality

First, anthropologists I swear
to seasons have been far too near
Immersed in culture, rain or dry
they have not seen the clouds pass by

And sociologists, even worse
with questionnaires and questions terse
snatch instant truth, one-off. It's rare
to find them survey all the year

Nutritionists with careful plan
conduct their surveys when they can
be sure the weather's fine and dry,
the harvest's in, food intake high

Malariologists can claim
their pattern is not quite the same
Superior in virtue they
migrate to *face* the rainy day

Economists, that super breed
show seasonal supplies exceed
demand; result — the landless poor
for less and less work more and more

And statisticians too declare
they have a seasonal nightmare
An average is but a dream
With seasons means aren't what they seem

Geographers — complacent crew —
will say — of course *they* always knew
what others now just come to know
that seasons come and seasons go

Appendix: Ode to the Seasons Conference

Contrariwise plant-breeders say
not seasons but the length of day
is critical; the key they've seen
's a photoperiodic gene

Demographers now wonder why
we do it when it's cool and dry
Conversely, when it's wet and hot
it seems we tend to do it not

Now epidemiologists
will say the worst is when it's poured
with rain for that's when vectors vect
and swarms of small insects infect

Then students seeking Ph.Ds
believe that everyone agrees
that rains don't do for rural study
suits get wet and shoes get muddy

And bureaucrats, of urban type
wait prudently till crops be ripe
before they venture far afield
to ask politely: what's the yield?

The international experts' flights
have other seasons; winter nights
in New York, Paris, Brussels, Rome
are what drive them, in flocks, from home

And Northern academics too
are seasonal in their global view
For they are seen in third world nations
only during long vacations

The rural people — I forgot
know what some others still know not
long life and leisure, food and health
belong the those who have the wealth

They do not need research to show
the troubles they already know
oppressed by sickness, hunger, debt
they know the worst is when its wet

But wealthy ones dislike life dry
The poor may thirst but we'll get by
eating and drinking (within reason)
steadily through the conference season

Robert Chambers

LIST OF CONTRIBUTORS

Tim Bayliss-Smith, Lecturer, Department of Geography, University of Cambridge CB2 3EN

R.A.E. Barrell, Bacteriologist, Public Health Laboratories, Withington Hospital, West Didsbury, Manchester M20 8LR

Stan Becker, International Centre for Diarrhoeal Disease Research, Bangladesh, G.P.O. Box 128, Dacca 2, Bangladesh

David Bradley, Professor of Tropical Hygiene and Director of Institute, Ross Institute of Tropical Hygiene, London School of Hygiene and Tropical Medicine, Keppel Street (Gower St.), London WC1E 7HT

R.S. Bray, Formerly Director of MRC Laboratories, The Gambia, and now member of staff of MRC, Imperial College Field Station, Silwood Park, Ashurst Lodge, Ascot, Berkshire SL5 5DE

Ian Carruthers, Reader in African Development, Wye College, University of London, Nr. Ashford, Kent TN25 5AH

Robert Chambers, Fellow, Institute of Development Studies, University of Sussex, Brighton BN1 9RE

Rafiqul Huda Chaudhury, Senior Research Demographer, Bangladesh Institute of Development Studies, Adamjee Court, Motijheel Commercial Area, Dacca 2, Bangladesh

Lincoln C. Chen, Scientific Director, International Centre for Diarrhoeal Disease Research, Bangladesh, G.P.O. Box 128, Dacca 2, Bangladesh

A.K.M. Alauddin Chowdhury, International Centre for Diarrhoeal Disease Research, Bangladesh, G.P.O. Box 128, Dacca 2, Bangladesh

Edward J. Clay, Fellow, Institute of Development Studies, University of Sussex, Brighton BN1 9RE

Nigel Crook, Lecturer, Dept. of Economics, School of Oriental and African Studies, University of London, Malet Street, London WC1E 7HP

W.A.M. Cutting, Formerly Senior Lecturer, Tropical Family Health, Ross Institute of Tropical Hygiene, London School of Hygiene and Tropical Medicine, now, Senior Lecturer, Dept. of Child Life and Health, University of Edinburgh, Scotland

B.S. Drasar, Senior Lecturer, Department of Medical Microbiology and Nutrition, London School of Hygiene and Tropical Medicine, Keppel Street (Gower St.), London WC1E 7HT

List of Contributors

Tim Dyson, Formerly Research Fellow, Centre for Population Studies, London School of Hygiene and Tropical Medicine, now Lecturer in Population Studies, London School of Economics, Houghton Street, London WC2A 2AE

Richard Feachem, Senior Lecturer in Tropical Public Health Engineering, Ross Institute of Tropical Hygiene, London School of Hygiene and Tropical Medicine, Keppel Street (Gower St.), London WC1E 7HT

James P. Goetz, Formerly Lecturer, Dept. of Community Health, Muhimbili Medical Centre, University of Dar es Salaam, now Medical Director, Oak Orchard Community Health Center, 80 West Avenue, Brockport, N.Y. 14420, USA

John Harriss, Lecturer, School of Development Studies, University of East Anglia, Norwich NR4 7TJ

Barbara Harriss, Economist, Nutrition Policy Unit, London School of Hygiene and Tropical Medicine, Keppel Street (Gower St.), London WC1E 7HT

Margaret Haswell, Rural Development Consultant, formerly at St. Hugh's College, Oxford

Sandi Huffman, International Centre for Diarrhoeal Disease Research, Bangladesh, G.P.O. Box 128, Dacca 2, Bangladesh

Melanie Hutton, formerly Nutritionist, Dunn Nutrition Unit, Milton Road, Cambridge CB4 1XJ

P.K. Kymal, Executive Director, Food and Nutrition Board, Krishi Bhavan, New Delhi, 110001, India

Richard Longhurst, formerly Research Associate, Dept. of Agricultural Economics, Ahmadu Bello University, now Consultant on Rural Development, c/o Institute of Development Studies, University of Sussex, Brighton BN1 9RE

Sheila Macrae, Demographer, 37 West Hill Court, Millfield Lane, Highgate, London N6 6JJ

Simon Maxwell, Agricultural Economist, British Mission in Tropical Agriculture, Casilla 359, Santa Cruz, Bolivia

Elisabeth Müller, formerly Nutritionist, Dunn Nutrition Unit, Milton Road, Cambridge CB4 1XJ

R. Muller, Senior Lecturer, Dept. of Helminthology, London School of Hygiene and Tropical Medicine, Keppel Street (Gower St.), London WC1E 7HT

D.K. Ndagala, Ministry of National Culture and Youth, Directorate of Research and Planning, City Drive, Tancot House, P.O. Box 4284, Dar es Salaam, Tanzania

Simeon R. Onchere, Department of Agricultural Economics, University of

Reading, Earley Gate, Whiteknights, Reading RG6 2AR

Arnold Pacey, Freelance writer and technical editor on technology and rural development, 53 Millway Close, Upper Wolvercote, Oxford OX2 8BL

Ingrid Palmer, Freelance economist interested in women and development

Alison Paul, Nutritionist, Dunn Nutrition Unit, Milton Road, Cambridge CB4 1XJ

Philip Payne, Head, Nutrition Policy Unit, Department of Human Nutrition, London School of Hygiene and Tropical Medicine, Keppel Street (Gower St.), London WC1E 7HT

Pu-ai Pei, Freelance writer and technical editor on technology and rural development, 53 Millway Close, Upper Wolvercote, Oxford OX2 8BL

Michael J. Porter, formerly USAID Office, Lahore, Pakistan, now 10B Prideaux Road, Eastbourne, Sussex BN21 2ND

A.M. Prentice, Nutritionist, Dunn Nutrition Unit, Milton Road, Cambridge CB4 1XJ

Philip Raikes, Fellow, Centre for Development Research, 9 Ny Kongensgade, DK-1472, Copenhagen K, Denmark

S. Rajagopalan, Officer on Special Duty, Ministry of Agriculture and Irrigation, Department of Food, Tamil Nadu Nutrition Project, 7A Gopalapuram First St., Madras 86, India

Henry Rempel, Professor, Department of Economics, University of Manitoba, Winnipeg, Canada R3T 2N2

M.G.M. Rowland, Paediatrician/Project Leader, Dunn Nutrition Unit, Milton Road, Cambridge CB4 1XJ

M.A. Sardar, International Centre for Diarrhoeal Disease Research, Bangladesh, G.P.O. Box 128, Dacca 2, Bangladesh

Emmy B. Simmons, Agricultural Economist, Agency for International Development, Washington D.C. 20523, USA

R. Slooff, Health Ecologist, Department of Tropical Hygiene, Royal Tropical Institute, Mauritskade 63, Amsterdam, The Netherlands

B.A. Southgate, Senior Lecturer, Ross Institute of Tropical Hygiene, London School of Hygiene and Tropical Medicine, Keppel Street (Gower St.), London WC1E 7HT

R.N.P. Sutton, Consultant Virologist, Virology Dept., Withington Hospital, West Didsbury, Manchester M20 8LR

Jeremy Swift, Research Fellow, Institute of Development Studies, University of Sussex, Brighton BN1 9RE, currently seconded to International Livestock Centre for Africa, P.O. Box 60, Bamako, Mali

Andrew Tomkins, Consultant Physician, Clinical Nutrition and Metabolism

List of Contributors

Unit, Hospital for Tropical Diseases, 4 St. Pancras Way, London NW1 2PE

B.B. Waddy, formerly specialist in epidemiology, Colonial Medical Service, 8 Salters Acres, Winchester, Hants.

R.P.D. Walsh, Lecturer, Department of Geography, University College of Swansea, Singleton Park, Swansea SA2 8PP

Michael Watts, Associate Professor, Department of Geography, University of California, Berkeley, California 94720, USA

R.G. Whitehead, Director, Dunn Nutrition Unit, Milton Road, Cambridge CB4 1XJ

INDEX

absolute seasonality, 15-16
administrative aspects, 225-6, 226-38
Afghanistan
  malaria in, 118-19
Africa
  deaths in, and seasonality, 145;
  disease in, 130, 175-7;
  food supply in, 48-50;
  health in, 164;
  malaria in, 118;
  rural economy of, and seasonality, 67-73;
  savannah areas in, 5;
  welfare in, 164.
  See also East Africa; Sub-Saharan Africa; North Africa; West Africa
agricultural cycle
  and fertility, 137-9;
  in Solomon Islands, 155
agricultural employment, 92-100.
  See also agricultural labour requirements.
agricultural labour requirements, 34-7, 74-6, 84-5, 92-100, 160-1, 186-90, 197-9, 199-201, 211-14, 220, 227, 232.
  See also energy.
agricultural production, 31-8, 67-8
  in Gambia, 38-41;
  in Nigeria, 74-6
agricultural technology, 92, 95-8
agricultural wages, 54-5, 90, 93
agricultural work
  and energy requirements, 38-41;
  in Nigeria, 74-6;
  in Tamil Nadu, India, 156-61.
  See also agricultural labour requirements.
agriculture
  and food, 229-30;
  and health, 235-6;
  and nutrition, 52-61, 229-30, 235-6
  and poverty, 235-6;
  and seasonal labour requirements, 34-7
  and women, 197-8
anthropometric data, 45, 166
Asia
  monsoon climates in, 5;
  seasonality in, 6.
  See also South Asia.
Australia
  diarrhoeal diseases in, 111-12

Bagamoyo District, Tanzania, 22, 24, 26, 182-6, 186-91
Bangladesh
  agricultural employment in, 92-100;
  cholera in, 106;
  diarrhoeal diseases in, 111;
  energy intakes in, 49-50;
  fertility in, 137, 138;
  food storage in, 230;
  landlessness in, 199;
  migration in, 137;
  poverty in, 164;
  prices in, 87-92;
  seasonality in, 23-4, 220-3;
  wages in, 87-92;
  women in, 199
bilharzia
  See schistosomiasis.
births
  in Matlab thana, Bangladesh, 150-2;
  and seasonal patterns, 135-62, 196-7, 233;
  in Solomon Islands, 154-6;
  in Tamil Nadu, India, 156-61.
  See also fertility.
blindness, 179
Brazil
  seasonality index for, 14;
  tropical climatic types in, 20-1
breast feeding, 42-3, 54-7, 59, 61, 62, 108-11, 112, 138, 152, 164, 166-7, 169-70, 172, 178-9, 195, 219

camels, 81-4
Caribbean
  births in, seasonality of, 142-4
cash crops, 40, 42, 44, 62, 74, 78-80, 195, 204, 212-13, 229.
  See also crops.
cattle, 74-80, 81-4, 187-9
Central America
  diarrhoeal diseases in, 110;
  malnutrition in, 110;
  onchocerciasis in, 123;
  seasonality in, 6
cereal crops, 31, 34, 39-40, 49-50, 63, 180.
  See also crops.
cerebrospinal meningitis (CSM), 175-7, 180

Index

Ceylon
    malaria in, 117.
    See also Sri Lanka.
children
    and diarrhoeal diseases, 44-5;
    and diseases, 102-5, 107, 108-11, 111-12, 115, 119-20, 128, 160-1, 182-6;
    in Gambia, 164-75;
    growth of, 164-75;
    and malnutrition, 46, 178;
    and mortality, 152;
    and nutrition, 44, 52-61, 62, 180;
    and poverty, 191, 231-3;
    in rainy season, 219;
    and seasonal burdens, 194;
    welfare of, 163-4;
    and work, 195
cholera, 57, 106, 148, 177
classification
    and rainfall seasonality, 18-21;
    of tropical climates, 17-22, 31
climate, 1-2, 9-29, 86, 154-5
    and seasonal fertility, 135-7;
    and skin diseases, 115-16
cooperatives
    See farming cooperatives.
Costa Rica
    diarrhoeal diseases in, 112;
    water pollution in, 108
crop storage, 42-4, 52, 76-7, 100, 190, 203, 230-1.
    See also food storage.
crops, 10-11, 26, 30-7, 38-40, 41-5, 49-50, 62, 63, 68, 73-80, 86-7, 87-9, 93-100, 146-8, 156-7, 180, 186-90, 195, 203-4, 212-13, 218, 220, 229, 230-1
cultivators, 218-19
    and pastoralists, 188-91
cultural influences
    and seasonal health patterns, 111, 179-82

data
    and anti-seasonal bias, 4
deaths, 196-7
    in Matlab thana, Bangladesh, 150-4;
    and seasonal patterns, 135-62, 196-7;
    in Tamil Nadu, India, 159.
    See also mortality.
debt, 5, 91, 204-6, 219
demography, 135-62.
    See also births; deaths; fertility; mortality.
dengue fever, 114, 130, 233-4
dependence, 206-10, 238
diarrhoeal diseases, 44-5, 52, 57-8, 61, 102-12, 129-30, 145, 170, 174, 180, 184-5, 190, 233-4
diet, 47-8, 61, 165-70.
    See also food; nutrition.
diseases, 41-5, 63, 102-34, 129-30, 146, 163, 165, 166-7, 170, 173, 175-7, 177-81, 182-6, 213-14, 219
dysentery, 107

East Africa
    measles in, 114;
    onchocerciasis in, 123;
    seasonality in, 24, 26.
    See also Africa.
ecology, 9-11
economic relations
    and seasonality, 67-101, 193-217, 223;
    and technology, 62-3
Egypt
    diarrhoeal diseases in, 103-4, 107;
    filariasis in, 121
employment, 60-1, 80, 87, 92-100, 201, 227-30, 236
energy
    and food, 30-66;
    and nutrient requirements, 47-8;
    and nutrition, 52-61;
    requirements, 37-8, 39-41, 62, 77-8, 196-7, 230;
    and seasonality, 30-66, 170-1;
    storage mechanisms for, 50-2.
    See also agricultural labour requirements.
England
    births in, and seasonality, 144;
    diarrhoeal diseases in, 103, 107, 111, 112;
    food poisoning in, 105;
    mortality in, 139-41;
    respiratory diseases in, 113.
    See also United Kingdom.
evaporation, 9-10

families, 194-5, 231-3
farming cooperatives, 200-1
farming systems, 229-30
fertility, 135-9, 149.
    See also births.
filiarial infections, 121-4, 130
finance
    and rural projects, 226-7
food, 30-66, 68-70, 73-80, 87-92, 148, 160-1, 163, 164, 201-6, 218-19, 229-30
    consumption, 38-41;
    contamination, 174;
    intake, 166-70;
    poisoning, 105;
    prices, 5, 54-5, 89, 187, 210, 219, 220, 231;
    production, 232;
    storage, 42-4, 55, 60, 86, 92, 100, 186, 189.
    See also cereal crops, crop storage, crops.
Fulani (of Nigeria), 180-1

255

Gambia
  children in, 164-75;
  diarrhoeal diseases in, 111;
  food and work study in, 38-41;
  malaria in, 117-20;
  malnutrition in, 46;
  seasonality in, 27, 28, 220-3;
  skin diseases in, 114-15
gastroenteritis, 108
Genieri, Gambia, 22, 27, 28, 38-41
Ghana
  disease in, 175-6;
  energy intakes in, 49-51;
  fertility in, 138;
  guinea-worm infection in, 127;
  malnutrition in, 46-7
gifts, 78-80, 202-3
goats, 81-4
government, 224-6
Guatemala
  diarrhoeal diseases in, 103, 107, 112
guinea-worm infection, 10, 102, 125-7, 129, 130, 176, 177, 181, 233-4

Hanwa village, Nigeria, 22, 73-80
Hausa (of Nigeria), 201-6
health, 163-92, 235-6
health services, 181, 186, 233-4
high-yielding varieties, 62, 92, 197
Hong Kong
  births in, and seasonality, 144;
  fertility in, 137
housing, 175-7

Ilbarguyu (of Tanzania), 187-8
income, 163, 199, 214, 232
India
  births in, and seasonality, 135, 144, 145-8;
  deaths in, and seasonality, 145-8;
  dependence and seasonality in, 206-10;
  diarrhoeal diseases in, 105, 111;
  fertility in, 138, 149;
  filariasis in, 121;
  food storage in, 230-1;
  food subsidies in, 231;
  guinea-worm infection in, 125-7;
  irrigation in, 3;
  malaria in, 116;
  migration in, 135;
  mortality in, 141;
  typhoid fever in, 106.
  See also Asia; Indian Subcontinent; South Asia.
Indian Subcontinent
  diseases in, 130;
  irrigation in, 6;
  seasonality in, 6;
  seasonality index for, 14-15;

tropical climatic types in, 20-1
International Centre for Diarrhoeal Disease Research, Bangladesh (ICDDR,B), 52, 57, 58, 61, 149, 150
irrigation, 3, 6, 24, 28, 30-1, 50, 62, 68, 92, 95, 118-19, 156, 205, 208, 220, 229-30

Jamaica
  malnutrition in, 46
Japan
  fertility in, 138
Java
  agricultural labour requirements in, 197-8, 200;
  seasonality in, 22

kala-azar, 121-4, 130
Kel Adrar Twareg (of Mali), 81-7
Keneba, Gambia, 22, 27, 28, 115-16, 164-75
Kenya
  diseases in, 41-5;
  energy intakes in, 49;
  kala-azar in, 123-4;
  migration in, 211;
  nutrition in, 41-5

labour
  and agriculture, 34-7;
  and economic relationships, 67-101;
  and energy, 30-8, 62;
  and food, 30-41;
  output, and food consumption, 38-41;
  and pastoral economies, 80-7;
  and seasonality, 30-41, 67-101.
  See also agricultural labour requirements.
land reform, 92, 200, 207-8, 238
landlessness, 92, 100, 199, 201, 207-9, 212, 220, 223-4
Latin America
  mortality in, 145.
  See also South America.
Lesotho
  diarrhoeal diseases in, 105, 107, 108;
  typhoid fever in, 106
loans, 91.
  See also debt.

Machakos District, Kenya, 22, 24, 26, 41-5, 211
malaria, 10, 102, 116-20, 129, 130, 148, 170, 176-7, 178, 180, 184-6, 233-4
Malaysia
  fertility in, 138
Mali
  seasonality in, 22, 27, 28
malnutrition, 30, 45-8, 108, 110-11, 130, 164, 178, 184-5, 190-1, 229
Malumfashi, Nigeria, 22, 27, 28, 177-81
marriage, 138, 144, 150-2, 206

Index

Matlab thana, Bangladesh, 22-4, 52-61, 87, 149-54
measles, 113-14, 180, 183-4
mechanisation, 37, 62, 72, 195, 197-8, 201
Mexico
  diarrhoeal diseases in, 104;
  fertility in, 139;
  migration from, 211-13;
  migration in, 137-8
migration, 91, 135, 137-8, 210-14
  in Bangladesh, 152;
  in Mexico, 137-8;
  in Nigeria, 203;
  in Solomon Islands, 155-6
milk production, 80-7, 188, 189, 218
mortality, 135, 139-41, 149, 151, 165, 174, 229.
  See also deaths.
Moslem communities, 52-61, 73-80, 195, 212
mosquitoes, 114, 116-20, 121-2, 130, 186

Nigeria
  diarrhoeal diseases in, 108, 110;
  energy intakes in, 49;
  food shortages in, 201-6;
  guinea-worm infection in, 126-7;
  health in, 177-81;
  malaria in, 119;
  measles in, 113-14;
  seasonality in, 27, 28, 220-3;
  skin diseases in, 114;
  typhoid fever in, 106
nomadism, 118-19.
  See also pastoral economies.
North Afica
  births in, and seasonality of, 142-3.
  See also Africa.
North Arcot District, India, 22, 24-5, 37, 156-60, 208
North Yemen
  onchocerciasis in, 123
nutrients, 47-8, 52-61
nutrition
  and agriculture, 52-61, 229-30, 235-6;
  and diseases, 41-5, 108-10;
  and fertility, 138;
  and food, 229-30;
  and health, 235-6;
  in Kenya, 41-5;
  in Matlab thana, Bangladesh, 52-61;
  in Nigeria, 178;
  and poverty, 235-6;
  and seasonality, 45-52;
  in Tamil Nadu, India, 156-61

onchocerciasis, 121-3, 176
oxen, 40, 41, 62-3

Pakistan
  guinea-worm infection in, 127.
  See also Indian Subcontinent.
Papua New Guinea
  skin diseases in, 115;
  water pollution in, 108
pastoral economies, 80-7, 164
pastoralists, 180-1, 186-91, 218
patriarchy, 199-200
patron-client relationships, 91, 206-10
Philippines
  rice cultivation in, 34-5
ploughs, 62, 63
policy implications, 6, 60-1, 80, 86-7, 91-2, 98-100, 149, 174-5, 186, 200-1, 214, 218-40
political mobilisation, 208-10
political organisation, 238
poverty, 1-2, 4-6, 86-7, 98-100, 130-1, 163-4, 174, 175-7, 181, 189-91, 210-14, 218, 223, 227-8, 235-7
pregnancy, 135-9, 142-5, 145-8, 150-2, 155-6, 157-61, 170-5, 178-9, 195, 219, 233.
  See also births.
prices, 87-92.
  See also food prices.
production systems, 68-73
protein-energy malnutrition (PEM), 30, 44, 160, 178, 185, 219
public works, 60, 227-9
Puerto Rico
  births in, seasonality of, 144-5

rainfall
  and agricultural cycle, 137;
  and disease, 108;
  and fertility, 135-7;
  and mortality, 148;
  and seasonality, 9-10, 11-21, 156, 223
redistribution, 202-3
'relative seasonality', 13-15
respiratory diseases, 112-14, 183-4
rice, 34-8, 39-40, 52, 54-5, 62, 87-9, 93-8, 118-19, 156, 159, 161, 197-8
'river blindness'
  See onchocerciasis.
roads, 3
rotavirus infection, 111-12
rural development, 218, 224-6, 226-38
rural industries, 92
rural works programmes, 92, 100

Sahel, 80-7.
  See also Africa.
Sarawak
  rice cultivation in, 34-5
savings, 231

257

schistosomiasis, 10, 126-31
'seasonal ecology', 102-34
seasonal mapping, 235
seasonal variability, 67-8
seasonality index, 14
sheep, 81-4
Singapore
  fertility in, 137
skin diseases, 114-16
smallpox, 146, 148
social aspects, 72-3, 100, 193-217, 223-4
  and migration, 213;
  and mortality, 141, 152
solar energy, 30-1, 33-4
solar radiation, 9-10
Solomon Islands
  births in, and seasonality, 154-6;
  seasonality in, 22-3
South Africa
  births in, and seasonality, 144;
  deaths in, and seasonality, 145;
  malnutrition in, 46
South America
  births in, and seasonality, 142-4;
  diarrhoeal diseases in, 110;
  malnutrition in, 110;
  onchocerciasis in, 123;
  seasonality in, 6.
  See also Latin America.
South Asia
  dependence and seasonality in, 206-10.
  See also Indian Subcontinent.
Sri Lanka
  dependence and seasonality in, 208;
  fertility in, 139;
  food subsidies in, 231.
  See also Ceylon.
Sub-Saharan Africa
  dry months in, 16;
  seasonality in, 6;
  seasonality index for, 14-15;
  tropical climatic types in, 18-20
subsistence farming, 34-8, 44, 61, 62-3, 80-7, 165, 186-91, 220
Sudan
  dry season research in, 3
Swaziland
  energy intakes in, 49-50

Tamil Nadu, India
  agricultural work in, 156-61;
  births in, 156-61;
  dependence and seasonality in, 207-10;
  nutrition in, 156-61;
  rice cultivation in, 37;
  seasonality in, 24-5
Tanzania
  health in, 182-6;
  poverty in, 186-91;
  rice cultivation in, 34-5;
  welfare in, 182-6
tax collection, 227
technology, 61-3, 198, 232.
  See also agricultural technology.
temperature
  and agricultural cycle, 137;
  and fertility, 135-7, 146-7
Thailand
  malnutrition in, 46
Thanjavur District, India, 22, 24-5, 160, 207, 208-9
Trinidad
  respiratory diseases in, 113
tropical areas
  and crop production, 33;
  and seasonality, 9-29, 67-73
typhoid fever, 105-6, 177

Uganda
  fertility in, 137, 138;
  malnutrition in, 46
underemployment, 93, 100
United Kingdom
  diarrhoeal diseases in, 103-4
United States
  diarrhoeal diseases in, 112;
  migration to, 211-13;
  typhoid fever in, 106
Upper Volta
  filariasis in, 121-2

village studies, 1, 3, 28, 38-41, 48-50, 73-80, 164-75, 177-86, 201-6, 208-9

wages, 87-92
water supply, 107-8, 118-19, 127, 128, 141, 165, 167, 170, 174, 180, 185, 186, 238
welfare, 163-92
West Africa
  energy intakes in, 49;
  guinea-worm infection in, 125-7;
  malaria in, 117, 119;
  malnutrition in, 110;
  measles in, 114;
  migration in, 210-14;
  onchocerciasis in, 123;
  seasonality in, 26-8.
  See also Africa.
women
  and agricultural work, 75-6, 146, 157-8, 163, 220, 232;
  and crop processing, 100;
  and energy expenditures, 39, 62;

Hausa (of Nigeria), 180;
Maguzawa (of Nigeria), 180;
and migration, 212-13;
and nutrition, 52-4, 56-7, 59, 108;
and pastoralists, 187;
and poverty, 231-3;

and seasonal burdens, 194-5, 195-201

yaws, 176

Zaria, Nigeria, 22, 27, 28, 49, 73-80, 177-81, 220